SHAKESPEARE SURVEY

ADVISORY BOARD

1 Shakespeare and his Stage
2 Shakespearian Production
3 The Man and the Writer
4 Interpretation
5 Textual Criticism
6 The Histories
7 Style and Language
8 The Comedies
9 *Hamlet*
10 The Roman Plays
11 The Last Plays (with an index to *Surveys 1–10*)
12 The Elizabethan Theatre
13 *King Lear*
14 Shakespeare and his Contemporaries
15 The Poems and Music
16 Shakespeare in the Modern World
17 Shakespeare in his Own Age
18 Shakespeare Then Till Now
19 *Macbeth*
20 Shakespearian and Other Tragedy

21 *Othello* (with an index to *Surveys 11–20*)
22 Aspects of Shakespearian Comedy
23 Shakespeare's Language
24 Shakespeare: Theatre Poet
25 Shakespeare's Problem Plays
26 Shakespeare's Jacobean Tragedies
27 Shakespeare's Early Tragedies
28 Shakespeare and the Ideas of his Time
29 Shakespeare's Last Plays
30 *Henry IV* to *Hamlet*
31 Shakespeare and the Classical World (with an index to *Surveys 21–30*)
32 The Middle Comedies
33 *King Lear*
34 Characterization in Shakespeare
35 Shakespeare in the Nineteenth Century
36 Shakespeare in the Twentieth Century
37 Shakespeare's Earlier Comedies

Aspects of *Macbeth*
Aspects of *Othello*
Aspects of *Hamlet*
Aspects of *King Lear*
Aspects of Shakespeare's 'Problem Plays'

SHAKESPEARE SURVEY

AN ANNUAL SURVEY OF
SHAKESPEARIAN STUDY AND PRODUCTION

37

EDITED BY
STANLEY WELLS

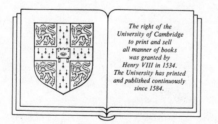

The right of the
University of Cambridge
to print and sell
all manner of books
was granted by
Henry VIII in 1534.
The University has printed
and published continuously
since 1584.

CAMBRIDGE UNIVERSITY PRESS

CAMBRIDGE

LONDON   NEW YORK   NEW ROCHELLE

MELBOURNE   SYDNEY

Published by the Press Syndicate of the University of Cambridge
The Pitt Building, Trumpington Street, Cambridge CB2 IRP
32 East 57th Street, New York, NY 10022, USA
296 Beaconsfield Parade, Middle Park, Melbourne 3206, Australia

First published 1984

Shakespeare Survey was first published in 1948. For the first
eighteen volumes it was edited by Allardyce Nicoll.
Kenneth Muir edited volumes 19–33

Printed in Great Britain
by the University Press, Cambridge

Library of Congress catalogue card number: 49–1639

British Library Cataloguing in Publication Data
Shakespeare Survey
37
1. Shakespeare, William – Societies, periodicals, etc.
I. Wells, Stanley
822.3'3 PR2885
ISBN 0 521 26701 3

EDITOR'S NOTE

The main theme of this volume is Shakespeare's earlier comedies, up to and including *The Merchant of Venice*. The next volume (which will be at press by the time this volume appears) will have as its theme 'Shakespeare and History'. We hope to include a number of papers given to the International Shakespeare Conference at Stratford-upon-Avon in 1984. Volume 39 will have as its theme 'Shakespeare on Film and Television'; we shall also be happy to consider articles on other aspects of Shakespeare in adaptation. Submissions should reach the Editor at 40 Walton Crescent, Oxford OX1 2JQ, by 1 September 1985 at the latest. Many articles are considered before the deadline, so those that arrive earlier have a greater chance of acceptance. Please either enclose return postage (overseas, in International Reply Coupons) or send a non-returnable xerox. A style sheet is available on request. All articles submitted are read by the Editor and by one or more members of the Advisory Board, whose indispensable assistance the Editor gratefully acknowledges.

With this volume we thank George Walton Williams for his six years of service, and welcome MacDonald P. Jackson in his place.

In attempting to survey the ever-increasing bulk of Shakespeare publications our reviewers have inevitably to exercise some selection. Review copies of books should be addressed to the Editor, as above. We are also very pleased to receive offprints of articles, which help to draw our reviewers' attention to relevant material.

S.W.W.

CONTRIBUTORS

N. W. BAWCUTT, *Senior Lecturer in English, University of Liverpool*

JOHN BLIGH, *Associate Professor of English, Guelph University*

DAVID DANIELL, *Lecturer in English, University College, London*

KENNETH GARLICK, *Keeper of Western Art, Ashmolean Museum, Oxford*

KEITH GEARY, *Oxford*

BRIAN GIBBONS, *Professor of English Literature, University of Zürich*

WERNER HABICHT, *Professor of English, University of Würzburg*

MacDONALD P. JACKSON, *Associate Professor of English, University of Auckland*

MICHAEL NEILL, *Senior Lecturer in English, University of Auckland*

R. B. PARKER, *Professor of English, Trinity College, Toronto*

LOIS POTTER, *Senior Lecturer in English, University of Leicester*

PETER SACCIO, *Professor of English, Dartmouth College, Hanover*

NICHOLAS SHRIMPTON, *Fellow of Lady Margaret Hall and Lecturer in English, University of Oxford*

JOHN W. SIDER, *Professor of English, Westmont College, Santa Barbara*

WILLIAM W. E. SLIGHTS, *Professor of English, University of Saskatchewan, Saskatoon*

K. TETZELI VON ROSADOR, *Professor of English, Westfälische Wilhelms-Universität, Münster*

ROGER WARREN, *Lecturer in English, University of Leicester*

R. S. WHITE, *Lecturer in English Literature, University of Newcastle-upon-Tyne*

ROSEMARY WRIGHT, *Salisbury*

CONTENTS

List of Illustrations   *page* viii

Criticism of the Comedies up to *The Merchant of Venice*: 1953–82 *by* R. S. WHITE   I

Plotting the Early Comedies: *The Comedy of Errors, Love's Labour's Lost, The Two Gentlemen of Verona by* K. TETZELI VON ROSADOR   13

The Good Marriage of Katherine and Petruchio *by* DAVID DANIELL   23

Shrewd and Kindly Farce *by* PETER SACCIO   33

Illustrations to *A Midsummer Night's Dream* before 1920 *by* KENNETH GARLICK   41

The Nature of Portia's Victory: Turning to Men in *The Merchant of Venice by* KEITH GEARY   55

Nature's Originals: Value in Shakespearian Pastoral *by* WILLIAM W. E. SLIGHTS   69

'Contrarieties agree': An Aspect of Dramatic Technique in *Henry VI by* ROGER WARREN   75

Falstaff's Broken Voice *by* JOHN W. SIDER   85

'He who the sword of heaven will bear': The Duke versus Angelo in *Measure for Measure by* N. W. BAWCUTT   89

War and Sex in *All's Well That Ends Well by* R. B. PARKER   99

Changing Places in *Othello by* MICHAEL NEILL   115

Prospero's Lime Tree and the Pursuit of *Vanitas by* ROSEMARY WRIGHT   133

Shakespearian Character Study to 1800 *by* JOHN BLIGH   141

How German is Shakespeare in Germany? Recent Trends in Criticism and Performance in West Germany *by* WERNER HABICHT   155

Shakespeare Performances in Stratford-upon-Avon and London, 1982–3 *by* NICHOLAS SHRIMPTON   163

The Year's Contributions to Shakespearian Study: 175

   1   Critical Studies *reviewed by* BRIAN GIBBONS   175

   2   Shakespeare's Life, Times and Stage *reviewed by* LOIS POTTER   188

   3   Editions and Textual Studies *reviewed by* MACDONALD P. JACKSON   202

Index   221

ILLUSTRATIONS

1   *The Meeting of Oberon and Titania*. Plate to Rowe's first edition of Shakespeare (1709), vol. 2   *page* 42

2   *The Meeting of Oberon and Titania*. Plate to Rowe's later edition of Shakespeare (1714), vol. 2   42

3   F. Gravelot, plate to Theobald's second edition of Shakespeare (1740), vol. 1   43

4   E. Edwards, plate to Bell's edition of Shakespeare, 1773   43

5   *Miss Barsanti in the Character of Helena*. Plate to Bell's edition of Shakespeare, 1776   44

6   J. H. Ramberg, *Miss Farren in the Character of Hermia*. Plate to Bell's edition of Shakespeare, 1785   44
    [*Reproduced by courtesy of the Shakespeare Centre Library, Stratford-upon-Avon*]

7   L. Schiavonetti, engraving after *Puck* by Sir Joshua Reynolds for Boydell's *Graphic Illustrations of the Dramatic Works of Shakespeare* (1802)   46
    [*Reproduced by courtesy of the Ashmolean Museum, Oxford*]

8   J. Parker, engraving after *Puck* by H. Fuseli for Boydell's *Graphic Illustrations of the Dramatic Works of Shakespeare* (1802)   47
    [*Reproduced by courtesy of the Ashmolean Museum, Oxford*]

9   P. J. de Loutherbourg, plate to Bell's edition of Shakespeare, 1785   47
    [*Reproduced by courtesy of the Shakespeare Centre Library, Stratford-upon-Avon*]

10   L. S. Ruhl, plate to *The Gallery of Shakespeare, or, Illustrations of his Dramatic Works* (Ackermann and Tilt, 1829)   48
    [*Reproduced by courtesy of the Shakespeare Centre Library, Stratford-upon-Avon*]

11   David Scott, *Puck fleeing before the Dawn*, 1837–8   49
    [*Reproduced by courtesy of the National Galleries of Scotland, Edinburgh*]

12   Sir Joseph Noel Paton, *The Quarrel of Oberon and Titania*, 1849   49
    [*Reproduced by courtesy of the National Galleries of Scotland, Edinburgh*]

13   Richard Dadd, *Contradiction. Oberon and Titania*, 1854–8   50
    [*Reproduced by courtesy of Messrs. Sotheby Parke Bernet*]

14   E. A. Abbey, illustration to act 1, scene 1 for *Harper's Bazaar*, 1893–4   51
    [*Reproduced by courtesy of the Shakespeare Centre Library, Stratford-upon-Avon*]

15   W. Heath Robinson, illustration to act 1, scene 1, 1914   51
    [*Reproduced by courtesy of the Bodleian Library, Oxford*]

16   Arthur Rackham, *Helena*, 1908   52

17   T. A. Dean, engraving after *Hermia and Helena* by John Wood   52
    [*Reproduced by courtesy of the Shakespeare Centre Library, Stratford-upon-Avon*]

18   *The Pedlar Robbed by Apes*. Florentine engraving, *c.* 1470–90   135

LIST OF ILLUSTRATIONS

19 *The Pedlar Robbed by Apes.* Engraving by Pieter van der Heyden after Pieter Breughel the
    Elder, 1562   136

20 *The Dream.* Flemish (?), early seventeenth century (formerly in the David Richardson
    Collection, Cambridge, Mass.)   138

21 *Twelfth Night,* Royal Shakespeare Theatre, 1983. Zoë Wanamaker as Viola and Miles
    Anderson as Orsino
    [*Photo: Donald Cooper*]   165

22 *Twelfth Night,* Royal Shakespeare Theatre, 1983. Daniel Massey as Sir Andrew Aguecheek,
    Gemma Jones as Maria, and John Thaw as Sir Toby Belch   166
    [*Photo: Donald Cooper*]

23 *The Taming of the Shrew,* Royal Shakespeare Theatre, 1982. Petruchio (Alun Armstrong) and
    Katherine (Sinead Cusack), with Baptista (David Waller)   167
    [*Photo: Donald Cooper*]

24 *The Comedy of Errors,* Royal Shakespeare Theatre, 1983. Luce (Frankie Cosgrave) refuses
    admission to Dromio of Ephesus (Henry Goodman, left), watched by Dromio of Syracuse
    (Richard O'Callaghan)   169
    [*Photo: Alastair Muir*]

25 *Henry VIII,* Royal Shakespeare Theatre, 1983. John Thaw as Cardinal Wolsey   171
    [*Photo: Donald Cooper*]

26 *Antony and Cleopatra,* The Other Place, 1982. Michael Gambon as Antony and Helen
    Mirren as Cleopatra   172
    [*Photo: Mark Williamson*]

ERRATUM

We regret that in *Shakespeare Survey 36*, page 46, column 2, line 9 was inadvertently repeated, replacing line 11 which should have read 'them in the only possible way, by the act of suicide.'

CRITICISM OF THE COMEDIES
UP TO 'THE MERCHANT OF VENICE':
1953–82

R. S. WHITE

Since John Russell Brown in 1955 surveyed criticism of Shakespearian comedy,[1] there has been such a wealth of information and interpretation that the job of bringing his work up to date has had to be divided amongst contributors. M. M. Mahood in 1979 looked at 'A Generation of Criticism' on *Much Ado About Nothing, As You Like It* and *Twelfth Night*,[2] whilst the present essay will cover the comedies leading up to this great trio. Obviously one cannot talk about the later plays without having an eye to the earlier, and Professor Mahood has made it unnecessary to attend to certain general aspects which the plays have in common. In the group examined here we have a couple of assured masterpieces and some plays which either have been or may become battlegrounds where 'experimental' approaches will fight for recognition. At first sight, however, the plays do not fall readily into a coherent grouping.

The Comedy of Errors, The Two Gentlemen of Verona, Love's Labour's Lost, The Taming of the Shrew, A Midsummer Night's Dream, The Merry Wives of Windsor,[3] and *The Merchant of Venice*: a thoroughly professional, classical farce, a comic romance, a courtly entertainment, a robustly unsentimental marriage-play, a piece of faery mingled with courtly interlude, a genial glimpse of provincial life, and a dark, 'problem' comedy which brings us close to death on the stage. Nothing much in common there, except the utter difference of each from its neighbour. Indeed, no other group of plays in the canon so firmly defies categorization, and all that the collection displays, if anything, is the dramatist's virtuoso control over a diversity of modes and materials loosely called 'comic'.

I. SCHOLARLY MATTERS

The plays share also a notorious difficulty for scholars who wish to ascertain dates of composition. No other selection of plays is so consistently disputed on this score. Now, just as we had begun to rest upon a general orthodoxy, E. A. J. Honigmann in *Shakespeare's Impact on his Contemporaries* (1982) shakes our complacency by arguing strongly for Shakespeare's 'early start', pushing some of the plays back to the mid 1580s. His thesis demands the greatest respect, and therefore throws into doubt the dating of all our plays except perhaps the *Dream* which seems fairly indisputably placed in 1595 or 1596. The debate will have to be carried on, and its outcome affects questions of sources, chronology, Shakespeare's development as an artist, and his literary relationships with contemporaries. Luckily, it is not I who must adjudicate, but somebody in thirty or so years' time. In the meantime, just to be on the safe side and to prevent the play disappearing into a *Shakespeare Survey* black hole between *The Merchant* and 'the middle comedies', I am taking *The Merry Wives of Windsor* under my wing. It would be a shame to let such a

---

[1] John Russell Brown, 'The Interpretation of Shakespeare's Comedies: 1900–1953', *Shakespeare Survey 8* (Cambridge, 1955), 1–13.

[2] M. M. Mahood, 'Shakespeare's Middle Comedies: A Generation of Criticism', *Shakespeare Survey 32* (Cambridge, 1979), 1–13.

[3] See below for my admittedly tenuous reasons for including this play. The various scholarly editions describe the difficult problems concerned with its date, and see William Green, *Shakespeare's 'Merry Wives of Windsor'* (Princeton, 1962).

friendly child become a homeless waif, and although nobody has seen the need to argue that the play is earlier than *The Merchant*, they may well have both been composed in 1597.

It is to be hoped (and expected) that any redating will not invalidate the monumental labours of Geoffrey Bullough in collecting the known sources for the plays. His *Narrative and Dramatic Sources of Shakespeare* (8 vols., 1957–75) may turn out to be amongst the most significant works done since Chambers on a whole range of scholarly issues. As well as collecting together a wealth of sources and analogues, he provides in the respective introductions masterly analyses of other problems for scholarly inquiry. Bullough has done for source study what the indefatigable S. Schoenbaum has more recently done for the study of Shakespeare's biography and the tribe of Greg and McKerrow for textual and bibliographical study of the whole canon. Kenneth Muir's *The Sources of Shakespeare's Plays* (1978), more modest in its scope, gives a compact survey of the field. L. G. Salingar in *Shakespeare and the Traditions of Comedy* (Cambridge, 1974) provides much specialist information on what might be called 'structural analogies' in Italian comedy, and at the end of the book he applies these to the study of Shakespeare's comedies, including *The Merchant of Venice*. We shall have to wait for his proposed sequel, which will deal more directly with Shakespeare, to judge fairly whether his emphasis on things classical and Italian (at the expense of romance traditions) helps to illuminate the comedies radically enough to enforce reinterpretation.

The early comedies, like many of Shakespeare's plays, have been well served in the last thirty years by vigorous and clear-headed editors. The new Arden has produced texts of each play with the scrupulous editorial attention and judicious reviews of criticism that we have come to expect from the series. Some have already dated, but one can happily single out the most long-awaited and most welcome, Harold Brooks's *A Midsummer Night's Dream* (1979), as likely to stand unchallenged for many years. Now that a fresh series from Oxford is on the road there may be some competition, but judging from H. J. Oliver's *The Taming of the Shrew*

(Oxford, 1982), appearing more or less at the same time as Brian Morris's Arden (1981), these will complement rather than compete. The 'newer' New Variorum is beginning slowly to come to life. Nobody could complain that too little is being done on textual, bibliographical, and historical matters. A welcome addition to the repertory is the appearance of all of our plays in the uncluttered series of New Penguin editions, with their sensible, lucid introductions and annotations.

2. GENERAL CRITICAL INTERPRETATION

Much of the work done over the last thirty years on the comedies as a group has consolidated one position that Brown himself helped to establish. No longer do we need to confess in furtive whispers that we find them 'serious' and worthy of close analysis. No longer can they be brushed aside as 'happy', lightweight works which might be destroyed by systematic analysis. In fact, even the most ardent initiates must have wondered at the boldness of the vanguard which attempted to move the plays right into the heavyweight division. With a breathtaking speed that took everybody by surprise, even *The Comedy of Errors* swiftly became a meeting place for Old and New classical comedy, a Jungian archetype from the collective unconscious and a play troubled with the *angst* of identity-crisis. Supporters trembled in anticipation as C. L. Barber brought the tablets down from the cloudy mountain inhabited by Northrop Frye. Their plays had come out!

Frye's 'The Argument of Comedy' (*English Institute Essays 1948* (1949), 58–73) had already appeared when Brown wrote his retrospective, but it was only a taste of things to come, especially in *A Natural Perspective* (1965) and *Anatomy of Criticism* (Princeton, 1957). Although one might now feel impatient with the sweeping range of his generalizations, Frye remains seminal because he established two basic positions: comedy, romance, and tragedy all have intimate formal and visionary links with each other, and comedy can be every bit as serious as tragedy. Without somebody saying these things, the study of Shakespearian comedy could have remained these thirty years the domain of charming, weightless *belles-lettres*. Judged purely as a critic, rather than as a contributor to the history of ideas, C. L. Barber seems to have weathered better, though for a reason which the 'anthropological' critics may not have expected. He never allows the portentousness of ideas to overshadow the sense of a play as an individual work of the imagination. The theoretical section of *Shakespeare's Festive Comedy* (Princeton, 1959), where he examines the pattern of saturnalian release implicit in the comic pattern, seems now as distant from the plays as Frye's unveiling of the mythos of spring. On the other hand, Barber's interpretations of the plays still yield surprises and increased respect for his acute sensitivity to tone. His work has not been swept aside by an avalanche of precocious innovators taking advantage of his pioneering work. Indeed, a recent, radical book, *The Woman's Part: Feminist Criticism of Shakespeare*[4] is dedicated to the memory of his inspiration. Meanwhile, Frye's influence is still alive in more hardheaded fashion, as evidenced by Ruth Nevo's *Comic Transformations in Shakespeare* (1980), a book which takes the pattern of Roman New Comedy as its point of departure.

After these critics who wished to interpret the comedies in more ambitious ways than their predecessors had laid foundations in the 1950s, we found in the 1960s a new breed of upstart crow amongst the ranks. Responding perhaps to something in the 'spirit of the age' (or to something publishers had decided was timely), these critics liberally sprinkled their titles with words like 'social', 'role-playing', and 'metadrama'. The plays often became case-studies for the social scientist or behavioural psychologist. These critics had their feet on the ground, not in the clouds of archetypes and mantras, and their touchstone was 'relevance'. A book which, although appearing much later, elegantly brings to maturity one aspect of these approaches is Thomas van Laan's *Role-Playing in Shakespeare* (Toronto, 1978). It is most adequate in its treatment of the early comedies, where the approach seems to fit the subject like a glove, showing Shakespeare's characters conversing and acting in response to a complex awareness of social roles. In such works, there is little talk of mythic significance or even 'release'. Everything becomes accessible to sober analysis in terms of social pressures, restrictions, and self-images imposed upon the characters. In extreme cases, we are reminded of the panel of social workers investigating why the 'delinquent' has 'deviated' (two more words popular at the time). Even when dealing with the play as illusion, 'the idea of the play' in Anne Righter's phrase from the title of her book,[5] 'discrepant awareness' (Bertrand Evans in 1960[6]) or 'metadrama' (J. L. Calderwood's field of inquiry), these critics refused to be 'taken in', insisting that playwright and audience alike are perfectly aware that they are engaged in the enactment of an artefact whose capacities for enchantment and willing suspension of disbelief must not be taken for granted but closely analysed. If Frye and Barber had made the comedies 'social' in the sense of recreating traditional, folk experience shared by all the community, the later critics took away the inverted commas, seeing social behaviour in the comedies in terms of rationally explicable patterns of behaviour and self-reflective illusions. Perhaps critics with these kinds of interests recognized their own pioneer when the essays of James Smith, some written in the 1940s, were reprinted as *Shakespearian and Other Essays* (Cambridge, 1974). Reading this book reminds us that even before the flood there were critics of remarkably searching capacity who could find quite enough to be serious about in the comedies. His delicate awareness of how revealing even a short snatch of dialogue can be helps us to understand better the phenomenon of tonality in works written for the stage, and to respect Shakespeare's skill in giving us people who actually converse responsively with each other instead of (as in the plays of many Elizabethan dramatists) speaking in rhetorical set-pieces, ellipses or indirections.

Since the analytical days of the 1960s, innovative streams of criticism have developed the stance of

---

[4] Carolyn Lenz, Gayle Greene and Carol Neely (eds.), *The Woman's Part: Feminist Criticism of Shakespeare* (Urbana, 1980).

[5] Anne Righter (Anne Barton), *Shakespeare and the Idea of the Play* (1962).

[6] Bertrand Evans, *Shakespeare's Comedies* (Oxford, 1960).

wary scepticism, sometimes in a way that may strike the conservative as threatening the citadel itself, the 'universality' which institutionalized Shakespeare has always been credited with. The new demystifiers have warned us that Shakespeare was himself the product of his historical context, and that he could not avoid ingrained cultural and political assumptions which are not necessarily universally shared and should be closely inspected for degree of bias. Marxist critics, so far represented in this field by Elliot Krieger in *A Marxist Study of Shakespeare's Comedies* (1979), remind us that the view of the world in the comedies holds a class structure which discriminates the privileged and aristocratic from the bourgeois and those who can be said to 'work', such as clowns, servants, constables, artisans and bawds. A growing body of feminist critics, their own model being Juliet Dusinberre's *Shakespeare and the Nature of Women* (1975), submit to critical scrutiny the (invariably male) lecturer's commonplaces that 'Shakespeare understood women' and believed in their liberation. Do not the comedies confirm in their structure that Shakespeare's women are made for marriage, that their liberation is brief and confined to courtship, and is conceived anyway in male concepts of freedom? Are not Katherine and Portia characters drawn to reinforce certain male stereotypes of perverse or 'strong' womanhood, rather than distinctively female? The significance of these 'alternative' approaches lies in the fact that fundamental questions are being asked, and the history of Shakespearian criticism has surely shown that Shakespeare can survive such a test. Some Marxists and some feminists respectively will say that Shakespeare, because of his class-bias and his appropriation of women to male expectations, is a dangerously reactionary influence when enshrined in school syllabuses and revered for his 'universality'. However, other critics of the same persuasions will argue that if we read the plays with a new astuteness to such concerns we will find just as much inbuilt criticism of the prevailing world-view as tacit support for it, and that Shakespeare may indeed be giving us patterns of liberation from conventional expectations in ways that will emerge as debate goes on. Each argument is likely to be carried out most fiercely over *The Merchant of Venice* and *The Taming of the Shrew* respectively, and we shall return to these plays. Certainly, the new approaches cannot be ignored, and writing with a mind to the reader in thirty years' time, I must recognize that it has often happened that heterodoxies of today's Shakespearian criticism are assimilated into the orthodoxies of tomorrow's. As Jaques reminds us, 'Out of these convertites / There is much matter to be heard and learn'd.' If it is possible to generalize about such matters, I should guess that the general current of thought amongst the younger critics is turning away from matters of form and imaginative vision towards an inspection of the deeper ethical assumptions underlying each play, and underlying the notion of criticism itself.

Of course, the little map which I have drawn of those trends in criticism most appropriate to the early comedies has been partial and personal. It is important to remember that probably a majority of writers would claim allegiance to no 'school', and are modestly attempting to explain their pleasures in the comedies by presenting patient and respectful explorations of particular problems in interpretation, and dealing with the plays as individual works of art with their unique idioms and effects. Not everyone wishes to be Apollo to Hyperion, or Hyperion to a satyr in the grand march of intellect. Alexander Leggatt's *Shakespeare's Comedies of Love* (1974), beginning with the apparently limited subject of Shakespeare's discrimination between different speech-modes in the comedies, manages to develop quietly sensitive accounts of each play as a unit. The eminently sensible Kenneth Muir, in *Shakespeare's Comic Sequence* (Liverpool, 1979), stays safely up the beach, judiciously sifting the sand of old critical problems, rather than risking himself on the ocean of current controversy. Many, such as D. P. Young in *The Heart's Forest* (New Haven, 1972) and Rosalie Colie in *Shakespeare's Living Art* (Princeton, 1974), have expanded our understanding by choosing to begin with Elizabethan conventions of the pastoral genre and its linguistic patterns. In conducting a revaluation of one of Shakespeare's contemporaries, G. K. Hunter in *John Lyly: The Humanist as Courtier* (1962) provides much insight into Shakespeare's own early comedies. We should remind ourselves also that the last thirty years have seen the appearance of works that nobody would claim as innovations of theory but many have found refreshing: John Russell Brown's own *Shakespeare and his Comedies* (1957), J. Dover Wilson's *Shakespeare's Happy Comedies* (1962), F. P. Wilson's 'Shakespeare's Comedies',[7] and the brief but interesting Writers and Their Works pamphlets by D. A. Traversi[8] and G. K. Hunter.[9] E. M. W. Tillyard's *Shakespeare's Early Comedies* (1966), a sturdy standby for students, has some sound things to say on individual plays, and is particularly adequate on *The Comedy of Errors*. Generally speaking, it is to these kinds of critics that we turn in surveying the work done on each play in the multiplicity of articles from journals and the occasional book-length study. Of course, it is necessary to be highly selective, and the fact that I do not refer to any single, seminal essay from such a journal as *Shakespeare Studies*, for example, does not mean that it has not provided over the years many helpful insights. Furthermore, although a thorough exploration is impossible in this piece, we cannot ignore the often profound effect on critical approaches caused by revolutionary performances of each play. Peter Brook's production of *Love's Labour's Lost* in 1946 inspired a critical rediscovery of the play and a new attention to the significance of its ending, whilst his more recent *A Midsummer Night's Dream* (1970) has also had an incalculable influence upon all critics who have written since on the play. There is now a more intimate and symbiotic relationship between what happens on the stage and what is written than ever before, and this is possibly most true for the comedies. Until one sees how effective and thought-provoking a play can be on stage, one is tempted to retreat to the older tendency of regarding serious analysis of the comedies as being an exercise in breaking a butterfly upon a wheel.

3. THE PLAYS

'Nobody will want a demonstration that *Twelfth Night* and *As You Like It* are better plays than *Two Gentlemen of Verona* and *Comedy of Errors*.' So writes Frank Kermode in his essay on 'The Mature Comedies' in *Early Shakespeare*.[10] One's sympathies are immediately aroused for the underdogs, which are apparently so insignificant that their names can be truncated without disrespect, and whose general inferiority is considered to be so patently obvious. They have occasionally had large claims made for them, but almost invariably by critics who have their sights set on later, and therefore higher, things, on the assumption that the child is father to the man. Nevill Coghill in 'The Basis of Shakespearian Comedy' (*Essays and Studies*, 3 (1950), pp. 1–28) and Stanley Wells in 'Shakespeare and Romance' (*Later Shakespeare*, ed. J. R. Brown and B. Harris, Stratford-upon-Avon Studies, 8, 1966), both present *The Comedy of Errors* and *The Two Gentlemen of Verona* as blueprints for later comedy, and excellent as these essays are, their authors would not claim to be giving the plays a qualitatively higher place in the canon than Kermode. Frye uses both plays as items of furniture in the vast room which for him is Shakespearian romance, and his goal is really the last plays. C. L. Barber does not grace either with a chapter in *Shakespeare's Festive Comedy*, and his essay on 'Shakespearean Comedy in *The Comedy of Errors*' in *College English*, 25 (1964), although enlightening, is accurate to the proportions of its title. Stanley Wells, in one of the best essays on the other play, registers some sense of defeat in his title, 'The Failure of *The Two Gentlemen of Verona*' (*Shakespeare Jahrbuch*, 99 (1963), 161–73).

Even the critics who believe the early plays have their music too, and advocate that we think not of the later, have expected little more than modest success in their evangelism. The respective Arden editors, R. A. Foakes (1962) and Clifford Leech (1969), praise the formal qualities of the plays, and emphasize some of the 'serious' elements, but they carefully refrain from making any special claims. Stanley Wells, who has contributed as much as

---

[7] F. P. Wilson, 'Shakespeare's Comedies' in *Shakespearian and Other Studies*, ed. Helen Gardner (Oxford, 1969).

[8] D. A. Traversi, *Shakespeare: The Early Comedies* (1960).

[9] G. K. Hunter, *Shakespeare: The Later Comedies* (1962).

[10] *Early Shakespeare*, ed. J. R. Brown and Bernard Harris, Stratford-upon-Avon Studies, 3 (1961), 211–27; p. 211.

anybody to the critical understanding of both comedies, does so, at least when editing *The Comedy of Errors*, by insisting that we should be looking for virtues other than 'the range, the variety, the subtlety, the richness of plays that [Shakespeare] was soon to compose', and he proposes different criteria for *Errors*:

But it would also be wrong to write of it as if it were not both the most brilliant comedy that had so far been written in English, and also – lest this imply merely relative success – a completely assured work for which no excuses need be made.

(New Penguin edition, Harmondsworth, 1972, p. 8)

Another critic who has fondly made these plays his domain, Harold Brooks, has emphasized the sheer craftsmanship and good fun of both plays, in 'Themes and Structure in *The Comedy of Errors*' (*Early Shakespeare*, pp. 55–71) and then in an essay whose genially meandering title suits its subject: 'Two Clowns in a Comedy (to say nothing of the dog): Speed, Launce (and Crab) in *The Two Gentlemen of Verona*' in *Essays and Studies*, 16 (1963), pp. 91–100. The play must attract long titles, for we have also Inga-Stina Ewbank's careful essay, '"Were man but constant, he were perfect": Constancy and Consistency in *The Two Gentlemen of Verona*' (*Shakespearian Comedy*, ed. Malcolm Bradbury and David Palmer, Stratford-upon-Avon Studies, 14, 1972).

Cinderellas or ugly sisters? Will their day ever come? At least among critics in general, it has not come yet. They have attracted the attentions of the fine critics mentioned above, but otherwise they are regarded as caviar to the general. Since 1953 several essays can be reported which have increased our admiration for the skill exhibited in the plotting of these plays, and we have witnessed some rather frustrated attempts to read at least *The Two Gentlemen of Verona* as a sustained parody of its romance materials, but nothing more solid which might shake the generally demeaning attitude to the play. It seems fairly clear that as long as we look for what Leavis called a 'deep centre' to plays, so long will these two early comedies (as well as *Cymbeline*, in discussing which Leavis coined his phrase), have to wait for revaluation. In the meantime, no doubt

audiences will continue to be delighted by fondly presented productions, although in making this judgement we can probably have more confidence in *Errors*, judging from the uninspiring stage history of *The Two Gentlemen*.

The Taming of the Shrew nowadays is acquiring a kind of perverse celebrity, not because it is seen to contribute to any particular model for Shakespearian comedy, nor because its poetic quality is undergoing any radical reassessment, but because it is a good play to start arguments. One argument used to rage (amongst those whose passions are aroused by such problems) about whether it preceded or post-dated *The Taming of a Shrew*, although now the consensus is that *The Shrew* came first. The critical, or ideological, argument centres upon how we are to read Kate's last speech. Is it a piece of conventional, Elizabethan advice on the duties of wives, a 'more or less automatic statement...of a generally held doctrine' as Robert Heilman puts it in his essay 'The *Taming* Untamed, or, The Return of the Shrew' (*Modern Language Quarterly*, 27 (1966), p. 147), or is it a sophisticated, ironic triumph over the more conventional people around Katherine and Petruchio? Does it show a patriarchal society vindicated or undermined? Is individual personality destroyed or created in the process of 'taming'? At least the days when one could describe the play as a 'farce' and gratefully turn to other matters, even though this policy is still adopted occasionally, seem to be numbered. Now we have 'the emergence of a humanized heroine against the background of depersonalizing farce unassimilated from the play's fabliau sources' (John C. Bean in *The Woman's Part: Feminist Criticism of Shakespeare*, p. 66), and Ralph Berry's version which finds in the play a 'synthesis of farce and comedy':

The kernel of the play is, if one likes, a fairly brutal sex farce; the formula of man taming woman is one to agitate primitively the minds of all audiences. But the play contains also a subtle account of two intelligent people arriving at a modus vivendi.

(*Shakespeare's Comedies*, 1972, p. 54)

The argument is fought also over Petruchio's speech in which he likens his practice towards Kate to the taming of a hawk. Does this passage reveal a brutal area of Shakespeare's own thinking which should make us wary of finding 'universal truth' everywhere in his words, or can we in some way maintain an ironic distance from the sentiments? The problems are compounded (or, if some bright critic could make something of it, clarified) by the Induction involving Christopher Sly, and raising characteristically Shakespearian doubts about the authenticity of illusion. To what extent is the play a projection of Sly's own attitudes towards women, expecting them to be demure but cunning (Bianca), shrewish or, preferably, obedient wives? If such an approach could in fact be sustained, it might lead us to claim that Shakespeare is challenging all conventions about women, rather than implicitly supporting any one of them. Whatever the answers to these questions may turn out to be (if settlement is ever reached), the fact that they are being vigorously raised has given new life to a play which had been regarded as too simple, or too poetically impoverished, to merit the serious discussion which has marked the criticism of Shakespearian comedy in recent years.

Love's Labour's Lost and *The Merry Wives of Windsor* are the most friendly (rather than happy) plays in the canon. Both present pictures of community, the one where Costard as 'a member of the commonwealth' trades jokes with a princess, the other showing a tightly knit township, integrating those willing to accept its godfearing and commercial values, and closing ranks against outsiders who threaten its stability. There is much to engage the attention of the 'serious' critics. The unconventional separation of lovers and the introduction of death at the end of *Love's Labour's Lost* are by no means dramatically unprepared for, as Bobbyann Roesen (Anne Barton) argues ('*Love's Labour's Lost*', *Shakespeare Quarterly*, 4 (1953), 411–26). The shadows lengthen as afternoon turns to evening, and there is, as other critics have emphasized, an element of nastiness in the way the courtiers disrupt the play put on for their entertainment, there is considerable immaturity in their treatment of the women, and there is a justified, retaliatory testing of the men performed by the women through mockery, ridicule and a form

of passive non-co-operation. The play's preoccupation with language itself, too, has serious implications, as J. L. Calderwood has pointed out in '*Love's Labour's Lost*: A Wantoning with Words' (*Studies in English Literature 1500–1900*, 5 (1965), 317–32), Ralph Berry in 'The Words of Mercury' (*Shakespeare Survey 22*, 1969, 69–77), and W. C. Carroll in a book-length treatment, *The Great Feast of Language in 'Love's Labour's Lost'* (Princeton, 1976). None of these enriching elements has, however, distracted audiences from wholeheartedly appreciating the cohesiveness of the sparkling comedy of manners. The play has triumphantly come into its own on the stage in recent years, after lying in relative obscurity for some two centuries. In the last fifteen or so years I have seen some ten productions, all highly successful, and although belief in 'the School of Night' has been eroded, there is still something in the play which draws its admirers together in a spirit of benign cabbalism.

The Merry Wives of Windsor has also been shown recently by the Royal Shakespeare Company to be eminently stageworthy, but critics have found difficulty in dealing seriously with it. F. P. Wilson called it 'the least worthy comedy',[11] and few will risk celebrating the play publicly. This is partly because its mode is perceived to be different from the norm of 'love comedy' and Leggatt, for example, leaves it aside for separate brief treatment in his *Citizen Comedy in the Age of Shakespeare* (Toronto, 1973). Barber and Berry, among others who have written books on the comedies, do not deal with it at all. Another reason for the lukewarm response is that no genuine 'difficulty' has been found in the play. I have a suspicion, however, that its unproblematical nature is an assumption that deserves to be challenged. It almost certainly stems from a lazy reading that places Falstaff at the centre, regards him as a sadly diminished figure, and dismisses the rest as secondary. If, however, we pursue other lines of interest, the play is found not only to be extraordinary in the complexity of its construction, as Chambers pointed out back in 1925, but also full of problems that can attract the

---

11 'Shakespeare's Comedies', p. 88.

attention of critics interested in the treatment of underlying ideologies in Shakespeare's drama. There is a thoroughly 'serious' thematic preoccupation with exploitation and jealousy in marriage (despite the comic tone), while the feminist could find material for exploring the double functions of women in Shakespeare's comic world, at once treated as commodities and as holding some kind of moral authority in their own right. The Marxist could recognize a community where class and economic motivations are not side-issues but central to the action and the vision. Before these lines of approach are developed, however, we must see through Shakespeare's joke, and take Falstaff away from the centre of our gaze. His very clumsiness in the economically 'middling' society of Windsor which deprives him of his wit, when seen in this light, might make us more appreciative of his mastery of comic tone in his own domain of Cheapside in the *Henry IV* plays. When somebody systematically places centrally the township of Windsor with its presentation as an entity in itself, made up of individuals but larger than each in its prevailing attitudes, then we shall be in a position to make pronouncements on the play's artistic value. Of course, there have been commentators who have appreciated aspects of *The Merry Wives*. Bertrand Evans found much to praise in the structure, whilst Brian Vickers in *The Artistry of Shakespeare's Prose* (1968) finds the unique range of linguistic modes of interest. M. C. Bradbrook writes well on the unity of the play in *Shakespeare the Craftsman* (Cambridge, 1969). If the partial leads made by these critics are followed, *The Merry Wives of Windsor* may yet have its day of critical acclaim as in many ways equal to, although very different from, the 'middle comedies'.

It is dangerous for a critic to be clever about *A Midsummer Night's Dream*. The play is quite clever enough itself. If we try earnestly to find logical reasons for the contradictions in its time-span, we find ourselves implicitly on Theseus' side, questioning things which are 'true' in an imaginative and theatrical sense, and we are uneasily aware that his point of view is undercut by the action we witness. On the other hand, if we simply accept the tricks

and the fairies as delightful products of the imagination and laugh into silence all the awkward questions, then we are just as likely to underestimate the intellectual toughness displayed by the dramatist in bringing off his conjuring tricks which unite three such different societies. Puck's final challenge remains as baffling as ever, rivalling the last words of *Tristram Shandy* and the last lines of Keats's 'Ode on a Grecian Urn' in its impenetrable lightness of attitude:

> If we shadows have offended,
> Think but this, and all is mended,
> That you have but slumb'red here
> While these visions did appear.
> And this weak and idle theme,
> No more yielding but a dream.

After all, it is only a poet's 'dream' dealing with the common 'dreams' of young love, such impossibilities as transformation of a man into an ass, and explaining the notorious changeability of the English weather by absurdly positing a realm of fairies whose emotional states are reflected in the natural world. Simple, to the point of simple-mindedness. Or is it? The play teases us out of thought as does eternity, only to tease us back into thought as does a mystery.

One theory that promises an analytical entrance to the glittering experience of the *Dream* is Norman Rabkin's notion of 'complementarity':

For the first time Shakespeare has turned his complementary vision in *A Midsummer Night's Dream* to a full examination of art itself, and with his characteristic ambivalence toward the irrational he sees it simultaneously as 'base and vile' yet of the highest 'form and dignity'.

(*Shakespeare and the Common Understanding*, New York, 1967, p. 205)

'Ambivalence', the concept used so effectively by A. P. Rossiter in his essays on the history plays, does seem appropriate to the *Dream*, with its obvious polarities between the rational and the irrational, the imaginative and the commonsense, the world of night and the world of morning, but only if we agree that the central subject or theme is 'art' itself. Others have been proposed.

The play has always been felt to have such a tight unity that it has offered a field day for 'theme hunters'. The diversity of suggestions, however, makes it startlingly clear that we do not really agree on what a 'theme' is. Does Harold Brooks tell us much when he says in his Arden introduction that 'Until the play nears its end, the theme of love and marriage holds without a rival the centre of attention?'[12] Or is he really defining a *subject*, equally applicable to plays as diverse as *Othello* and *The Taming of the Shrew*? Does it obscure the formal neatness and straightforwardness of the narrative to look a little more conceptually at the idea of 'imagination', which is a faculty ultimately creating the multi-layered illusion itself, with its various orders and disorders? Although Brooks suggests that this subject is merely 'contributory' to the theme which he finds, others have found it a productive starting-point. In the most ambitious book-length treatment of the play, D. P. Young's *Something of Great Constancy* (New Haven, 1966), and in one of the most perceptive articles, 'Imagination in *A Midsummer Night's Dream*' by R. W. Dent (*Shakespeare Quarterly*, 15 (1964), 115–29), the significance of imagination in the action and the vision of the play is found to be consistent and central. However, nagging doubts remain. Is 'the workings of the imagination' a theme of the play or an (imaginative or imaginary) idea projected on to the play by critics who, in the heyday of metadramatic theory, were themselves centrally interested in ideas of illusion, and in the medium of drama sometimes at the expense of its content? Indeed, the critic most associated with this general approach to Shakespeare's drama, J. L. Calderwood, makes many of his most interesting comments on this play in '*A Midsummer Night's Dream* and the Illusion of Drama' (*Modern Language Quarterly*, 26 (1965), 506–22), as if it were something of a *locus classicus* for his general theory. Now that McLuhan and Marcuse are not such prominent presences in academic thinking, the approach has lost a little of its freshness. Other themes have been persuasively argued, such as dream itself (despite the fact that Hermia's is the only actual dream in the play,[13] and that a fairly insignificant one), or metamorphosis. It is salutary to remember

that Northrop Frye also found the play important to the development of his own methodology, hinging on the ideas of the 'green world' being a place for self-discovery through alternative experiences that lead to 'clarification', and on the structural pattern of comedy showing a healthy flouting of an irrational ('authoritarian' might be a less debatable word) law; whilst C. L. Barber finds in the play a demonstration of his crucial distinction between the logic of everyday reality and the release of the holiday spirit. It seems that the *Dream* can be all things to all critics, and yet there is still something left over from all analyses. Oh dear, yes, we sigh, *A Midsummer Night's Dream* has a theme, but what on earth is it? The play wins again in a love match. We are tempted to flounder back to Dover Wilson, call it a 'happy' comedy and leave it at that, were it not that even this escape-route has been sealed off by Michael Taylor who argues that the play is no such thing in his brief but interesting article, 'The Darker Purpose of *A Midsummer Night's Dream*', published in *Studies in English Literature*, 9 (1969, 259–73). The partial validity of some of his perceptions was given ocular proof by Peter Brook, whose memorable production emphasized the potentially disturbing aspect of the scenes in the forest. Helena, for example, has a terrible time, and I cannot help feeling sorry for the humble bees whose honey-bags are stolen, and the painted butterflies whose wings are plucked off, merely to please Bottom.

It must be a relief for a critic at least to begin with a firm topic, without the immediate need to make any large statement about the play as a whole. Some of the most illuminating treatments have been pragmatic in this sense. K. M. Briggs in *The Anatomy of Puck* (1959), Enid Welsford in *The Court Masque* (1927), and Alan Brissenden in *Shakespeare and the Dance* (1981), although beginning with particular points on the map, manage to light up many other areas with a subtlety absent from more

---

[12] *A Midsummer Night's Dream*, ed. Harold F. Brooks (1979), pp. xciii–xciv.

[13] One might argue that there is at least an ambiguity over Bottom's 'I have had a dream...'

theoretical approaches. The same goes for Moelwyn Merchant's 'Visual Re-Creation' of the play, as he examines the stage history in the light of artistic representations in the Stratford-upon-Avon Studies volume, *Early Shakespeare* (pp. 165–85).

The Merchant of Venice has come more and more to be seen as a play which introduces into Shakespearian comedy a range of disturbing tones. While the other plays respect the limits of illusion, never letting us forget that we are watching a creation of the imagination, *The Merchant* presents a challenge from a particularly bloodthirsty representative of 'reality'. Even if we allow structure to dominate, arguing that love wins over hatred, and that Shylock is primarily a function of the overall design, there are too many disquieting elements to allow any complacency. Shylock, far from being a mere plot-device, is a character of considerable dramatic power, and he is presented as embodying an intractable mixture of racial vulnerability and obdurate insistence upon the inviolability of commercial and legal facts. At the same time, the Christians, although undoubtedly representing an ethic derived from comic love conventions, are seen at times in states of boredom (Portia), melancholy (Antonio), mercenariness (Bassanio), and vindictiveness (Gratiano). Even Launcelot Gobbo and his blind father do not provide quite the robust entertainment of, say, Launce, Speed and Crab, but rather a seedy kind of black humour. This is a play which the 'serious' critics feel fully justified in dwelling upon. It is, for example, significant that Freud's comments, so limited in themselves, are invariably reproduced in anthologies of criticism, because however we define its nature, the play does seem at points to reach into some dark recesses of the mind. A. D. Moody, in his short and challenging monograph *Shakespeare: 'The Merchant of Venice'* (1964), concludes by comparing 'the experience of the play' with the experience of those who witnessed the rise of Nazism in the 1930s: 'it has a relevance to life beyond anything we might expect of romance' (p. 56). His argument proceeds to such a commitment because Moody, probably more than any other critic, is prepared fully to face up to the moral deficiencies in all the characters,

instead of seeing them under the control of overriding romantic conventions or literary stereotypes. For him, the play is centrally concerned with 'deceptions and delusions' that reach out of the world of play.

It is possible that recent criticism has changed its focus in a more specific way. Rather than taking the 'problem' to be Shylock, who had been the universal preoccupation of commentators from the time of Lamb, we are now inclined to stress the centrality of the commercial imperative. John Russell Brown, in his introduction to the Arden edition (1955) and in his book on the comedies, probably influenced by L. C. Knights, writes at length on the presence throughout the play of hard economic concerns. Not surprisingly, Elliot Krieger, in his Marxist study (see p. 4), begins with *The Merchant of Venice*, although I find the distinctions he uses (between a 'first world' and a 'second world') oddly conventional in their closeness to Frye's, and a limitation upon what we should expect from a rigorously Marxist interpretation. Even within the limits of his own argument, Krieger is unconvincing on some points of comparison between Venice and Belmont. This is not to dismiss the approach itself. It seems unarguable, given the play's own preoccupation with money and class, that Marxist criticism could sharpen our perceptions here, as well as reminding us that these subjects held an almost hypnotic effect on the Elizabethan and Jacobean imagination. (The Cave of Mammon is one of Spenser's most powerful evocations, and from *The Jew of Malta* to *Volpone* and citizen comedy in general, acquisitiveness was seen as a suitable dramatic subject.) For a start, one could begin from the observation that for all its continental setting and colourful characters, the play gives us sharply distinguished portraits of economic 'types' very common in Shakespeare's England under the effects of monetary inflation. We see an example of the secure, landed gentry in Portia who can afford to repay the borrowed sum twelve times over but who is still emotionally trapped by impositions of heredity; of the insecure merchant at the mercy of fortune (Antonio, almost a Raleigh figure, waiting with melancholy and some desperation for his fortunes to change); of the urban aristocracy, titled but unmoneyed (Bassanio), the secure, thrifty usurer who could financially exploit inflation by demanding high interest rates or rackrenting property, insisting on laws of the marketplace (Shylock); and even of the massive numbers of recently unemployed agricultural and urban workers, willing to take any job (Gobbo). As an apparently fairly acquisitive man himself, and an occasional moneylender to boot, Shakespeare must have had a shrewd knowledge of such types in his own society.

Although a great deal has been written on *The Merchant of Venice* in the last thirty years, it is difficult to pick out anything which has proved particularly seminal. One still finds the occasional piece on Shylock, but E. E. Stoll's essay of 1911[14] still deserves to hold the field. Some accounts reflect the modern desire to find 'themes', such as Frank Kermode's piece on judgement, redemption and mercy ('The Mature Comedies' in *Early Shakespeare*) and Sigurd Burckhardt's lively discussion of 'The Gentle Bond' in *Shakespearean Meanings* (Princeton, 1968), but even these do not encompass the sheer diversity of the dramatic experience offered by the play. More than any other comedy, *The Merchant* covers a range of conflicting tones, and although Alexander Leggatt does justice to some of the more obvious contrasts in linguistic expression, he perhaps does not capture the richly coloured sombreness of mood as well as James Smith in his powerful and sensitive essay. It would appear that *The Merchant of Venice*, whilst undoubtedly catching the attention of recent critics, has so far eluded their grasp, not because of any dazzling qualities shared with the *Dream* but because of something disagreeable in its subject-matter and functionally clumsy or awkward

in its structure and general execution. (I think, for example, of the long last act.) If the suspicion I hold is correct, that younger critics are retreating from an interest in themes and artifice, and moving towards an inquiry into the ethical complexities of situations faced by individuals in compromised or conscientious positions, then perhaps *A Midsummer Night's Dream* will attract fewer commentators in the future whilst *The Merchant of Venice* (with *The Shrew* and *The Merry Wives of Windsor*) will loom larger.

One expects shifts of emphases in critical thinking over thirty years. Looking back, the shifts have been more subtle and gradual than, for example, the spectacular changes wrought in the 1950s when comedy itself was reassessed. Although the plays dealt with in this essay still seem as separate and individual as ever, at least we have been given fresh insight into each, reminded constantly that although light in tone they have serious undercurrents, and shown that their diversity remains the product of one writer's imagination which has certain preoccupations and recurrent attitudes. In looking forward, I suggest that it is to the underlying consistencies and complexities of these attitudes that critics in the coming years will address themselves. Writers like Dowden, Thorndike and Parrott (with whom Brown opened his retrospective essay), might turn in their graves, but the days when we were advised to do little more than 'bask in the sunshine' of Shakespeare's comedies now belong to a lost innocence of criticism.

---

[14] E. E. Stoll, 'Shylock', *Journal of English and Germanic Philology*, 10 (1911), 236–79. It should be mentioned that Olivier's performance in the 1970s was not particularly successful in its attempt to place Shylock back at the centre.

PLOTTING THE EARLY COMEDIES: 'THE COMEDY OF ERRORS', 'LOVE'S LABOUR'S LOST', 'THE TWO GENTLEMEN OF VERONA'

K. TETZELI VON ROSADOR

Dealing with plot in terms derived and adapted from Aristotle and the Terentian theorists, and applying it to the *protasis* of Shakespeare's early comedies, requires some explanatory, if not apologetic, introductory remarks. For plot, a few recent critical efforts notwithstanding,[1] is not an accepted critical tool. We may no longer be guilty of the downright denunciation formulated by an anonymous mid-Victorian critic who levelled the charge of puerility against plot: 'Few men', he stated apodictically, 'feel interested in a plot after nineteen.'[2] What we are guilty of is something possibly even more deadly – neglect. Plot, for Aristotle the soul of drama, has virtually disappeared from critical vocabulary, as is evidenced in P. G. Phialas's statement: 'Of the components of drama, structure, theme, and character are the most important.'[3] The relegation of plot to the status of 'the most primitive of guides to our experience of a play'[4] by another recent critic of Shakespeare's comedies illuminates the esteem plot-analysis currently enjoys. The reason for this neglect, if not contempt, of plot and the art of plotting by twentieth-century novelists, dramatists, and critics alike can be traced to definitions such as R. G. Moulton's. For him plot is 'the purely intellectual side of action', any play's ultimate 'reduction to order'.[5] From reduction, it is but a short step to reductiveness, to regarding plot as an intellectual contrivance, a blueprint for mechanical construction. (And from reductiveness, it is but a short step to Virginia Woolf's typically modern aversion to all those 'neat designs of life that are drawn up on half sheets of note paper'.[6])

To free plot from modern critical neglect and the odium of reductiveness, to transform it again into an important category of dramatic analysis, a return to, and adaptation of, Aristotle's concept of plot seems advisable. Neither for Aristotle nor for the Terentian theorists from Donatus to Scaliger is the meaning of plot confined to a rational ordering of subject-matter. All of them conceive of plot as having – and this is the basic assumption of this essay – a thematic dimension and an inexorable movement forward.[7] The latter is inherent in the

---

[1] Joan Rees, in *Shakespeare and the Story. Aspects of Creation* (1978), analyses Shakespeare's art of story-telling which undoubtedly includes problems of plotting. The interchangeability of plot, action, and story as descriptive terms illustrates the state of discussion. For Ruth Nevo, *Comic Transformations in Shakespeare* (London and New York, 1980), 'the Donatan formula for comic plots' is one of the two variables, the other being the battle of the sexes, which, fused, go to create Shakespearian comedy (chap. 1). The *Jahrbuch* of the *Deutsche Shakespeare Gesellschaft West* for 1981 is dedicated to plot-analyses of the tragedies. Madeleine Doran's two chapters on the fable in *Endeavors of Art: A study of form in Elizabethan drama* (Madison, 1954) are still indispensable.

[2] *Fraser's Magazine*, 43 (1851), p. 88.

[3] *Shakespeare's Romantic Comedies* (Chapel Hill, 1966), p. xiii.

[4] Ralph Berry, *Shakespeare's Comedies: Explorations in Form* (Princeton, 1972), p. 12.

[5] *Shakespeare as a Dramatic Artist. A Popular Illustration of the Principles of Scientific Criticism* (Oxford, 1906), p. 356.

[6] This is the complaint of Bernard, the novelist, in Virginia Woolf's *The Waves*. It is directed against the use and inevitability of 'stories' and thus, by implication, even more radically against plots.

[7] Though a thematic dimension belongs ineradicably to the Aristotelian concept of plot, Aristotle himself has unwittingly prepared the ground for emptying the concept of plot of this dimension. Of the three terms he

axiom of necessary sequence,[8] in, to use Aristotle's seemingly simple words, the dictum that a play must have a beginning, a middle, and an end. Both the thematic dimension and the forward movement of plot can be illuminated through the Renaissance theorists' use of the concept of *turbae*,[9] which denotes the perturbation, error, peril, anguish, in brief the complication and potential tragedy of comedy. Such *turbae*, most Terentian exegists hold, should be introduced as early as the *protasis*, the beginning of the play, to be developed during the *epitasis*, characterized by Evanthius as the 'incrementum, processusque turbarum'. Thus the *protasis* is not only intended to impart introductory information about the play's setting and characters but also has to awaken the audience's expectations. Even retrospection, therefore, must make the spectator look ahead; not only the end of the play but also the movement towards it must be contained within the beginning. Plotting the *protasis*, the dramatist must neglect neither the evolution of the theme, the planting and unfolding of the *turbae*, nor the arousal and retention of the audience's forward-directed interest. What is demanded of him is therefore more than an art of anticipation and preparation (a subject which Wolfgang Clemen has discussed[10]). What is demanded is an art of precipitation, of preparing a concerted forward movement, which is met, on the part of the spectator, with what William Archer has called 'the characteristic mental attitude of the theatrical audience', namely 'a stretching out, a stretching forward, of the mind'.[11] It is this art of precipitation, of prefiguring within the *protasis* both the play's middle and its end, which is to be discussed.

That *The Comedy of Errors* is, generally speaking, plotted according to the model of Roman New Comedy there can be no reasonable doubt, Shakespeare using Plautus' *Menaechmi* and *Amphitruo* as his primary sources. Nor can there, after Madeleine Doran's detailed discussion,[12] be much doubt that such romance elements as the shipwreck, the dispersal of the family, and Egeon's search were seen, by Elizabethan eyes, to be in no way inimical or alien to the world of Terentian or Plautine

comedy. Even so, the integration of these romance elements into the farcical atmosphere prevailing in Shakespeare's Ephesus demands consideration. That, as far as Egeon's recapitulation of the events preceding Solinus' doom of death is concerned, this integration is somewhat loosely achieved seems to be the widely held critical opinion. What else, in the last analysis, do all those comments mean which speak of the opening scene as only a prologue, as part of a frame? – which view the tragic potential of Egeon's fate only as a background or foil to the farcical turbulence to follow, various efforts to demonstrate an aesthetic unity of frame and the Ephesian plot of mistaken identities notwithstanding? Among the unifying arguments advanced, Gāmini Salgādo's and Leo Salingar's seem the most persuasive. While the first emphasizes the existence of natural, regenerative forces within Egeon's fated course, such as marriage and childbirth, the latter points out that the marked insistence of Egeon's repeated references to the losing of various members of his family first arouses the audience's expectation that these members will be found again during the two hours' traffic of the stage and then transforms it to near certainty.[13] Comic precipitation is thus achieved. This precipitation is strengthened for those knowledgeable members of the audience who have

---

uses in his *Poetics* – the terminological multiplicity itself not promoting perfect clarity – to denote the plot, *mythos*, *praxis*, and 'composition or structure of incidents' (σύνθεσις τῶν πραγμάτων), it is above all the last which possesses, in C. S. Lewis's terminology, a 'dangerous sense'. If plot is viewed as a *synthesis* the qualities of linear, temporal progression are neglected, those of a spatial construct, its formal aspects, are stressed. In this it differs markedly from the meaning of *mythos*, the very etymology of which implies a thematic notion.

8 Cf. Gerald F. Else, *Aristotle's Poetics. The Argument* (Leiden, 1957), p. 282.

9 Cf. M. T. Herrick, *Comic Theory in the Sixteenth Century* (Urbana, 1950), *passim*.

10 *Shakespeare's Dramatic Art* (1972), pp. 1–95.

11 *Play-Making. A Manual of Craftsmanship* (1912), p. 148.

12 *Endeavors of Art*, pp. 174–82.

13 '"Time's Deformed Hand": Sequence, Consequence, and Inconsequence in *The Comedy of Errors*', *Shakespeare Survey 25* (Cambridge, 1972), 81–91, p. 83; *Shakespeare and the Traditions of Comedy* (Cambridge, 1974), p. 62.

read their Donatus or Scaliger or are acquainted with the main tenets of Renaissance poetics by hearsay: from a play's beginning in trouble, confusion, and peril, they would confidently look forward to a comic catastrophe.

But it is above all the plotting of Egeon's life-story and of the first scene which by indirection ensures the audience that what they are watching is a comedy and which pitches their minds forward to a comic conclusion. Moreover, this is a kind of plotting which informs the rest of the play as well. The life of Egeon and his family from the moment they embark is patterned on a variant of the approved romance model of never-ceasing reversals from happiness to unhappiness to happiness. It consists of a plot-movement which, again and again, builds up dangers, unendurable suffering or mortal peril, only to bypass irrevocable consequences at the last possible moment. A minor event in Egeon's extensively related curriculum vitae provides the first illustration and epitomizes the play's plot. Soon after leaving Epidamium on shipboard Egeon is threatened by wind and waves with 'immediate death', which, rather surprisingly, he 'would gladly have embrac'd' (1.1.68–9)[14] – yet his wife and children make him give battle to fate – successfully, as it turns out. What is implicit in this incident, namely, that happy chance or one's own activity suffices to circumvent suffering or even death, is made explicit by repetition: Egeon and his family are left behind by the sailors on a ship 'then sinking-ripe' (l. 77) – they find 'a small spare mast' (l. 79) and the sea waxes calm; the mast bursts against 'a mighty rock' (l. 101) – they are all rescued, if separately; the Draconian laws of Ephesus promise death to any Syracusan not able to pay the considerable ransom of a thousand marks – Egeon is not put to death straight away, although his 'substance, valued at the highest rate, / Cannot amount unto a hundred marks' (ll. 23–4); the Duke protests that it were 'against our laws, / Against my crown, my oath, my dignity' (ll. 142–3) to soften the law's rigidity – he favours Egeon in what he can and grants a day's reprieve. The same idea informs the plotting in all these instances: suffering and death are imminent, in the twinkling of an eye they are

evaded.[15] No final happiness results, however, from such temporary evasion but the repeated postponement of danger ensures a definitive one sooner or later. All these subdued reversals further the comic precipitation of the plot. The question is no longer whether the plot is moving towards a happy ending, but how many corners it will have to turn before the happy ending will come into sight, for how long the dramatist will manage to keep the audience's attention stretched forward by such twists and turns. For it is easy to evade suffering and death in *The Comedy of Errors*; how easy is shown by the fact that a rather simple bit of advice guarantees the safety of Antipholus of Syracuse (and might have ensured that of Egeon): 'Therefore give out you are of Epidamium' (1.2.1).

Thus the first scene establishes a plot-pattern which Shakespeare employs over and again in *The Comedy of Errors*: dangers threaten, the tension increases, only to be quickly averted or to be, at the least, made ineffectual for the time being: the money Antipholus of Syracuse thinks lost soon turns up again (2.1 and 2.2); Antipholus of Ephesus eventually listens to advice and does not break into his own house by main force (3.1); Dromio of Syracuse escapes the claims of the monstrously spherical kitchen-wench, as does his master the siren-like enchantments of Luciana (3.2); Angelo, the goldsmith, is arrested, to find himself soon afterwards at liberty again (5.1) – no word of explanation is given and none is needed, the plot-pattern accounts for all; Antipholus and Dromio of Syracuse with drawn swords chase the Ephesians, who escape easily (4.4); a duel is opportunely averted (5.1). In the Duke's one-line granting of liberty and life to Egeon against all the laws of Ephesus and all the Duke's oaths (5.1.391) the pattern finds its most concentrated (and ironical?) expression. Thus essentially identical elements make up the plot of *The Comedy of Errors*,

---

[14] All quotations from Shakespeare's plays are taken from *The Riverside Shakespeare*, ed. G. Blakemore Evans (Boston, 1974).

[15] As a 'pattern of apparently discontinuous behavior' this has been studied by J. Dennis Huston, *Shakespeare's Comedies of Play* (New York, 1981), pp. 24–6.

a plot of repeated evasion or postponement of danger. But danger continuously evaded or postponed, never resolved, is liable to leave a considerable residue of potential, latent tension.[16] In *The Comedy of Errors*, however, this tension is left residual and never wrecks the comic precipitation. Shakespeare uses another plotting device over and again to keep the farcical balance: the threat of an outburst of violence and aggression hovering over many a scene is either turned aside or finds an outlet. This is an outlet which never breaks the bounds set by the genre of a comedy of errors. It is the numerous beatings the two Dromios receive which channel aggression in a fashion appropriate to farcical comedy. The more elaborate punishment of Dr Pinch, the pompous exorcist, serves the same function. Latent dangers are diverted from the protagonists to minor figures – certainly a convenient strategy for keeping the comic spirit intact.

Reduced from picture to diagram the plot of *The Comedy of Errors* thus oscillates regularly between the building up of danger and its evasion. It also oscillates between, in musical terminology, accelerando and ritardando. And this oscillation, too, is of a fairly regular character. Again the *protasis* provides both model (1.2) and first variation or rather repetition (2.1). The opening dialogues of both scenes serve multiple yet identical functions: they impart information; they introduce the figures in their typicality (the traveller and his servant, the shrewish wife and her confidante); they allude to or discuss important themes of the play, the problem of identity through Antipholus of Syracuse (1.2.33–40), that of marital obedience through the highly patterned *débat* between Adriana and Luciana (2.1.1–42). The easy introduction of stereotyped figures and the quiet unfolding of relevant themes are abruptly brought to an end through the entrance of another figure, in both scenes a servant. Now misunderstandings ensue and characterize the following part of each scene: orders are given which will move the action forward, tension and aggression accumulate and find a vent in the beatings the Dromios suffer. The violence and turbulence of the centre is then contrasted with the finale of each scene. Both scenes close with rather meditative, subdued passages of thematic interest:

Antipholus evokes the aura of magic which ever since the Apostle Paul's days has been attributed to Ephesus (1.2.97–105) and Adriana pours out her jealous lament (2.1.87–115). This tripartite division remains the governing principle of scenic structure henceforward. Even if from the fourth act onwards the oscillation negates the scene divisions, the movement of the plot still pulsates regularly between turbulence and calm, is alternately speeded up and slowed down. (And appropriate changes of metre or movement between verse and prose underline these differences in scenic quality.)

Clearly, these two plotting devices, the building up of danger and its sudden, easy evasion, the tripartite scene-division with its regular alternation between turbulence and calm, work together and mutually enforce the comic precipitation of the play. Thus, the opening section of each scene may dramatize the conditions which give rise to danger or violence, the middle their imminent or actual outbreak, the last their evasion and the establishment of a new, precarious balance. Both scenes dealt with (1.2, 2.1), and others besides,[17] are plotted according to this formula. But even in a farce formulaic plotting may be overdone, mechanization may be carried too far (a truth which must be asserted, even at the danger of sounding like Mr Brooke of *Middlemarch* on poetics). Shakespeare employs two plot strategies to counteract such mechanization. First, there is the repeated reporting of events dramatically presented earlier on. The Ephesian Dromio's report (2.1.45–74) of the meeting with his presumptive master in the market-place to fetch him home to dinner first instances this plot-device. The incident is related again, if my count is correct, on three further occasions through three different speakers.[18] More than a third of the whole play is taken up by the narration of events which the spectator has

---

16 This provides some justification for interpretations which stress the near-tragic status of *The Comedy of Errors*, e.g. Gwyn Williams, '"The Comedy of Errors" Rescued from Tragedy', *Review of English Literature*, 5 (1964), 63–71.

17 Most clearly 2.2, 3.1, 4.1–3.

18 2.2.7–19; 2.2.154–64; 3.1.6–14.

witnessed before in the flesh.[19] The fourth scene of act 4 is almost totally, act 5 in large part given to such reporting. Consequently, different and radically differing perspectives of the dramatis personae refract all the events of the play.[20] These refractions of what has happened by those to whom it has happened provide glimpses of the suffering, jealous, choleric, greedy, mercantile humanity behind the swiftly moving plot. Some humanization is the result, enough to add to the interest of the audience, not enough to raise problems either about the moral status of this world of farce or about the ultimate ruthlessness of this kind of plotting with its emphasis on mechanical virtuosity. The other strategy Shakespeare employs to counterweigh the dehumanizing effects of formulaic plotting consists in providing explanatory models for all the twists and turns of the plot. Again the *protasis* lays the groundwork. The strange behaviour of his servant and the loss of his money make Antipholus of Syracuse remember widely believed rumours, namely, that 'the Ephesians were infamous for their Magicall practises':[21]

> They say this town is full of cozenage:
> As nimble jugglers that deceive the eye,
> Dark-working sorcerers that change the mind,
> Soul-killing witches that deform the body,
> Disguised cheaters, prating mountebanks,
> And many such-like liberties of sin:
>
> (1.2.97–102)

Dromio of Ephesus, on the other hand, can only find reason in unreason for his master's outrageous conduct: 'Why, mistress, sure my master is horn-mad' (2.1.57). Henceforward, magic and madness reign in Ephesus. They offer seemingly plausible explanations for what is going on, add a further level of misunderstanding and thus contribute to the entanglements of the plot, and, by implication, insinuate what, in essence, motivates and shapes a farcical plot. Put formulaic plotting, *Errors*-like, into unmitigated practice: surely, that way madness lies.

Love's Labour's Lost, by a consensus most unusual in Shakespeare criticism, possesses only vestiges of action, is ballet-like or musical in structure and devoted to the self-conscious presentation of stylistic and verbal extravagancies. Yet one of the finest essays on the play, written at a time when it was still mainly regarded as a linguistic and historical conundrum, has ascribed to it 'an inexorable movement forward'.[22] The analysis of Shakespeare's strategies of plotting the *protasis* proves this view correct – and the general consensus not wrong. The *protasis* of *Love's Labour's Lost* is plotted along totally different lines from that of *The Comedy of Errors*. With only a little exaggeration it can be claimed that the *protasis* is contained within the introductory dialogue of the four lords (1–180), with slightly more exaggeration that it consists of the first fourteen lines of the play, Navarre's edict: action and theme are all enclosed there as in a nut-shell. This protatic function of Navarre's speech I shall discuss here. Both central concepts and much of the imagery of *Love's Labour's Lost*, both the structural pattern and the plot, are prefigured or epitomized in these fourteen lines. As a full analysis of Navarre's speech, if my premise is correct, must inevitably lead to an interpretation of the comedy in its totality, I shall limit myself to a few examples. The imagery of warfare, for instance, which is variously and consistently employed throughout the play,[23] is first evoked by Navarre, the three lords being rather prematurely designated by him as

> brave conquerors – for so you are,
> That war against your own affections
> And the huge army of the world's desires.
>
> (1.1.8–10)

---

[19] According to G. Salgādo, '"Time's Deformed Hand"', p. 82, more than 700 lines in a play of about 1700 lines are taken up by such reporting.

[20] Bertrand Evans, *Shakespeare's Comedies* (Oxford, 1960), pp. 1–9, has analysed this phenomenon in its relation to genre and audience reaction, as has Manfred Pfister in *Studien zum Wandel der Perspektivenstruktur in elisabethanischen und jakobäischen Komödien* (Munich, 1974), pp. 60–86, with regard to theme and the mutual relationship of the dramatis personae as well.

[21] Alexander Roberts, *A Treatise of Witchcraft* (1616), p. 61.

[22] Bobbyann Roesen (Anne Barton), '*Love's Labour's Lost*', *Shakespeare Quarterly*, 4 (1953), p. 413.

[23] Cf. the discussion in William C. Carroll's brilliantly stimulating monograph, *The Great Feast of Language in 'Love's Labour's Lost'* (Princeton, 1976), pp. 98–9. I am much indebted to Carroll's study.

And, to point to just one other example, the problem of knowing and ruling one's 'affections' (l. 9) figures prominently in Navarre's proclamation, to be then repeatedly discussed, augmented, criticized in the course of the play: the wit- and witticism-combats between the lords and ladies revolve almost exclusively about the nature and value of affection and its bastard offspring, affectation.

The analysis and criticism of concepts or problems, however, are not limited to the verbal level in *Love's Labour's Lost*. The central concepts find their concrete embodiments or are dramatically acted out. Act 4, scene 1 contains a striking example. It is Navarre who, in his first speech, expresses his striving after eternal fame through a metaphor of the chase; he seeks 'fame, that all hunt after' (l. 1). Subsequently, Navarre's verbal heart's desire finds a sort of fulfilment. What was merely words with no regard paid to consequences is tested against its enactment, against its reality of flesh and blood. A real chase is presented and the Princess most explicitly points the moral:

Glory grows guilty of detested crimes,
When for fame's sake, for praise, an outward part,
We bend to that the working of the heart;
As I for praise alone now seek to spill
The poor deer's blood, that my heart means no ill.
(4.1.31–5)

Beyond its fairly obvious thematic relevance as a criticism of one of the play's central concepts (fame) and themes (words versus action) this passage, in its relation to Navarre's opening speech, epitomizes the working of the play's plot: Navarre announces a programme full of untested concepts and ideals, a programme of words. The words turn into actions, but into actions which in various ways run counter to the intention of the speaker. They enact not what has been desired but what has been denied. In Freudian terminology, the plot of *Love's Labour's Lost* fully acts out the return of the repressed.

The supreme importance of antithesis for the play's plotting derives from this. Antitheses structure the play on all levels[24] and Navarre's speech is studded with them. It opposes 'lives' to 'tombs' and 'death', 'cormorant devouring Time' to 'eternity', 'grace' to 'disgrace', 'court' to 'academe', 'still' to 'living'. Navarre's whole thinking is rigidly dualist, dividing mind from body, opting for a *vita contemplativa* divorced from all activity. Half of life is thus negated or repressed. Compulsorily, this half returns and gives battle to Navarre's and his lords' intentions. This is the 'inexorable movement forward' of *Love's Labour's Lost*, its comic precipitation. The arrival of the French Princess and her ladies is part of this forward movement. It becomes inevitable the moment Navarre neglects his court, abdicates his princely duties, and, prefiguring Dukes Vincentio and Prospero, considers his academe dukedom large enough. 'Still and contemplative' an Elizabethan prince may not live, be he never so unwilling to stage himself to the public eye. His political position and function demand a different, an active life. This is what the arrival of the French Princess confronts Navarre with. Moreover, he and his lords are pitilessly confronted with everything else they have negated, most importantly with the fact and consequences of time, mutability, and death. To give a single example each: Navarre's intention to live in a very specific sense *sub specie aeternitatis*, to abolish, as it were, Time for an eternity of fame must perforce collide with nature's own time-scheme which all flesh is subject to, the seasonal cycle. Indeed, from Berowne's verses in the beginning

At Christmas I no more desire a rose
Than wish a snow in May's new-fangled shows;
(1.1.105–6)

to the *débat* of spring and winter, cuckoo and owl, at the end, the movement of *Love's Labour's Lost* is governed by natural, cyclical time.[25] Navarre's analogous intention to escape the effects of mutability is, in the high comic vein, mocked by Rosaline. Her 'thus change I like the moon' is the necessary counterpoint to the King's brazen fixity as asserted in his opening speech. Finally, 'the

---

24 Cf. the catalogue of antitheses in Carroll, *The Great Feast of Language*, p. 171.
25 Cf. for a comprehensive treatment John Kerrigan, '*Love's Labour's Lost* and the Circling Seasons', *Essays in Criticism*, 28 (1978), 269–87.

disgrace of death' which he attempts to banish from his court and life is called into the lists against him: Marcade is its embodiment. Death returns on Navarre and his dearest wish with a vengeance; it even halts the comic precipitation of the play, 'the scene begins to cloud' indeed (5.2.721) and Jack must go without Jill for a year and a day.

Thus the antitheses of Navarre's opening speech define the plot-movement of *Love's Labour's Lost*. The tension between the opposite poles of the antitheses is resolved as the repressed or negated part is first conjured into being and action (or rather counteraction) and then triumphs over the initially preferred attitude. The plot of *Love's Labour's Lost* can therefore also be described as a long ironic reversal of Navarre's rigid and illusive programme. The eavesdropping scene (4.3) is the most striking theatrical emblem for these reversals, the four lords turning in a trice from mortification and study to sensual gratification and love, from being 'brave conquerors...That war against...affections' (1.1.8–9) to 'affection's men-at-arms' (4.3.286).

As a postscript something more speculative may be added. Is it mere chance that in a play which bountifully employs sonnets and sonnet-like forms, which promotes its male protagonists to sonneteers, in which Don Armado is sure that he will literally 'turn sonnet' (1.2.184), which presents, discusses, and criticizes much of the contents and attitudes of the (courtly) love-poetry which the sonnet epitomizes – is it mere chance that the programme of such a play is contained in fourteen lines?[26] If not, Navarre's 'sonnet' may serve as another structural emblem of *Love's Labour's Lost*. For this is surely a sonnet with a difference. If its *volta* is but slightly out of place, in line 8 instead of line 9, it entirely lacks another distinguishing characteristic of the sonnet-form, namely the appropriate rhyme-scheme. Its form is plainly defective. It is exactly this formal deficiency, however, which may be considered to be structurally programmatic. For as this 'sonnet' is a sonnet in only one essential, but otherwise corrupts and destroys traditional form, so do other episodes of the play. The defective sonnet anticipates the corruption and destruction of form in the Masque of the Muscovites, in the Pageant of the Nine

Worthies, and, most important, in the comic movement of the play itself. The sonnet, the masque, the pageant, the comedy itself: they all exist but as 'form confounded' (5.2.519), a not unusual result of the return of the repressed.

The Two Gentlemen of Verona, if a frequency count proves a reliable basis for evaluation, is the least attractive of Shakespeare's comedies: it has, comparatively speaking, been seldom discussed by critics and even more rarely performed. Shakespeare's plotting seems to have contributed its fair share to the play's failure.[27] The *protasis* of *The Comedy of Errors* builds up the play's comic precipitation by a continuous interplay between the creation of dangers and their evasion, the plot of *Love's Labour's Lost* is contained within Navarre's opening speech and acts out, by means of ironic reversals, the return of the repressed, whereas the *protasis* of *The Two Gentlemen of Verona*, instead of rousing the audience's attention and pitching it forward to a comic conclusion, sends it on various wild-goose chases. Nonetheless, the opening dialogue between Valentine and Proteus appears, at first sight, to be most promising from a dramatic point of view. It contains much that, developed, might spark off a dramatic conflict. It states a theme – love – which might function as the basis for the plot and presents two characters differentiated by their attitudes towards this love-theme. Even if, as Inga-Stina Ewbank has convincingly demonstrated, these attitudes shrink to mere attitudinizing in the course of the play,[28] a Lylyan dramaturgy, the facetting of

---

[26] That the number of lines in the programmatic part of Navarre's speech and of the Elizabethan regulation sonnet are identical has been pointed out by Karl-Heinz Wendel, *Sonettstrukturen in Shakespeares Dramen* (Bad Homburg, 1968), p. 139, and, independently, by L. A. Montrose, '"Folly, in wisdom hatch'd": The Exemplary Comedy of *Love's Labour's Lost*', *Comparative Drama*, 11 (1977/78), p. 149.

[27] As has the restriction of speech to the soliloquy, the duologue, and the aside noted by Stanley Wells: 'The Failure of *The Two Gentlemen of Verona*', *Shakespeare-Jahrbuch*, 99 (1963), 161–73, pp. 163–5.

[28] '"Were man but constant, he were perfect": Constancy and Consistency in "The Two Gentlemen of Verona"',

a theme through various characters and situations in the mode of *Endimion*, might be the entertaining result. Sure enough, the unfolding of the theme continues when Julia, in the first lines of the second scene, quite programmatically takes it up:

> But say, Lucetta, now we are alone,
> Wouldst thou then counsel me to fall in love?
>
> (1.2.1–2)

But where is the conflict, where is a plot-propelling force? The names of the male protagonists offer the sole clue. A faithful lover named Proteus, a despiser of love named Valentine – an ironic reversal is with certainty to be expected. And, pat it comes with Valentine's dotage (2.1) and Proteus's faithlessness (2.4). Thus, by the middle of the second act and still within the *protasis*, the reversal has already occurred and the one tension inherent in the protagonists' attitudes towards love has been resolved. New motives must now be looked for to move the play forward (and Proteus's soliloquy, 2.4.192–214, speedily supplies the want).

The nucleus of yet another plot and conflict seems to be enclosed within the opening dialogue between Valentine and Proteus. It is epigrammatically stated by Proteus in his soliloquy: 'He after honor hunts, I after love' (1.1.63). Valentine and Proteus, honour and love, are contrasted, two sets of possibly conflicting values which rule human behaviour are evoked. The contrast widens as Proteus, still during his soliloquy, sets worldly achievements, 'studies', 'good counsel', and, finally, 'the world at nought' (ll. 67–8) – and all for love. This basic contrast is further enriched and developed into a rudimentary plot and a potential conflict by the plans of the elder generation to make Proteus, who hunts after love, follow the course of Valentine 'to seek preferment out' (1.3.7). The audience's expectation that this is the matter which will constitute the conflict and plot of *The Two Gentlemen of Verona* may have been additionally strengthened by some knowledge of dramatic convention or theatrical history. For the conflict of love and honour belongs firmly to the repertoire of Elizabethan comedy. Both Alexander's conduct in Lyly's *Campaspe* and Edward's in Greene's *Friar Bacon and Friar Bungay*, to name but

two examples, are defined by it. Internal and external factors, therefore, mutually enforce each other and create some comic precipitation. But in *The Two Gentlemen of Verona* the conflict between seeking worldly preferment and thinking the world well lost for love leads nowhere. With Valentine abandoning the thought of a worldly career the matter is quietly dropped. And again the need for some new plot-propelling force arises.

If the *protasis* of *The Two Gentlemen of Verona* does not set going an action which encompasses the whole play, what then does? What is the basic idea behind, the thematic dimension of, the plot? It was R. G. Moulton who first pointed out,[29] and most critics have agreed with him, that the play's action does not spring from the character or conduct of the dramatis personae and that for internal, temporal progression external, spatial journeyings and changes of location have been substituted. The *protasis* provides the model for this, if for nothing else: Valentine leaves for the Emperor's court in the first scene and he is followed by Proteus at the beginning of the second act. Proteus, in turn, is followed by Julia between acts 2 and 3. Between the third and the fourth acts Valentine has to go into exile, followed, in the beginning of the fifth act, by Silvia who is herself followed by the whole court. No doubt this multiple journeying is a device to structure the play, especially to mark the act-divisions.[30] No doubt, too, that such journeying is the traditional hallmark of romance.[31] Yet the journeys have hardly any thematic or emblematic significance. They neither serve to express the character's change or growth nor to illuminate the

---

in *Shakespearian Comedy*, ed. D. J. Palmer and M. Bradbury, Stratford-upon-Avon Studies, 14 (1972), pp. 51–2.

29 *Shakespeare as a Dramatic Thinker* (1907; repr. New York, 1969), pp. 222 ff.

30 The insistent use of journeys and, additionally, mythic allusions and letters elicits high praise of the play's structure from W. L. Godshalk, 'The Structural Unity of *The Two Gentlemen of Verona*', *Studies in Philology*, 66 (1969), p. 169.

31 This is fully discussed by Clifford Leech in his Introduction to the (new) Arden edition of the play (1969), pp. lviii–lix.

ways of the world or of the powers ruling them. They offer the amusement of frequent change to the spectator. They are *ersatz*: external movement usurps the place of plot and action.

Just as a thematically based plot is replaced by frequent changes of location, so sudden changes of mind take the place of motivation. The *protasis* contains the first instance: Proteus is commanded by his father to follow Valentine to the Emperor's court at once. No reason for this command is allowed to Proteus, although the search for worldly preferment had occupied the thoughts of the elder generation in a preceding dialogue. On the contrary, Antonio stresses the arbitrary and authoritarian suddenness of his decision:

> Muse not that I thus suddenly proceed;
> For what I will, I will, and there an end.

> (1.3.64–5)

With the same abrupt suddenness the whole movement of *The Two Gentlemen of Verona* jerks on: Proteus's wooing is as suddenly granted (1.3.45–7) as he is suddenly commanded away by his father; Valentine suddenly does not despise love any longer, but is its ardent devotee (2.1.3–5); Proteus suddenly proves true to name and type (2.4.192–5); in 4.3 a noble knight, Sir Eglamour, is with a flick of the wrist produced from the wings, only to be, in the fifth act, abruptly metamorphosed into a downright coward. And the mental and emotional quick-changes of the two so-called gentlemen in the forest-maze are too well known to need recital. Does the arbitrary suddenness of change describe the movement of the comedy? Does it precipitate the play to its comic conclusion? In a sense, yes. Still, the effect on the audience is not, in William Archer's words, a stretching forward of the mind but, to a large extent, bewilderment. For the arbitrary changes are consistent in nothing but their arbitrariness, they do not move the play in any expected direction but whither it listeth. And to make matters worse, there is no motivation, no reason for either the arbitrariness or the suddenness of the reversals. Valentine and Proteus are not even Fortune's fools. They are puppets on a string, moving perforce according to the whimsical pulls and jerks of the master-puppeteer.

The conclusions to be drawn from the dramatization of the *protasis* in these three early comedies suggest themselves. Restless experimentation, according to John Russell Brown the characteristic feature of all the comedies,[32] is certainly to be discerned in Shakespeare's treatment of the introductions. In the way they pursue identical aims they are all utterly unlike. This is the more remarkable as Graeco-Roman New Comedy, the Terentian plot-formula and act-division, provides the overall structure for each of the plays. In *The Comedy of Errors* and *Love's Labour's Lost*, Shakespeare has fully exploited one of the Terentian theorists' premises, namely that the *protasis* is not only to be given over to introductory information about the setting and the dramatis personae but has also to rouse the audience's expectation and stretch it forward towards a comic catastrophe. What is possibly more important and helps to define Shakespeare's dramatic genius: in both cases he has also extended the traditional function of the *protasis*. It now contains, in nucleic and highly concentrated form, the play's structure, theme, and plot. While the *protasis* of *The Comedy of Errors* establishes a model, a pattern both for plot and scene to be repeated with little variation throughout the play, *Love's Labour's Lost* formulates a programme which is then dramatically unfolded by means of ironic reversals. In both plays plot and theme are indissolubly linked and mutually enforce each other. The possibility of evading even mortal danger functions as the thematic underpinning of the plot in *The Comedy of Errors*, the return of the repressed sums up the plot's meaning in *Love's Labour's Lost*.

It is here, in the relationship of plot, theme, and structure, that *The Two Gentlemen of Verona* fails. Opportunities to establish such a relationship are wasted more than once in the course of the *protasis*. Episodic, sprawling romance material may prove less amenable to the high degree of concentration achieved in the two other plays. But there is nothing in the inherent nature of romance material to

---

[32] *Shakespeare and His Comedies* (1957), p. 27.

prevent plots from possessing a thematic dimension and pointing clearly forward towards the comic catastrophe, as *The Tempest* magically demonstrates. The *protasis* of *The Two Gentlemen of Verona*, however, nowhere provides such comic precipitation. The movement of the play does not spring from the nature of the dramatis personae, nor is it governed by Fortune, the traditional goddess of romance. From the very beginning the play ambles along without clear direction. Mechanical substi-tutes, the frequent changes of location and the sudden changes of mind, have to be introduced to give some appearance of dramatic movement. Behind this flimsy appearance the constantly interfering dramatist becomes visible, the puppeteer who every now and again has to provide a new stimulus, a new motive, location or character to keep the action from grinding to a dead halt. In this, Sir Eglamour is the play's quintessential figure.

THE GOOD MARRIAGE OF KATHERINE AND PETRUCHIO

DAVID DANIELL

Nowadays, *The Taming of the Shrew* is taken in its entirety, without mutilation, crude business with whips (imported by Kemble) or announcements of the embarrassing incompetence of the prentice Shakespeare. It is winning increasing praise, for the structure of its interlocking parts among other things, and is becoming understood as a fast-moving play about various kinds of romance and fulfilment in marriage.[1]

Problems remain, of course, particularly with Katherine's final speech: modern solutions making it a statement of contemporary doctrine, or of male fantasy, or of almost unbelievably sustained irony, do not any of them seem to suggest that there is much for Katherine and Petruchio to look forward to in marriage. The speech is a disappointment after the tender moment of 'Nay, I will give thee a kiss' (5.1.133) which suggested that something was coming with a lot of good feeling in it, an impression later supported by her having the wit to win Petruchio's wager for him. Moreover, submission, as it is first, and strongly, presented in the play, in the Induction, scene 1, is denigration, a game played by pretended attendants; and *wifely* submission, shown even more strongly in the following scene, is sport by a page dressed as the sham wife of a ridiculously deceived 'husband'. It is all a pastime, and false.

Sly, however, disappears for good, and this is surely right in view of the serious point about marriage which can be seen to be made at the end of the play by Katherine. I want to suggest that it is a truly Shakespearian marriage-play, and as such takes marriage seriously and makes as high a claim for the state of matrimony as, from experience of

him elsewhere, we should expect Shakespeare to do. The way into this, I suggest, is through the play's special sense of theatricality, linked with an understanding that it is wrong to think of such a marriage-play having a firmly closed ending.

That *The Taming of the Shrew* is imbued with a fresh excitement about the potentials of theatre now needs little elaboration. The most modern commentators take that as understood, and indeed enlarge on the matter with some precision. G. R. Hibbard in the New Penguin edition refers to

bravura pieces, conscious displays of the rhetorical arts of grotesque description, farcical narrative, and inventive vituperation. Language is being deliberately exploited for effect; and what, in another context, might well appear cruel, outrageous, or offensive is transformed into comic exuberance by a linguistic virtuosity that delights in the exercise of its own powers.

Brian Morris in his Arden edition notes among much else a contrast of 'physical violence with the eloquence of persuasions and the rituals of debate'. H. J. Oliver sums up a major part of the introduction to his Oxford Shakespeare edition with the words 'Shakespeare certainly plays with the subject of theatrical illusion, and through the Induction and elsewhere seems to warn his audience of the ambiguity of "belief".'[2] Theatricality is

---

[1] Brian Morris concludes the Introduction to his Arden edition (1981) with a long section 'Love and marriage', pp. 136–49.

[2] G. R. Hibbard, *The Taming of the Shrew* (Harmondsworth, 1968), p. 8; Brian Morris, p. 105; H. J. Oliver, *The Taming of the Shrew* (Oxford, 1982), p. 57.

everywhere. The Bianca plot works because people dress up as other people and assume roles. Petruchio, as is now frequently said, plays a part like an actor until he has subdued Katherine. It is universally agreed that the Induction spells out clearly that theatrical illusion can have powerful effect, and that this is important for the rest of the play. In the Lord's two long speeches which so dominate the play's first 136 lines he shows himself to be obsessed with the notion of acting, particularly with the careful creation of an illusion of a rich world for Sly to come to life in. This is even more developed in the following scene as his servants get the hang of the idea and fantasize freely about what sensual delights are in their power to offer. By the time Lucentio and Tranio enter to start the specially mounted play some quite large areas of the capability of theatre to create illusion have been coloured in.

Two things should reinforce the importance of this stress on theatricality itself for the rest of the play. The first is that the opening two scenes are not, in Folio, quite as detached as they are often assumed to be. The labels 'Induction, scene 1' and 'Induction, scene 2' used in virtually all modern editions, though in some senses technically correct (if un-Shakespearian) only go back as far as Pope.[3] The Folio text begins firmly 'Actus primus. Scoena Prima.' (and then forgets all about divisions until 'Actus Tertia'). Though the non-appearance of Sly in the Folio after the end of the first scene of the Bianca plot causes worry to some critics, the Folio arrangement of the scenes might prevent a general tendency to detach him too far. As I shall show, it is not true to say that Sly's concerns are later absorbed into the main action – that Katherine's arrival in a new world created for her has, as it were, consummated Sly's action. But the relentless insistence on the creation of controlled illusion from 'Actus primus. Scoena Prima.' does, as we shall see, have an important effect on the main actions, and particularly on the relation between Petruchio and Kate.

Secondly, it is difficult to miss the point about theatrical illusion when two early moments of transition in the first scene are so odd. It is peculiar that the hunting Lord's first thought on seeing the 'monstrous beast' (having apostrophized death in one line) should be to play such an elaborate trick. That is hardly an expected response. Then, to cap that, he hears a trumpet, and confidently expects 'some noble gentleman that means, / Travelling some journey, to repose him here'. But it is no such thing. It is 'players / That offer service to your lordship'. Their arrival, in view of the game of 'supposes' that he has in hand, is altogether too apt.

The two opening scenes bring together three of the play's chief concerns: hunting, acting, and the creation of an illusion of a powerfully rich world. As the second play-within-the-play begins (the first is 'Sly as lord') Lucentio and Tranio are caught up in a business which carries all three things forward. Lucentio has no doubt of the richness of Bianca: '...I saw sweet beauty in her face...I saw her coral lips to move, / And with her breath she did perfume the air' (1.1.162, 169–70). With Tranio, he is going to hunt her down: 'I burn, I pine, I perish, Tranio, / If I achieve not this young modest girl' (ll. 150–1). And he is soon involved in a situation which makes play-acting both essential and exciting. The direct wooing of Bianca is forbidden by her father, and there are rivals. Indeed, disguise and part-playing are positively invited, as Baptista encourages the rivals to produce 'schoolmasters' who will be kept 'within my house'. The theatrical game spins merrily, with Tranio playing Lucentio, Lucentio playing 'Cambio', Hortensio playing 'Licio' – and Bianca playing the adorable young girl. Presently a Pedant plays Vincentio. At the end of the play all the disguises have come off. Lucentio is himself and successfully wedded to Bianca who, married, is not quite as she appeared to be when wooed. Tranio is himself, and seems to have been forgiven, as he comports himself boldly. The Pedant and the real Vincentio have, in a good deal of wonderfully rapid

3 'His contemporaries found the implied play metaphor of the induction device extremely attractive; Shakespeare himself seems to have preferred the less artificial form of the play within the play.' Anne Righter, Shakespeare and the Idea of the Play (1962), p. 104.

business, faced each other out and the truth has triumphed.

All this, however, is more a matter of simple change of name. The Pedant does not even need a disguise. Lucentio is disguised, and Tranio puts on Lucentio's finery ('*Enter Tranio brave*', 1.2.214). Hortensio dresses up. But the deceptions that are practised lack depth, and belong to the very fast-moving world of amorous intrigue. Everyone receives the appropriate reward, and the two who are married at the end of this plot, Lucentio and Hortensio, have wives who, as G. R. Hibbard says of Bianca, have realized that 'deception is a woman's most effective weapon'.[4]

Inside this action is the other, that of Katherine and Petruchio. This can also be seen in the primary colours of hunting, acting and a special richness. It is so clearly set inside, like a jewel in a mounting, that the resulting extension of the significances comes to be unmistakable. By this device, the action is moved on to another plane, as it were: almost on to another dimension. If *The Taming of the Shrew* is seen as a set of Chinese boxes, then the opening of the last one has some magic qualities. Katherine is most firmly inset. Consider: the audience is in a theatre watching a play about a Lord who makes a play for a tinker who watches a play about two young Italians who watch 'some show to welcome us to town' (1.1.47) inside which is a play about the surreptitious wooing of an *amorosa* by a love-sick hero and his rivals. Inside that is set another play about, by contrast, the very blatant wooing of her sister. Katherine does not say very much; compared with Rosalind, or even Beatrice, she is positively silent; but she is undoubtedly the heart of the play. She is introduced at five removes, it might be said, from street-level. At each remove the illusion increases. (We might note that Petruchio's very late entry into the action could well be said to make a sixth remove; the play has run for 524 lines at his entry, before which he is not even mentioned.)

On this interior plane, displacements are not of name or clothes, but of two entire personalities, a very different thing altogether. Indeed, Petruchio has announced himself vigorously from his first entry into the action, and he bombards Katherine,

in the very first seconds of their first meeting, with her own name – eleven times in seven lines. He forbids his wife the new cap and gown the Tailor has provided, and his change of clothes for the wedding makes a mockery of dressing-up.

Nor are the displacements, like the others, temporary. Katherine, her 'lesson' learned, will not revert to being a shrew. Petruchio, having tamed her, will not revert to bullying. Except that I do not believe that Shakespeare's play says anything quite so obvious, or so final. If, rather than dramatic life on a different plane, there were a straight parallel here with the Bianca plot, it would have to be argued that Petruchio was 'really' a gentle person who put on roughness only while he was wooing Kate. To say so is to forget that he enters the play knocking his servant about and his servant calls him, twice, quarrelsome and mad (1.2.13–32). It is to argue too that Kate is 'really' an emotionally mature young woman ready for marriage thrown temporarily into desperation by her impossible father and sister. But within thirty-five lines of meeting someone who has come to woo her, who announces 'Good Kate; I am a gentleman' she is crying 'That I'll try' and '*She strikes him*' (2.1.216). Both have strong violent streaks. Katherine says she will not be made a puppet (4.3.103) to be knocked about, or not, for ever after. Rather, as the further inside, the more the increase of illusion, so the illusion now is of a greater 'reality', not less. Unlike 'Cambio' and 'Licio', Katherine and Petruchio are 'real' people. *Their* theatrical dimension allows them to do something quite different, and much more interesting. Katherine and Petruchio can be seen to grow to share an ability to use theatrical situations to express new and broadening perspectives in a world as unlimited as art itself.

I want to come at this now from another direction. Brian Morris, in the introduction to his Arden edition, says 'There are few points of possible comparison between *Shrew* and the first tetralogy of history plays.'[5] I feel that this is not quite true. There

---

[4] Hibbard, p. 35.

[5] Morris, p. 59.

may well turn out to be quite a number – certainly more than it is possible to comment on here. In the first place, there are large areas of superficial similarity in the use of verse, where so often the rhythms of the lines of the *Henry VI* plays are clearly from the same mind as made *Shrew*. Equally generally, there are similarities in certain single lines where the reader, meeting the line on its own, would be hard put to it to place the line in the right play. Thus 'I see report is fabulous and false' might be from either a history play or *Shrew*. It is *1 Henry VI*, 2.3.18, where, like *Shrew*'s 'And now I find report a very liar' it is in a sexually charged two-hander in the first heat of a meeting.

> Thus have I politicly begun my reign,
> And 'tis my hope to end successfully

taken alone, would be put in the first tetralogy; it is of course Petruchio at 4.1.172–3, though it resembles *2 Henry VI*, 3.1.341, and the tenor of the 'jolly thriving wooer' at *Richard III* 4.3.36–43. The *2 Henry VI* line, 'Well, nobles, well, 'tis politicly done' also comes early in a soliloquy announcing a programme of action to win a personal triumph, and has the only other use of 'politicly' in Shakespeare. The game can be continued. I suppose 'Cease, cease these jars and rest your minds in peace; / Let's to the altar' might be mistaken for *Shrew* instead of *1 Henry VI*, 1.1.44–5. Stamping a hat under a foot does not just belong to Kate – Gloucester does it to Winchester's hat at *1 Henry VI*, 1.3.49. There are some similarities of situation. The duel of wits between Petruchio and Kate might be said to parallel the duels between Joan la Pucelle and the Dauphin, or Joan and Talbot, in *1 Henry VI*, act 1, scenes 2 and 5, or more plausibly between Richard's outrageous wooing of Anne, and Elizabeth, in *Richard III*, act 1, scene 1, and act 4, scene 4. Eyes dazzled by the sun – in particular relation to a dramatically significant father – are the basis of special wordplay and action in both *Shrew* act 4, scene 5, and *3 Henry VI* act 2, scene 1. The 'martial' quality of Joan and the bluff chivalry of Talbot suggests casting the same kind of actors as Katherine and Petruchio. Fancy can multiply parallels and

echoes. It is odd that the only early plays of Shakespeare not mentioned by Francis Meres are the three parts of *Henry VI* and *Shrew*. Further analysis of what they might have in common, especially audiences, needs to be done.

Yet it is not entirely fanciful to see that from the moment of Petruchio's Richard-like soliloquy ('Thus have I politicly begun my reign') the Petruchio–Katherine relationship brushes against the world of the history plays, and indeed with their principal source. The other main plots, concerning Lucentio and Bianca, and the Lord and his servants, are Ovidian in tone and reference, as can be easily demonstrated. Katherina, however, suffers in a different key. Her description of herself as 'starv'd for meat, giddy for lack of sleep; / With oaths kept waking, and with brawling fed' (4.3.9–10) belongs more to Shakespeare's world of war than to anything remotely like the Ovid found elsewhere in the play. The 'Beggars that come unto my father's door' who 'Upon entreaty have a present alms' of the same speech suggest the same world, of displaced soldiery. She feels herself threatened with 'deadly sickness or else present death'. Her violent reaction to Grumio's tantalizing game with beef and mustard is to beat him, with words which could be from a woman in the later plays of the tetralogy:

> Sorrow on thee and all the pack of you
> That triumph thus upon my misery!

Her experience of noise and violence and hunger and misery belongs to the earlier history plays.

Petruchio's courtship moves through several areas of reference. Just before he met Katherine, he saw his wooing in Petrarchan terms (2.1.169–72). He can flatter her with classical affinities – 'Dian', 'Grissel', Lucrece; and carry on like any swashbuckler (3.2.229–35). It is only from the end of act 4, scene 1 that he hopes to end his 'reign' both 'politicly' and 'successfully', and the idea of the warlike is never far away after that. Even his violence about the gown is in battlefield terms: ''Tis like a demi-cannon...up and down, carv'd...snip and nip and cut and slish and slash...' (4.3.88–90). Lucentio, indeed, presently thinks he announces the end of a civil war.

> At last, though long, our jarring notes agree;
> And time it is when raging war is done
> To smile at scapes and perils overblown.
>
> (5.2.1–3)

Petruchio won his first victory some time before that, in Katherine's apparent submission over the matter of the sun and the moon: 'What you will have it nam'd, even that it is' (4.5.21), and at that point Hortensio thinks all is over: 'Petruchio, go thy ways, the field is won' (l. 23). Petruchio, however, has not finished. Almost at once, Vincentio enters, and Petruchio greets him as 'gentle mistress':

> Tell me, sweet Kate, and tell me truly too,
> Hast thou beheld a fresher gentlewoman?
> Such war of white and red within her cheeks!
>
> (ll. 28–30)

For the moment, Kate has agreed no more than to play his game of pretence. It has cost her a good deal, no doubt, and it is a real step forward, which he acknowledges. But he himself goes 'forward, forward' (l. 24) from the 'war of white and red' to something more than one victory, more even than 'peace...and love, and quiet life, / An awful rule, and right supremacy...what not that's sweet and happy' (5.2.108–10) when she has won his wager for him. He does not know the full measure of his success until she has spoken her last, and famous, speech.

It is hard not to see in that 'war of white and red' a hint of the Wars of the Roses, however well-worn the notion of white and red cheeks was for Elizabethans. The probable dates of the writing of the first tetralogy encompass the likely dates for the writing of *The Taming of the Shrew*. Certainly, close to the time of writing the comedy, Shakespeare put on the stage a symbolic scene in which an imaginary origin is given for the name of the wars, an incident in the Temple Garden when English lords and others pluck red and white roses.

Plantagenet.
> Meantime your cheeks do counterfeit our roses;
> For pale they look with fear, as witnessing
> The truth on our side.

Somerset.   No, Plantagenet,
> 'Tis not for fear but anger that thy cheeks
> Blush for pure shame to counterfeit our roses,
> And yet thy tongue will not confess thy error.
>
> (1 Henry VI, 2.4.62–7)

In Shakespeare, these wars end with a marriage, a union. His principal source, Hall's Chronicle, is properly entitled *The Union of the Two Noble and Illustre Famelies...*, and Hall's direction is not just visible in his title. His brief preface, setting out the necessity and value of the writing of history, concludes his address to Edward VI with references to the marriage which healed the national split.

> Wherefore...I have compiled and gathered (and not made) out of diverse writers, as well forayn as Englishe, this simple treatise whiche I have named the union of the noble houses of Lancaster and Yorke, conjoyned together by the godly mariage of your most noble graundfather, and your verteous grandmother. For as kyng henry the fourthe was the beginnyng and rote of the great discord and devision: so was the godly matrimony, the final ende of all discencions, titles and debates.[6]

These matters would be merely curious were it not for the metaphoric strain of Katherine's last speech, which is either the proper climax to a marriage-play or it is nothing. Here, indeed, she is speaking in terms which could also be lifted from Shakespeare's earlier history plays.

> Fie, fie! unknit that threatening unkind brow,
> And dart not scornful glances from those eyes
> To wound thy lord, thy king, thy governor.
>
> (5.2.136–8)

She refers to 'thy lord, thy life, thy keeper, / Thy head, thy sovereign' (ll. 146–7) who 'craves no other tribute at thy hands / But love, fair looks, and true obedience' (ll. 152–3). There is owed 'Such duty as the subject owes the prince' (l. 155): if not, the result is 'a foul contending rebel / And graceless traitor...' (ll. 159–60). She is ashamed that women 'offer war where they should kneel for

---

6 Edward Hall, *The Union of the Two Noble and Illustre Famelies...*(1548), pp. vi, vii.

peace; / Or seek for rule, supremacy, and sway...'
(ll. 162–3).

Why Katherine chooses such language is the heart of the problem of her last speech. Is she really saying that a disobedient woman is a 'foul contending rebel and graceless traitor'? Partly she is, because she is specifically addressing two women, Bianca and the Widow, who have been 'disobedient' and who have seemed to have got the upper hand by an unpleasant kind of deception. But the dynamic of the play assuredly means that she has to be saying something private to Petruchio as well. Whatever happened between them, they have been together, and not with the others, all through the play, as a rule. They are spectators, merely, of the wild complications of the Pedant–Vincentio scene, act 5, scene 1, in which the rest of the plots of the play are resolved, and their enjoyment has included enjoyment of each other, so much that at the end Katherine can kiss Petruchio, even in public, adding 'now pray thee, love, stay' to which her husband replies 'Is not this well? Come, my sweet Kate...' (ll. 133–4).

H. J. Oliver has noticed how the matter of Katherine and Petruchio keeps becoming too *well-understood* for farce. 'It is as if Shakespeare set out to write a farce about taming a shrew but had hardly begun before he asked himself what might make a woman shrewish anyway...We sympathize with Katherine – and as soon as we do, farce becomes impossible.'[7] This is right, but I take it far further than Oliver would have approved. *The Taming of the Shrew* is a play unusually about marriages as well as courtships, and the quality of the marriage of Katherine and Petruchio might be expected to depend, as I said at the beginning of this essay, on more than a wink and a tone of irony, or a well-delivered paper on the necessity of order in the State. I am suggesting that a special quality of mutuality grew between Katherine and Petruchio as the play progressed, something invisible to all the others in the play and sealed for them both by Kate's last speech. It is surely unsatisfactory for Kate simply to flip over from one state into its opposite, or for Petruchio to have 'really' been gentle all along. I suggest that they have found, led by Petruchio, a way of being richly together with all their

contradictions – and energies – very much alive and kicking. Beatrice and Benedick go into their marriage at the end of *Much Ado About Nothing* as witty and spirited as ever, but together and not apart. I believe that Katherine and Petruchio do the same, and do it through an understanding of the power of acting, of being actors.

That Petruchio sets out to play a part is now commonly understood. Theatricality, however, attaches to him rather more than has been seen. He is an actor – a man who loves acting with a full-spirited craftsmanship far ahead of the Lord's thin-blooded connoisseurship. He has a violent streak, and is impetuous: but he has an actor's power of control, as well as an actor's apparent sudden switch of mood. He arrives quarrelling with his servant and is still smouldering when Hortensio has parted them (1.2.1–45). But presented instantly with Hortensio's offer of a 'shrewd ill-favour'd wife' (which is only Hortensio's thirteenth line) Petruchio shows excellent manners, saying like any easy guest 'Sure I'll go along with it'. More, he says it as if he were Pistol, in high style full of classical tags:

> Be she as foul as was Florentius' love,
> As old as Sibyl, and as curst and shrewd
> As Socrates' Xanthippe or a worse.
>
> (ll. 67–9)

We then watch him move, step by step, towards Katherine. He learns that their fathers knew each other, so he is on visiting terms. He discovers that she has a wider reputation as 'an irksome brawling scold' (l. 184) but is loud in his claim not to be put off: indeed, he speaks like a mini-Othello:

> Think you a little din can daunt mine ears?
> Have I not in my time heard lions roar?
> Have I not heard the sea, puff'd up with winds,
> Rage like an angry boar chafed with sweat?
> Have I not heard great ordnance in the field,
> And heaven's artillery thunder in the skies?
> Have I not in a pitched battle heard
> Loud 'larums, neighing steeds, and trumpets' clang?
>
> (1.2.196–203)

---

[7] Oliver, p. 51.

Of course he hasn't: or at least, some of it is unlikely. He has only just left home by his own confession, apparently setting off for the first time (ll. 48–56). He is using one of his voices. We soon hear another one, in the one delicious sentence from the sideline with which he sums up Tranio's posturing (as opposed to acting) – 'Hortensio, to what end are all these words?' (l. 246). He visits Baptista to present 'Licio' (Hortensio) and sees for himself the peculiarities of the household. He understands the 'little wind' with which the father and sister increase Katherine's fire, and offers himself, in another voice, as a 'raging fire'.

He quickly takes two big steps towards her, first when Hortensio enters '*with his head broke*' (2.1.140) and then when he hears as it were a tape-recording of her voice in Hortensio's report ('"Frets, call you these?" quoth she "I'll fume with them"') and finds that she can make a theatrically appropriate strong action while saying a witty line, and that she has a liberated tongue ('with twenty such vile terms') – in other words, she could well turn out to have the stuff of actors too. He is eager to see her, and sets up in soliloquy a programme not based on violence ('raging fires') but on his actor's ability to present her with a new world for her to live in ('I'll tell her plain / She sings as sweetly...').

They meet, and fall in love. Both are taken aback. Petruchio is surprised to lose some rounds of the wit-contest on points. But he holds to his purpose, though she has struck him and made him forget the part he is acting ('I swear I'll cuff you, if you strike again', 2.1.217).

Thereafter it is possible to watch him acting his way through his relationship with her, and with everyone else. From the moment of meeting, he is hunting, and in deadly earnest. He uses all his skills to make worlds for her to try to live in, as he does, as an actor, even in what appears to be bullying.[8] (She seems, pretty well from the start, to understand him as an actor. 'Where did you study all this goodly speech?' she asks (2.1.255).) In all his dealings with her, he acts out a character, and a set of situations, which present her with a mirror of herself, and in particular her high-spirited violence and her sense of being out in the cold and deprived. She who had

tied up her sister's hands – apparently because she was dressed up (2.1.3–5) – finds her own hands tied, as it were, in the scene with the Tailor, where she can't actually get her hands on the finery that was ordered. The speed of all this action in the central scenes, in the third and fourth acts, helps by presenting not so much development of 'character' as a set of projected slides, almost cartoons, of the wedding, the journey, the honeymoon, and so on. Katherine is not alone in finding it all 'unreal': it is part of a play.

But the play has a clear direction. It is always worth asking what Shakespeare does *not* do. Brian Morris points out what can be learned by seeing what appealed to the young playwright looking for ideas in the old Italian comedy. Shakespeare's Lucentio is not desperate for money, and has not seduced Bianca and got her pregnant, as Erostrato, his equivalent in *Supposes*, has done. Instead, he is seen 'to fall instantly, rapturously, romantically in love with her at first sight...It is this potential for romance, for love leading to marriage, which Shakespeare detected and exploited in Gascoigne's work.'[9] Indeed, no one in *Shrew* is desperate for money. There is no seduction or rape. The horrifying violence of such folk-tales of shrews tamed as have been sometimes produced as 'sources', or even analogues, is removed far away, mercifully, as is any tone of cynicism.

The direction of the play, for Katherine and Petruchio, is towards marriage as a rich, shared sanity. That means asserting and sharing *all* the facts about one's own identity, not suppressing large areas. Sly, floundering in the Lord's trickery, tried to assert himself like that (Induction 2.17–23). But then he sinks into illusion and is never undeceived. That is important. He 'does *not* become what others pretend him to be'.[10] Nor does Katherine. If she is a true Shakespearian heroine, in marriage she becomes herself only more so: in her case, almost

---

[8] John Russell Brown, in *Shakespeare and his Comedies* (1957), p. 98, comes near to making this point, but then veers off to something else.

[9] Morris, pp. 82, 83.

[10] Oliver, p. 38.

as capable of future strong, witty, over-verbalized action as Beatrice. Marriage is addition, not subtraction: it is a sad let-down if the dazzling action of the play produces only a female wimp. But at the end of the play she shows that she shares with Petruchio an understood frame for both their lives. Whatever Petruchio has done, he has given her his full attention in action; she has learned to act too, in both senses. This, with the special ability of acting to embrace and give form to violence, is the mutuality they share.

Her first clear step was when she learned that simple deception worked (something her sister had, infuriatingly, known by instinct). She privately called the sun the moon, and then publicly greeted Vincentio as a 'Young budding virgin, fair and fresh and sweet' (4.5.36). Soon after this, she and Petruchio are shown not only married, but tenderly in love (the kiss). Her final step is when she shows to Petruchio that she has understood that they, the two of them, can contain violence and rebellion in their own mutual frame.

Now civil wounds are stopp'd, peace lives again –
That she may long live here, God say amen!
              (*Richard III*, 5.5.40–1)

are the last lines of the Roses tetralogy. The 'war of white and red' ends in a true union of strong, almost over-strong, dynasties, and not in the impoverishment of one side. (Sly had suggested such a link in the fourth line of the play – 'Look in the chronicles'.)

Muriel Bradbrook made clear what a new thing Shakespeare was making. 'Katherine is the first shrew to be given a father, the first to be shown as maid and bride...'

Traditionally the shrew triumphed; hers was the oldest and indeed the only native comic rôle for women. If overcome, she submitted either to high theological argument or to a taste of the stick... Petruchio does not use the stick, and Katherine in her final speech does not console herself with theology.[11]

Instead of the stick, or theology (which is certainly present at that point in *A Shrew*) Shakespeare makes Kate move herself further into, rather than out of, a play-world. Her final deed is to act a big theatrical set-piece, speaking the longest speech in the play, its length totally disrupting the rhythms presented by the other plot. 'Women', she says – that is, the conventionally married in front of her – are to be submissive. But she has been hunting with Petruchio as a couple for some time now, and she sends him, inside the speech, a message about themselves, Katherine and Petruchio, in the language of dramatized civil war. The play would founder – which it doesn't – if Katherine had merely surrendered to a generalization about 'women', and said nothing intensely personal about herself and Petruchio.[12]

She concludes, and starts the final run of couplets, by admitting that women are weak in such wars, and must accept it, and indeed, with a startling theatrical gesture she demonstrates it ('place your hands below your husband's foot'). She has successfully acted a long speech with interior reference to an imaginary history play, though only Petruchio can appreciate that. Partly she is telling him that the civil war in her is over, and she will not fight her rescuer. Partly she is rejoicing in their new world.

Brian Vickers demonstrates 'the speed and fluidity with which Shakespeare can modulate from one medium to the other as his dramatic intention requires'. He comments on the last lines of *Shrew* act 5, scene 1 ('kiss me, Kate'). He also analyses the verse and prose of the Sly scenes, making an excellent point about the 'new' Sly's blank verse, 'a step up to an assumed dignity and style', which is then exploited 'by inserting into this new frame fragments of the old Sly that we used to know...The incongruity between style and subject-matter is now so marked that it re-creates on the plane of language the visual effect of Sly sitting up

---

11 M. C. Bradbrook, 'Dramatic Role as Social Image; a Study of *The Taming of the Shrew*', *Shakespeare-Jahrbuch*, 94 (1958), pp. 139, 134–5.

12 The play would go down even faster if she were using the forty-four lines to declaim a thesis about 'order', as maintained by G. I. Duthie, *Shakespeare* (1951), p. 58, and Derek Traversi, *An Approach to Shakespeare I: Henry VI to Twelfth Night* (1968), p. 89.

in bed, newly washed and nobly attired.'[13] I see a much developed and mature incongruity in the violence with which Katherine uses, in a speech about the experience of marriage, the vocabulary and rhythms of a contentious claimant to a throne from a history play. It is right that it is incongruous. The married state of Katherine and Petruchio has, from the end of the play, no connection with the married state of Lucentio and Bianca or Hortensio and his Widow. ('If she and I be pleas'd, what's that to you?' (2.1.295).) For them, as Lucentio fatuously said, the war was over. For Katherine and Petruchio, it has barely started. This is the play which is beginning. *The Taming of the Shrew* has shown us ('So workmanly the blood and tears are drawn' (Induction 2.58)) a conflict of very close relationship – in play terms. Petruchio, having met her, 'thought it good' that she should 'hear a play' (Induction 2.131). Now she shows that she has understood. They go back to the beginning, as it were, to watch a play that they are creating. That is the true Shakespearian touch, going back at the end of a comedy, in a spiral movement, to the same point only higher. Thus Portia and Bassanio *begin*,

at the end of *Merchant*, in a Belmont modified by the play-scene of the trial in Venice. Thus Beatrice and Benedick, at the end of *Much Ado*, start again ('Then you do not love me?...No, truly, but in friendly recompense'), but now together and changed by the play-scene at the church.

Together, Katherine and Petruchio have filled-in many more areas of the capability of theatre than seemed possible at the beginning. In particular they have, like Beatrice and Benedick after them, created an open world for each other; they are themselves, only more so being now together. Their mutuality is based on the power of acting. Kate's speech is rivalled in length only by those of the Lord in the Induction when he is setting up a play-world. This shared power can encompass continual challenges for sovereignty, and even violence, together. Far from such things splitting their marriage apart, they will bring them into closer union. 'We three are married, but you two are sped.'

---

[13] Brian Vickers, *The Artistry of Shakespeare's Prose* (London and New York, 1968), pp. 13, 14.

SHREWD AND KINDLY FARCE

PETER SACCIO

If Shakespeare's plays exemplify what humankind can achieve at its most vital, most thoughtful, and most sympathetic, not only a source of received wisdom but also a resource for those at odds with the received culture, *The Taming of the Shrew* remains an embarrassment to many who profess and call themselves Shakespearians.[1] In our century a brisk revisionism has flourished. Two major series of scholiasts, the first generally modern and psychological, the second specifically feminist, have argued variously that the shrew never really was a shrew but a woman responding understandably to the abuse of a dreadful family, that she is not really tamed, and that her final speech on wifely obedience is a piece of extended irony that dupes perhaps Petruchio and certainly the other characters.[2] Standing nearly alone in recent academic commentary, but supported by many theatrical productions, Robert Heilman has attempted to combat this taming of *The Taming of the Shrew*. Although he allows that Katherine and Petruchio are persons of wit and imagination rather than mere harridan and whip-wielder, Heilman insists that the play is a farce straightforwardly handling the matter named in its title, and dismisses revisionism as 'a critical falconry that endeavors to domesticate [the play] within the confines of recent sensibility'.[3] This dispute, which will surely continue, at present stands bracketed by two documents, comparison of which illuminates what it has and has not achieved.

In 1897, George Bernard Shaw praised those elements of the play he found 'realistic':

Petruchio is worth fifty Orlandos as a human study. The preliminary scenes in which he shews his character by pricking up his ears at the news that there is a fortune to be got by any man who will take an ugly and ill-tempered woman off her father's hands, and hurrying off to strike the bargain before somebody else picks it up, are not romantic; but they give an honest and masterly picture of a real man, whose like we have all met. The actual taming of the woman by the methods used in taming wild beasts belongs to his determination to make himself rich and

---

[1] An earlier version of this paper was delivered at the annual meeting of the Shakespeare Association of America in Minneapolis, Minnesota, in April 1982. Quotations from *The Shrew* come from the new Arden edition, ed. Brian Morris (London and New York, 1981).

[2] The twentieth-century critical fortunes of *The Shrew*, to the mid-sixties, have been well summarized by Robert B. Heilman in 'The *Taming* Untamed, or, The Return of the Shrew', *Modern Language Quarterly*, 27 (1966), 147–61. Pre-World War II commentary often deplores the play's apparent doctrine; postwar commentary by Nevill Coghill, Margaret Webster, Harold Goddard and others finds Shakespeare more in sympathy with modern opinions on women. Postdating Heilman's article is the major wave of feminist commentary, well represented by Coppélia Kahn, ' *The Taming of the Shrew*: Shakespeare's Mirror of Marriage', *Modern Language Studies*, 5 (1975), 88–102; Marianne L. Novy, 'Patriarchy and Play in *The Taming of the Shrew*', *English Literary Renaissance*, 9 (1979), 264–80; John C. Bean, 'Comic Structure and the Humanizing of Kate in *The Taming of the Shrew*', in *The Woman's Part: Feminist Criticism of Shakespeare*, ed. Carolyn Ruth Swift Lenz *et al.* (Urbana, 1980), pp. 65–78; and Irene G. Dash, *Wooing, Wedding, and Power: Women in Shakespeare's Plays* (New York, 1981). Kahn is unique in suggesting that, while Katherine's final speech is ironic, Petruchio is not duped but knows he is being taken in and prefers it that way.

[3] Heilman, p. 161.

comfortable, and his perfect freedom from all delicacy in using his strength and opportunities for that purpose. The process is quite bearable, because the selfishness of the man is healthily goodhumored and untainted by wanton cruelty, and it is good for the shrew to encounter a force like that and be brought to her senses....[But] the last scene is altogether disgusting to modern sensibility. No man with any decency of feeling can sit it out in the company of a woman without being extremely ashamed of the lord-of-creation moral implied in the wager and the speech put into the woman's own mouth.[4]

In 1980, Professor John Bean reversed the terms precisely: he defended Katherine's final speech and deplored the taming. Bean rightly points out that the obedience speech does not imply a lord-of-creation moral. That notion of male supremacy, with its analogy between the husband and the Christian God and its theological argument from the story of Adam's rib and Eve's fall, can be found in the parallel place in *The Taming of A Shrew*, but not in the Folio play. The religious language of Shakespeare's heroine echoes the marriage service of the Book of Common Prayer, not the doctrine of Creation. She expounds marriage as a non-tyrannical political hierarchy in which the partners have distinctive roles co-operating in mutual love, a notion reflecting humanist ideas on marriage and constituting a considerable change from medieval male autocracy. Bean further admires the romantic thread of the play, 'those elements that show Kate's discovery of her inward self through her discovery first of play and then of love'. What Bean finds hateful is the taming: the throwing about of food and bedclothes, the abuse of the tailor, and – though not the obedience speech itself – the way in which Katherine is induced to say it, responding to Petruchio's directions like 'a trained bear'. Here, according to Bean, is 'depersonalizing farce unassimilated from the play's fabliau sources'.[5]

The precision of this reversal is useful. Although male, both writers have considerable credentials as feminists. Were he still living, the creator of Vivie Warren and St Joan might well have been persuaded to contribute to the volume in which Professor Bean's essay appears, *The Woman's Part*. Yet Shaw, who normally detested farce and damned Garrick's revision of the script, found farce realistic and bearable in this instance, while condemning the final doctrine. Bean finds the doctrine not only historically excusable but innovative for its time – a step forward by the Life Force, one might say – and tolerates the action insofar as it is romantic, while condemning Petruchio's motives and farcical methods. Thus the whirligig of time brings in his revenges. The villain in Padua is now not male autocracy but farce. Bean finds it so offensive that he supposes that Shakespeare was confused in intention, did not fully know what he was doing. In this dislike he joins other feminist critics of the play, Coppélia Kahn and Irene Dash, who also attack what Kahn calls 'the mechanism of farce'.[6] His view is carried to an extreme in the firm pronouncement of H. J. Oliver. In the introduction to his otherwise admirable edition of *The Shrew*, Oliver describes the play as 'a young dramatist's attempt, not repeated, to mingle two genres that cannot be combined'. 'Characterization and farce are, finally, incompatible.'[7]

Since a few Shakespearians have been reluctant to admit the Bard's connection with anything so low as farce, it would be well to assert firmly the view of this essay, that the play is definitely (though not exclusively) farcical. Tranio exemplifies the trickery and disguise so prominent in Roman farce; Gremio illustrates devices of characterization used in the Commedia dell'Arte; Petruchio and his servants display the physical knockabout that occurs in farce of all ages. The verbal wit is often farcical. Compared, say, to the lyrical strain and sinuous sophistication of Rosalind's speeches in *As You Like It*, the wit of *The Shrew* comes near wisecracking. The funny lines are stychomythic exchanges and sharp retorts, as in the courting scene; grotesque

4 *Shaw on Shakespeare*, ed. Edwin Wilson (Harmondsworth, 1969), pp. 197–8.
5 Bean, pp. 71, 74, 66.
6 Bean, p. 74; Kahn, as reprinted in *The Authority of Experience: Essays in Feminist Criticism*, ed. Arlyn Diamond and Lee R. Edwards (Amherst, 1977), p. 99.
7 H. J. Oliver, ed., *The Taming of the Shrew*, The Oxford Shakespeare (Oxford, 1982), pp. 56, 52.

catalogues such as Biondello's list of the diseases of Petruchio's horse and Petruchio's abuse of the tailor; accounts of physical roughhouse such as the story of the horse in the mud and Petruchio's plan to rip apart the bedchamber. Stage productions are usually full of bustling activity. Even when this is not dictated by explicit directions in the script, it responds to the character of the script, to the brisk competitiveness of the lines. We may reasonably complain of productions in which directorial inventiveness overstresses knockabout at the severe expense of other qualities in the text, but an absence of knockabout subverts the text even more drastically.

Farce, of course, has long had a bad press. The Elizabethans did not have the word, but they had the thing, most notably in the jigs performed as afterpieces and dismissed by intellectuals like Prince Hamlet when he wanted to sneer at Polonius's taste: 'He's for a jig or a tale of bawdry'. Dryden, who had the word, said that farce consisted of 'unnatural events'.[8] That is the keynote of the bad press: the negative description. Nearly every effort to define or describe farce since Dryden – carefully collected in Leo Hughes's *A Century of English Farce* – has been couched in negatives.[9] These definitions met their justified rebuke when, in 1958, Eric Bentley anatomized the entry on farce offered by *The Oxford Companion to the Theatre* and found 'the whole article based on the...assumption that farce consists of defects without qualities'.[10] When, as in *The Shrew*, farce is combined with a romantic element, the farce may receive even harsher treatment because of the contrast. Thus Hughes, providing what he calls an 'acceptable definition of farce' for *The Princeton Encyclopedia of Poetry and Poetics*, remarks 'Its object is to provoke the spectator to laughter, not the reflective kind which comedy is intended to elicit, but the uncomplicated response of simple enjoyment.'[11] Freudian critics such as Bentley and Barbara Freedman argue that the enjoyment of farce is hardly that simple, but even they do not help when the farcical effects are allied with 'the reflective laughter which comedy is intended to elicit', as is certainly the case with *The Shrew*, since their analysis concerns psychoanalytic

insights that (by definition) cannot be the object of our conscious reflection as long as we are attending to the literal story enacted on the stage.[12] The apparent incompatibility between farce and humane attention to character appears most sharply in feminist criticism, and reasonably so. Critics explicitly devoted to the identification, examination, and exposure of stereotypes will naturally disdain a genre considered particularly dehumanizing. The editors of *The Woman's Part* speak flatly of 'the rigidities of farce'.[13]

Farce need not be rigid, and is not rigid in *The Shrew*. The unattractive features of the genre have been overstated, and the overstatements have been perpetrated most devastatingly by the one prominent defender of the farcical *Shrew*, Robert Heilman, whose description of farce fuels the attacks of Bean and Kahn. According to Heilman, farce deals with 'limited personality that acts and responds in a mechanical way and hence moves toward a given end with a perfection not likely if all the elements in human nature were really at work'. 'Those who have this personality are not really hurt, do not think much, are not much troubled by scruples.' 'They lack, largely or totally, the physical, emotional, intellectual, and moral sensitivity that we think of as "normal".' Farce 'simplifie[s] life by a selective anaesthetizing of the whole person'.[14] Each of these sentences, and many another in Heilman's essay, is

---

[8] Preface to *An Evening's Love, The Works of John Dryden*, ed. H. T. Swedenberg, Jr, *et al.*, vol. 10 (Berkeley, 1970), p. 203.

[9] *A Century of English Farce* (Princeton, 1956), esp. chapter 1.

[10] Eric Bentley, 'The Psychology of Farce', in *Let's Get a Divorce! and Other Plays* (New York, 1958), p. viii.

[11] *Princeton Encyclopedia of Poetry and Poetics*, ed. Alex Preminger *et al.*, enlarged edition (Princeton, 1974), p. 271.

[12] See Barbara Freedman, 'Errors in Comedy: A Psychoanalytic Theory of Farce', in *Shakespearean Comedy*, ed. Maurice Charney (New York, 1980), pp. 233–43. This fascinating analysis ends with the remark that the errors of *The Comedy of Errors* are really 'no errors at all', an observation that indicates that the story and characters as such have dissolved completely.

[13] *The Woman's Part*, p. 8.

[14] Heilman, pp. 160, 154, 152.

couched in negatives or privatives: limit, without, not, lack, simplify, anaesthetize. Since no work of art can contain all the possibilities of life, since all simplify by selection and emphasis, one could describe any genre this way and thus make it unattractive to those concerned with doing justice to the full range of human character. What would happen if tragedy were subjected to such descriptive habits? Tragedy concerns persons unnaturally ready to rush to extremes; who do not pause to reflect (cf. *King Lear*); or who, reflecting, do so faultily (cf. *Othello*); who, by a selective anaesthetizing of the whole person, lack a sense of humour or balance about their problems (cf. *Macbeth* or *Coriolanus*); who will not sit down with a sympathetic friend or a good therapist or at least a valium to get to the root of the matter, but instead dash about with drawn swords; in short, a collection of paranoid hysterics who refuse to live like sensible adults. As for moving toward a given end with a perfection foreign to human nature, what real royal court has ever (short of war or armed revolution) suffered the complete and simultaneous extermination that occurs at Elsinore?

The farce presented in Petruchio's wooing of Katherine and in the efforts of Tranio and Biondello to win Bianca for Lucentio deserves a positive description. That farce arises within a relatively realistic situation. As many have noted, Bianca's popularity and Baptista's favouritism credibly motivate Katherine's shrewish behaviour. As George Hibbard has splendidly argued, the premises of the plot 'reflect life as it was lived', specifically the marital customs of Elizabethan England.[15] A wealthy father, properly seeking husbands for his daughters, tries to even the odds between the popular girl and her unwanted elder sister by vowing that the former shall not marry before the latter, and thereby creates a frustrating and distressing stalemate for everyone concerned. Within this situation, farce celebrates the virtues of energy, ingenuity, and resilience, virtues that disrupt the static dilemma and work to resolve it. The energy is obvious in the eagerness of the male characters arriving in Padua to take on a set of problems regarded by the Paduans as hopeless, and in the demands they confidently

make upon themselves in order to cope with them.[16] It is verbally elaborated in Petruchio's speeches of resolution: when he boasts of his career amid roaring lions and clanging trumpets he sounds rather like Tamburlaine. Ingenuity — mental independence and resourcefulness — lies in the suitors' adoption of unconventional means to gain their ends, notably in Petruchio's behaviour at the wedding and in his pretence of being a greater shrew than Katherine, but also in the fertile inventiveness of Lucentio and his servants. By resilience I refer to a special combination of stubbornness and adaptability. This virtue is often overlooked in farcical characters. We are too ready (with or without the explicit aid of Bergson) to describe farce as mechanical or rigid, and thus condemn farcical behaviour as subhuman. The ability to initiate or endure repeated confrontations, pratfalls, and beatings can be testimony to the determination of the characters, and the determination loses its mechanical quality when it is combined with the cleverness, the ready resourcefulness displayed by Petruchio in the taming and by the variety of 'supposes' in the Bianca plot. In civilized life, of course, most adults avoid the physical activities of farce — the shouting and the knockabout — but the energy, ingenuity, and resilience embodied in such activities are valuable qualities. We do not honour lassitude, mental barrenness, and defeatism.

It may be objected that I have attributed these farce-displayed virtues only to male characters. That, indeed, is the heart of the current feminist case: Professor Kahn regards farce as the elaboration of a male fantasy of domination, and Professor Bean sees Katherine as the victim of farce.[17] But Katherine is also an initiator. Her verbal and physical energy

---

[15] George R. Hibbard, ' *The Taming of the Shrew*: A Social Comedy', in *Shakespearean Essays*, ed. Alwin Thaler and Norman Sanders, *Tennessee Studies in Literature*, Special Number 2 (Knoxville, 1964), pp. 15–28.

[16] I am indebted to the ingenious variation on Northrop Frye's theory of comedy presented by Sherman Hawkins in 'The Two Worlds of Shakespearean Comedy', *Shakespeare Studies*, 3 (1967), 62–80.

[17] Kahn, p. 85; Bean, p. 74.

in resisting humiliation mark her first two appearances on stage; indeed, they make her the attractive and interesting character that she is. When she meets Petruchio in her third scene, she initiates both the wit combat and the physical brawling. At this moment, her behaviour has a strain of compulsiveness not shared by Petruchio or Tranio: she has the energy, but her resilience is more stubborn than adaptable, and her ingenuity relies heavily on the use or threat of physical violence. But that is precisely the point: her liberation from raging shrewishness, from compulsiveness and destructiveness, is marked by her growth in farcical range. Petruchio teaches her to play, as many critics have noted,[18] but what she plays is the energetic, resilient, ingenious games of farce – the farcical wit of the sun/moon scene and the farcical actions of 'swingeing' Bianca and the Widow forth and treading on her own cap. The romantic humanization of Katherine is expressed, not in such reflective speeches as might be given to Viola, but through the resilience and energy of her co-operation with Petruchio's madcap words and actions. One verbal example is particularly revealing. Early in the play Petruchio elaborates a farcical catalogue of Katherine's supposed virtues:

'Twas told me you were rough, and coy, and
    sullen,
And now I find report a very liar;
For thou art pleasant, gamesome, passing courteous,
But slow in speech, yet sweet as spring-time
    flowers.
Thou canst not frown, thou canst not look askance,
Nor bite the lip, as angry wenches will,
Nor hast thou pleasure to be cross in talk....
Why does the world report that Kate doth limp?
O slanderous world! Kate like the hazel-twig
Is straight and slender, and as brown in hue
As hazel-nuts and sweeter than the kernels.

                    (2.1.237–49)

The energy of Petruchio's adjective-lists, and the rural vividness and tang of his hazel imagery, contrast sharply with Lucentio's praise of Bianca, heavy as it is with bookish mythology and the conventional sonneteer's talk of coral lips and sweet breath (1.1.150–76). Late in the play Katherine

splendidly adopts Petruchio's mode of farcical blazon:

Young budding virgin, fair, and fresh, and sweet,
Whither away, or where is thy abode?
Happy the parents of so fair a child,
Happier the man whom favourable stars
Allots thee for his lovely bedfellow.   (4.5.36–40)

Here her striking and ludicrous invention tops Petruchio's more conventional description of eyes like stars and 'war of white and red within her cheeks' (4.5.30–2).

Katherine eventually becomes an expert farceur. Her initiation into the full freedoms of farce, moreover, corresponds to the developing pattern of farce in the play itself, to the larger dramatic rhythms. Dramatic rhythm is a matter largely neglected by recent commentary on the play: the feminist concern with social roles has tended to treat the play as case history, where behaviour may be investigated principally as it reveals the sociological assumptions of the playwright and the age. But dramatic events exist within a structure and rhythm of episodes, and that rhythm governs our apprehension of them. Timing is part of the nature of farcical events, in the overall pace of the play as well as in the execution of local business. In *The Taming of the Shrew*, broadly funny episodes are carefully rationed, with some of the most notable knockabout taking place off stage: the lute-breaking, the wedding service. With the Induction and the elaborately rendered first entrances of Lucentio and Petruchio, the opening scenes are leisurely, slowly introducing the persons and leading only gradually to their engagement with each other. By the time Petruchio woos Katherine and we feel thoroughly into the matter, fully forty per cent of the play has elapsed. Thereafter the pace quickens. The third and fourth acts give us the scenes of outrageous pretence, bizarre costume, physical violence, and disruption of household order characteristic of farce.[19] I emphasize

---

[18] See Novy, 'Patriarchy and Play', and J. Dennis Huston, '"To Make a Puppet": Play and Play-Making in *The Taming of the Shrew*', *Shakespeare Studies*, 9 (1976), 73–87.

[19] Brian Morris, p. 142, suggests that the wedding and country-house scenes 'would be farcical' if Petruchio did

this accelerating pattern because it is not the usual rhythm of later Shakespeare, the rhythm Bernard Beckerman has taught us to recognize in Shakespeare at the Globe.[20] In most of the Globe plays, as Beckerman notes, there is a mid-play plateau, a sequence of high dramatic excitement, followed by a stretch of lower-intensity story-telling. Perhaps the most conspicuous feature of this design, at least for modern audiences, is the fourth-act sag foreign to modern expectations of dramatic rhythm. Modern audiences are apt to get restless, and modern producers to cut heavily, during the scenes of Laertes's rebellion, the scenes between the blinding of Gloucester and the return of Cordelia, and the later prison scenes of *Measure for Measure*. But *The Shrew* accelerates in the later acts, rushing eagerly through hurry and confusion in both its plots, precipitating a comic catharsis through which the characters come to new recognition of their relationships. The accelerating rhythm works on a dynamic of repetition and variation: Katherine is thrice frustrated over food, twice over clothing; she is tested twice in rapid succession over the sun and the old man. The alternating scenes of the sub-plot (4.2 and 4.4) are each built as diptychs: they increase the pace by each handling two problems or two phases of the same problem, the second of which arises unexpectedly in the middle of the scene and calls for a further stretch of ingenuity from the plotters. The final scene of the sub-plot (5.1) builds an hilarious climax out of the true Vincentio's rapid, progressive confrontations with the false Vincentio, Biondello, Tranio and Baptista, and finally the young lovers. The true Vincentio, in his first appearance, is flabbergasted twice, first by being hailed as a nubile virgin and then by Petruchio's bland revelation that 'thy son by this hath married'.[21] The accelerating pace of scenes is matched on the local, verbal level, by rhetorical schemes of repetition leading to climax – anaphora, epistrophe, ploce – schemes that Katherine adopts from Petruchio and uses increasingly. Of particular importance in reinforcing this pace is the sense of improvisation. Although nothing in theatre requires more painstaking rehearsal, farce presents itself as impromptu, spontaneous. Exactly such improvisa-

tion, such invention upon unexpected demand, characterizes Petruchio from early on:

Katherine.
Where did you study all this goodly speech?
Petruchio.
It is extempore, from my mother-wit.

(2.1.256–7)

This is the skill that Katherine learns to exercise in greeting Vincentio, and her practice of it is very carefully rendered: 'Young budding virgin, fair, and fresh, and sweet – '. She starts with fine hyperbolic inventiveness, in a vigorous six-stress line. But then her ingenuity momentarily staggers: 'Whither away, or where is thy abode?' That's a flat line, a dull line unworthy of its predecessor. No word adds colour to the idea, the questions are uninteresting, and the flaccid structure created by the weak 'or' helps the line to get nowhere. She is gagging, groping for the next bright idea. Then it comes to her, and without waiting for a reply to her dull questions she produces a sustained outburst of inventiveness, elaborating the fantasy to a wonderfully ridiculous extreme:

> Happy the parents of so fair a child,
> Happier the man whom favourable stars
> Allots thee for his lovely bedfellow.

This rhythmic pattern in the play, rising to frenzy in the later scenes, creates the setting in which the quieter, more romantic moments have their telling impact. When Katherine and Petruchio kiss in the street, defiant of decorum but very much in love,

---

not have a serious purpose. The remark neatly illustrates the prejudice against farce: why should the purpose make the actions less farcical or less funny?

[20] Bernard Beckerman, *Shakespeare at the Globe, 1599–1609* (New York, 1962), chapter 2, esp. pp. 34–5.

[21] 4.5.62. No production I have seen has exploited the surprise that must occur to Vincentio here. Editors who comment on the line (e.g. Morris both in a footnote and in his Introduction, p. 19, and Hibbard in the New Penguin Shakespeare) are concerned only with Petruchio's passing on information he could not possibly have. In a play concerned with the proper arrangement of marriages, with a character who exists almost entirely to be subjected to comic shocks, surely this is a notable moment.

'we recognize triumph, we sympathize with surrender; we experience satisfaction in the completion of a long pattern, and we regret that an interesting fight seems finished'.[22] That fulfilment would lack its rich savour were it not preceded by the climactic confusions of the sub-plot, the vigorous confrontations of Katherine and Petruchio, and the notable off-stage kiss, the 'clamorous smack' that had made the church echo at the wedding (3.2.176). Even more, Katherine's obedience speech, with its elaborate appeal to political and social sanctities, would lack its sense of full-chord resolution if it punctuated something less energetic than farce.

It will be clear by now that I cannot agree with the common modern view that seeks to revise the plain doctrine of Katherine's last speech under the all-saving name of irony. Bean's enrichment of the historical context is helpful here. Discussion of the speech has been vexed by two principal confusions. The first is theatrical: an actress may undercut the sense, vulgarly with a wink at the audience, or elegantly by playing in the high Congrevean manner of Edith Evans. But that is not the point. Such subversion can be practised, according to skill, by any performer on any passage in Shakespeare. It is a familiar form of theatrical humour, delightful at cast parties. With a playwright whose liars and deceivers regularly announce their intentions, however, we must seek some textual basis for supposing that Katherine does not mean what she says. The second confusion, encountered when we seek such textual basis, lies in ignoring the difference between local verbal ironies and a massive irony of intent extending through forty-four lines. Verbal ironies certainly flicker in particular lines. To suggest that Petruchio 'commits his body / To painful labour both by sea and land' is to exaggerate the undoubted work of a country gentleman in managing his estate into something that sounds suspiciously like digging the ditches.[23] Katherine's reference to a wife who lies 'warm at home' is rich in private irony for herself and her husband, but not for the guests who are ignorant of the events of her honeymoon. This verbal playfulness she has learned from her husband, and it valuably lightens what

might otherwise be an intolerably long oration, but it does not contradict the doctrine she expounds or the gesture with which she concludes the speech. To argue that the sheer length of the speech contradicts its meaning[24] is to cast wanton doubt on everything in the highly rhetorical Elizabethan drama, and also to ignore Katherine's energy in all undertakings, Petruchio's request for such a speech, and the dramatic value of a full statement. Furthermore, verbal irony is far less important in drama than irony of event. Long doctrinal speeches in Shakespeare – the fable of the belly in *Coriolanus*, the divine-right speeches of *Richard II* – are often subject to ironic examination by the events of the play, but Katherine's speech is the only such sermon in Shakespeare occurring so late in its play that no further event can challenge it. We do not even need to deplore, as Bean does, the means by which the speech is introduced. Petruchio does not impose it as a further test or taming. The wager has already been won, and husband and wife are playing a game whose object is to demonstrate their superiority as a couple to their scornful relatives.[25]

The rhythmic pattern I have described, of a leisurely opening followed by gathering farce leading to an unusually late climax and a richly toned conclusion, makes possible the blending of farce and romantic development of character that Oliver deems unworkable. Shakespeare evidently thought so: contrary to Oliver's assertion, he did repeat the blend and the pattern, in a subtler and more varied form, in *Twelfth Night*, a play also combining a romantic story of wooers and disguisers with a farcical effort to tame a shrewish person. Although a Globe play, *Twelfth Night* does not manifest the

---

22 Morris, p. 108: he is discussing 4.5, the sun/moon scene, but his fine remark is also applicable to the kiss passage the end of 5.1.

23 Two recent Petruchios, Raúl Juliá at the New York Shakespeare Festival (1979) and Alun Armstrong of the Royal Shakespeare Company (1982–3), both responded to the line with surprise and a gesture of humorous denial.

24 'It fairly shouts obedience, when a gentle murmur would suffice' (Kahn, p. 99).

25 See Morris, pp. 145–9, and Ralph Berry, *Shakespeare's Comedies: Explorations in Form* (Princeton, 1972), p. 70.

pattern of mid-play plateau and fourth-act sag that Beckerman describes. Instead, like *The Shrew*, its plot begins with great leisureliness; its theatrical excitement derives from a series of farcical complications that start in the cakes-and-ale scene and accelerate through the letter, yellow-stockings, and duel scenes; and its farce heightens the moments of still romantic wonder late in the love plot. Petrarchanism is set off and energized by the honest mean habiliments of farce.

The Taming of the Shrew is a farce both shrewd and kindly. It is shrewd in many senses. Both hero and heroine are turbulent people. Both, indeed, have the characteristics of real shrews – energy, irascibility, and noise.[26] Katherine is also beshrewed, 'curst', afflicted by having a sly sister and a father whose relatively good intentions are not supported by much real intelligence about coping with his daughters. She is also shrewd in the sense of being ill-reported, of having a reputation somewhat in excess of her real behaviour.[27] And the play itself, especially in acts 3 and 4, is shrewd: noisy, energetic, sharp, piercing, keen. But it is also kindly. This word (which, with its relatives, occurs twenty times in the play) is crucial to the effect. Were it more noticed, feminist critics might be less unhappy. Particularly in the Induction and the final scene, 'kindly' is heavily emphasized in the range of meanings that encompasses 'natural', 'dutiful', 'compassionate', 'gentle', 'beneficent' – the range of meanings so important in *King Lear*. In the Induction, the Lord commands his practical joke on Christopher Sly to be done 'kindly', with 'gently' and 'friendly' as synonymous directions (Induction 1.44, 64, 70, 101, 116). In the final scene, both Baptista and Lucentio welcome the wedding guests with 'kindness' (5.2.5, 13). Petruchio responds with a compliment to everyone present, 'Padua affords nothing but what is kind' (l. 14). Katherine begins her great speech with, 'Fie, fie! Unknit that threatening, unkind brow' (l. 137; if the Elizabethans pronounced the 'k' of 'unknit,' the combination of 'unknit'/ 'unkind' would gain prominence by virtue of the complex sound-echo). The play enacts a transformation from shrewdness into kindness, from what is turbulent, curst, keen, and noisy – natural in the sense of fallen nature – to what is generous, gentle, dutiful, and loving – natural in the sense of belonging properly to human relationships in families and communities. It is almost a transformation from Edmund's nature to Cordelia's. There is no confusion of purpose here, no failure to assimilate inherited material to the new purpose. It is of the essence of *The Taming of the Shrew* that it be both a shrewd and a kindly farce.

---

26 Morris, pp. 120–2, stresses Shakespeare's presumed knowledge of the real animal.

27 Kahn, pp. 90–1, discusses the inflation of her reputation. In defining 'shrewd', *OED* includes 'Of reputation, opinion, meaning: Evil, bad, unfavourable' (3b): examples cited make clear that a shrewd reputation need not be justified.

ILLUSTRATIONS TO 'A MIDSUMMER NIGHT'S DREAM' BEFORE 1920

KENNETH GARLICK

It is somewhat – if not wholly – presumptuous to present a piece on the subject of illustrations to one play of Shakespeare when the groundwork for the study of illustrations to the whole of Shakespeare has already been so carefully achieved by W. Moelwyn Merchant in his book *Shakespeare and the Artist*, published by the Oxford University Press in 1959, and by T. S. R. Boase in his *Illustrations of Shakespeare's Plays in the Seventeenth and Eighteenth Centuries*, a detailed contribution to the *Journal of the Warburg and Courtauld Institutes* in 1947. This short article could not have been prepared without them. I shall confine myself to illustration in the strict interpretation of the word, that is to a selection – by no means comprehensive – of illustrations in published texts and to drawings and paintings which represent episodes from the play. I shall not discuss representations of actual stage productions or designs for sets or costumes. In the case of *A Midsummer Night's Dream*, which did not become a widely popular subject until well into the nineteenth century, and which at all times has been better known for its 'fairy' content than its court-and-love intrigue, the illustrations range from the ethos of the baroque masque through the academic restriction of the late eighteenth century to the kind of historical and un-Shakespearian approach of the mid and late nineteenth century which is implied in the word 'revival'. Much the same comment could no doubt be made of a historical sequence of illustrations to any one of Shakespeare's plays, but in the case of the *Dream* the coalescence of English romanticism and German fairy sentiment produced for several decades a popular image of the play which has become almost a part of our folk-lore, and recent productions which, perhaps in a kind of despair, have tried to be different and to underplay or even ignore the enchantment, have by doing so lost significance. The 'story' is not enough. It never was.

In 1692 *The Fairy Queen*, part opera, part masque, part dramatic spectacle, the music by Henry Purcell, the dances by Josias Priest, was produced in London at Dorset Garden Theatre (or the Queen's Theatre, as it was renamed in 1689) down by the Thames. It was based on *A Midsummer Night's Dream*, but it was in no sense a production of the play. Enchantment however there would have been in all senses of that word, and it must have remained for long vivid in the minds of those who saw and heard it. Is there some memory of it, or even reference to it, in the first illustration to the *Dream* that has come down to us, the frontispiece to the play in volume 2 of Nicholas Rowe's edition of Shakespeare, published by Tonson in 1709 (fig. 1)? Here in a wood near Athens, 'ill met by moonlight', Oberon and Titania are depicted according to the stage instructions 'OBERON at one door with his TRAIN, and TITANIA, at another, with hers'. They are dressed in the height of late seventeenth-century baroque operatic fashion, with plumed headgear, mock Roman military costume for the men and a kind of half-William-and-Mary or Anne court dress for the women. The full moon rides high, the powerful shadows fall to the right and there is a suggestion of summer lightning in the sky. It is a crudely cut illustration but it evokes successfully the theatre of aria and spectacle and drop-cloth transformations.

1. *The Meeting of Oberon and Titania.* Plate to Rowe's first edition of Shakespeare (1709), vol. 2

2. *The Meeting of Oberon and Titania.* Plate to Rowe's later edition of Shakespeare (1714), vol. 2

This Oberon and Titania seem to sing rather than speak. Five years later, in the 1714 edition of Rowe, all kinds of changes have occurred in the same plate (fig. 2). The composition of the landscape is reversed. The figures are enlarged. The shadows – presumably to balance the composition – fall in opposite directions. There is a loss of impact on the eye of the reader, but a gain in sylvan unreality. Who was responsible for the first design? Possibly Michael van der Gucht, who came over from Antwerp to work for Tonson in the 1690s, and who signed the frontispiece for the 1709 edition. Hanns

Hammelmann,[1] on the other hand, believes that it was not van der Gucht but François Boitard (who illustrated Tonson's edition of Beaumont and Fletcher). Whoever it was must have had the quality of his designs much diminished by the unsophisticated cutting of the wood block, and perhaps for this reason Tonson employed Louis du Guernier, a Frenchman who worked in England from 1712 until

---

[1] Hanns Hammelmann, *Book Illustrators in Eighteenth-Century England*, edited and completed by T. S. R. Boase (New Haven and London, 1975).

3. F. Gravelot, plate to Theobald's second edition of
Shakespeare (1740), vol. I

4. E. Edwards, plate to Bell's edition of Shakespeare, 1773

his death in 1716, to modify the 'cuts' of 1709 for
the edition of 1714. In the case of the *Dream*, the
modification is no remarkable improvement.

Lewis Theobald's *Shakespeare* (which corrected
Pope's of 1725) appeared in seven volumes, 1733–4,
and went through numerous editions into the 1770s.
For this there were new plates, some of which were
also used by Sir Thomas Hanmer for his six-volume
*Works of Shakespeare...carefully revised and corrected
by the former editions* (1743–4). These were mostly
engraved by François Gravelot from the designs of
Francis Hayman but occasionally the designs were
Gravelot's own, and this is so with the plate for the
Dream (fig. 3) which shows a very English and
Elizabethan Puck in a kind of jester's motley (a new

interpretation of 'I jest to Oberon and make him
smile'?) about to squeeze the juice of Love-in-
idleness upon the eyelids of a vaguely Greek
Lysander. Gravelot, who had the distinction of
being for short periods the pupil of Boucher and the
master of Gainsborough, had come over from Paris
between 1732 and 1733, presumably already trained
as a book illustrator, and from his studio in Covent
Garden he spread some knowledge of the French
rococo to a previously uninstructed audience.
Gainsborough absorbed it into his whole being and
without it might have developed as a more parochial
artist. Gravelot was not alone as a French visitor to
London, and his importance must not be exaggerated, but he certainly brought to the art of engraving

MISS BARSANTI in the Character of HELENA.
And will you rent our ancient Love asunder
to join with Men in scorning your poor Friend?

5. *Miss Barsanti in the Character of Helena.* Plate to Bell's
edition of Shakespeare, 1776

6. J. H. Ramberg, *Miss Farren in the Character of Hermia.*
Plate to Bell's edition of Shakespeare, 1785

in this country a decorative elegance it had lacked hitherto. Figs. 1 and 3 speak for themselves. There is however no gainsaying that while fig. 1 evokes the theatre quite forcibly, fig. 3 does not. It is an illustration to a book and not a record of a stage performance. It is difficult to accept with any conviction that the English actor of the 1740s took up on stage poses of such grace as Gravelot has invented. One imagines stage performances to have been more in line with Edward Edwards's illustration to act 3, scene 2, which appeared in Bell's edition of Shakespeare, 1773 (fig. 4), the first edition to appear with new plates since Theobald and Hanmer. Edwards, who that very year was elected

ARA, is more remembered now for his *Anecdotes of Painters*[2] than his work as artist and engraver. In fact, he was a dull artist. We can however believe that in the theatre of the day Bottom and his artisan associates wore a kind of contemporary costume which made concessions to the sixteenth century by way of puffed and slashed sleeves and doublet, as is here shown, and that their gestures were of the stock kind which Edwards records. More amusing is the tiny recumbent figure in the middle distance, a fairy presumably, but totally unlike the fairy of tradition, a mannerist Lilliputian who might have been lifted and diminished from some Parmigianinesque allegorical composition. She gives no clue to the appearance of any stage fairy of this date, nor to my knowledge is there any pictorial representation that

---

[2] Edward Edwards, *Anecdotes of Painters who have resided or been born in England...a continuation to the Anecdotes of Painting by the late Horace Earl of Oxford* (1808).

does. It is however the fairy world of the *Dream* that increasingly takes over from the human narrative in the field of illustration from about this time. Apart from the occasional representation of an actress in her part – Miss Barsanti as Helena in full contemporary fig, 1776 (fig. 5), or Miss Farren as Hermia, arch as her admirers always wished her to be, her dress loosely classical, 1785 (fig. 6) – it is Puck, Titania, Oberon and the fairies who edge out the lovers and the mechanicals. Johnson remarked of Shakespeare and the *Dream* 'Fairies in his time were much in fashion' as if in his own, Johnson's time, they had quite gone out, but Johnson was writing in 1765. By the last quarter of the century fairies were well in again. The first evidence of this is Boydell's Shakespeare Gallery.[3] Boydell's great venture is too well known and too well documented elsewhere for an account of it to be necessary here. The *Dream* was allocated four paintings, three by Fuseli and one by Reynolds, one by each artist being a *Puck* (Reynolds perhaps rather typically preferring to call him Robin Goodfellow), the second and third Fuselis being the enormous *Titania and Bottom in the Wood*, now in the Tate Gallery, and the equally large *Titania's Awakening* in the Kunstmuseum at Winterthur. The Reynolds is an odd and, in comparison with the Fuseli, a pretty picture.[4] Reynolds, a bachelor, doted (if that is quite the right word for this level-headed man) on small children. His child portraits are among his most natural and successful. When however he strayed into literature or fantasy (*The Infant Dr Johnson*[5] is the most extreme example) sentiment turned to sentimentality or absurdity. This Puck (fig. 7), 'an ugly little imp but with some character' wrote Horace Walpole, is not the Puck of the play. He is too much an infant to realize the part. And what does one make of the naked female lying some paces away from Bottom? Is she a mature fairy? Titania? Perhaps. She cannot be Helena or Hermia unless Reynolds chose to ignore the proprieties, which is to say the least unlikely. Fuseli's *Puck*[6] (fig. 8), on the other hand, is of the stage stagey. He has no age. He is capable of thoughtlessly causing disaster wherever he goes. He cannot by any stretch of the imagination be regarded as human, pretty, or even

impish in the Reynolds sense. He is a much more potent invention. Shakespeare indeed sparked the wit of Fuseli to its complete fulfilment. Apart from the two paintings for Boydell he made others of the *Dream* for Woodmason's Shakespeare Gallery[7] and others again from other Shakespeare plays which were not specific commissions. The Fuseli exhibition in the Tate Gallery in 1975 brought together a number of them and the catalogue has a useful section devoted to Fuseli and Shakespeare.

Puck was indeed interpreted and depicted in such variety that he would make the subject of an essay in himself. A further selection of three created between 1789 and 1837 will illustrate this point concisely. In Bell's edition of Johnson and Steevens's *Shakespeare*, Ramberg's *Miss Farren as Hermia* (fig. 6) is uncomfortably bound into the book facing a vision of 'I'll put a girdle round the earth' (fig. 9) by Philip James de Loutherbourg, an artist with a greater actual experience of stage work and design than any who had yet attempted to illustrate a Shakespeare play. In 1773 he became a stage and scenery designer to Garrick and at a later date his moving panorama known as the 'Eidophusikon' played with vast distances and theatrical effects of the phenomena of nature. It is entirely in character that in this plate to the *Dream* de Loutherbourg's Oberon should stand on what appears to be a cloud a foot's pace from dry land. He is part of some kind of transformation scene. Puck on the other hand skims into the empyrean with a skill no number of ropes or theatre engines could effect. This is an old-fashioned rendering. Oberon in Turkish costume takes us right back to Purcell and the masque – or at least to the French stage of that date – and Puck, winged, shoots away with a vigour that goes back to the Sistine ceiling. He is a guardian angel rather

---

[3] W. Moelwyn Merchant, *Shakespeare and the Artist* (Oxford, 1959), pp. 66–76.

[4] Collection Earl Fitzwilliam.

[5] Hyde Collection, USA.

[6] Present location unknown. See Gert Schiff, *Johann Heinrich Füssli* (Zurich, 1973), vol. 1, p. 494; vol. 2, plate 186.

[7] Robin Hamlyn, 'An Irish Shakespeare Gallery', in *The Burlington Magazine*, 120 (1978), 515–29.

7. L. Schiavonetti, engraving after *Puck* by Sir Joshua Reynolds for Boydell's *Graphic
Illustrations of the Dramatic Works of Shakespeare* (1802)

than a fairy creature, basically a derivation from the Italian baroque. De Loutherbourg, who was an ambitious and complex character, painted a variety of subjects, literary, biblical, and historical, for the annual exhibitions of the Royal Academy, and this illustration is conceived in terms of an old-masterish picture. In contrast, forty-four years later Ackermann and Tilt moved, if rather awkwardly, with the times when they published *The Gallery of Shakespeare, or, Illustrations of his Dramatic Works. 'Midsummer-Night's Dream', in six etchings, on steel,*

from Ruhl; to which are annexed descriptions of the plates, in 1829. This was a translation of the first part of a series of engraved illustrations to Shakespeare by Moritz Retzch and Ludwig Sigismund Ruhl, published in Leipzig 1828–45. The plates were accompanied by explanatory texts more or less outlining the 'story' by such luminaries of the day as C. A. Boettinger, Carl Borromaeus von Miltitz, and Professor D. Hermann Ulrici. They are line engravings of the pure if insipid style that remained popular through to the middle of the century for the

8. J. Parker, engraving after *Puck* by H. Fuseli for Boydell's *Graphic Illustrations of the Dramatic Works of Shakespeare* (1802)

9. P. J. de Loutherbourg, plate to Bell's edition of Shakespeare, 1785

kind of book of literary illustration that was certainly not 'coffee table' but also not quite 'library', a style which derived from Flaxman's *Classical Outlines*. There were French translations as well as English. It is difficult for a 1980s Englishman to assess the precise nature of the intended humour in the Puck (fig. 10) who, with robust limbs but wearing an acorn cap and sporting useless butterfly wings, sweeps up as Shakespeare directed: 'I am sent with broom before / To sweep the dust behind the door.' Again, as Shakespeare directed, Oberon and Titania .enter with their trains. Titania's attendants carry things which look like brooms too. They may however be meant to be oriental and Cleopatra-like.

Is it a heavy German joke? The Renaissance palace setting is certainly not Athenian but that again may be a misfire that was seriously intended. The illustration is, as it were, Fuseli below par, but good to be seen in England where by this time Fuseli's work was forgotten and out of tune with the times. How far did Retzch and Ruhl lead into the acceptance of a fairy world which the marriage of Queen Victoria with Prince Albert of Saxe-Coburg-Gotha popularized and ultimately sanctified? It would be nice to think that they helped. Certainly by the late thirties and the forties the fairy world began to inspire work of a higher order than any we have considered so far. In 1838 David Scott, an

10. L. S. Ruhl, plate to *The Gallery of Shakespeare, or, Illustrations of his Dramatic Works* (Ackermann and Tilt, 1829)

artist of frustrated power and promise, whose death at the age of forty-three in 1849 was one of the more poignant losses to the visual arts by early death of this romantic period, showed at the Royal Scottish Academy *Puck fleeing before the Dawn* (fig. 11) with the quotation:

> And we fairies that do run,
> By the triple Hecate's team,
> From the presence of the Sun
> Following darkness like a dream
>
> (5.1.372–5)

This composition, highly original, but at the same time growing out of Fuseli, brings Boydell as it were up to date. A Boydell of the 1830s would not have hesitated to include it in his Gallery. Scott had spent some years in Italy. The garden with its cypress and its balustraded terrace is Italian. The sea is the Mediterranean. It is the nearest we have so far got to the Aegean and to Athens and to that extent the impact of the fairy world is diminished. Fairies do not belong to the south and indeed the flying ring

of winged creatures following in Puck's wake is more like a buzz of fireflies than Titania and her attendants. It is a strange picture, perhaps illustrating unawares the way the historic conscience was already beginning to work on Shakespearian stage production. Charles Kemble's production of *King John* in 1823 was 'historical'. Shakespeare himself, of course, was in this respect wholly capricious and the relation of fairyland to geographical location or historical time meant nothing to him. Why should it?

Sir Joseph Noel Paton (he was knighted in 1867), Scott's junior by fifteen years, takes us into the fairyland of Fuseli devitalized by saccharine. In Fuseli fantasy runs riot and borders on nightmare. Here we have dream-land only. Paton's mother, we are told in the *DNB*, 'was an enthusiast for fairy-tales and the traditions and legends of the Highlands', and by good fortune he chose to work on *Midsummer Night's Dream* subjects early in life. His later religious paintings are Nazarene diluted to sentimentality. His interpretations of the *Dream* – *The Reconciliation of Oberon and Titania*, 1846–7, and *The Quarrel of Oberon and Titania* (fig. 12), 1849 – are, however, in their glossy way, pleasingly light-hearted and fantastic, all of a piece with the fashion of the day for shine and prettiness and convolvulus colour, especially as it was popularized in the work of Daniel Maclise. They are, too, captivating in detail, and as pictures that were and continue to be immensely pleasing to the public, of the first importance in the iconography of the play. As late as 1895 a writer in *The Art Journal*[8] described *The Quarrel* as the most popular picture in the Scottish National Gallery. Slightly before Paton's entry into the fairy field, Richard Dadd, who was only four years his junior, had established himself as a painter of this theme. *Come unto these yellow sands*, a concept nearer to Scott than Paton, was exhibited at the Royal Academy in 1842. But Dadd lost his reason, murdered his father in 1843, and was admitted to Bethlem Hospital in 1844. Those of his pictures which are now most universally admired and which, not surprisingly, show signs of originality of a kind

---

8 Alfred T. Story, 'Sir Noel Paton: His Life and Work', *The Art Journal* (1895), 97–128.

11. David Scott, *Puck fleeing before the Dawn*, 1837–8

12. Sir Joseph Noel Paton, *The Quarrel of Oberon and Titania*, 1849

13. Richard Dadd, *Contradiction. Oberon and Titania*, 1854–8

that could flourish only in a disordered mind, were painted after this date. His *Contradiction. Oberon and Titania*[9] (fig. 13) was painted 1854–8. The overflowing details of Paton (Dadd might have read of Paton's *Dream* pictures, but could not have seen them) here are almost out of control. A huge butterfly rests on an outsize water-lily leaf, and ears of barley, grown beyond the ambitions of any organizer of a harvest-festival, flop where they do not belong. Oberon and Titania confront one another across giant convolvuli. Lysander and Hermia enter on the right, out of context. Something like a malachite ostrich egg is suspended in mid-air. One can see the picture dissolving and reintegrating into Bosch. Is this not much nearer in spirit to

Shakespeare than Paton? It is one of the masterpieces the *Dream* has inspired.

Mendelssohn's enchanted and enchanting overture to *A Midsummer Night's Dream* was given its first public performance at Stettin in 1827, just before the appearance of the first number of Retzch and Ruhl, and composers and artists alike sought Shakespearian subjects increasingly throughout Europe during the nineteenth century. Even the idea of a Shakespeare Gallery was revived in Florence in 1861 by one Caetano Giucci who, in a pamphlet,[10] proposed four subjects for *A Midsummer Night's Dream* – Hermia

---

9 Sotheby's sale, London, 15 March 1983, lot 25.

10 Library of the Shakespeare Centre, Stratford-upon-Avon.

14. E. A. Abbey, illustration to act 1, scene 1 for *Harper's Bazaar*, 1893–4

15. W. Heath Robinson, illustration to act 1, scene 1, 1914

refusing the husband proposed by her father, Hermia and Helena asleep, Lysander and Demetrius draw their swords, and *Titania caressing Bottom in his Ass's Head*. The Titania and Bottom subject had been popularized by Landseer around 1850 (and therefore contemporaneously with Paton) in a picture now in the National Gallery of Victoria, Melbourne, but the interesting thing about Giucci's four subjects is that three of them relate to the basic plot of the play and to the Athenian mortals. It is from about this time that illustrators began to some extent to desert the fairy element and to visualize productions of the play in historically 'accurate' terms. Later in the century Shakespearian subjects, in oil and water-colour or as book illustration, careful, detailed costume pieces bearing all the marks of the increasingly popular local English pageant – steeple hats, long scalloped sleeves, pointed medieval shoes – were in great demand from such artists as J. Byam Shaw, F. Cadogan Cowper and, a little later, Eleanor Fortescue-Brickdale, whose work is now being reassessed and merited more deservedly. There is space here to consider only one or two of this generation. Edwin Austin Abbey, a native of Philadelphia who settled in England around 1880, is perhaps the most notable. He made a series of

16. Arthur Rackham, *Helena*, 1908

17. T. A. Dean, engraving after *Hermia and Helena* by
John Wood

illustrations to the comedies of Shakespeare, commissioned by *Harper's Bazaar*, which was completed in 1896 and, later, a series for the tragedies. He longed to be 'accurate' – 'In the case of the Comedies the scenes of which are laid in Venice, Padua, Tuscany, etc., I should like to go to these places which I have never seen.'[11] His *Enter Theseus* (fig. 14) 'with pomp, with triumph and with revelling' sets the scene on a grand stage. It might be the Mediterranean corner which Puck streaks over in David Scott's painting – would that Scott had had the opportunity to make designs for the *Dream* on a gigantic scale – but it is not an imaginative concept in that sense. It is carefully researched 'revival' for a stirring, visually exciting, expensive production of the kind which is

unfashionable now but must have been enormously enjoyable at that time, and would indeed be so today. The masque element so apparent in the plate to the *Dream* in Rowe's edition of 1709 has here developed into spectacle that leads us on to Cecil B. de Mille. It is surprising to find William Heath Robinson, in the next generation, whom one associates almost exclusively with elaborate, humorous (and ultimately rather boring) ingenuities on the theme of fantastic home-made machinery, continuing the E. A. Abbey approach in his illustrations to the *Dream* of 1914 (fig. 15). Aesthetically he

---

11 E. V. Lucas, *Life and Work of Edwin Austin Abbey RA*, 2 vols. (London and New York, 1921), vol. 1, p. 168.

descends from Beardsley and his plates in colour and black-and-white make the book a period decorative piece, a pleasure to handle, a dream in quite another sense than Shakespeare's, a day-dream if you like, a reverie (a word so utterly of that time) that renders the text remote. Heath Robinson was a contemporary of Arthur Rackham whose fantasies were in some ways like his own, but of a more remarkable order. Rackham indeed is spiritually in the direct line from Retzch and Ruhl. His spiky imagination is Germanic. Grimm's *Fairy Tales* were after his own heart as material for illustrations. Rackham's *Dream*, 1908, produced like Heath Robinson's as a drawing-room gift book or a book to be kept on the shelves of a glass-fronted bookcase, and treated with great care, is at its most successful in its depiction of Bottom the monster and the lovers lost in entangled copses. But as a production of its time and an example of how inevitably the artist interprets Shakespeare through the eyes of his period, it is Rackham's Hermia and Helena who are most revealing. *Helena* (fig. 16) with her Edwardian hair-style, her bracelets, and her cloak is a kind of Mrs Ramsay, a decade or so too soon, waiting for the cab to take her out to dinner or the play, just as almost a century earlier John Wood's *Hermia and Helena* (fig. 17), with their ringlets and jewelled clasps and regency Grecian garments, would have been more at home turning the pages of an album of engraved portraits of beauties than taking part in a stage production of Shakespeare where they would certainly have behaved too well.

THE NATURE OF PORTIA'S VICTORY:
TURNING TO MEN IN
'THE MERCHANT OF VENICE'

KEITH GEARY

Critics have often approached Portia's disguise as Balthazar with expectations implicitly shaped by the disguises of Julia, Rosalind, and Viola. Peter Hyland remarks that in *The Merchant of Venice* 'Shakespeare was still at the stage of experiment and his use of disguise here is less successful than it was in *The Two Gentlemen of Verona*'.[1] Juliet Dusinberre expresses the widely held opinion that 'Shakespeare evaded in *The Merchant of Venice* the problems that he created for himself in *Twelfth Night* and *As You Like It*'.[2] Such comments assume that the dramatic nature of sexual disguise must necessarily be the same in all contexts. What is most striking about Portia's disguise as Balthazar is the absence of the psychological and sexual ambiguity that informs the disguises of the other heroines. If we turn to Portia's disguise looking for this quality we will inevitably conclude that it is poorer in conception and execution than the other disguises. Critics have rarely considered the possibility that Shakespeare, confronting different problems in *The Merchant of Venice*, conceived sexual disguise in different terms. The dramatic relation between Balthazar as a role and Portia as a character is fundamentally different from that between the other heroines and their disguises. We need to examine anew the place of Portia's performance as Balthazar in the play's treatment of the love-versus-friendship *débat*-theme, attending closely to the *ambivalence* built into the part of Portia–Balthazar and the way that it is resolved in the much-abused fifth act.

Critical writing on *The Merchant of Venice* can boast, as Norman Rabkin has shown,[3] opposed and apparently contradictory interpretations of every important character and incident in the play. We must, critics tell us, take sides either with Shylock or with Portia and the Christians, and stand by our choice, for 'How can we for a moment sympathize with Shylock unless at the same time we indignantly turn, not only against Gratiano, but against Portia, the Duke, and all Venice as well?'[4] The black-and-white judgement that E. E. Stoll's question encourages seems peculiarly inappropriate to a play that argues the falsity of such neat and absolute distinctions. *The Merchant of Venice* deals in shades of grey and continually raises the problem of appropriate response and judgement, most acutely, of course, in relation to Shylock, who has consistently polarized both audiences' responses and critics' interpretations: diabolical monster or tortured scapegoat? The audience's problem with Shylock is like that of Launcelot Gobbo who, prompted to different courses of action by his conscience and the fiend, puzzles over the 'right' response to the Jew. An episode such as Shylock's conversation with Tubal in act 3, scene 1, with its extraordinary shifts and reversals of Shylock's mood, his transformation from caricature stage Jew,

---

[1] Peter Hyland, 'Shakespeare's Heroines: Disguise in the Romantic Comedies', *Ariel*, 9 (1978), 23–39; p. 31.

[2] Juliet Dusinberre, *Shakespeare and the Nature of Women* (1975), p. 267.

[3] See Norman Rabkin, 'Meaning and Shakespeare', in Clifford Leech and J. M. R. Margeson, eds., *Shakespeare 1971: Proceedings of the World Shakespeare Congress, Vancouver, August 1971* (Toronto, 1972).

[4] E. E. Stoll, *Shakespeare Studies* (New York, 1927), p. 318.

the miserly malevolent villain, to the deserted, tormented father, the widower mourning the loss of Leah's ring, denies the audience a single, simple response. He is both caricature and human being, both torturing monster and tormented victim.[5] Like Janus, by whom Gratiano swears, Shylock is 'double-headed': the design of the character is fundamentally ambivalent. By manipulating this ambivalence Shakespeare makes Shylock a touchstone: our response to him at a particular moment partly defines our response to the other characters and especially to the goings-on in Belmont and Antonio's relation to them.

Reappearing in Belmont in the final scene, Portia likens the light of a candle to the shining of 'a good deed in a naughty world' (5.1.91).[6] Nerissa replies:

When the moon shone we did not see the candle.
Portia.
So doth the greater glory dim the less, –
A substitute shines brightly as a king
Until a king be by, and then his state
Empties itself, as doth an inland brook
Into the main of waters: – music – hark!
Nerissa.
It is your music (madam) of the house.
Portia.
Nothing is good (I see) without respect, –
Methinks it sounds much sweeter than by day.
Nerissa.
Silence bestows that virtue on it madam.
(5.1.92–101)

This discussion of the relative nature of goodness is especially resonant in a play so concerned with judgement and justice, reward and punishment. In a sense, Portia's words also illuminate a central aspect of Shakespeare's dramatic technique in *The Merchant of Venice*. Shylock's presence in the play allows Shakespeare to present the literal and metaphorical contracts of friendship and marriage in a manner unusually cynical for one of his comedies, without appearing to undermine their value totally. In Shakespeare's exploration of the materialism of human relationships, both business and personal, Shylock's ambivalent presence protects the other characters at the same time as it comments on them: his materialism shields them from the full effects of

the admissions that the play makes about them and their society. As Portia says, 'Nothing is good (I see) without respect', and Shylock is there to deflect on to himself the brunt of the audience's censure.

Ambivalence is not, of course, a characteristic of Shylock alone. In the final scene, accusing Bassanio of infidelity and rejecting his oath of innocence sworn by 'thine own fair eyes / Wherein I see myself' (5.1.242–3), Portia declares:

Mark you but that!
In both my eyes he doubly sees himself:
In each eye one, – swear by your double self,
And there's an oath of credit.
(5.1.243–6)

All the main characters in the play have double selves, and so sustain the apparently contradictory critical readings that Rabkin has noted, one predominating, then the other, making our responses and judgements difficult, shifting, relative. This Janus-like duality is built into the larger design of the play. *The Merchant of Venice* contains a number of 'tricks' – elements that appear to mean one thing but turn out to mean another or, more exactly, to have two meanings simultaneously. Shylock's bond, Antonio's generosity, the law in the trial and the gift of the ring share this quality, but it is most fully embodied in the ambivalent 'double self' of Portia and Balthazar, the lady and the lawyer.

In shaping Portia, Shakespeare made a number of significant changes to the figure he found in his major source, Ser Giovanni's *Il Pecorone*. In Ser Giovanni's story the Lady of Belmont is a beautiful widow who has, the sea-captain tells Giannetto (Bassanio), ruined many gentlemen. She has made a law 'that anyone who arrives must sleep with her, and if he can possess her he must take her for his wife and become lord of the port and all that country. But if he fails, he

---

[5] See Rabkin, pp. 90–1, on this scene. For an interesting account of Shylock in the theatre, see John Russell Brown, 'The Realization of Shylock: A Theatrical Criticism', in John Russell Brown and Bernard Harris, eds., *Early Shakespeare*, Stratford-upon-Avon Studies, 3 (1961).

[6] All references are to the texts of the new Arden editions of the plays.

loses everything that he has.'[7] In *The Merchant of Venice* Shakespeare has Portia's father make the law, makes Portia a virtuous daughter, replaces the sexual test with the lottery of the caskets, and discards the mercenary motive – Portia stands to gain nothing except a husband. The lady's situation becomes a paradigm of a daughter's position as her father's property to be bestowed on a husband of his choosing. Portia complains 'O me the word "choose"! I may neither choose who I would, nor refuse who I dislike, so is the will of a living daughter curb'd by the will of a dead father: is it not hard Nerissa, that I cannot choose one, nor refuse none?' (1.2.22–6). The arranged marriage, which caused Hermia and Juliet such problems, becomes a lottery in which Portia, like a princess in a fairy-tale, is literally the prize. The appalling constraints of her situation and her enforced passivity are stressed repeatedly: 'the lott'ry of my destiny / Bars me the right of voluntary choosing' (2.1.15–16), she tells Morocco. Silvia's literal imprisonment in *The Two Gentlemen of Verona*, locked in a tower by her father, becomes in Portia's situation a more terrible metaphorical imprisonment.

The overnaming of the suitors in the first scene in Belmont recalls Julia's first scene in *The Two Gentlemen of Verona*. There it is Lucetta who comments on the suitors whilst Julia listens. Here it is Portia who comments and, unlike Lucetta, she offers criticism not praise: Nerissa names the suitors and Portia mocks them wittily. We laugh with her at their expense, as we do later when, knowing what she thinks of her other suitors, we hear her assure Morocco that he stands 'as fair / As any comer I have look'd on yet / For my affection' (2.1.20–2). All her suitors, those named and those who appear in person to condemn themselves out of their own mouths, are made to look conceited fools, braggarts, nincompoops. The 'casket' scenes emphasize Portia's superiority to her suitors and her ability to deal with them directly, without the aid of other men; there is no Boyet or Lafew or even Touchstone in Belmont. At the same time they underline the powerlessness of her situation: 'I had rather be married to a death's-head with a bone in his mouth, than to either of these: God defend me

from these two' (1.2.49–51). He must, for she cannot – and will not – refuse if either should choose correctly. In the 'casket' scenes the world of Belmont is clearly defined as feminine, yet ironically governed by the will of a dead man. Shakespeare stresses the relaxed, harmonious intimacy of Portia and Nerissa – they do not come to blows like Julia and Lucetta; they present a united front to the world of men and to the seemingly interminable stream of suitors.

Portia's satiric description of youthful masculinity when she announces to Nerissa her plan to disguise is similar, in its high-spirited pleasure at the thought of playing a man, to Rosalind's speech on her intended disguise at the end of act 1 of *As You Like It*. Portia declares:

> When we are both accoutered like young men,
> I'll prove the prettier fellow of the two,
> And wear my dagger with the braver grace,
> And speak between the change of man and boy,
> With a reed voice, and turn two mincing steps
> Into a manly stride; and speak of frays
> Like a fine bragging youth: and tell quaint lies
> How honourable ladies sought my love,
> Which I denying, they fell sick and died.
>
> (3.4.63–71)

She could be describing Ganymede with his captivating vitality and balance of masculine and feminine. But this description has nothing in common with the sober doctor of laws of '*so young a body with so old a head*' (4.1.160–1) in the court scene. It is far removed from the ruthlessly efficient lawyer dispensing justice with the utmost rigour and in accordance with the minutest details of the letter of the law. Portia's speech creates expectations that are then flatly unfulfilled: we are given something very different. And not only is Balthazar very different from Portia's description of how she will play a man but there is nothing in the doctor of laws to remind us of this 'unlesson'd girl, unschool'd, unpractised' (3.2.159), as she rather modestly terms herself. Shakespeare gives Portia more pre-disguise scenes than any of the other disguised heroines,

---

[7] Geoffrey Bullough, ed., *Narrative and Dramatic Sources of Shakespeare*, 8 vols. (1957–75), vol. I (1957), p. 21.

firmly and extensively establishing her character before she disguises. Furthermore he returns her to female dress for the entire fifth act, unlike the other heroines. The emphasis in the 'casket' scenes on both Portia's resilient femininity and her ability to cope efficiently with men has the double effect of preparing the audience to accept more readily her disguise as a lawyer – she is an intelligent, capable woman – and of making the transformation into Balthazar sexually all the more miraculous. There is an absolute distinction between Portia and Balthazar.

Portia's disguise, unlike those of the other heroines, reveals no interest in exploring the psychological consequences of a sexual disguise. This is a crucial difference. The sustained use of dramatic irony by which Shakespeare emphasizes the psychological and sexual ambiguities of the heroines' disguises in the other comedies – for instance, in Julia's meeting with Silvia (4.4) or in Rosalind–Ganymede's wooing-game scenes with Orlando – is absent in the trial. The 'special intimacy'[8] that the other heroines share with the audience is never established. Portia speaks only as Balthazar, not in a 'double voice' as Julia does to Silvia or as Viola does so poignantly in the 'Patience on a monument' scene with Orsino (2.4). Portia plays one role unambiguously and continuously. Only once in the trial does Balthazar speak so as explicitly to remind the audience that he is really Portia: after Bassanio's offer to sacrifice 'life itself, my wife, and all the world' (4.1.280) to save Antonio:

Your wife would give you little thanks for that
If she were by to hear you make the offer.

(4.1.284–5)

By reminding the audience that Balthazar *is* Bassanio's wife these words stress the completeness of her transformation into Balthazar. The entirely different identity she has assumed is wholly masculine, wholly Balthazar's; she is transformed into a new character and, most importantly, a man. The theatrical fact of the boy actor in the Elizabethan theatre makes Portia's sexual transformation complete, for the boy actor simply discards the female dress and characteristics of Portia, dons

a lawyer's gown and plays Balthazar, a young doctor of laws. Balthazar is, in Rosalind's words, 'all points like a man' (1.3.112) because that is what he actually is.

Samuel Pepys's comment on the performance of Kynaston, one of the last boy actors to play women, in the title role of Jonson's *Epicoene, or The Silent Woman* is illuminating in this context. He is particularly struck by Kynaston's appearing first 'the prettiest woman in the whole house' and then 'the handsomest man'. We may compare his slightly wonder-struck comments on Nell Gwyn's performance as a boy: 'She comes in like a young gallant; and hath the motions and carriage of a spark the most that ever I saw any man have.'[9] What fascinates him in each case is the extraordinary completeness of the sexual transformation. It is, we may assume, this kind of transformation that the boy actor in the Lord Chamberlain's Men effected in playing first Portia, then Balthazar, and then Portia once more.

The sexual transformation effected by Portia's disguise is central to the treatment of the love-versus-friendship *débat*-theme in *The Merchant of Venice*. Shakespeare pits the claims of the legal bond of marriage against those of masculine friendship, whose primacy was sanctioned by the still powerful medieval code of 'god-like amity' (3.4.3). Portia's disguise, her performance in the trial, and her recovery of the ring enforce the sexual dimension of the conflict centred on Bassanio's divided loyalties. Through Portia's disguise Shakespeare adapts the *débat*-theme framework to dramatize the struggle between heterosexual love and homosexual love in the triangle of Portia, Bassanio, and Antonio. The relationship between Antonio and Bassanio is not so easily fitted into the conventional friendship category of the love-versus-friendship *débat* as earlier critics of the play believed and as, indeed, still appears to be the case to some.[10]

8 Hyland, p. 23.
9 Samuel Pepys, *Diary*, entries for 7 January 1660/1 and 2 March 1666/7, repr. in Helen McAfee, *Pepys on the Restoration Stage* (New Haven, 1916), pp. 225, 244.
10 See Lawrence Danson, *The Harmonies of 'The Merchant of Venice'* (New Haven, 1978).

Certainly the feeling of Antonio, 'a tainted wether of the flock' (4.1.114), for Bassanio – Solanio says 'he only loves the world for him' (2.8.50) – resists accommodation within such a scheme, even taking into account the repeatedly asserted intensity and emotionalism of Renaissance friendships. We need only glance at Proteus and Valentine in *The Two Gentlemen of Verona* to realize how much more intense and less immature is the relationship of Antonio and Bassanio. It is perhaps more appropriate to think of a Renaissance friendship such as that of James I and Buckingham. Much critical ingenuity has been expended in evading this conclusion.[11] D. J. Palmer has commented that 'critics who try like Salerio and Solanio to discover the cause of Antonio's sadness are wilfully ignoring its dramatic point: "In sooth, I know not why I am so sad."'[12] If this is so, we must conclude that Shakespeare fritters away the first 113 lines of the play by having the characters discuss something that is irrelevant and in which we are not intended to be the least interested. The dramatic point is precisely the uncertainty surrounding the cause of Antonio's sadness. Palmer's comment conflicts with the effect of the opening scene and the way in which Shakespeare has dramatized the audience's first encounter with Antonio and Bassanio.

It cannot be denied that the play *does* begin by focusing our attention on the 'marvellously chang'd' (1.1.76) Antonio, on speculation as to the cause of his sadness, or that the scene does indeed offer the audience an explanation. Salerio's suggestion that the cause is Antonio's concern about his business affairs is flatly rejected. Solanio's suggestion that he is in love receives a 'Fie! Fie!' (l. 46), 'an exclamation of reproach rather than a clear negative'.[13] Solanio immediately changes tack, offering a comic – and uncontentious – explanation: 'let us say you are sad / Because you are not merry' (ll. 47–8). At the appearance of Bassanio, accompanied by Lorenzo and Gratiano – 'better company', 'worthier friends' (ll. 59, 61) – all but Gratiano show themselves eager to leave Antonio and Bassanio tactfully alone together, a response which Bassanio is quick to notice, seeming a little reluctant to be left alone with his friend: 'You grow exceeding strange: must it be so?' (l. 67). Once alone

with Bassanio, Antonio brushes aside idle chit-chat and comes straight to the point:

> Well, tell me now what lady is the same
> To whom you swore a secret pilgrimage –
> That you to-day promis'd to tell me of?
>
> (ll. 119–21)

Bassanio answers Antonio's directness with elaborately indirect and slightly embarrassed requests for yet more money. Twice Antonio reproaches him for this long-winded beating about the bush – 'herein [you] spend but time / To wind about my love with circumstance' (ll. 153–4) – and affirms his unquestioning generosity:

> My purse, my person, my extremest means
> Lie all unlock'd to your occasions.
>
> (ll. 138–9)

Bassanio then proceeds to describe his projected journey to Belmont less in terms of intended marriage than as if it were a business venture, emphasizing that both he and Antonio will profit materially from it. Antonio immediately agrees to rack his credit 'even to the uttermost' (l. 181), and the scene ends. The first half of the scene invites the audience to ponder the cause of Antonio's sadness and the second half presents that cause: his imminent separation from Bassanio. To Antonio Bassanio 'owe[s] the most in money and in love', but his purpose is 'to get clear of all the debts I owe' (ll. 131, 134). The scene is tense with an unspoken loosening of ties.

This is not to say that the scene is a love-scene. There has been a trend in recent productions to make this scene and other moments in the play explicitly homosexual. Jonathan Miller emphasized this aspect in his National Theatre production (1970) with Laurence Olivier, and it is now common for Antonio and Bassanio to kiss in this scene and others.

---

11 See, for example, Alice N. Benston, 'Portia, the Law, and the Tripartite Structure of *The Merchant of Venice*', *Shakespeare Quarterly*, 30 (1979), 367–85.

12 D. J. Palmer, '*The Merchant of Venice*, or The Importance of Being Earnest', in Malcolm Bradbury and D. J. Palmer, eds., *Shakespearian Comedy*, Stratford-upon-Avon Studies, 14 (1972), p. 103.

13 John Russell Brown, note on this line in his new Arden edition of the play, p. 7.

Such directorial touches both recognize an important element in the play and falsify the manner in which Shakespeare presents it. There is no justification in the text for such intimate physical contact – behaviour which on the Elizabethan stage would direct the audience's anti-homosexual feelings against the characters involved, a response on which the design of Marlowe's *Edward II* is founded. What the text does make clear is that the relationship between Antonio and Bassanio is of great intensity, of love, most importantly on Antonio's side, and strong enough for its claims to counterbalance those of Bassanio's newly established relationship with Portia – indeed proving to be the more powerful allegiance at vital moments in the play. Several of Shakespeare's alterations to *Il Pecorone* increase the importance of the Antonio-character and embody in him an explicit and potent threat to Portia's sway over Bassanio's heart. Shakespeare makes his Antonio Bassanio's friend instead of his godfather, thus importing into the story the love-versus-friendship *débat* in the first place. The action of the play hinges as much on the conflict between Antonio and Portia for the possession of Bassanio's love as on that between the Christians, led by Portia, and Shylock. But the nature and extent of Antonio's feeling for Bassanio and of his challenge to Portia's position as wife become clear to the audience only gradually. At the beginning of the play Antonio remarks of his sadness:

> how I caught it, found it, or came by it,
> What stuff 'tis made of, whereof it is born,
> I am to learn. (1.1.3–5)

Like Antonio, the audience learn what stuff his sadness is made of and whereof it is born. The nature of his feeling for Bassanio becomes apparent by stages: in his instant agreement to Shylock's 'merry bond' (1.3.169); in the moving account of the friends' emotional parting (2.8); in the power of his letter (3.2); and, finally, in his readiness to sacrifice himself in the trial scene, 'a tainted wether of the flock, / Meetest for death, – the weakest kind of fruit' (4.1.114–15) in an otherwise virile, hetero-sexual society. At the opening of the play, however, Antonio appears the embodiment of the virtues of friendship, the paragon of boundless generosity, only too ready to 'give and hazard all he hath' (2.7.9).

When arranging his loan in act 1, scene 3, Antonio, as exemplar of 'god-like amity', instructs Shylock:

> If thou wilt lend this money, lend it not
> As to thy friends, for when did friendship take
> A breed for barren metal of his friend? (1.3.127–9)

Antonio argues that there are distinctly separate codes for personal relationships and business relationships. Shylock, however, blurs the distinctions, treating all alike and applying the terms of love and friendship to commercial transactions:

> I say
> To buy his favour, I extend this friendship, –
> If he will take it, so, – if not, adieu,
> And for my love I pray you wrong me not. (1.3.163–6)

Such phrasing is not confined to Shylock. In *The Merchant of Venice* love is consistently described in financial or commercial terms: debts, bonds, bargains, contracts. Salerio observes that

> ten times faster Venus' pigeons fly
> To seal love's bonds new-made, than they are wont
> To keep obliged faith unforfeited! (2.6.5–7)

Bassanio owes Antonio

> the most in money and in love,
> And from your love I have a warranty
> To unburthen all my plots and purposes
> How to get clear of all the debts I owe.
> (1.1.131–4)

Antonio demonstrates his love by racking his credit to the uttermost. Bassanio declares that Portia is 'nothing undervalu'd / To Cato's daughter, Brutus' Portia' (1.1.165–6). Morocco asks (rhetorically) 'shall I think in silver she's immur'd / Being ten times undervalued to try'd gold?' (2.7.52–3). Contemplating his expedition to Belmont, Bassanio's 'mind presages me such thrift / That I should questionless be fortunate' (1.1.175–6). Shylock speaks of 'my bargains, and my well-won thrift /

Which [Antonio] calls interest' (1.3.45–6). Verbal links between love and commerce are made again and again, and the economic aspects of all the main relationships in the play are continually emphasized. Shakespeare punningly invokes the various forms of making suit: for love, for money, for justice. Bassanio, Morocco, and Arragon make suit to Portia, and Gratiano to Nerissa, Lorenzo to Jessica. Bassanio and Antonio make suit to Shylock: 'moneys is your suit' (1.3.114). Shylock pursues 'a losing suit' (4.1.62) against Antonio in the trial. Seeking a new master, Launcelot makes suit to Bassanio – 'thou hast obtain'd thy suit' (2.2.137) – and Gratiano, too, appeals to Bassanio: 'I have suit to you' (2.2.169). Shakespeare is especially insistent on the relation between finance and marriage, and his presentation of the relationships of Portia and Bassanio and Jessica and Lorenzo develops this connection most extensively. In a play that contains an almost programmatic definition of love in the motto on the leaden casket – 'Who chooseth me, must give and hazard all he hath' (2.7.9) – it is striking that the lovers' adherence to this principle is not unambiguous. As Morocco remarks, in a rare moment of insight, 'men that hazard all / Do it in hope of fair advantages' (2.7.18–19). Bassanio, Portia, Jessica, and Lorenzo share a sound grasp of what they have to gain from their marriages.

The Jessica and Lorenzo sub-plot is not in *Il Pecorone*, although it is to be found in a different form in another possible source, Masuccio's *Il Novellino*. The conduct of the relationship of Jessica and Lorenzo parallels and contrasts with that of Portia and Bassanio: both relationships involve a casket, a disguise, and a ring. The sub-plot shows a woman escaping the restrictions of her position as daughter and making the choice of her husband for herself:

> O Lorenzo
> If thou keep promise I shall end this strife,
> Become a Christian and thy loving wife!
> (2.3.19–21)

Jessica's evasion of the will of her father, whose motto 'Fast bind, fast find, – / A proverb never stale in thrifty mind' (2.5.53–4) applies as much to his daughter as to his other property, underlines the narrow constraints endured by Portia, who cannot choose, but must obey the will of her 'virtuous' and 'holy' father, whose 'good inspiration' (1.2.27, 28) of the lottery is little more than a fairy-tale version of Shylock's attitude. But Jessica's elopement has another aspect. Lorenzo promises to assist his friends when it is their turn 'to play the thieves for wives' (2.6.23), and indeed the elopement is also a robbery: Jessica throws down the casket of jewels and gold to Lorenzo and then goes back inside the house to 'gild myself / With some moe ducats' (2.6.49–50). The elopement of these unthrift lovers involves urgent economic considerations: they need ready money. Furthermore, for Jessica there is a religious profit to be gained by marriage to Lorenzo: 'I shall be sav'd by my husband, – he hath made me a Christian!' (3.5.17–18). Shakespeare holds the two aspects of the escape in tension. Lorenzo's eulogy on 'wise, fair, and true' Jessica (2.6.56), whilst she fetches the ducats, counterbalances the impression of the elopement as a robbery, quelling any niggling suspicions that perhaps he is interested only in her money.

The relationship between the financial and romantic aspects of marriage which Shakespeare emphasizes in his handling of the elopement of Jessica and Lorenzo is most fully developed in the scene of Bassanio's choice of the casket which is permeated by the language of commerce. Shakespeare prepares extensively for this scene, particularly in his presentation of Bassanio. In no other Shakespearian comedy do the chief lovers meet for the first time so late in the play. This reflects the play's stress on the initial situations of the lovers: Portia bound by her father's will, and Bassanio in debt and virtually penniless. Bassanio's money troubles – a problem he shares with Jessica and Lorenzo – set him apart from the other romantic heroes of the comedies. Orsino, Benedick, Berowne, and the others never have to worry about finding money as Bassanio does (though 'Hath Leonato any son, my lord?' (1.1.256) is one of the first questions the dubious Claudio asks about Hero); they are all conveniently equipped with private fortunes or the assurance of a good inheritance. But Bassanio, unable to manage his financial affairs efficiently, needs money, and the easiest and quickest way to get it is by finding himself a rich wife. The opening scene of the play establishes him as a fortune-hunter. He describes his expedition to Belmont as a business enterprise in which Portia, 'a lady richly left' and of great 'worth', is the 'golden fleece', the 'thrift' (1.1.161, 167, 170, 175). Shakespeare then gradually prepares the audience to accept Bassanio as a suitor worthy of Portia. In the first scene itself, his mercenary aspect is slightly qualified: Portia is singled out not only because she is rich but also because 'sometimes from her eyes / I did receive fair speechless messages' (1.1.163–4). Portia's praise of Bassanio at the end of her first scene is lent weight by her earlier ridicule of her other suitors. The rowdy Gratiano is manipulated as a foil for Bassanio whose ready granting of his friend's suit (2.2) before he knows what it is, though a slight matter, recalls Antonio's earlier magnanimity. The granting of Gratiano's request allows Bassanio to appear as the spokesman for restraint and decorum: 'pray thee take pain / To allay with some cold drops of modesty / Thy skipping spirit' (2.2.176–8). On the announcement, after Arragon's departure, of the imminent arrival of another suitor Nerissa remarks 'Bassanio, Lord Love, if thy will it be!' (2.9.101). And, of course, it is. The action moves towards the inevitable 'casket' scene and Shakespeare draws on the audience's awareness of how the fairy-tale convention works: the third suitor is always successful. Bassanio's 'casket' scene is immediately preceded by Shylock's conversation with Tubal — the long scene is framed by two of Shylock's five appearances in the play — which shows the ascendancy of materialist values in personal, indeed in familial, relationships as well as in business relationships. Shylock bewails the loss of 'two thousand ducats in that, and other precious, precious jewels; I would my daughter were dead at my foot, and the jewels in her ear' (3.1.79–81). The contrast provided by Shylock's materialism here makes the emphasis on finance in the succeeding 'casket' scene appear in a better light, at the same time as it enforces the audience's recognition of a connection.

The contrast between the emotional texture of Bassanio's 'casket' scene and the scene with Shylock before it is striking. This scene has an emotional and poetic richness, a sense of joy welling up as the scene moves to Bassanio's choice of the casket — a movement accompanied by the first sounds of music in the play — that differs greatly from anything so far. The half-bored, yet impatient, tone of Portia's dealings with her previous suitors has gone:

> I could teach you
> How to choose right, but then I am forsworn,
> So will I never be, – so may you miss me, –
> But if you do, you'll make me wish a sin,
> That I had been forsworn. Beshrew your eyes,
> They have o'erlook'd me and divided me,
> One half of me is yours, the other half yours, –
> Mine I would say: but if mine then yours,
> And so all yours. (3.2.10–18)

Portia's new love strains against submission to the rules of the lottery; her refusal to cheat makes the scene all the more tense and lays all hopes on Bassanio alone. His long speech of deliberation displays motives impeccably ideal and disinterested. His 'And here choose I, – joy be the consequence!' (3.2.107) can be an electric moment in production, and Portia's words of exalted joy (3.2.108–14) crown the moment as Bassanio discovers her portrait and begins another persuasively romantic and idealistic speech. But this speech concludes with the diction of legal contracts:

> So (thrice-fair lady) stand I even so,
> As doubtful whether what I see be true,
> Until confirm'd, sign'd, ratified by you.
> (3.2.146–8)

Portia, wishing that she were fairer, richer, and so would 'Exceed account', defines 'the full sum of me' (3.2.157) and describes her forthcoming marriage as if it were a business transaction, presenting herself as a piece of property with a new owner:

> Myself, and what is mine, to you and yours
> Is now converted. But now I was the lord
> Of this fair mansion, master of my servants,
> Queen o'er myself: and even now, but now,
> This house, these servants, and this same myself

cold

Are yours, – my lord's! – I give them with this
    ring,
Which when you part from, lose, or give away,
Let it presage the ruin of your love,
And be my vantage to exclaim on you.

(3.2.166–74)

The courtly mistress becomes the subordinate wife,
and the transition from daughterhood to wifehood
is a movement from one dependent economic
relationship to another. Portia gives Bassanio the
ring, the symbol both of their love in its ideal aspect
and of the legal bond that embodies it, and spells out
the conditions of the contract, to which Bassanio
swears adherence:

> when this ring
> Parts from this finger, then parts life from hence, –
> O then be bold to say Bassanio's dead!

(3.2.183–5)

In hazarding all Bassanio has certainly realized 'his
fair advantages' (2.7.19). The language of the
fortune-hunter reappears, but now it is Gratiano, not
Bassanio, who boasts of the marriage as the 'bargain
of your faith' and declares: 'We are the Jasons, we
have won the fleece' (3.2.193, 240). While still
impressing the financial aspect of the marriage on
the audience, Shakespeare spares Bassanio from taint
and allows him once again to be the spokesman for
decorum and responsibility: 'And do you Gratiano
mean good faith?' (3.2.210).

It is into this mood of harmony and imminent
sexual pleasure – Gratiano wants to 'play with them
the first boy for a thousand ducats' (3.2.213–14) and
seems keen to set about winning his wager as soon
as possible – that the messenger from Venice
intrudes. The arrival of Salerio with Antonio's letter
to Bassanio prevents the sexual consummation of the
relationship between Portia and Bassanio. Bassanio's
dilemma of conflicting loyalties is settled by Portia's
taking an active initiative: she offers to match
Antonio's financial generosity twenty times over 'to
pay the petty debt' (3.2.306) and then declares:

> First go with me to church, and call me wife,
> And then away to Venice to your friend:
> For never shall you lie by Portia's side
> With an unquiet soul. (3.2.302–5)

This scene differs from the story Shakespeare found
in *Il Pecorone* in two points: the lovers' relationship
is consummated before the Bassanio–character
returns to Venice, indeed before they are married;
and there is no letter. It is also worth noting that
in the source the Antonio–character not only does
not intervene but also does not know the true
purpose of his godson's expeditions. These changes
increase the influence of the absent Antonio.
Shakespeare gives the letter great prominence; first
its contents are made clear to the audience and then
it is read aloud:

> *my bond to the Jew is forfeit, and (since in paying it, it is
> impossible I should all live), debts are clear'd between you
> and I, if I might but see you at my death: notwithstanding,
> use your pleasure, – if your love do not persuade you to
> come, let not my letter.* (3.2.315–20)

Antonio's appeal to Bassanio's love for him makes
clear the exact nature of his bond with Shylock and
contrasts sharply with his words at their leave-taking
when, Salerio says, he told Bassanio to

> 'stay the very riping of the time,
> And for the Jew's bond which he hath of me –
> Let it not enter in your mind of love.'

(2.8.40–2)

The bond with Shylock is revealed to have a
profound emotional significance for Antonio. It is
a desperate attempt to hold on to Bassanio, to bind
the young man to him. It is his response to the threat
to their friendship posed by the expedition to
Belmont and to the prospect of Bassanio's drifting
away from him which it implies – hence his
immediate and apparently carefree readiness to agree
to the 'merry sport' (1.3.141) of the bond. Antonio's
letter claims the payment of Bassanio's debt of love,
fusing the languages of love and commerce in a way
that he has earlier condemned in Shylock.

Shylock's repetitive raving about his determination to have his bond in the next scene is placed
immediately after the reading of Antonio's letter
which also calls in that bond and is instrumental in
shattering the joyous mood of the scene in Belmont.
Clearly the effect of this scene is hostility towards
Shylock and sympathy with Antonio. But, at the

same time, the audience are made to recognize that Antonio, too, will have his bond: Bassanio is being forced to place the claims of Antonio and the code of friendship before his marriage. Shylock's malevolent fury shields Antonio by making his letter-of-the-law adherence to the bond in the sphere of personal relationships appear less reprehensible by contrast. Antonio may indeed 'give and hazard all he hath' for Bassanio's sake, but he has his 'hope of fair advantages' (2.7.9, 19). His letter creates a direct conflict with Portia's marriage to Bassanio. But that relationship is an investment that Portia is determined to protect: 'Since you are dear bought, I will love you dear' (3.2.312). In packing her husband off to Venice and Antonio she concedes her claim on his love – the legal claim of a wife – only to reassert it absolutely in the court scene and the last act.

The sexual innuendo of Nerissa's question after Portia announces her plan to disguise, 'Why, shall we turn to men?' (3.4.78), is extremely relevant to the disguise and to the action of the final two acts. Portia and Nerissa are, in effect, dressing as men to get their husbands, at last, into bed. To win them back from the all-male business world of Venice – where the men 'converse and waste the time together' (3.4.12), as Portia says, attending business-men's dinner parties and indulging in the 'shallow fopp'ry' (2.5.35) of gentlemen's revelry – the women must take on the appearance of men. The strongly masculine atmosphere of Venice contrasts with that of Belmont which, though initially governed by the will of Portia's dead father, gradually becomes dominated by the women. In the final act it is Portia herself who resolves the complications of the situation; there is no male figure such as the Duke in The Two Gentlemen of Verona. In breaking free of her restrictive situation by eloping with Lorenzo, Jessica – the only woman to appear (briefly) dressed as such in Venice in the entire play – has to dress as a young man. It is appropriate that a wind favourable to Bassanio's departure for Belmont causes the cancellation of a dinner party and planned revelry: 'No masque to-night, – the wind is come about' (2.6.64). Venturing into the world of Venice, Portia must

deal with a more specific threat to her marriage than an excess of masculine bonhomie: Antonio. In her disguise she adopts a masculine sexual identity to enable her to operate actively in Venice and so to displace Antonio's hold on Bassanio's affections and loyalty. In the love-versus-friendship structure of The Two Gentlemen of Verona Julia's disguise is ultimately a means of indirect intervention by which she recovers Proteus. Portia's disguise allows her to intervene directly to recover her husband, not, of course, from another woman, but from another man. That the play deals with the breaking of the marriage bond, not a bond between lovers, is a crucial difference. Portia, unlike Julia, has no qualms about disguising as a man; she intervenes strictly on her own terms – those of a wife – and rigorously imposes these on the two men in acts 4 and 5.

The action of the great court scene is double. Its basis is the dual nature of Antonio's bond with Shylock: the financial bond with the Jew is also a personal bond with Bassanio. When Shylock calls in his bond with Antonio, the latter, in turn, calls in his with Bassanio. But the court scene also sets Shylock's bond against Portia's bond of marriage. The scene's action is in two stages. Shylock's bond focuses the trial itself: the marriage bond, the ring episode that concludes it. Portia is pitted against Shylock to save Antonio and pitted against Antonio to save Bassanio. In defeating Shylock's design she is also defeating that of Antonio, who is almost as eager as Shylock that the apparently inevitable judgement should be given and the condition of the bond fulfilled:

> Make no moe offers, use no farther means,
> But with all brief and plain conveniency
> Let me have judgment, and the Jew his will!
> (4.1.81–3)

Antonio is to be a man saved against his will. With Portia's words 'Why then thus it is, – / You must prepare your bosom for his knife' (4.1.240–1), Shylock and Antonio appear to be on the point of receiving the judgement they both want, giving Shylock Antonio's heart and by this sacrifice allowing Antonio a final grand proof of his love for

Bassanio, so reaffirming the bond between them and Bassanio's debt of love:

> Grieve not that I am fall'n to this for you:
> For herein Fortune shows herself more kind
> Than is her custom: it is still her use
> To let the wretched man outlive his wealth,
> To view with hollow eye and wrinkled brow
> An age of poverty: from which ling'ring penance
> Of such misery doth she cut me off.
> Commend me to your honourable wife,
> Tell her the process of Antonio's end,
> Say how I lov'd you, speak me fair in death:
> And when the tale is told, bid her be judge
> Whether Bassanio had not once a love:
> Repent but you that you shall lose your friend
> And he repents not that he pays your debt.
> For if the Jew do cut but deep enough,
> I'll pay it instantly with all my heart.
>
> (4.1.262–77)

In Antonio's words the loss of his 'wealth' is less the loss of his fortune than the loss of Bassanio to Portia. Antonio, finally, applies the diction of finance to love more completely than any other character. He will literally pay Bassanio's debt with all his heart. Antonio sets his sacrifice and his love in explicit opposition to Portia's love for Bassanio. And Bassanio, whose new-found generosity is emphasized in this scene (4.1.112–13, 205–8, 315, 323), responds instantly:

> life itself, my wife, and all the world,
> Are not with me esteem'd above thy life.
> I would lose all, ay sacrifice them all
> Here to this devil, to deliver you.
>
> (4.1.280–3)

The threat to Portia's position implicit in Bassanio's generosity is crystallized and recognized:

> Your wife would give you little thanks for that
> If she were by to hear you make the offer.
>
> (4.1.284–5)

Unknown to Antonio and Bassanio, Portia is literally 'judge' and she proceeds to give sentence – in favour of Shylock.

For the first two-thirds of the scene Shylock is the caricature stage Jew of other moments in the play. His preparations with scale and knife, his horrifying

enthusiasm (4.1.248–50), his exultant praise of Balthazar – all present him as the comic, diabolical stage villain, the butt of the audience's hostility: 'I cannot find it, 'tis not in the bond' (4.1.258). With Shylock in absolute ascendancy, convinced of his triumph, spurred on by the 'Daniel come to judgment', Portia suddenly turns the tables on him and on Antonio: 'Tarry a little, there is something else, – ' (4.1.219, 301). This is the turning-point of the scene. Portia's quibble defeats Shylock, and the audience responds with relief and pleasure – it is indeed the sport to have the enginer hoist with his own petar. But then Balthazar goes further. Shylock's adherence to the letter of the law in the first movement of the scene has its mirror image in Balthazar's even more rigorous adherence to it in the second movement. The audience's admiring delight in Balthazar's ingenuity mixes with awe at his ruthless, merciless efficiency. The young doctor of laws has a second trump card up his sleeve: 'The law hath yet another hold on you' (4.1.343). This unexpected hold on Shylock allows the inhuman 'mercy' (4.1.374) of the forced conversion which Antonio inflicts on him.

Portia frustrates Antonio's attempts to sacrifice himself as a final gesture of his love for Bassanio, relentlessly applying the letter of the law to protect her own bond with Bassanio. By the end of the trial, her comment

> For as thou urgest justice, be assur'd
> Thou shalt have justice more than thou desir'st
>
> (4.1.311–12)

applies as much to Antonio, with his eagerness for 'judgment', as to Shylock. Antonio and Portia act in their own interests, each asserting the primacy of his or her bond. Shylock declares:

> The pound of flesh which I demand of him
> Is dearly bought, 'tis mine and I will have it.
>
> (4.1.99–100)

His words echo Portia's description of Bassanio as 'dear bought' (3.2.312). Like Shylock, she will have her pound of flesh: she will protect her investment, imposing the terms of her marriage contract, just as earlier she adhered so exactly to the law of her father's will. Shylock is punished for the kind of rigidity that both Antonio and Portia practise in their dealings with Bassanio. Antonio forces the men-before-women principle of the friendship code on Bassanio, and Portia must be equally rigid to recover her husband. The men's behaviour forces her to play their game according to their own rules, pressing her claim in Shylockian fashion. In the trial itself, Portia prevents Shylock's attempt to cut out Antonio's heart. In the ring episode, she goes on to complete her own design: she cuts Bassanio out of Antonio's heart.

Critics have almost unanimously dismissed the ring episode – and so one-fifth of the play! – as 'but superficial matter'[14] after the court scene. This verdict fails to recognize that the ring episode is almost a re-enactment of the trial itself, but focusing this time on the play's second bond, the marriage bond. That Balthazar is really Portia asserting her claim as wife on Bassanio is the only reason for act 5; a genuine Balthazar – or, for that matter, aged Bellario, the shadowy legal expert who hovers behind Portia's triumph – could have saved Antonio and Bassanio could have returned to Belmont. Only the conflict in the triangle of Portia, Bassanio, and Antonio necessitates the ring episode. In Balthazar's request for the ring Bassanio received from Portia, the conflict between Bassanio's feeling for Portia and for Antonio is again explicitly raised. The audience are reminded of the ring's significance and of Bassanio's vow:

> Good sir, this ring was given me by my wife,
> And when she put it on, she made me vow
> That I should neither sell, nor give, nor lose it.
>
> (4.1.437–9)

In *Il Pecorone* Giannetto grants the request of his own accord. But Shakespeare has Bassanio refuse at first and then send the ring after Balthazar at Antonio's request:

> My Lord Bassanio, let him have the ring,
> Let his deservings and my love withal
> Be valued 'gainst your wife's commandement.
>
> (4.1.445–7)

Once again Antonio sets the claims of his love in opposition to Bassanio's marriage with Portia, and Bassanio, agreeing immediately to his request, again puts his feeling for his friend before his wife and his vow to her. Ironically, in reaffirming his continuing influence over Bassanio, Antonio plays into Portia's hands. What the concluding scene in Belmont will reveal to Antonio and Bassanio is the extent to which they are bound not to Balthazar, as the Duke thinks (4.1.403), but, unknowingly, to Portia. The tactic that worked for Balthazar in the trial works again for Portia in this scene – the lady has learnt from the lawyer: she pulls the trump card of Balthazar's identity from her sleeve, as she earlier produced the quibble and the law depriving Shylock of his property.

The long final scene completes Portia's judgement of Antonio begun in the court scene. In that scene she prevented his sacrifice of 'all [his] heart' (4.1.277) for Bassanio's sake. In this scene she asserts her total possession of Bassanio and asserts it in explicitly sexual terms. The ring — like the sword, one of the commonest symbols of a sexual organ — is the source of the scene's innuendo and talk of infidelity. John Doebler, in his study of iconic imagery in Shakespeare, interprets the ring in *The Merchant of Venice* in religious terms as a symbol of chastity and argues that 'the literal ring becomes a figurative circle in which chastity is returned to itself'.[15] Such an interpretation does not take proper account of the circumstances under which the ring was originally given away and misrepresents the scene's references to the ring, which are bawdy precisely because the scene concerns, not an ideal chastity, but sexuality and infidelity:

> Well, while I live, I'll fear no other thing
> So sore, as keeping safe Nerissa's ring.
>
> (5.1.306–7)

The ring in this episode is the ring of fabliau. *Mery*

---

[14] H. B. Charlton, *Shakespearian Comedy* (1938; repr. London and New York, 1966), p. 59. See also C. L. Barber, *Shakespeare's Festive Comedy* (Princeton, 1959), p. 186; Palmer, p. 116; and Anthony B. Dawson, *Indirections: Shakespeare and the Art of Illusion* (Toronto, 1978), p. 15.

[15] John Doebler, *Shakespeare's Speaking Pictures: Studies in Iconic Imagery* (Albuquerque, New Mexico, 1974), p. 52.

Tales and Quick Answeres, a miscellany published in 1567, includes the following tale:

A man that was ryght iolous of his wyfe, dreamed on a nyght as he laye a bed with her and slepte, that the dyuell aperd vnto him and sayde: woldest thou nat be gladde, that I shulde put the in suretie of thy wyfe? Yes, sayde he. Holde, sayde the dyuell, as longe as thou hast this rynge vpon thy fynger, no man shall make thee kockolde. The man was gladde thereof, and when he awaked, he found his fynger in ★★★★★★★★.[16]

The ring in *The Merchant of Venice* – as well as being the symbol of the marriage contract – is similarly a comic sexual symbol. The bawdy to which it gives rise brings us back to the sexual transformation of Portia's disguise.

It is in act 5, scene 1 that we find the kind of dramatic irony that is, as we have seen, absent in the court scene during Portia's performance as Balthazar. Portia responds to Bassanio's infidelity by threatening to commit a like infidelity with the doctor of laws: an eye for an eye, a tooth for a tooth. We are repeatedly reminded of Portia's sexual transformation in the earlier scene. Bassanio declares:

No woman had it, but a civil doctor,
Which did refuse three thousand ducats of me.
(5.1.210–11)

Portia retorts:

I will become as liberal as you,
I'll not deny him any thing I have,
No, not my body, not my husband's bed.
(5.1.226–8)

Portia endows Bassanio's gift of the ring with an explicitly sexual significance. In adopting her disguise as Balthazar, Portia sacrifices her body as Antonio offers to sacrifice his body in the bond with Shylock. She turns to a man – assumes a wholly masculine identity – and receives the ring from Bassanio as such – as Balthazar and not as Portia. Her prediction is proved accurate: the men do indeed 'think we are accomplished / With that we lack' (3.4.61–2). Bassanio's symbolic gesture of infidelity is committed with a man at Antonio's request. By her disguise Portia crystallizes a dual sexuality that matches the 'double self' (5.1.245) that

she perceives in Bassanio; she shows her capacity to be both woman and man, wife and friend to him, as Bassanio recognizes when he says: 'Sweet doctor, you shall be my bedfellow' (5.1.284). By the sleight of getting the ring as Balthazar, Portia has fastened the homoerotic tendency of Bassanio's sexuality and the obligations of masculine friendship on to herself. Consequently there is no room for Antonio, 'th'unhappy subject of these quarrels' (5.1.238). The bond Antonio gives in this scene parallels his original bond to Shylock, but whereas the earlier bond was an attempt to hold on to Bassanio, this bond relinquishes any hold on him:

Antonio.

I once did lend my body for his wealth,
Which but for him that had your husband's ring
Had quite miscarried. I dare be bound again,
My soul upon the forfeit, that your lord
Will never more break faith advisedly.

Portia.

Then you shall be his surety: give him this,
And bid him keep it better than the other.

Antonio.

Here Lord Bassanio, swear to keep this ring.
(5.1.249–56)

That Portia gives Antonio the ring to return to Bassanio does not show, as Alexander Leggatt asserts, that 'he has a share in their happiness'.[17] In returning the ring Antonio acknowledges that he is excluded from that happiness – he is not married off at the last minute like his counterpart in *Il Pecorone* – and that Portia has defeated him and displaced him in Bassanio's heart. Accordingly he can stand bound for Bassanio's future fidelity to Portia. Significantly, Portia accepts Antonio's bond as Bassanio's 'surety' and not any renewed oath from her husband. Portia's judgement of Antonio is completed by the letter she gives him. The casualness of her announcement that his argosies have survived – 'You shall not know by what strange

---

16 Repr. in W. Carew Hazlitt, ed., *Shakespeare's Jestbooks* (London, 1874), quoted in Russell J. Meyer, 'Keeping Safe Nerissa's Ring', *American Notes & Queries*, 16 (1978), 67.

17 Alexander Leggatt, *Shakespeare's Comedy of Love* (1973), p. 148.

accident / I chanced on this letter' (5.1.278–9) – creates the impression that Portia herself is in some mysterious way responsible for their reappearance: she pays off the remaining debt and Antonio's final claim on Bassanio is removed. Antonio's words 'Sweet lady, you have given me life and living' (5.1.286) recall Shylock's words at his moment of greatest desolation: 'you take my life / When you do take the means whereby I live' (4.1.372–3). The trump card of Balthazar's identity leaves Antonio as the trump card of the law left Shylock. While appearing to return to Antonio all that he began with – except Bassanio – Portia leaves him, like Shylock, with nothing. He has 'outlive[d] his wealth, / To view with hollow eye and wrinkled brow / An age of poverty' (4.1.265–7). In asserting her claims as a wife Portia, the 'unlesson'd girl, unschool'd, unpractised' (3.2.159), ultimately proves herself the most adept businessman of them all.

NATURE'S ORIGINALS:
VALUE IN SHAKESPEARIAN PASTORAL

In matters of origin, literature is [...]
evolutionary. Whether we vi[...] re accompanies and
literary forms and works as imi[...] n the action of the
against previous generations o[...] nd the romances it
hand of the individual autho[...] hic resonance.
generative force. No literar[...] poetry appear to be
radically yet retained so mu[...] al child abandoned in
under the hand of individua[...] ed eventually as the
from Theocritus to Rob[...] rth and proven virtue.[4]
inherited the pastoral in m[...] d in the directness and
and Renaissance anti-forms, [...] orld that proves more
into tones ranging from the soft pastoral o[...] om which the child was
Midsummer Night's Dream to the hard pastoral of [...] re familiar to us in its
King Lear, but the most characteristic action in his Christian v[...] lowly shepherds find the
pastoral plays involves characters retrieving or royal child who will be cast out so that by His death
reinventing their origins in a natural setting. all men may discover a new paradise within the self
and beyond nature. These stories of noble, innocent

A frequent accusation against the pastoral is that children discovered apart from decadent, envy-
its emphasis on withdrawal from society serves only ridden civilization have power to charm audiences
to glorify nostalgia and moral lassitude. Friedrich because of the wish we all harbour to retrieve a
Schiller, for example, asserted that pastoral idylls better self, if not a Golden Age, amid nature's
'cannot vivify, they can only soften' because of the tranquillity. In his pastoral sequences Shakespeare
value they traditionally attach to *otium*.[1] In a similar uses a wide variety of narratives to transform these
vein Renato Poggioli begins his major study of myths of high virtue in humble surroundings into
pastoral saying 'The psychological root of the
pastoral is a double longing after innocence and
happiness, to be recovered not through conversion
or regeneration, but merely through a retreat.'[2]
However morally flabby the retreats of later
pastorals may have become, those strategic with-
drawals in Shakespeare's plays nearly always are
movements *towards* something immensely invigor-
ating: nature (Greek *physis*) in its 'etymologically
primary' sense of genesis, birth, and, hence, the
'congenital ... talents of a person'.[3] The act of

A shorter version of this essay was presented at the 1982
annual convention of the Shakespeare Association of
America.
[1] Friedrich Schiller, 'On Simple and Sentimental Poetry',
in *Essays Aesthetical and Philosophical* (1910), p. 315.
[2] Renato Poggioli, 'The Oaten Flute', *Harvard Library
Bulletin*, 11 (1957), p. 147.
[3] A. O. Lovejoy and F. Boas, *Primitivism and Related Ideas
in Antiquity* (Baltimore, 1935), p. 447.
[4] For the myth's possible relation to the earliest pastoral
verse see Frank Kermode's introduction to *English
Pastoral Poetry from the Beginnings to Marvell* (1952), p. 20.

mostadept busines women

sophisticated drama, and during his playwriting career he moves generally towards a more direct, mythic representation of human origins in his pastoral work.

In the earliest of his green-world comedies Shakespeare both uses and parodies the story of the noble child banished to the woods. The Duke of Milan scornfully denigrates Valentine's origins when he catches the young gentleman fumbling with letters and ladders:

> Wilt thou reach stars, because they shine on thee?
> Go, base intruder, overweening slave,
> Bestow thy fawning smiles on equal mates,
> And think my patience (more than thy desert)
> Is privilege for thy departure hence.
>
> (*Two Gentlemen of Verona*, 3.1.156–60)[5]

Valentine quickly takes advantage of the 'privilege' to leave. He repairs to the forest and is shortly discovered there by the same Duke, who, with laughable disregard for consistency, proclaims the former 'base intruder' now a 'gentleman and well deriv'd' (5.4.146). Though the young man has earned the Duke's respect by his spirited denunciation of Thurio, his social derivation remains unchanged. The myth of innate nobility revealed amid rusticity resolves the obstacle to a happy ending and at the same time is the source of the joke on the convention-bound comic father.

A far more persistent set of conflicts is transported from court to woodland in *A Midsummer Night's Dream*. The lovers' departure for the green world creates pastoral expectations that are never fully realized. While Shakespeare includes one undisguised myth of origins in *A Midsummer Night's Dream*, it explains more about the perpetuation of old jealousies and rivalries than it does about the beginnings of new love such as we will see characterizes the pastoral experience of the later comedies and romances. The midsummer's myth of dissension in nature belongs to Titania:

> thorough this distemperature, we see
> The seasons alter: hoary-headed frosts
> Fall in the fresh lap of the crimson rose,
> And on old Hiems' thin and icy crown
> An odorous chaplet of sweet summer buds
> Is, as in mockery, set; the spring, the summer,
> The childing autumn, angry winter, change
> Their wonted liveries; and the mazed world,
> By their increase, now knows not which is which.
> And this same progeny of evils comes
> From our debate, from our dissension;
> We are their parents and original.
>
> (*A Midsummer Night's Dream*, 2.1.106–17)

Shakespeare has a woodland deity moralize certain violent anomalies in the weather not, as René Girard has argued, as a way of disguising human responsibility for a 'progeny of evils' but as a way, metaphorically, of expressing the pains of false labour that characters in the play bring upon themselves by mistaking jealous emulation for love.[6] As Girard himself points out, acts 2 and 3 of *A Midsummer Night's Dream* are not about revitalizing love in a pastoral setting but rather about 'choos[ing] love by another's eyes' (1.1.140) and, as a result, quarrelling with rivals in the darkened pathways of the Athenian wood. The pastoral retreat of *A Midsummer Night's Dream* transports the contention of the Athenian court into the woods and there increases the volume and intensity of the discord. Rather than discovering the vitality of loving co-operation, the four young Athenians simply co-opt the language of love to use as a weapon to assault their various unwilling partners. When Helena proposes metaphorically to use her heart of true steel as an instrument to split open Demetrius's heart of adamant (2.1.195–7) and Demetrius, 'Pierc'd through the heart with [Hermia's] stern cruelty' (3.2.59), offers to skewer Lysander's heart on his sword, the latent hostility in Petrarch's *Rime petrose* threatens to shatter all pastoral ease. Whenever a note of tenderness or genuine concern does creep into the pursuer's voice, it is met with derision and the charge of inauthenticity. The charge gains some force in the

---

[5] Throughout I quote from *The Riverside Shakespeare*, ed. G. B. Evans *et al.* (Boston, 1974).

[6] René Girard, 'Myth and Ritual in Shakespeare: *A Midsummer Night's Dream*', in *Textual Strategies: Perspectives in Post-Structuralist Criticism*, ed. Josué V. Harari (Ithaca, 1979), pp. 189–212.

audience's mind because of the lovers' vulnerability to the fickleness so easily and naturally induced by Puck. Far more authentic than their rhetoric of love is the language of scorn, anger, envy, and rivalry. What Shakespeare dramatizes in acts 2 and 3, then, is the opposite of a model of society revitalized through respect and mutuality. The resolution of conflict comes suddenly, more from exhaustion than understanding. Demetrius simply avers that he has returned to his original or 'natural taste' (4.1.174) for Helena, and Hermia speaks confusedly of a dreamy double vision (ll. 189–90) akin to the 'natural perspective, that is and is not' at the end of *Twelfth Night*. The ending of *A Midsummer Night's Dream*, however, does without the startling revelation that clarifies the vision in *Twelfth Night*. Instead, Shakespeare relies heavily on Hippolyta's claims for the transforming power of imagination (5.1.23–7) to encourage the audience to share the hope for generative love that is celebrated in the final blessing of the marriage beds. The pastoral value of new beginnings is not, then, fully integrated into the narrative of *A Midsummer Night's Dream*.

Shakespeare more convincingly reshapes myths of renewable origins through mimesis in *As You Like It*. Taking as starting points the theatrical convention of disguise (itself a kind of imitation-within-an-imitation) and the literary conventions of Petrarchism and allegory, Shakespeare paradoxically gives us a version of pastoral renewal at its most believable. Rosalind, who wants more than simply to be discovered as a noble child banished to the woods, creates an entire set of fictional origins for herself when Orlando asks 'Ganymede',

Where dwell you, pretty youth?
Rosalind. With this shepherdess, my sister; here in the skirts of the forest, like fringe upon a petticoat.
Orlando. Are you native of this place?
Rosalind. As the cony that you see dwell where she is kindled.
Orlando. Your accent is something finer than you could purchase in so remov'd a dwelling.
Rosalind. I have been told so of many; but indeed an old religious uncle of mine taught me to speak, who was in his youth an inland man, one that knew courtship too well, for there he fell in love. I have

heard him read many lectures against it, and I thank God I am not a woman, to be touch'd with so many giddy offences as he hath generally tax'd their whole sex withal.

(*As You Like It*, 3.2.334–50)

Rosalind's opening metaphors, 'skirts of the forest' and 'fringe upon a petticoat', function both to make her sex-reversing disguise translucent with girlish analogy and also to locate the pastoral borderland symbolically between the barbaric deep-wood and the civilized 'inland', or in Freudian terms, between the deep recesses of the id and the shallow glosses of the super-ego.[7] This is the land of pure, innocent ego, freed of all constrictive parentage, however elevated. The question of Rosalind's nativeness to (or, as she interprets Orlando's second question, her nativity in) the pastoral margin, gives rise to the witty analogy with the cony who passes her life in the place where she was 'kindled'. Alexander Pope may be partly excused for mistaking the line-ending hyphen in F4 and Rowe for the compound 'kind-led', since not only is the cony-kind led by its nature to reproduce (or 'to kindle'), but in inventing the tale of her nativity, Rosalind is rediscovering her own kind or essential nature.[8] Like her made-up, surrogate father, she embodies civilization's highest virtues (rhetorical skill directed towards pious ends) and eschews its chief deficiency (envious imitation).

As though anticipating Schiller's objection that pastoral idylls can carry our minds only backwards to a lost childhood, Rosalind exclaims, 'But what talk we of fathers, when there is such a man as Orlando?' (3.4.38–9). Her nascent love requires a new language, and so Rosalind turns satirist, leading Orlando to love her gentle wit by mocking the legacy of Petrarchan love-talk. His eternal love-sickness becomes the 'quotidian of love' (3.2.365), its daily-passing smart. Attempting to rehearse time-tried lovers' speeches on a supposed youth, Orlando finds himself twitted for his grandiose claims and reduced to the level of the least romantic

---

[7] The same idea is expressed more literally in the phrase 'purlieus of this forest' at 4.3.76.

[8] On the textual history of this line see *A New Variorum Edition of As You Like It*, ed. Richard Knowles (New York, 1977), p. 179.

of animals: 'I had as lief be woo'd of a snail' (4.1.52). Rosalind's mouth, like Gargantua's, contains a jumbled world of wisdom and emotion ranging from fanciful emblems to teasing mythological anthologies to wheedling instruction in manners and punctuality.[9] The purpose of this rhetorical *mélange* is to make a convention-ridden lover stop imitating others' desires and start talking openly about the new feelings, problems, and hopes that pastoral separation from history and civilization has generated in the young couple.

While Rosalind makes up a new genesis for herself through disguise and benign lies, her lover's brother, Oliver, experiences a spiritual rebirth that he describes in richly mixed allegorical–pastoral language. The 'old oak, whose boughs were moss'd with age / And high top bald with dry antiquity' (4.3.104–5) may suggest the spiritual aridity and meanness of his earlier persecutions of Orlando, but it also suggests the antiquity of their common ancestral line – a family tree that may yet bear fruit in this pastoral haven. The 'green and gilded snake' (l. 108) has possible resonances of Edenic myth, and the 'lioness with udders all drawn dry' (l. 114) may well allude in complicated and ambiguous ways to the aridity of the sleeping Oliver or to the Herculean nobility of his rescuer or to both. Finally, a familial love from happier times is rekindled when Orlando decides to risk his own life to save his brother's.

> *Oliver.* . . . kindness, nobler ever than revenge,
> And nature, stronger than his just occasion,
> Made him give battle to the lioness,
> Who quickly fell before him, in which hurtling
> From miserable slumber I awaked.
>
> (4.3.128–32)

The inadvertent confession in the last line is one consequence of Oliver's spiritual awakening and gives rise to the paradox of ''Twas I; but 'tis not I' (l. 135) that lends vitality to even a stock character, once he has been touched by the power of re-creative myth.

We would be limiting our understanding of Shakespearian pastoral unnecessarily if we concluded from the foregoing discussion that he fabricated myths of personal and familial genesis solely as a means of resolving comic plots. The pastoral mode cuts across generic lines and encompasses not only the joy of rebirth but also its pain. As several recent critics have shown us, *King Lear* is a hard pastoral, and we might expect to glimpse there the dark side of the kindling of mankind.[10] Shakespeare reserves his explicit discussion of the pangs of birth for Lear's lowest moment of pastoral alienation, his interview with the sightless Gloucester in the open country near Dover.

> I know thee well enough, thy name is
>   Gloucester.
> Thou must be patient; we came crying hither.
> Thou know'st, the first time that we smell the air
> We wawl and cry. I will preach to thee. Mark.
>   *Lear takes off his crown of weeds and flowers.*
> *Gloucester.*
>   Alack, alack the day!
> *Lear.*
>   When we are born, we cry that we are come
>   To this great stage of fools.
>
> (*King Lear*, 4.6.177–83)

Like his earlier association with the Fool, Lear's simplified syntax, so different from his orotund pronouncements of act 1, scene 1, signals his change to a new form of childishness (*not* senility, however), and the 'wawl and cry' of all new-born infants will be hideously echoed in Lear's howl at 5.3.258. But Lear has relentlessly moved back towards primal inarticulateness and nakedness (the 'poor, bare, fork'd animal') in search not of an ending but a healthier beginning for life. In doing so, he has rediscovered his human kindness through taking pity on all 'poor naked wretches'. Evil, on the other

---

9 See the allusion to Gargantua's mouth at 3.2.225 and Erich Auerbach's essay on 'The World in Pantagruel's Mouth' in *Mimesis: The Representation of Reality in Western Literature*, trans. Willard R. Trask (Princeton, 1953), pp. 262–84.

10 Maynard Mack, *King Lear in Our Time* (Berkeley, 1965), pp. 63–6; David P. Young, *The Heart's Forest: A Study of Shakespeare's Pastoral Plays* (New Haven, 1972), pp. 76–8; Nancy R. Lindheim, '*King Lear* as Pastoral Tragedy', in *Some Facets of 'King Lear': Essays in Prismatic Criticism*, ed. Rosalie L. Colie and F. T. Flahiff (Toronto, 1974), pp. 169–84; Susan Snyder, *The Comic Matrix of Shakespeare's Tragedies* (Princeton, 1979), pp. 142–4.

hand, is intimately connected with the violation of personal origins. As Albany tells the adulterous Goneril,

> That nature which contemns it origin
> Cannot be bordered certain in itself.
>
> (4.2.32–3)

Integrity depends, in other words, on acknowledging and sustaining one's parents, sole authors of congenital talents. By the time he '*takes off his crown of weeds and flowers*' in act 4 (an admittedly controversial stage direction), Lear has dragged the ancient myth of the royal child discovered in the wilderness kicking and screaming into time-present and the harsh light of reality. Though there is something of Macbeth's self-inflicted nihilism in Lear's negative use of the world–stage metaphor,[11] the destructive forces in Lear's bleak pastoral world mine beneath even its villains, making perversity seem the essence of divine as well as human nature. The speech on every man's extended birth trauma is, ironically, prelude to the temporary reprieve of act 4, scene 7, where Cordelia's reciprocated charity marks Lear's return from the pastoral desert to court and family. After this moment, Lear retreats into a myth of womb-like insularity that creates a possible future, but only in his mind.

> So we'll live,
> And pray, and sing, and tell old tales, and laugh
> At gilded butterflies. (5.3.11–13)

His world of imagination is not despicable, but it is immediately anticipated and frustrated by human perversity in the form of Edmund's execution order. The future vanishes, along with the pastoral language of natural artifice ('gilded butterflies'), leaving Lear to howl in his crushingly paradoxical end-of-the-world nativity.

In *King Lear* human realities finally swallow up mythic possibilities, but the myth re-emerges boldly, intact in the final romances. Admittedly artificial dramaturgy, frankly pastoral wedding celebrations, divinely inspired riddles, and transparently mythic rediscoveries of identity are central to *The Winter's Tale* and *The Tempest*, as Northrop

Frye and others have shown.[12] In act 4 of *The Winter's Tale*, for example, the lost royal child, Perdita, exchanges her humble pastoral garb for the flowered splendour of Flora as she plays Queen of the May (4.4.1 ff.). Both garments disguise her real identity as King Leontes's cast-away daughter, but both also reveal ideal parts of her being: her natural honesty and her royal grace, which are expressed through the mythic trappings of pastoral. Furthermore, Perdita's several fathers provide a convenient anthology of Shakespeare's techniques of celebrating new life (not just past glories) in his idylls. First, there is her biological father, the king who learns to replace envy with love through the exercise of memory and wonder; next, her pastoral father, the shepherd whose plainness mocks and is mocked by court sophisticates; and finally her made-up father, the Libyan King Smalus, whose fictional paternity of Perdita is the young couple's desperate attempt to begin their married life free of the blight of Leontes, the former killer of marriage and generation.[13] Thus, Shakespeare, as it were, reviews for us the course of his pastoral career from literal assertions of one's origins to mimetic constructions of new origins and mythic treatments of rebirth.[14]

The Tempest, too, may be seen as a résumé of Shakespeare's literal, mimetic, and mythic explorations of human origin in a pastoral setting. First, Miranda is told of her literal parentage, birthright, and banishment. This requires looking into the 'dark backward and abysm of time' (1.2.50), there to find Prospero's virtuous wife and his perfidious

---

11 *Macbeth*, 5.5.19–28.
12 See especially Frye's *A Natural Perspective: The Development of Shakespearean Comedy and Romance* (New York, 1965) and Hallett Smith's warning against invalid forms of myth-criticism in the appendix ('Myth, Symbol and Poetry') to his book *Shakespeare's Romances* (San Marino, 1972), pp. 197–209.
13 Northrop Frye suggests that Perdita has a fourth father, her putative one, in Polixenes. See 'Recognition in *The Winter's Tale*', in *Essays on Shakespeare and Elizabethan Drama in Honor of Hardin Craig* (Columbia, Missouri, 1962), pp. 235–46.
14 Compare the final theatrical coup of *The Winter's Tale*, the living statue.

brother. Using the language of generation, Prospero describes the genesis of usurpation in his dukedom:

> my trust,
> Like a good parent, did beget of [Antonio]
> A falsehood in its contrary, as great
> As my trust was. (1.2.93–6)

Truth, always older than Falsehood, still must suffer under her younger sibling's tyrannical ambition. These bitter events of a dozen years earlier, and not the ideals of a false Golden Age, so lovingly rehearsed by Gonzalo in his famous ideal commonwealth speech (2.1.148–69), provide the time-frame for the present action. Antonio's earlier treachery is abortively repeated in his plot with Sebastian to murder Alonso and parodied in the Caliban–Stephano–Trinculo mock-usurpation plot.

Once the crucial political time-frame has been established and Miranda apprised of her true origins, Shakespeare introduces the temporarily orphaned Prince Ferdinand. Miranda charms him with her beauty and innocence, Prospero with his magic. The effect of these charms is to reduce him in the social hierarchy to the status of a menial, bearing logs in humble service to his new-found mistress. This action mimetically re-presents Miranda's own enforced debasement from princess (and her father's from duke) to exile, artificially suspending Prince Ferdinand's courtly origins and offering him a fresh start in love's natural polity. He explains the renovating power of this new condition eloquently and sincerely:

> I am, in my condition,
> A prince, Miranda; I do think, a king
> (I would, not so!), and would no more endure
> This wooden slavery than to suffer
> The flesh-fly blow my mouth. Hear my soul speak:
> The very instant that I saw you, did
> My heart fly to your service, there resides,
> To make me slave to it, and for your sake
> Am I this patient log-man. (3.1.59–67)

Prospero assures us from his vantage point that this is indeed the beginning of a new life: 'Heavens rain grace / On that which breeds between 'em' (3.1.75–6).

In addition to the mimetic reconstruction of personal beginnings in the lives of Ferdinand and Miranda, Shakespeare reworks, in Prospero's forgiveness of his brother, the mythic material of man rediscovering his basic human kindness that we saw in the cases of Oliver and Lear. Like Miranda, Prospero has now learned the wonder of pastoral innocence, marvelling that Ariel can feel such compassion for the political transgressors.

> Hast thou, which art but air, a touch, a feeling
> Of their afflictions, and shall not myself,
> One of their kind, that relish all as sharply
> Passion as they, be kindlier mov'd than thou art?
> (The Tempest, 5.1.21–4)

The experience of pastoral exile has taught Prospero to be fully human by adding forgiveness to his powers of natural magic. Prospero's failure as ruler of his own passions and Milan's had its roots in the time of Miranda's childhood, when he misapplied the pastoral value of *otium* in his own bookish studies. As *The Tempest* nears its end, the importance of contemplation is reasserted ('Every third thought shall be my grave', 5.1.312), now as a necessary counterweight to the heady, active life of Milan's newly betrothed governors.

From *The Two Gentlemen of Verona* to *The Tempest* the endings of Shakespeare's pastorals, far from being stagnant or flaccid, as Schiller feared pastorals might be, remain lively and thought-provoking by variously presenting myths of human regeneration. The power of the pastoral plays and sequences I have been considering resides in the liberation of self that is instigated when one is prepared either to trace his or her life back to its origins in human kindness or to imagine a fresh version of genesis consonant with pastoral peace and natural piety.

'CONTRARIETIES AGREE': AN ASPECT OF DRAMATIC TECHNIQUE IN 'HENRY VI'

ROGER WARREN

Half-way through the *Henry VI* trilogy, as Jack Cade's army swarms into London, the Lord Mayor sends to the Tower for help against the rebels. Lord Scales replies that while he is very willing to help, 'I am troubled here with them myself' (*Part Two*, 4.5.7); he suggests instead that the citizens should gather head in Smithfield, 'And thither I will send you Matthew Gough' (4.5.10). This, as it turns out, is no great help, for twenty lines later, after a brief intervening scene for Cade, there comes the terse stage direction: '*Alarums. Matthew Gough is slain, and all the rest*' (4.7.0).[1]

This tiny episode is based on a fuller treatment in Edward Hall's Chronicle. Hall explains that Lord Scales appointed Matthew Gough 'to assist the Mayor and the Londoners, because he was both of manhood and experience greatly renowned' but that, while the King's forces defended London Bridge 'all the night valiantly', the rebels were victorious, and slew many, including 'Matthew Gough, a man of great . . . experience in feats of chivalry, the which in continual wars had valiantly served the King . . . beyond the sea'. Beside this detailed information which Hall provides about Matthew Gough, Shakespeare's Gough is a ghost character. There is, indeed, no way in which an audience could pick up who he is when he appears only to be killed immediately. Does this, then, provide an example of Shakespeare's 'prentice work' in *Henry VI*, an immature grasp of dramatic technique in lifting bodily from the Chronicle an episode which an audience couldn't be expected to follow? I think it shows something quite different, and much more interesting.

In their preface to the First Folio, Heminges and

Condell said that Shakespeare's 'mind and hand went together'; and here, Shakespeare seems to be working so quickly that he hasn't made quite clear the point of the episode which he is shaping from Hall's material, though it is obvious what that point is: the only reason that he mentions Matthew Gough by name is that, in the chronicles, Gough is an experienced military leader who might, therefore, be expected to withstand Jack Cade. Shakespeare is raising the expectation of Cade's defeat – only to shatter that anticipation almost immediately by having Gough killed the moment he appears. And the very fact that he hasn't properly established Matthew Gough as an identifiable dramatic character may serve to give us a glimpse of Shakespeare working out, not quite successfully here, an aspect of dramatic technique which he uses a great deal during the *Henry VI* trilogy, that of setting one extreme against another, and especially of leading the audience to expect a particular consequence, and then reversing that expectation by presenting a quite different result, often the complete opposite of the one expected.

I

There is a particularly effective example of such reversal of expectation in the second scene of the trilogy, where the Dauphin is besieging Orleans:

Sound, sound alarum; we will rush on them.
Now for the honour of the forlorn French!
Him I forgive my death that killeth me
When he sees me go back one foot or fly.

---

[1] All quotations from *Henry VI* are from the New Penguin edition, ed. Norman Sanders, 3 vols. (Harmondsworth, 1981). The passages quoted from Hall and Holinshed may also be found in the notes to this edition.

The Dauphin and his troops leave the stage; but instantly, says the stage direction, '*They are beaten back by the English with great loss*'; and far from forgiving his men, the Dauphin cries

> Who ever saw the like? What men have I!
> Dogs! Cowards! Dastards! I would ne'er have fled
> But that they left me 'midst my enemies.
>
> (*Part One*, 1.2.18–24)

The dramatic effect depends upon the fact that the Dauphin's extravagant vow that he will not fly and that his men can kill him if he does should be followed *immediately* by his ignominious retreat, and by his violent verbal attack on those men whom he said he would forgive for killing him if he did what he has in fact done. In short, the expectation established so emphatically by the language is instantly contradicted by the stage action.

Later in the scene Shakespeare uses the device again to emphasize the prowess of Joan of Arc. The Dauphin offers another military challenge:

> Only this proof I'll of thy valour make:
> In single combat thou shalt buckle with me...

Joan's reply does not raise any great expectation that she will prove a dangerous opponent. Shakespeare borrows two phrases from Holinshed, that Joan discovered her sword 'among old iron' and that it was 'with five flower-de-luces . . . graven on both sides', and bases her speech upon the contrast between the two. The detail about the fleur-de-lis, the royal emblem of France, invests the sword with a grandeur which Joan promptly deflates by saying that she found it among 'old iron'. Her deflating sense of humour is very characteristic of Shakespeare's portrayal of her:

> I am prepared; here is my keen-edged sword,
> Decked with five flower-de-luces on each side,
> The which at Touraine, in Saint Katherine's
>   churchyard,
> Out of a great deal of old iron I chose forth.

Charles and Joan are sharply contrasted in the language they speak, both here and in their single lines as they prepare to fight. His line is characteristically vaunting: 'Then come, a God's name; I fear no woman.' Hers is characteristically ribald and humorous: 'And while I live, I'll ne'er fly from a man.' But it is the humorous country girl who wins, and the Dauphin suffers his second military reversal in this scene:

> Stay, stay thy hands; thou art an Amazon,
> And fightest with the sword of Deborah.
>
> (1.2.94–105)

Such reversals of expectations are used a great deal in *Part One*, from the opening funeral of Henry V, where messenger after messenger interrupts the solemn tributes to Henry's conquests with reports of the loss of those conquests:

> Henry the Fifth, thy ghost I invocate;
> Prosper this realm, keep it from civil broils;
> Combat with adverse planets in the heavens!
> A far more glorious star thy soul will make
> Than Julius Caesar or bright –

But Bedford's ritual invocation is shattered in mid-line by the messenger's report of the harsh facts:

> My honourable lords, health to you all!
> Sad tidings bring I to you out of France,
> Of loss, of slaughter, and discomfiture;
> Guienne, Champaigne, Rheims, Rouen, Orleans,
> Paris, Gisors, Poitiers, are all quite lost.
>
> (1.1.52–61)

The list of towns comes across like a series of hammer-blows shattering Bedford's hopes of future prosperity. The effect is repeated twice. Bedford calls for his armour –

> Wounds will I lend the French instead of eyes,
> To weep their intermissive miseries

– only to hear even worse news from a second messenger:

> France is revolted from the English quite,
> Except some petty towns of no import.
>
> (1.1.87–91)

And when Bedford proclaims that

> An army have I mustered in my thoughts,
> Wherewith already France is overrun

a third messenger at once brings news of 'a dismal fight / Betwixt the stout Lord Talbot and the French'. Winchester expresses the customary expectation they have of Talbot – 'What? Wherein Talbot overcame, is't so?' – only to have that dashed: 'O, no; wherein Lord Talbot was o'erthrown' (1.1.101–8). The unthinkable has happened.

Such effects recur frequently during the long sequence in which Shakespeare dramatizes the fluctuating fortunes of the French and English forces. 'Now it is supper-time in Orleans', remarks Salisbury casually to Talbot as they overlook the city from '*the turrets*', imagining that at such a time there can be no danger; but a '*Boy with a linstock*' unexpectedly shoots Salisbury down (1.4.59–69); then Joan relieves Orleans and beats Talbot back; but the fortunes of war swing the other way when Talbot and his forces scale the walls of Orleans, and '*the French leap over the walls in their shirts*' (2.1.38); and the episode ends with the broadly humorous incident of an English soldier crying 'À Talbot! À Talbot!' and causing Joan and the Dauphin to break off their mutual recriminations and flee, '*leaving their clothes behind*' (2.1.77). Much of the later warfare is summarized by Talbot's line about Rouen, 'Lost and recovered in a day again!' (3.2.115), and by Joan's caustic dismissal of her own eloquence in persuading Burgundy to defect from the English, 'Done like a Frenchman – turn and turn again' (3.3.85). The whole process is summarized at the death of Talbot. Sir William Lucy spends twelve lines in building up a ceremonial catalogue of Talbot's many titles, culminating in:

> Lord Cromwell of Wingfield, Lord Furnival of
> Sheffield,
> The thrice-victorious Lord of Falconbridge,
> Knight of the noble Order of Saint George,
> Worthy Saint Michael, and the Golden Fleece,
> Great Marshal to Henry the Sixth
> Of all his wars within the realm of France[.]

But this celebration of Talbot's achievements is utterly deflated by Joan's grimly factual statement of his fate:

> Him that thou magnifiest with all these titles
> Stinking and flyblown lies here at our feet.
>
> (4.7.66–76)

Such jarring contrasts may perhaps seem a simple, even primitive dramatic technique; but the contrasts are clearly very deliberately worked out, and they are extremely effective in performance. Here they are bold and simple; but Shakespeare also uses contrasts in a somewhat different way, in the creation of entire characters and in the structure of whole scenes, particularly in his treatment of Joan and Margaret.

II

In his first presentation of Joan, Shakespeare makes use of the two opposed views (roughly, the French and English views) of Joan as saint and sorceress to create a varied, interesting dramatic character. Indeed, Joan presents two views of herself when she first appears. She claims that she has been transformed by her visions:

> Lo, whilst I waited on my tender lambs
> And to sun's parching heat displayed my cheeks,
> God's Mother deignèd to appear to me...
> In complete glory she revealed herself.

But Joan combines these holy associations with a humorous awareness of herself and of her origins:

> And whereas I was black and swart before,
> With those clear rays which she infused on me
> That beauty am I blessed with which you may see.
>
> (1.2.76–86)

She may claim to have been transformed by her vision, but she has lost none of her clear-eyed peasant directness in the process. At the end of the play, Shakespeare specifically identifies her spirits as demons; it is through their power that she has been 'the English scourge'; and at this point Shakespeare sets one female 'English scourge' against another: for no sooner has Joan been dragged off the stage than Suffolk enters '*with Margaret in his hand*'; and just as Shakespeare uses contrasts for his portrait of Joan, he uses them again for the basic structure of the whole scene between Margaret and Suffolk.

Suffolk is so overcome by his infatuation with Margaret that he chivalrously offers to let her go – with the immediate result that he has to stop her when she takes him at his word and starts to leave:

> Be not offended, nature's miracle;
> Thou art allotted to be ta'en by me....
> Yet, if this servile usage once offend,
> Go and be free again as Suffolk's friend.
> *She is going*
> O, stay! (*Aside*) I have no power to let her pass;
> My hand would free her, but my heart says no.
>
> (5.3.54–61)

The first part of the scene is built upon humorous cross-purposes, with both characters addressing the audience rather than one another. Suffolk debates how he may avoid letting her go; she reacts to his self-absorption with a mixture of bewilderment and mockery:

> *Suffolk.* (*aside*)
> She's beautiful, and therefore to be wooed;
> She is a woman, therefore to be won.
> *Margaret.*
> Wilt thou accept of ransom, yea or no?
> *Suffolk.* (*aside*)
> Fond man, remember that thou hast a wife.
> Then how can Margaret be thy paramour?...
> *Margaret.*
> He talks at random. Sure the man is mad.
> *Suffolk.*
> And yet a dispensation may be had.
> *Margaret.*
> And yet I would that you would answer me.
> *Suffolk.*
> I'll win this Lady Margaret. For whom?
> Why, for my king! Tush, that's a wooden thing!
> *Margaret.*
> He talks of wood. It is some carpenter.
>
> (5.3.78–90)

That joke about wood may not show any very subtle wit, but it works in performance, just as the unsubtle but effective interruptions of Henry V's funeral in the first scene work; and indeed, this scene with its constant use of anticlimax is a humorous version of the violent reversals elsewhere. In the second half of the scene, Margaret turns the tables on Suffolk by using his own technique against him:

> *Margaret.*
> Hear ye, captain? Are you not at leisure?

> *Suffolk.* (*aside*)
> It shall be so, disdain they ne'er so much.
> Henry is youthful and will quickly yield. –
> (*To her*) Madam, I have a secret to reveal.
> *Margaret.* (*aside*)
> What though I be enthralled? He seems a knight
> And will not any way dishonour me.
> *Suffolk.*
> Lady, vouchsafe to listen what I say.
> *Margaret.* (*aside*)
> Perhaps I shall be rescued by the French,
> And then I need not crave his courtesy.
> *Suffolk.*
> Sweet madam, give me hearing in a cause –
> *Margaret.* (*aside*)
> Tush, women have been captivate ere now.
> *Suffolk.*
> Lady, wherefore talk you so?
> *Margaret.*
> I cry you mercy, 'tis but *quid* for *quo*.
>
> (5.3.97–109)

Margaret's witty use of *quid pro quo* suggests a perfect balance between them, and anticipates the way in which banter expresses relationship in later plays (Hotspur and Kate, Berowne and Rosaline, Beatrice and Benedick). The cross-purposes which, at the start of the scene, began by isolating Margaret and Suffolk from each other gradually come to suggest collusion. Shakespeare clinches the point as Margaret leaves the stage. After Suffolk has plighted her his faith on Henry's behalf, he calls her back again and asks her for a kiss, ostensibly as a 'token to his majesty'; but after giving him the kiss, Margaret proves to be a perfect match for him as she shows that she understands his real meaning and the facts of the situation in her lightly mocking, teasing reply:

> That for thyself. I will not so presume
> To send such peevish tokens to a king.
>
> (5.3.185–6)

The humour and the formal balance of the scene emphasize the mutual interest of Margaret and Suffolk, paving the way for *Part Two*.

Those contrasts which Shakespeare uses for individual episodes and for characterization in *Part One* help to provide the structure for the entire central action of *Part Two*, the destruction of Duke Humphrey and its consequences. Margaret, Suffolk and Winchester conspire to ensnare Duke Humphrey and also to send York 'packing with an host of men', as York himself ironically points out (3.1.342). But their plans have quite different consequences from those they hoped for, and recoil upon their own heads: Humphrey's death leads directly to Suffolk's enforced parting from the Queen, and to his and Winchester's own violent ends; and York's return from Ireland with that army leads to the outbreak of the Wars of the Roses, with its ultimately fatal consequences for Margaret herself.

Margaret's parting from Suffolk in some ways counterpoints, in a sad minor key, their first meeting; certainly some of the same devices recur. In her fury with the King, Margaret asks Suffolk if he lacks the spirit to curse his enemies; Suffolk responds with an elaborate evocation of poisons, basilisks, and screech-owls which gets so out of control that Margaret herself has to break in on his speech to stem the tide, with the result that he points out the anticlimactic irony of the situation: 'You bade me ban, and will you bid me leave?' (3.2.307–33). But she calms him, and bids him a moving farewell. She tells him to go – only to call him back again at once, an exact parallel, in a more sombre vein, to the technique which Suffolk used with her in their first scene:

Queen.
  O, let me entreat thee cease. Give me thy hand
  That I may dew it with my mournful tears;
  Nor let the rain of heaven wet this place
  To wash away my woeful monuments....
  Go, speak not to me; even now be gone.
  O, go not yet. Even thus two friends condemned
  Embrace and kiss and take ten thousand leaves,
  Loather a hundred times to part than die.
  Yet now farewell, and farewell life with thee....
  To France, sweet Suffolk! Let me hear from
     thee;
  For wheresoe'er thou art in this world's globe,
  I'll have an Iris that shall find thee out.
Suffolk.
  I go.

Queen. And take my heart with thee....
Suffolk.
  This way fall I to death.
Queen.   This way for me.
                         (3.2.339–412)

Their parting in opposite directions is a formal reversal of the formality of their first meeting. In that scene, the cross-purposes which seemed to separate them in fact expressed their coming together. Here, similar formality expresses their drawing apart. Such writing is often said to be 'artificial'; if so, its artifice makes central use of contrasts, establishing a point and then reversing it. And this artifice is carefully worked out to communicate character and situation. It is at once artificial and moving in human terms. It is also typical that Shakespeare should treat even people like Suffolk and the Queen, who behave so badly, even criminally, with compassion. Whatever their faults, they are not monsters, but human beings.

'This way fall I to death': Suffolk's death scene itself is a striking instance of the technique of reversal. On the one hand, Suffolk is alarmed at hearing Walter Whitmore's name, pronounced 'Water', for it was prophesied 'that by water I should die' (4.1.35): it suggests to him that his death is near. But on the other hand, he expresses elaborate incredulity that he could possibly die at such hands:

  Obscure and lousy swain, King Henry's blood,
  The honourable blood of Lancaster,
  Must not be shed by such a jaded groom....
  It is impossible that I should die
  By such a lowly vassal as thyself.
                   (4.1.50–2, 110–11)

What Shakespeare is doing here is plain: he is 'writing up' Suffolk's speeches so that 'Suffolk's imperial tongue' reaches new heights of arrogance and hubris in order that his fall may seem the greater from the new pinnacle to which his speeches have raised him; but his protestations are starkly juxtaposed with the brutal facts, as Whitmore re-enters with Suffolk's body and severed head, and crudely comments:

> There let his head and lifeless body lie,
> Until the Queen his mistress bury it.
>
> (4.1.144–5)

As if to emphasize that Winchester's doom, like Suffolk's, is the consequence of their conspiracy against Duke Humphrey, Shakespeare interrupts the parting of Margaret and Suffolk with the news

> That Cardinal Beaufort is at point of death;
> For suddenly a grievous sickness took him,
> That makes him gasp, and stare, and catch the air.
>
> (3.2.369–71)

Shakespeare stresses that Winchester was 'suddenly' taken ill, as if the illness fell like a visitation upon him; and he reinforces the suggestion by making the symptoms recall Warwick's description, earlier in the same scene, of how Humphrey himself appears to have struggled for life (3.2.160–76): it is as if what he arranged for Humphrey is now happening to him. Then, in the Cardinal's death scene, Shakespeare again makes dramatic use of frustrated hopes. The King desperately urges him:

> Lord Cardinal, if thou thinkest on heaven's bliss,
> Hold up thy hand, make signal of thy hope.

But all is in vain: 'He dies and makes no sign' (3.3.27–9). This powerful moment is a variation of the technique I have been describing: now it is not merely the expectations of the audience, but the hopes of Henry himself, which are raised and then frustrated. It intensifies a harrowing moment.

III

Part Three makes considerable use of contrasts and reversals, since they are obviously an appropriate way of representing the fluctuating fortunes of civil war, as one side gains the ascendancy, then gives way to the other. As Henry says of the battle of Towton,

> Now sways it this way, like a mighty sea
> Forced by the tide to combat with the wind;
> Now sways it that way, like the self-same sea
> Forced to retire by fury of the wind.
>
> (2.5.5–8)

Shakespeare tellingly uses the reversal of expectation to reinforce the pathos when Henry is joined on the battlefield by a son that has killed his father and a father that has killed his son. Both characters initially regard their victims merely as impersonal opponents. The son hopes for financial gain:

> This man whom hand to hand I slew in fight
> May be possessèd with some store of crowns.

But when he opens the helmet, he finds something quite different:

> Who's this? O God! It is my father's face,
> Whom in this conflict I, unwares, have killed.
>
> (2.5.56–62)

Likewise the father starts by regarding his victim merely as a difficult opponent who must now (literally) pay him for his labour:

> Thou that so stoutly hath resisted me,
> Give me thy gold, if thou hast any gold;
> For I have bought it with an hundred blows.
> But let me see: is this our foeman's face?
> Ah no, no, no, it is mine only son!
>
> (2.5.79–83)

The formality, even artifice, of the scene in no way detracts from its power; and an important element in this is certainly the device of arousing one expectation and then frustrating it with something which is not only quite unexpected but also quite unbearable in human terms.

As with the death of Suffolk in *Part Two*, Shakespeare prepares for the death of York by showing him at the height of his power in the opening scene of *Part Three*. This is emphasized by the stage action itself. York is seated in Henry's throne; Henry makes an uncharacteristic attempt to defy his enemies with 'frowns, words, and threats' (1.1.72), but it only takes a show of brute force from Warwick ('*He stamps with his foot, and the soldiers show themselves*', 1.1.169) for Henry's gesture of opposition to collapse completely:

> My lord of Warwick, hear but one word;
> Let me for this my lifetime reign as king.
>
> (1.1.170–1)

It is York's agreement to this which Margaret uses to prolong his agony in the staggering scene of his death. This scene uses contrasts for two purposes, to create both situation and character: the mock-coronation underlines the distance between what York has aimed for and what he has achieved; but it also develops the personality of Margaret herself, as she dwells upon the contrast between his aspirations to kingship and his actual situation, humiliated and at her mercy. She makes the point at the outset by contrasting the metaphorical mountains at which he aimed with the molehill on which she forces him to stand:

Come, make him stand upon this molehill here
That raught at mountains with outstretchèd arms,
Yet parted but the shadow with his hand.
What! Was it you that would be England's king?
Was't you that revelled in our parliament
And made a preachment of your high descent?

(1.4.67–72)

It is to provoke him into breaking down that she hits on the idea of the mock-coronation, which simultaneously expresses the ironical frustration of all his hopes and also her personality in her mocking commentary:

York cannot speak, unless he wear a crown.
A crown for York! And, lords, bow low to him;
Hold you his hands whilst I do set it on.
Ay, marry, sir, now looks he like a king!

(1.4.93–6)

But then she gradually turns the situation towards his death by referring back to the agreement which York forced upon Henry when he actually had the power of a real king:

But how is it that great Plantagenet
Is crowned so soon, and broke his solemn oath?
As I bethink me, you should not be king
Till our King Henry had shook hands with Death.

(1.4.99–102)

This leads eventually to the slaughter of York, which in turn leads to the ironies of the next scene, where York's three sons see the three suns in the sky and are just interpreting these as an encouraging omen when the messenger interrupts them with the news of York's death (2.1.25–47).

In the middle of *Part Three*, Shakespeare lightens the violent mood by making a somewhat different use of contrasts and reversals. It has often been pointed out that Richard of Gloucester's long soliloquy is the most colloquial speech in the play, the speech which most gives the impression of a man thinking. But Shakespeare achieves this effect partly by making Richard raise and then shatter expectation several times during the course of the speech itself. For instance, he enthusiastically sets out to prove a lover:

Well, say there is no kingdom then for Richard,
What other pleasure can the world afford?
I'll make my heaven in a lady's lap,
And deck my body in gay ornaments,
And 'witch sweet ladies with my words and looks.

But he soon calls a halt to that plan:

O, miserable thought! And more unlikely
Than to accomplish twenty golden crowns!

(3.2.146–52)

So he will have to aim for the crown after all, and he develops this idea at length:

Then, since this earth affords no joy to me
But to command, to check, to o'erbear such
As are of better person than myself,
I'll make my heaven to dream upon the crown.

But then he suddenly back-tracks again:

And yet I know not how to get the crown,
For many lives stand between me and home.

(3.2.165–73)

As the soliloquy develops, however, he lists his various accomplishments with increasing confidence:

Why, I can smile, and murder whiles I smile,
And cry 'Content!' to that which grieves my heart,
And wet my cheeks with artificial tears,
And frame my face to all occasions....
I can add colours to the chameleon,
Change shapes with Proteus for advantages,
And set the murderous Machiavel to school.

Once more, Richard arrests the flow of the speech, but this time he does not mock what he had said in order to contradict it, but in order to intensify its effect, to suggest that the talents required to gain a crown are no more than those he already possesses:

> Can I do this, and cannot get a crown?
> Tut, were it farther off, I'll pluck it down.
>
> (3.2.182–95)

The technique of the entire speech is based on an alternation of climax and anticlimax, in order to express Richard's thought processes, his mind moving backwards and forwards.

Earlier in the same scene, Shakespeare has lightened the mood in another way. When Lady Elizabeth Grey asks Edward IV to restore her husband's lands, Shakespeare reverts to the technique of humorous cross-purposes which he used for Margaret and Suffolk in *Part One*:

> *Lady Grey.*
> Why stops my lord? Shall I not hear my task?
> *Edward.*
> An easy task; 'tis but to love a king.
> *Lady Grey.*
> That's soon performed, because I am a subject.
> *Edward.*
> Why, then, thy husband's lands I freely give
>   thee.
> *Lady Grey.*
> I take my leave with many thousand thanks....
> *Edward.*
> But stay thee; 'tis the fruits of love I mean.
> *Lady Grey.*
> The fruits of love I mean, my loving liege.
> *Edward.*
> Ay, but I fear me in another sense.
>
> (3.2.52–60)

But whereas the cross-purposes of the Margaret/Suffolk scene suggested collusion, these indicate disagreement, with the result that Edward has to marry Elizabeth; and so this lightweight exchange, like the Margaret/Suffolk one, has serious consequences: for it alienates Warwick from Edward and so provokes the events of the remainder of the play.

It is indeed in the characterization and behaviour of Warwick that Shakespeare finds the technique of ironic reversal especially useful. When Warwick arrives at the French court to ask for Lady Bona as Edward's queen, he and Margaret soon fall to vigorous mutual abuse:

> Henry now lives in Scotland at his ease,
> Where having nothing, nothing can he lose.
> And as for you yourself, our quondam queen,
> You have a father able to maintain you,
> And better 'twere you troubled him than France.

Margaret gives as good as she gets:

> Peace, impudent and shameless Warwick, peace,
> Proud setter-up and puller-down of kings!
> I will not hence till, with my talk and tears,
> Both full of truth, I make King Lewis behold
> Thy sly conveyance and thy lord's false love;
> For both of you are birds of self-same feather.
>
> (3.3.151–61)

This dispute is interrupted by a '*Post blowing a horn within*' – literally interrupted in the Folio, which places the direction *before* Margaret's last line, so that the horn sounds even while she is angrily finishing her speech. The post, of course, brings news of Edward's marriage, and the text graphically expresses Margaret's and Warwick's contrasted reactions:

> I like it well that our fair Queen and mistress
> Smiles at her news, while Warwick frowns at his.
>
> (3.3.167–8)

Within ten lines, Warwick completely reverses his former position and abandons Edward, a volte-face beautifully expressed in his complete change of manner towards his 'quondam queen':

> My noble Queen, let former grudges pass,
> And henceforth I am thy true servitor.
> I will revenge his wrong to Lady Bona
> And replant Henry in his former state.

And Margaret changes her tune to match:

> Warwick, these words have turned my hate to
>   love;
> And I forgive and quite forget old faults,
> And joy that thou becomest King Henry's friend.
>
> (3.3.195–201)

This kind of ironic reversal strikingly recurs in two of Warwick's later scenes. His capture of Edward is preceded by a conversation for the three watchmen who guard Edward's tent. One of them points out the reason for Edward's careless encampment in the fields: ''Tis the more honour, because more dangerous.' Another watchman answers with a wry irony that fleetingly anticipates Falstaff:

> Ay, but give me worship and quietness;
> I like it better than a dangerous honour.

He goes on to make an equally practical, tactical point:

> If Warwick knew in what estate he stands,
> 'Tis to be doubted he would waken him.

'Unless', replies the first watchman, 'our halberds did shut up his passage', and the second watchman agrees:

> Ay, wherefore else guard we his royal tent,
> But to defend his person from night-foes?

Just how little their watch is worth is made plain at once, for Warwick and his men immediately burst in, 'and set upon the guard, who fly, crying "Arm! Arm!"' (4.3.15–27). Then Warwick brings out Edward in his night-gown, and removes his crown – a visual image of the Kingmaker at work. In this scene, it is Warwick who springs the surprise and takes advantage of the misplaced confidence of the sentries; but on the walls of Coventry, Warwick himself is caught out in a similar way:

> O, unbid spite! Is sportful Edward come?
> Where slept our scouts, or how are they seduced,
> That we could hear no news of his repair?
>
> (5.1.18–20)

And worse is to come with the arrival of Clarence. Warwick hails him in anticipation:

> lo, where George of Clarence sweeps along,
> Of force enough to bid his brother battle;
> With whom an upright zeal to right prevails
> More than the nature of a brother's love!
> Come, Clarence, come; thou wilt, if Warwick call.

So much for expectation; for Clarence replies

> Father of Warwick, know you what this means?
> Look here, I throw my infamy at thee

taking, as the Quarto puts it, 'his red rose out of his hat and throw[ing] it at Warwick' (5.1.76–82). These bold reversals are as much visual as verbal; but the most effective of them all is a verbal one. In Warwick's death-speech, the great Kingmaker realizes the full irony of his situation. He recalls his achievements in his days of power:

> For who lived king, but I could dig his grave?
> And who durst smile when Warwick bent his brow?

And he deliberately contrasts that glory with the inglorious reality he has now met with:

> Lo, now my glory smeared in dust and blood!
> My parks, my walks, my manors that I had,
> Even now forsake me, and of all my lands
> Is nothing left me but my body's length.
> Why, what is pomp, rule, reign, but earth and dust?
> And, live we how we can, yet die we must.
>
> (5.2.21–8)

When Warwick captures Edward at his insecure night camp and removes his crown, he calls him 'but the shadow' of a king (4.3.51). His words echo Talbot's to the Countess of Auvergne in *Part One*:

> I am but shadow of myself.
> You are deceived. My substance is not here.

The Countess comments:

> This is a riddling merchant for the nonce;
> He will be here, and yet he is not here.
> How can these contrarieties agree?
>
> (2.3.49–58)

Talbot shows her how by blowing his horn and summoning his soldiers. She thought that she held him, his 'substance', as her prisoner; but he turns the tables on her, and demonstrates that his real 'substance' is his army. In this way, 'contrarieties agree'; and by using this kind of dramatic effect in various different ways throughout the trilogy, Shakespeare himself makes 'contrarieties agree' as he dramatizes the expectations and disappointments, the switchback reversals, of the Wars of the Roses.

FALSTAFF'S BROKEN VOICE

JOHN W. SIDER

When Charles Mathews the Elder first appeared as Falstaff at the Theatre Royal, Haymarket, in 1814, a critic remarked: 'What was wanting to make it a perfect representation was the round volume of voice commensurate with the hollow of the frame from which it came.'[1] As far as I know, no critic or scholar has considered this requirement unreasonable; yet it contradicts what the texts say about Falstaff's voice. From both parts of *Henry IV* it seems clear that Falstaff was meant to speak not in deep, sonorous tones, but in a voice grown high and thin with advanced years – like the voice of Silence in the recent BBC television production, or the falsetto of William Hutt's Shallow at Stratford, Ontario, in 1965.

Though the texts make Shakespeare's conception clear beyond reasonable doubt, it is easy to see why it has been ignored. Our reading has been guided by our experience of stage Falstaffs, and audiences have expected a great voice answerable to the great body. At Drury Lane 'Harper's fat figure, full voice, round face, and honest laugh...fixed him at last in the jolly knight's easy chair'; and Quin had a 'happy swell of voice'.[2] The critics' strictures are as instructive as their praise. 'Charles Kemble...gave a bad performance of *Falstaff*. His voice was weak.' In *The Merry Wives of Windsor* at the New Theatre in 1910, Louis Calvert's Falstaff spoke in 'a thin, puny voice . . . diffusing a fog of dulness'.[3] George Bernard Shaw predicted that Herbert Beerbohm Tree would 'never be even a moderately good Falstaff'; he complained of a voice 'coarsened, vulgarized, and falsified without being enriched and coloured'.[4] Certainly a modern audience would be surprised to

see Shakespeare's intent realized in the theatre: a piping voice incongruously matched with a hulk of flesh.

In *1 Henry IV* the evidence of Shakespeare's conception has been overlooked because misunderstood. The Prince says: 'and, Falstaff, you carried your guts away as nimbly, with as quick dexterity, and roar'd for mercy, and still run and roar'd, as ever I heard bullcalf' (2.4.258–61).[5] Did Falstaff bellow 'like a young bull pricked in the haunches by swords or goads at a bull baiting', as John Dover Wilson suggests?[6] That interpretation would suit 'as ever I heard *bull*', but a bull*calf* cannot bellow: in *Much Ado About Nothing* (3.3.71–2) a calf 'bleats'. *Bullcalf* can mean only 'male calf'. Alexander Schmidt glosses it so;[7] and the combination appears in the *OED* with other instances of *bull* as attributive meaning 'male': *bull elephant*, *bull elk*, and *bull whale*. How does a calf 'roar'? In current usage *roar* seems invariably to denote deep sonority, but it was not necessarily so in Shakespeare's time or before. About 1400,

---

[1] William Winter, *Shakespeare on the Stage*, Third Series (1916), p. 344.

[2] Thomas Davies, *Dramatic Miscellanies*, 3 vols. (1783–4), vol. 1, p. 138; Francis Gentleman, *The Dramatic Censor*, 2 vols. (1770), vol. 2, p. 396.

[3] William Winter, *Shakespeare on the Stage*, pp. 345, 414.

[4] *Dramatic Opinions and Essays*, 2 vols. (London, 1907), vol. 1, pp. 431, 432.

[5] My text is *The Riverside Shakespeare*, ed. G. Blakemore Evans (Boston, 1974).

[6] *The First Part of King Henry the Fourth*, ed. John Dover Wilson (Cambridge, 1946), p. 151. See also Wilson's *The Fortunes of Falstaff* (Cambridge, 1943), p. 45.

[7] *Shakespeare-Lexicon*, 2nd edn., 2 vols. (Berlin, 1886).

Andromache was said to roar (*OED*, roar *sb.*¹ 1); so was a baby, about 1570 (*sb.*¹ 1β). Particularly revealing is a quotation in the *OED* (roar *v.* 2.b) from John de Trevisa's translation (1398) of *De Proprietatibus Rerum* by Bartholomaeus Anglicus: 'The lambe knoweth his owne moder in somoche that yf she rorith among many shepe in a flocke, anone by bletyng he knowyth the voys of his owne moder.' In Shakespeare's usage 'roar' usually denotes deep sonority; but he seems to equate it with 'piteous cry' in *The Winter's Tale* (3.3.90, 99). Certainly Hal's remark is a special case – one more jest at Falstaff's age and physical condition, turning on the nuances of *roar*. The proverb 'Roar like a bull' is at least as old as *Havelock the Dane* (*OED*, roar *v.* 1β); Falstaff will allude to it later: 'Come prick Bullcalf till he roar again' (*2 Henry IV*, 3.2.175–6). Here the Prince adds one syllable to the proverb and gives *roar* an ironic second meaning: Falstaff could not 'roar' in the usual sense; he bleated like a calf.

The evidence in Part 2 likewise has not been fully appreciated:

Chief Justice. Do you set down your name in the scroll of youth, that are written down old with all the characters of age? Have you not a moist eye, a dry hand, a yellow cheek, a white beard, a decreasing leg, an increasing belly? Is not your voice broken, your wind short, your chin double, your wit single, and every part about you blasted with antiquity? and will you yet call yourself young? Fie, fie, fie, Sir John!

Falstaff. My lord, I was born about three of the clock in the afternoon, with a white head and something a round belly. For my voice, I have lost it with hallowing and singing of anthems.

(1.2.178–90)

Of course Falstaff was joking when he set apart the Lord Chief Justice from 'us that are young' (1.2.174); to hold the sweet jest up he blames his broken voice on innocent, even praiseworthy, causes that have nothing to do with age. Registered as it is with 'all the characters of age', his broken voice should remind us of a similar description in Jaques's seven 'ages':

> The sixt age shifts
> Into the lean and slipper'd pantaloon,
> With spectacles on nose, and pouch on side,

His youthful hose, well sav'd, a world too wide
For his shrunk shank, and his big manly voice,
Turning again toward childish treble, pipes
And whistles in his sound.

(*As You Like It*, 2.7.157–63)

Can Falstaff's broken voice be anything but this?[8] He may seem older in Part 2 than in Part 1, but his age affects his voice throughout. The Lord Chief Justice is an especially reliable witness: he may be like other sorts of men in taking a pride to gird at Falstaff, but he is not the man to wrench the true cause the false way.

Without some contemporary witness we cannot be altogether sure that the first stage-Falstaff's execution matched this conception; yet three considerations establish a strong probability.

First, Elizabethan acting companies went to some trouble to hold the mirror up to nature in their costumes, props, sound effects, and the like. It would be odd if they made no effort to distinguish the voice of an old man from other voices. Certainly they distinguished other physical features of the elderly, as in *Much Ado About Nothing*:

Ursula. I know you well enough, you are Signior Antonio.
Antonio. At a word, I am not.
Ursula. I know you by the waggling of your head.
Antonio. To tell you true, I counterfeit him.
Ursula. You could never do him so ill-well, unless you were the very man. (2.1.112–18)

Benedick. I should think this a gull, but that the white-bearded fellow speaks it. Knavery cannot sure hide himself in such reverence.

(2.3.118–20)

Second, the idea of special voices for special characters was familiar. When Edgar neglects the character of poor Tom, the blinded Gloucester can hear the difference: 'Methinks thy voice is alter'd'

---

8 It might seem logical to call Falstaff's childish treble '*unbroken*', like a youth's voice before it 'breaks' by becoming deeper and stronger. But Shakespeare appears to be using *broken* more generally, to mean 'altered from one voice-register to another'. In that sense it denotes the raised pitch and weakened force of an old man's voice just as well as the deepening and strengthening of a young man's.

(*King Lear*, 4.6.7). Volpone's histrionic arts apparently include an altered voice, as in Voltore's presence:

'Tis well. My pillow now, and let him enter.
> [*Exit Mosca.*]
Now, my feigned cough, my phthisic, and my
> gout,
My apoplexy, palsy, and catarrhs,
Help, with your forcèd functions, this my posture,
Wherein, this three year, I have milked their hopes.
He comes, I hear him – uh! uh! uh! uh! O –
> (*Volpone*, 1.2.123–8)[9]

> I feel me going, uh! uh! uh! uh!
> I'm sailing to my port, uh! uh! uh! uh!
> And I am glad I am so near my haven.
> > (*Volpone*, 1.3.28–30)

Even Bottom has a voice as variable as his beards:

My chief humor is for a tyrant. I could play Ercles rarely, or a part to tear a cat in, to make all split.... And I may hide my face, let me play Thisby too. I'll speak in a monstrous little voice....Let me play the lion too. I will roar, that I will do any man's heart good to hear me....I grant you, friends, if you should fright the ladies out of their wits, they would have no more discretion but to hang us; but I will aggravate my voice so that I will roar you as gently as any sucking dove; I will roar you and 'twere any nightingale.
(*A Midsummer Night's Dream*, 1.2.28–30, 51–2, 70–1, 79–84)

Third, in both parts of *Henry IV* passages of the text depend for their effect on Falstaff's childish treble. Without it the Prince's wordplay on *bullcalf* would lose its point; and it is hard to imagine Shakespeare writing 'your voice broken' into the speech of the Lord Chief Justice in Part 2, without a stage precedent already established in the production of Part 1. On Shakespeare's stage, Falstaff probably sounded as Shakespeare intended.

On any view of Falstaff's character and functions, the two plays of *Henry IV* would be different plays if he spoke all those memorable and pregnant lines in an aged, high-pitched voice. It is difficult to foresee just how different he would seem on stage, but the shift in auditory meaning would surely alter visual meaning: it would be harder to ignore what Shakespeare says about Falstaff's general physical condition. Have we thought of him as robust:

clear-eyed, sturdy-sinewed, and red-cheeked?[10] If director and actor agreed to make his physical presence consonant with his voice, they would give him watery eyes, dwindled legs, yellow complexion, and other 'characters of age' specified in the catalogue of the Lord Chief Justice, along with the baldness and white beard already familiar on stage. The result could be less prepossessing than 'the burly form, the round, ruddy face, . . . the strong hard voice' which are usually regarded as 'perfect' attributes.[11] It would become more evident in the theatre that Falstaff is not young for his seventy-odd years, that he is called 'old Sir John' not by jesting exaggeration but as a simple matter of fact. It is a wonderful thing to see the semblable coherence of his recruits' names and his own condition: Shadow for his knighthood, Wart for his means of life (the Prince calls him a wen), Mouldy and Feeble for his physique, and Bullcalf for his voice. Modern criticism has rescued his character from romanticizing, but not his person.

A broken voice could invite us to place Falstaff differently among the older men of *1* and *2 Henry IV*. When he meets the Lord Chief Justice in the street, the contrast of their voices would magnify Falstaff's effrontery about his age. Were we inclined to believe his bantering professions, we might approve directors and actors who give him more physical vitality than the Lord Chief Justice, but Falstaff belongs to Jaques's sixth 'age', and the Lord Chief Justice quite clearly to the fifth:

> And then the justice,
> In fair round belly with good capon lin'd,
> With eyes severe and beard of formal cut,
> Full of wise saws and modern instances;
> And so he plays his part.
> > (*As You Like It*, 2.7.153–7)

Whereas stage productions have given Shallow and Silence childish trebles to set their decline apart from Falstaff's greater vigour, Shakespeare's conception would put them all in the same circle, accordingly

---

9 Ben Jonson, *Volpone*, ed. Alvin B. Kernan (New Haven and London, 1962).

10 E.g. D. B. Landt, 'The Ancestry of Falstaff', *Shakespeare Quarterly*, 17 (1966), 69–76, p. 69.

11 Winter, *Shakespeare on the Stage*, p. 358.

increasing Falstaff's distance from men like North-umberland, Glendower, and Henry IV.

A voice such as Shakespeare conceived could greatly alter the stage effect of Falstaff's lines. Some ironies would become more comic: 'They hate us youth' (Part 1, 2.2.85); 'His age some fifty' (Part 1, 2.4.424); 'I am only old in judgment and under-standing' (Part 2, 1.2.191–2). Whatever the Prince's intent, the Page certainly sets Falstaff off (Part 2, 1.2.12–14), and a kind of affinity in their voices could heighten the contrast of their sizes. Many speeches might seem more pathetic: 'more valiant, being as he is old Jack Falstaff' (Part 1, 2.4.477–8); 'I am wither'd like an old apple-john' (Part 1, 3.3.4); 'What, is the old king dead?' (Part 2, 5.3.120). The language of his follies and vices would appear more grotesque:

Come sing me a bawdy song, make me merry. I was as virtuously given as a gentleman need to be, virtuous enough: swore little, dic'd not above seven times – a week, went to a bawdy-house not above once in a quarter – of an hour, paid money that I borrow'd – three or four times, liv'd well and in good compass, and now I live out of all order, out of all compass.

(Part 1, 3.3.13–20)

Uttered in the voice of reverend age, Falstaff's moral pronouncements might appear even more obviously ill-sorted with his own life: no hole in hell were hot enough for Gadshill 'if men were to be sav'd by merit' (Part 1, 1.2.107); Bardolph is 'altogether given over' (Part 1, 3.3.36); Hal is to be dispraised before 'the wicked' (Part 2, 2.4.319). There could be fresh poignancy in his talk of death:

Doll. ... Thou whoreson little tidy Bartholomew boar-pig, when wilt thou leave fighting a' days and foining a' nights, and begin to patch up thine old body for heaven?

Enter, [*behind,*] PRINCE [HENRY] *and* POINS,
[*disguised*].

Falstaff. Peace, good Doll, do not speak like a death's-head, do not bid me remember mine end.

(Part 2, 2.4.231–5)

A voice so replete with years, but so empty of grace, could emphasize a theological second meaning in some speeches: 'Am I not fall'n away vilely?' (Part 1, 3.3.1); 'What need I be so forward with him that calls not on me?' (Part 1, 5.1.128–9). There's no reprobate like an old reprobate; even the language of Falstaff's wit might seem more like folly – how ill the quavering of age becomes a fool and jester! On the other hand, a childish treble could help to exalt a Falstaff portrayed as parodist or holy fool.[12]

An aged voice would change his theatrical effect – as much in *The Merry Wives of Windsor*, conceivably, as in the two parts of *Henry IV* – but perhaps not by resolving or even simplifying critical disagreements. For if Falstaff's voice from the stage incessantly reminded us that he is indeed a very old man, the romantics could admire him more, the cynics could deplore him more, and we would all have more cause to wonder at him. Zeffirelli has given us a Romeo and a Juliet who are authentic in their ages; are we ready for a yellow-cheeked, shrunk-shanked, broken-voiced Falstaff? At first Shakespeare's con-ception might be just as unsettling in the theatre as a black Othello once was to audiences who had always thought him brown – despite the difference of the prejudices. The romantic idea of Falstaff's person might die hard; or it might disappear quickly, if a broken voice and other 'characters of age' proved to be illuminating.

---

12 Roy Battenhouse, 'Falstaff as Parodist and Perhaps Holy Fool', *PMLA*, 90 (1975), 32–52.

'HE WHO THE SWORD OF HEAVEN WILL BEAR': THE DUKE VERSUS ANGELO IN 'MEASURE FOR MEASURE'

N. W. BAWCUTT

'Law', 'Mercy', and 'Justice' are three of the main concepts repeatedly used in *Measure for Measure*. There are no simple deductions to be made from this fact: the meaning of the play cannot be summed up as a kind of mathematical equation, Law plus Mercy equals Justice. The words themselves are not presented unambiguously. 'Law' is usually qualified by adjectives implying that Viennese law is harsh by its very nature – 'strict statutes and most biting laws' (1.3.19), 'the hideous law' (1.4.63), 'the angry law' (3.1.201) – but there is also a series of striking, sometimes faintly ludicrous, images suggesting that the law is despised and ineffective. Law is like 'an o'er-grown lion in a cave / That goes not out to prey' (1.3.22–3) or the 'threatening twigs of birch' (1.3.24) used to whip children; if not applied effectively it will be like the motionless scarecrow that the birds of prey regard as 'Their perch, and not their terror' (2.1.4), or will 'Stand like the forfeits in a barber's shop, / As much in mock as mark' (5.1.319–20). The result is a paradoxical double image: the law can frequently be ignored with impunity, but may suddenly and unpredictably inflict savage punishment, with a kind of arbitrariness that is half accepted and half resented, as in the opening speeches of Claudio.

'Mercy' also is qualified in a variety of ways: 'lawful mercy' (2.4.112) is quite different from the 'devilish mercy' (3.1.64) offered by Angelo to Isabella. For Escalus, too much mercy does more harm than good:

> Mercy is not itself, that oft looks so;
> Pardon is still the nurse of second woe.
>
> (2.1.280–1)

In its personified form mercy sometimes behaves very unlike the gentle creature we might expect it to be:

> Mercy to thee would prove itself a bawd.
>
> (3.1.149)

> This would make mercy swear and play the tyrant.
>
> (3.2.188–9)

> The very mercy of the law cries out
> Most audible, even from his proper tongue:
> 'An Angelo for Claudio; death for death.'
>
> (5.1.405–7)

The term 'justice' is not sharply distinguished from 'law', especially in the first half of the play, and when, in the concluding trial scene, Isabella calls for 'justice! Justice! Justice! Justice!' (5.1.26) against Angelo, 'a murderer . . . an adulterous thief, / An hypocrite, a virgin-violator' (5.1.41–3), it is clear enough that at this point in the scene, whatever may happen afterwards, she wants him to be severely punished.[1] (And we should perhaps bear in mind that many readers have regarded the final mercy shown to Angelo as very far from doing justice to his particular case.)

If the terms themselves are probed and examined in the course of the play, and sometimes overlap and sometimes oppose each other, this is all the more reason for not treating the play allegorically and assigning one abstraction exclusively to a single

---

[1] Isabella, it is true, knows perfectly well that Angelo has not in fact blackmailed her into sexual submission, but she genuinely believes that he has treacherously executed her brother.

character. Three of the most important characters – Claudio, Isabella, and Angelo – are tormented by divided loyalties and impulses, a turmoil so vividly presented that it is surely impossible to see any of them as a static personification. It is natural enough that we should compare the Duke to Angelo – both are judges and administrators faced with complex legal problems – but it seems a little too easy to say, as so many critics do, that Angelo stands for the Law, rigidly applied, while the Duke represents Mercy. It is not false, but it is an over-simplification. The differing attitudes of the two men towards the law and its application need a more thorough examination than has been made so far, and this will involve a consideration of certain words used in the play which tend to be overlooked, such as 'severe' and 'severity', and the group consisting of 'tyrant', 'tyranny', and 'tyrannous'.

Rather than work through the play consecutively, I want to begin in the middle and work outwards. The Duke learns of Angelo's attempt to blackmail Isabella in act 3, and when left to himself at the end of that act he meditates, in the light of Angelo's behaviour, on the duties of a ruler. This passage in couplets has almost always been treated unsympathetically. As recently as 1922 Dover Wilson was willing to endorse the common view that the lines were a spurious interpolation,[2] and even those who accepted them as genuine were often puzzled by their presence and felt obliged to devise some ingenious theory to account for their existence. A good example is provided by Mary Lascelles: 'One conjecture remains permissible; at some performance, Shakespeare's play was given in two parts, a pause intervening, and on this occasion it was judged prudent to remind the audience, on renewal of the performance, of the theme and situation.'[3] But there is not a scrap of evidence to support this, and even if we regard Measure for Measure as a kind of two-part play the section in couplets is surely as much an epilogue to Part I as a prologue to Part II.

There is no need to swing to the other extreme and regard the passage as the very core and centre of the play, the neglected key which will unlock the secret meaning of Measure for Measure. It is not great verse, and none of its lines embed themselves in the mind like 'man, proud man, / Dress'd in a little brief authority' (2.2.118–19) or 'Ay, but to die, and go we know not where' (3.1.117). It is written in a condensed and elliptical style which sometimes leads to obscurity, and parts of it may be textually corrupt, though most of the editorial tinkering inflicted on it has surely been quite unnecessary. Even so, we do not have to agree with Rosalind Miles that 'the Duke is only making appropriate sententious noises to close a climactic movement of the play.'[4] I prefer to assume that Shakespeare himself wrote the passage, intended it to occur at this particular point, and expected his audience to treat it as a necessary part of the play, demanding full and sympathetic attention.

J. W. Lever's analysis of the structure of the passage seems basically right to me.[5] It is plausible that a couplet has dropped out between lines 267 and 268; if so, the passage originally consisted of twenty-four lines which can be divided into four sections, each of six lines or three couplets. The first section is a generalized statement on the qualities required in a good ruler, while the second is a rebuke to Angelo for failing to show those qualities. The third section is a puzzle, especially if a couplet is missing. Lever feels that the Duke is 'asking how Angelo's abuses are to be rectified' and asserts that the 'idle spiders' strings' in line 268 are an allusion to 'the Renaissance commonplace . . . that the laws were like spiders' webs which caught the small flies but let the big insects break through'. To my mind the image is rather that of a heavy load or weight pulled along by threads which are as flimsy as a spider's web. The four sections of the Duke's meditation seem to alternate between the general and the particular: the first and third sections are generalizations applicable

[2] Measure for Measure, ed. A. Quiller-Couch and J. Dover Wilson, New Cambridge Shakespeare (Cambridge, 1922), pp. 139, 141.

[3] Mary Lascelles, Shakespeare's Measure for Measure (1953), p. 104.

[4] Rosalind Miles, The Problem of Measure for Measure (1976), p. 180.

[5] Measure for Measure, ed. J. W. Lever, the Arden Shakespeare (1965), pp. 93–4. All my references are to this edition.

to all men, the second and fourth are specifically about Angelo. The third section could perhaps be interpreted, with allowance for textual deficiencies, as the Duke's recognition in general terms that a guilty hypocrite can make important consequences follow from totally spurious appearances. In the final section the Duke decides to turn Angelo's own weapons against him: deception will be used to counter deception.

The Duke's meditation opens with a couplet that editors rarely discuss in any detail:

> He who the sword of heaven will bear
> Should be as holy as severe.   (3.2.254–5)

The sword is a symbolic instrument of punishment – even, presumably, of capital punishment. It is 'of heaven' and therefore has a divine origin or sanction.[6] This suggests that religion endorses punishment quite as much as it endorses mercy. The implications of the second line are slightly elusive. I take the primary meaning to be that anyone who wishes to wield the sword of justice should be holy in equal proportion to the degree of his severity. There is no condemnation of severity: it follows logically that he may be as severe as he wishes provided that he is correspondingly holy. The couplet is a gnomic utterance that can stand on its own, but it is also a condensation of an exchange between Escalus and the Duke a few lines earlier, where Escalus tells the Duke that he has pleaded in vain for clemency towards Claudio:

> I have laboured for the poor gentleman to the extremest shore of my modesty, but my brother-justice have I found so severe that he hath forced me to tell him he is indeed Justice.
> *Duke.* If his own life answer the straitness of his proceeding, it shall become him well: wherein if he chance to fail, he hath sentenced himself.
>
> (3.2.244–51)

The logic here is quite explicit: if the strictness of Angelo's private life corresponds to his strictness as a judge, his severity will be admirable. If it does not correspond, he ought to receive the same sentence himself.

There is plenty of evidence in the scene leading up to the Duke's meditation to indicate that he has no indulgence whatever to sexual licence. When Pompey is brought in charged with being a bawd, an accusation he makes no attempt to deny, the Duke attacks him furiously for living off the 'abominable and beastly touches' of prostitutes and their clients (3.2.23), and the Duke's description of prostitution as a 'filthy vice' (line 22) is a curiously close echo of a phrase used earlier by Angelo to Isabella, 'Fie, these filthy vices!' (2.4.42). When Lucio complains that Angelo 'puts transgression to't' (3.2.91–2), the Duke defends Angelo ('He does well in't', line 93), and answers Lucio's suggestion that Angelo might show 'A little more lenity to lechery' (line 94) by asserting the need for harshness: 'It is too general a vice, and severity must cure it' (line 96). This seems to echo or parallel the earlier comments of Escalus and the anonymous Justice at the end of act 2, scene 1:

> *Justice.*
>   Lord Angelo is severe.
> *Escalus.*   It is but needful.
>
> (2.1.279)

In these exchanges the Duke and Escalus both appear as upholders of severity. The theme becomes overtly comic in the Duke's horror and embarrassment when he himself is casually described by Lucio as a habitual libertine, who 'would mouth with a beggar though she smelt brown bread and garlic' (3.2.177–8). Pompey and Lucio are both disreputable characters whom the Duke would be unlikely to find congenial, but even in his discussion with the nobly penitent Juliet in an earlier scene he refers to her 'most offenceful act' three times as a 'sin' (2.3.19–31). If Angelo is to be called a puritan, so too is the Duke.

At first sight the Duke's conversation with Friar

---

6 The sword is of course a common attribute of justice, but in this context there may be a biblical allusion to the Epistle to the Romans, chapter 13, in which Christians are ordered to obey 'the powers that be'. Part of verse 4 reads as follows in the 1560 Geneva version: 'if thou do euil, feare: for he beareth not the sworde for noght: for he is the minister of God to take vengeance on him that doeth euil.'

Thomas in act 1, scene 3, would seem to prove irrefutably that the Duke approves of severity in certain circumstances. Angelo, we are told, has been put in charge of Vienna in the expectation that he will strictly enforce the neglected laws of the city, so the Duke can hardly blame him if he does precisely that. Here, however, we encounter a difficulty. Friar Thomas is merely a rather clumsy stage device used by Shakespeare to enable the Duke to share his thoughts with the audience without resorting to a soliloquy which would have been over fifty lines long. No other character in the play has any clear idea of the Duke's purposes; both his departure and his return are shrouded in mystery and confusion. As M. D. H. Parker notices, 'Angelo is not told to be rigorous';[7] indeed, the formality of the play's opening scene rather conceals the fact that neither Escalus nor Angelo is given a precise indication of how the Duke expects him to behave. Escalus is told that he already knows so much about law and administration that further advice would be super-fluous. Angelo is admonished in biblical language not to hide his light under a bushel or bury his talents; he is given exactly the same powers as the Duke, but it is twice made clear that he is totally free to use them as he wishes:

> In our remove, be thou at full ourself.
> Mortality and mercy in Vienna
> Live in thy tongue, and heart.   (1.1.43–5)

> Your scope is as mine own,
> So to enforce or qualify the laws
> As to your soul seems good.   (ll. 64–6)

It is hardly surprising that the two men should want to meet in order to clarify their position:

Escalus.
> A power I have, but of what strength and nature
> I am not yet instructed.
Angelo.
> 'Tis so with me.   (ll. 79–81)

Possibly the written commissions are detailed and specific, but they are not read out to the audience.[8] The only way I can put all this together is to assume that the Duke hopes and expects that Angelo will restore strict discipline to Vienna. But he has reservations about Angelo's integrity (see 1.3.50–4), and in order to make a genuine trial of Angelo the Duke must leave him completely free to expose his true nature.

The next four lines of the Duke's meditation help to bring out the implications of the opening couplet:

> Pattern in himself to know,
> Grace to stand, and virtue, go:
> More nor less to others paying
> Than by self-offences weighing.
>
> (3.2.256–9)

Lever's paraphrase of the first line, 'to know that the precedent for his judgements lies in his own conduct', is curiously muted, as though Lever is reluctant to acknowledge the full force of the line. 'Pattern' here is surely used in *OED*'s sense 1, 'an example or model deserving imitation': if the ruler wants a model of the right sort of human behaviour, he should be able to find it by looking into himself. The next line is a little more specific, if we expand it in the way most modern editors do: 'he must have grace in order to stand, and virtue in order to go'.[9] The ruler needs divine grace to keep him morally upright, but by itself this might seem merely passive, so he also needs virtue as an active principle. This helps to lead us forward to the second couplet, which deals with the ruler's attitude when he functions as a judge: he pays out, or inflicts, neither more nor less punishment to others than is determined by weighing up the amount of evil in

---

7 M. D. H. Parker, *The Slave of Life* (1955), p. 112.

8 Escalus is ordered not to 'warp' (diverge) from his commission (line 14), so presumably it gives him detailed instructions.

9 H. C. Hart, in the first Arden edition (1905), suggested that 'and virtue go' could mean 'if his virtue should fail him'. But the combination of 'stand' and 'go', in the senses of 'keep upright' and 'walk', seems to be a stock Elizabethan usage; compare a story in Thomas Lupton's *Siuqila: Too Good to be True* (Part II, 1581) in which a girl spends all night tied to a tree, sig. V2, 'I was neither able to goe nor stande', and V4, 'I vnbound hir', who was so frozen with the cold, that then she could neither go nor stand'. This book contains a version of the *Measure for Measure* story which may have been known to Shakespeare.

himself. (It is not, of course, specifically said that the 'paying' refers to punishment, but the reference to 'self-offences' in the next line makes this the most plausible interpretation.)

In this context 'weighing' clearly has a moral significance, and the concept of assessing or judging other people in terms of ourselves is central to the play. When Isabella tells Angelo, 'We cannot weigh our brother with ourself' (2.2.127) her remark appears to mean simply that we cannot judge everybody by a single standard, since those in authority can successfully commit offences which would be punished in ordinary people. It is little more than a piece of worldly wisdom, and Lucio is surprised to find her so shrewd ('Art avis'd o' that?', line 133). But when she urges Angelo:

> Go to your bosom,
> Knock there, and ask your heart what it doth know
> That's like my brother's fault. If it confess
> A natural guiltiness, such as is his,
> Let it not sound a thought upon your tongue
> Against my brother's life   (ll. 137–42)

her speech is a turning-point in the play, though its effect is ironically not what she intends. Angelo does look into his bosom, and finds that like Claudio he can feel urgent sexual desire, but the discovery does not prompt him towards sympathy or mercy. In the last scene of the play Isabella's earlier phraseology is picked up by the Duke in his pretended refusal to believe that Angelo could have behaved in this manner:

> it imports no reason
> That with such vehemency he should pursue
> Faults proper to himself. If he had so offended,
> He would have weigh'd thy brother by himself,
> And not have cut him off.   (5.1.111–15)

This provides, I think, a useful gloss or expansion of lines 259–60 in the couplet speech at the end of act 3.

It is characteristic of the play, and indeed of Shakespeare's normal dramatic technique, that there should also be comic treatment of the theme. Abhorson the executioner is shocked that he should be expected to use Pompey the bawd as his assistant ('he will discredit our mystery', 4.2.26–7), but the

Provost can see nothing to choose between them: 'Go to, sir, you weigh equally: a feather will turn the scale' (ll. 28–9).[10]

Lucio too has his own debased and simplified version of judging others in terms of oneself: as Lucio sees it, Angelo is severe simply because he is quite incapable of having sexual feelings. Lucio wants the Duke to return because the Duke is an old lecher whose experience of begetting bastards would make him more tolerant: 'He had some feeling of the sport; he knew the service; and that instructed him to mercy' (3.2.115–17). A related theme is that of putting oneself in another person's position, of seeing things from the opposite point of view; Isabella, for example, vividly imagines how first her brother and then she herself would have behaved if they had exchanged places with Angelo:

> If he had been as you, and you as he,
> You would have slipp'd like him, but he like
>   you
> Would not have been so stern.
>
> *Angelo.*   Pray you be gone.
>
> *Isabella.*
> I would to heaven I had your potency,
> And you were Isabel! Should it then be thus?
> No; I would tell what 'twere to be a judge,
> And what a prisoner.   (2.2.64–70)

This can easily be pushed a little further by Shakespeare and treated literally as a plot device of physical substitution, Angelo for the Duke, Mariana for Isabella, and so on.

In the light of all this evidence it surely becomes increasingly clear that the Duke, in terms of his own statements, does not differ from Angelo by advocating mercy, a word he rarely uses and completely omits from his meditation on the duties of a ruler. The difference is rather that the Duke, in contrast to Angelo, believes in a personal or reflexive view of the law: when faced with a prisoner the judge must

---

[10] This conjunction of 'weigh' and 'scale' suggests that Lever is right to gloss 'scaled' as 'weighed as in scales (his moral worth truly estimated)' at 3.1.256, where the Duke claims that Angelo, 'the corrupt deputy', will be 'scaled' if Isabella goes ahead with the bed-trick.

look into himself, and is disqualified from judgement if he is guilty of the same offence. If, however, the judge has been able to restrain his own tendency to a particular sin, he is perfectly entitled to punish that sin in other people. This attitude clearly emerges in a passage not mentioned so far, when the Duke and Provost are together in the prison at midnight, waiting in the hope that Claudio will be pardoned. The Provost criticizes Angelo ('It is a bitter deputy') but is rebuked by the Duke:

> Not so, not so; his life is parallel'd
> Even with the stroke and line of his great justice.
> He doth with holy abstinence subdue
> That in himself which he spurs on his power
> To qualify in others: were he meal'd with that
> Which he corrects, then were he tyrannous;
> But this being so, he's just. (4.2.77–83)

For Isabella, in an earlier scene, tyranny occurs when a ruler exercises his full powers of punishment to their uttermost:

> O, it is excellent
> To have a giant's strength, but it is tyrannous
> To use it like a giant. (2.2.108–10)

For the Duke, tyranny is not merely the infliction of harsh punishment; it is the infliction of harsh punishment by someone who is not in a moral position to do so. The same attitude underlies the Duke's explanation to Friar Thomas of why he has chosen Angelo to reform Vienna instead of himself:

> Sith 'twas my fault to give the people scope,
> 'Twould be my tyranny to strike and gall them
> For what I bid them do: for we bid this be done,
> When evil deeds have their permissive pass,
> And not the punishment. (1.3.35–9)

By being excessively lax in the past, the Duke has disqualified himself from exercising severity in the present.

Angelo explicitly rejects the personal view of law at the opening of act 2. His first speech, affirming that the law must be genuinely terrifying and not merely a scarecrow, seems to answer an off-stage plea from Escalus for mercy towards Claudio. Escalus then tries various approaches, one of which is to suggest, in a rather awkward and tentative

fashion, that Angelo himself might have committed the same offence if circumstances had been particularly favourable. In other words, he invites Angelo to put himself in Claudio's position. Angelo is unperturbed: for one thing, he knows perfectly well that he has never committed precisely the same offence as Claudio. In addition, even though some administrators of justice may be corrupt:

> I not deny
> The jury passing on the prisoner's life
> May in the sworn twelve have a thief, or two,
> Guiltier than him they try (2.1.18–21)

the fact has no great importance: 'What knows the laws / That thieves do pass on thieves?' (ll. 22–3). The tone appears to be contemptuous: 'why should you expect the law to be at all concerned about the fact that one thief is passing sentence on another?' For Angelo the whole process of the law is impersonal; crimes come to light, are punished by the appropriate law, and that is that. He is merely an agent, 'the voice of the recorded law' (2.4.61), and he feels no personal involvement in the sentence he has passed on Claudio: 'It is the law, not I, condemn your brother' (2.2.80). It is not until Angelo feels desire for Isabella that he makes any move towards the personal view of law: 'Thieves for their robbery have authority, / When judges steal themselves' (2.2.176–7); but the change is not powerful enough to alter his behaviour.

Angelo's conduct is so clearly shown to be wrong by the whole course of the play that it would seem perverse to argue in his defence, but it has to be said that most normal systems of law operate on principles closer to Angelo's than the Duke's. A sentence made by due process of law on adequate evidence could hardly be appealed against on the grounds that the judge himself had subsequently been discovered to be guilty of the offence for which he had sentenced the prisoner. The response would surely be that the judge himself must now stand trial, but his verdict need not be overturned. The Duke's insistence that a judge should be aware of his own human fallibility is admirable, but if pushed to extremes can lead to gross injustices. If you are convicted of a particular offence, the sentence you receive will not depend exclusively on the gravity of your offence, but also on the extent to which the judge has weaknesses of the kind for which you have been convicted. It is as though on each occasion the judge must put himself on trial as well as the prisoner, and in such circumstances there can be no uniformity of sentencing.

What is the Duke's response to Angelo's behaviour? The most explicit statement comes in the second section of his meditation at the end of act 3:

> Shame to him whose cruel striking
> Kills for faults of his own liking!
> Twice treble shame on Angelo,
> To weed my vice, and let his grow!
> O, what may man within him hide,
> Though angel on the outward side!
>
> (3.2.260–5)

The only point here that provokes much editorial discussion is 'my vice' in line 263; opinion is divided between a personal interpretation (the vice created by the Duke's negligence) and an impersonal (the vice of other people in contrast to Angelo's). The personal reading surely fits the context better and is much more powerful. The Duke is angry because the man he chose as his substitute, while busily weeding out the vice for which the Duke feels personally responsible, is simultaneously creating a fresh crop of his own. This brings out the main emphasis of the Duke's complaint: what he objects to is not Angelo's severity but his hypocrisy. It could be argued that 'cruel striking' and 'Kills' to some extent imply that the Duke regards the sentence on Claudio as inherently severe. This may be so, but the way the argument develops suggests that Angelo is cruel not just because he is rigorous but because he is punishing others for his own offences.

The problem of interpreting these lines prompts a question which has important implications, though at first sight it might seem a triviality of the 'How many children had Lady Macbeth?' type. When precisely does the Duke decide to intervene on Claudio's behalf, and why does he do so? It is assumed sometimes that the Duke makes up his mind to rescue Claudio as soon as he hears of Angelo's harsh sentence. For Bertrand Evans the turning-point is the Duke's examination of Juliet (act

2, scene 3): 'This is a crucial interview: if there is a precise point at which the Duke commits himself to the cause, it is here, when he finds Juliet's penitence honest, and, being so, to merit forgiveness.'[11] Evans may be right, but there is nothing in the scene to compel us to think so. The decisive and unmistakable intervention comes in act 3, at the point where Isabella is about to storm out in horror at her brother's willingness to prostitute her body to save his own. The Duke comes forward with a plan for coping with the problem, which must have been thought out beforehand, but he could quite easily have devised it only a few minutes in advance, while listening to the increasingly emotional debate between Claudio and Isabella. Indeed, the device he suggests, the 'bed-trick' substitution of Mariana for Isabella, would have been quite pointless at an earlier stage when Angelo was not lusting after Isabella. The conclusion seems to be that the Duke intervenes only at the point where he discovers that Angelo is a hypocrite who is in no position to condemn others. It might even be true that if Angelo had continued to behave with rectitude, the Duke would have allowed Claudio to go to his death. Of course it is foolish to speculate on what fictitious characters in a work of art might have done in different circumstances: I put it in this way only to bring out the full implications of the issue.

The exact way in which the Duke intervenes has a bearing on the way we respond to his character. The Duke is sometimes seen by those who dislike him as a cold-hearted manipulator, handling human beings rather as an experimental psychologist might treat the rats in his laboratory, subjecting them to unsuspected shocks in an arbitrary way that needs to be justified. It is true that in acts 4 and 5 he frequently allows the other characters to remain ignorant of the truth in a way that might cause undeserved suffering, as when Isabella is told, quite untruthfully, that her brother has been executed. The trial scene in act 5 proceeds for much of its length on assumptions that the Duke knows to be totally false, and he even persuades Isabella, some-

---

[11] Bertrand Evans, *Shakespeare's Comedies* (Oxford, 1960), p. 193.

what to her embarrassment (4.6.1–4), to pretend that she has been deflowered by Angelo. Now if we assume that the Duke decides to rescue Claudio and Juliet as soon as he learns of their predicament, it follows that his use of this kind of deception begins virtually as soon as he puts on the robes of a friar, and in particular, that his great speech attempting to reconcile Claudio to death is a kind of sham because he knows perfectly well that Claudio is not going to die. If, however, the Duke does not decide to intervene until Angelo's hypocrisy has been revealed, the interview with Juliet and the speech on death to Claudio can be taken at their face value. Until he overhears the agonized discussion between Claudio and Isabella in prison, the Duke knows no more than anyone else: Angelo might of course change his mind at the last minute, but all the signs suggest that Claudio is going to die, and the Duke bases his conduct on this assumption.

My argument also applies to an earlier scene in the play, the Duke's account to Friar Thomas in act 1, scene 3, of his motives for putting Angelo in charge of Vienna. It has become increasingly fashionable for sophisticated critics to invoke chapter 7 of Machiavelli's *The Prince* in this connection. When Cesare Borgia had gained control of the Romagna in Italy, he found it 'rife with brigandage, factions, and every sort of abuse' through the weak and avaricious behaviour of its previous rulers.

So he placed there messer Remirro de Orco, a cruel, efficient man, to whom he entrusted the fullest powers. In a short time this Remirro pacified and unified the Romagna, winning great credit for himself.

There were, however, dangers in allowing this efficient cruelty to persist too long; the servant's brutalities were making the master unpopular.

Cesare waited for his opportunity; then, one morning, Remirro's body was found cut in two pieces on the piazza at Cesena, with a block of wood and a bloody knife beside it. The brutality of this spectacle kept the people of the Romagna for a time appeased and stupefied.[12]

We are invited to compare this to *Measure for Measure* and to see the Duke as a kind of white, or perhaps

we should say grey, Machiavellian who tries to avoid unpopularity by getting a subordinate to do his dirty work for him. But there is no evidence that Shakespeare had read a word of Machiavelli or had the slightest admiration for him, and I cannot believe for a moment that Shakespeare would have expected or welcomed the comparison. If there are some similarities between the Duke's behaviour and Cesare Borgia's, there are also striking differences. The Duke's account of his motives for delegating power may not strike us as fully convincing, but it harmonizes so well with his deepest convictions about the way a ruler should behave that there is no need to regard his action as a repulsive duplicity.

I have already emphasized that the ideas discussed so far are not intended to provide a complete interpretation of the play. All the same, it would be natural, and legitimate, to ask whether the way we interpret the Duke's couplet speech at the end of act 3 has any bearing on our response to the second half of the play and in particular to the concluding trial scene which occupies the whole of act 5. When the Duke temporarily hands over his power at the beginning of the play, he has two motives for doing so: one is to test Angelo, the other is to bring about a stricter enforcement of the laws of Vienna. At the end it would seem that the first aim has been accomplished, with a negative result, while the second has been discreetly put aside and is not supposed to be present in the audience's mind. If, however, we take seriously the Duke's idea about personal justice, then his second aim is dependent on his first: the law cannot be enforced with severity if the man brought in to enforce the law proves to be corrupt. The danger of this sort of argument is that it can sound glib, and it must be admitted that the Duke never says anything of the kind explicitly. At the same time, there is nothing in act 5 to support those critics who argue that the play shows us an educative process in which the Duke, or Angelo, or possibly both together, learn that justice needs to be tempered with mercy, that the ideal is some kind of blend or balance. The alternatives at the end of the

---

12 Machiavelli, *The Prince*, translated by George Bull (Harmondsworth, 1961), pp. 57–8.

play are not light punishment and heavy punishment, but rather punishment in general as against mercy and forgiveness. In the opening scene the Duke had said to Angelo: 'Mortality and mercy in Vienna / Live in thy tongue, and heart' (1.1.44–5), and the play seems to offer us little between these two extremes, death on the one hand, and forgiveness on the other.

The disparity between the first half of *Measure for Measure*, up to the Duke's intervention, and the second half is a major critical problem of the play. The first half has an almost tragic intensity as the characters clash with each other in a way that painfully reveals their innermost character. Everything is spontaneous and unpredictable. In the second half, there is a strong sense of intrigue and manipulation: Shakespeare possibly wanted the trial scene in act 5 to have the same dramatic tension as the earlier scenes involving Claudio, Isabella, and Angelo, but in the trial scene there is an air of contrivance, with the Duke as both actor and director in a play-within-the-play. There are of course reasons for this shift of emphasis, even if they do not provide full artistic justification. In all other versions of the story the woman corresponding to Isabella goes to bed with the Angelo-figure, and it is she who complains to the judge's overlord when she realizes she has been duped. Shakespeare did not want his heroine to lose her virginity, so he provides a substitute, but he could hardly make Isabella herself suggest this device or provide her own substitute. Inevitably the Duke takes over as the organizer of the action.

The consequences of Shakespeare's decision may seem unfortunate, but the decision was consciously made. The last section of the Duke's meditation at the end of act 3 helps to prepare us for the intrigue of the last two acts:

> Craft against vice I must apply.
> With Angelo tonight shall lie
> His old betrothed, but despised:
> So disguise shall by th'disguised
> Pay with falsehood false exacting,
> And perform an old contracting.
>
> (3.2.270–5)

Clearly Angelo will be outwitted – the play will not end tragically – but the 'craft' used to counter his 'vice' will entail disguise and falsehood, so we need not be unduly surprised if the virtuous characters tell lies. The Duke could simply have revealed himself, but this would have brought the play to an abrupt conclusion, and more importantly, Angelo would not have been forced to experience intimately the deception and false appearances he has inflicted on other people. Angelo is thus receiving measure for measure, particularly if we gloss the word 'measure' according to sense 15 of *OED*, 'treatment meted out to a person, especially by way of retribution or punishment'. Those who dislike the second half of *Measure for Measure* will not be made to change their minds by any analysis, however subtle, of the Duke's meditation at the end of act 3. But if the evidence suggests, to a degree unusual in Shakespeare, that he deliberately and consciously altered the mode of his play, we ought to be cautious before passing judgement on it. Whatever artistic flaws there may be in *Measure for Measure*, they are not the result of carelessness or inadvertence on Shakespeare's part.

WAR AND SEX IN
'ALL'S WELL THAT ENDS WELL'

R. B. PARKER

I

I wish to pursue G. Wilson Knight's suggestion that *All's Well That Ends Well* is built on a conflict between the masculine concept of honour as prowess in war and the feminine concept of honour as chastity in love.[1] However, whereas Knight goes on to interpret the conclusion as an almost mystical victory for transcendent chastity in which 'sanctity aspires to sexuality' (p. 160), I propose to pick up his puzzling concept of Helena's 'bisexuality' to suggest instead that the conflict of the play is resolved by having each ideal – war and love – modify the other, so that the conclusion takes the form of a wry accommodation between them in which the purity of both ideals has had to be abandoned. As in *Troilus and Cressida* (echoed in *All's Well*) where there is a similar intercontamination of war and sex, this accommodation is seen through a consciousness of passing time. Shakespeare has added to his source[2] an important framework of death-haunted and nostalgic elders – the Countess, Lord Lafew, Lavache, and the melancholy King of France (who has a much more important part in the play than in Boccaccio) – which places the lovers' struggle in a perspective of succeeding generations, so that the young have to work out their relationships against their elders' fears and expectations for them. As Erik Erikson says in his essay 'Youth: Fidelity and Diversity':

It is the young who, by their responses and actions, tell the old whether life as represented by the old and as presented to the young has meaning; and it is the young who carry in them the power to confirm them

and, joining the issues, to renew and to regenerate [as Helena does], or to reform and to rebel [which is Bertram's first reaction].[3]

Thus, we constantly see the actions of Bertram and Helena through the affectionate tolerance, exasperation, hope, and need of their elders; and though this focus is not exclusive or without its own ironies (and should not, therefore, be accepted uncritically),[4] it does help to establish the note of cautious relief with which, as the title indicates, *All's Well* concludes.

The need for an accommodation between war and sexual love was an important and recurring motif in Renaissance art and thought. Edgar Wind illustrates this in his explication of such paintings as Veronese's *Mars and Venus*,[5] where Cupid's binding together of the legs of the two deities produces milk from Venus' breast while another Cupid playfully uses Mars' own sword to drive away his war-horse. Plutarch reports that 'In the fables of the Greeks, Harmony was born from the union of Venus and Mars: of whom the latter is fierce and contentious,

---

[1] G. Wilson Knight, 'The Triple Eye', in *The Sovereign Flower* (1958), pp. 93–160.

[2] 'Giletta of Narbona', the ninth story of the third day of Boccaccio's *Decameron* (1348–58), as translated by William Painter, *The Palace of Pleasure* (3rd edition, 1575).

[3] Erik Erikson, 'Youth: Fidelity and Diversity', in *The Challenge of Youth*, ed. Erik H. Erikson (Garden, NY, 1965), p. 24.

[4] As it tends to be in the otherwise very acute article by Josephine Waters Bennett, 'New Techniques of Comedy in *All's Well That Ends Well*', *Shakespeare Quarterly*, 18 (1967), 337–62.

[5] Edgar Wind, *Pagan Mysteries in the Renaissance* (revised edition, Harmondsworth, 1967), pp. 86 ff. (see plate 76).

the former generous and pleasing',[6] and this is restated by Aquinas in his *Summa Theologica* in terms of the concupiscible and irascible passions of man's middle, or 'sensible', soul: 'The passions of the irascible appetite counteract the passions of the concupiscible appetite: since concupiscence, on being roused, diminishes anger; and anger, being roused, diminishes concupiscence in many cases.'[7] Venus, the concupiscible, and Mars, the irascible, were thought to temper each other to produce Chastity, one of the virtues of temperance that stands not for virginity but for fruitful sexual union. And though, as Wilson Knight noted, Diana rather than Venus is the co-deity of *All's Well*, this is a Diana who is, as Helena tells the Countess, 'both herself and Love' (1.3.208)[8] – in other words, the combined Diana and Venus figure that Wind demonstrates was a recurrent Renaissance image for the combination of Chastity and Sex, in which perspicacity must surrender to passion and chastity itself can prove a weapon.[9]

My argument, then, will be that, as Bertram must be educated from war to accept first sexuality, then its responsibilities, so Helena too must learn to abandon the false religion of self-abnegation in sexual love and bring it to fruition by increasingly deliberate aggression. Such an approach allows both characters something closer to their proper due than is usual in criticism of the play. The extremes of both the irascible and the concupiscible are tolerated by the older generation as aberrations or 'sicknesses' natural to the young, and their accommodation brings the hero and heroine back to Roussillon to confirm and rejuvenate both family and state in a pattern that anticipates that of Shakespeare's Romances. *All's Well* is not one of the final plays, however, and the tone of its conclusion recognizes that such an accommodation may also have its losses and uncertainties.

II

For most people the chief stumbling block to *All's Well* is the hero's character; like Dr Johnson, they cannot reconcile themselves to Bertram.[10] As Helena's raptures over his 'hawking eye', his curls, and so forth indicate, one of Bertram's problems is

that he is so good-looking that people are ready to make excuses for him and eager to see a potential for nobility in him that he does not really possess. This then produces a more troublesome problem: people keep saying they hope he will live up to the virtues and achievements of his famous father. He is constantly called 'boy' – by his mother, by the King, by Lafew, and most often (with provocation) by his crony, the impostor Parolles – so we may assume he is still very young, probably in his late teens.

Like any adolescent whose widowed mother insists that he live up to a formidable father, Bertram wishes to escape from Roussillon in order to establish an identity for himself, first at the court, then, when that fails him, in a foreign war where the adolescent pressures of aggression and sexuality can find freer expression. At the beginning we do not see much of what he is like, only what others think of him; but, characteristically, he seems not even to have heard of the King's illness though Lafew says it is 'notorious' (1.1.33), and his eagerness to be gone from the 'dark house' of mourning slips awkwardly out when he interrupts his mother's conversation with Lafew (1.1.55), a breach of decorum that brings a mingled blessing and reproof from the Countess to her 'unseason'd courtier' (1.1.57–9, 67).

Bertram finds the court no freer than his home, however. It too is death-haunted, shadowed with nostalgia and distrust of the future. The King pushes his responsibility as guardian to the point of claiming 'My son's no dearer' (1.2.76), and goes even further than the Countess in lecturing him about his father's splendid example (1.2.19–22). Clearly, however, he fears that Bertram will turn out no better than the

---

6 *De Iside et Osiride*, 48 (*Moralia* 370D – 371A), quoted in Wind, p. 86.

7 *Summa Theologica*, I, Q.81, Art.2, trans. Fathers of the English Dominican Province, 21 vols. (1912–25).

8 Quotations from *All's Well* are from the new Arden edition, edited by G. K. Hunter (3rd edition, 1959).

9 Wind, pp. 74–80.

10 Samuel Johnson, *The Plays of William Shakespeare* (1765), in *Johnson on Shakespeare*, ed. Arthur Sherbo (New Haven and London, 1968), vol. 7 of *The Works of Samuel Johnson*, p. 400.

other young 'goers backward' at court (1.2.48), who, in the King's opinion, sacrifice honour to levity and the pursuit of fashionable clothes. Since we have seen that Bertram's chosen confidant is the impudent Parolles whose extravagance of dress is a subject of general remark, the foreboding seems well founded.

In lecturing Bertram about his father's virtues, the King especially emphasizes the elder Roussillon's soldiership; but irritatingly, when war breaks out between Florence and Siena, he forbids Bertram to take part in it because of his youth, yet at the same time encourages the other young courtiers to fight 'on either part', bidding them 'be . . . the sons / Of worthy Frenchmen' (2.1.11–12). It is at this point too, from the King himself, that the idea of war as a rival, or substitute, for sexuality is introduced. He bids the French volunteers,

> see that you come
> Not to woo honour, but to wed it, when
> The bravest questant shrinks: (2.1.14–16)

and warns them jocularly against

> Those girls of Italy, take heed of them;
> They say our French lack language to deny
> If they demand; beware of being captives
> Before you serve.   (2.1.19–22)

The comment is ironically placed, since the King will soon be insisting that Bertram, whom he has forbidden to serve, must marry against his inclination, and will himself deny all Bertram's attempts to protest.

Even before this happens, however, Bertram interprets the King's restraint as a denial of his virility by an effeminizing environment. 'I shall stay here the forehorse to a smock,' he complains, 'Till honour be bought up, and no sword worn / But one to dance with' (2.1.30–3). Parolles suggests he steal from court, in phrasing that reminds Bertram of his youth and has a martial–sexual pun on 'stand' – 'And thy mind stand to't, boy, steal away' (2.1.29) – and this is supported by the other volunteers in a typical scene of young male camaraderie. So before ever the marriage to Helena is raised, Bertram has come to see the court as a place of womanly restraint, with escape to war as a means to virile honour and to his acceptance as an equal by the young courtiers among whom he must establish his independent status.

This war–sex opposition is exacerbated when the King forces Bertram to marry Helena, after she has gone through a face-saving ceremony of rejecting the King's other wards. Whether these young Lords are ready to accept her, as their speeches suggest, or whether, as Lafew's rage at them implies, their responses show merely polite relief at not having been selected, it is important to notice the reasons which Helena gives for turning them down: one is too much above her in rank, another is too young to wish to marry, and to a third she says, 'I'll never do you wrong, for your own sake' (2.3.90). All these reasons apply equally to Bertram, and there is therefore considerable excuse for his shock when she bashfully fixes on him.

Bertram's reasons for rejecting Helena are complex. Like all Shakespeare's young lovers, he wishes to choose love for himself: 'In such a business give me leave to use / The help of mine own eyes' (2.3.107–8); but this is followed by a burst of snobbery meant to contrast with the courtesy to social inferiors his father has been praised for: 'A poor physician's daughter my wife!' (l. 115) – a protective insistence on rank hinted at earlier perhaps when, at his departure from Roussillon, he bade Helena 'Be comfortable to my mother, your mistress' (1.1.73). There are deeper reasons than these for the rejection, however. His 'I know her well: / She had her breeding at my father's charge' (2.3.113–14) shows that he associates Helena with the home he is trying to escape; and there may also be in this a covert fear of incest,[11] especially when we remember Helena's frantic, reiterated concern that the Countess should not regard Bertram as her 'brother' (1.3.150, 155, 157, 161).

But, most suggestive of all, in answer to the King's argument that he should marry Helena in gratitude for her having 'raised' his guardian from

---

[11] This point is developed in Arthur Kirsch, *Shakespeare and the Experience of Love* (Cambridge, 1981), chapter 5, and Richard Wheeler, *Shakespeare's Development and the Problem Play* (Berkeley, 1981), chapter 2.

a 'sickly bed', there emerges what appears to be a recoil from sexuality itself, a fear not out of keeping (in those days at least) with Bertram's comparative youth: 'But follows it, my lord, to bring me down / Must answer for your raising?' (2.3.112–13). He can remain adamant, therefore, to the King's disquisition on virtue and nobility precisely because that really is not the issue for him, and only succumbs when the monarch asserts his double authority as ruler and surrogate 'father', browbeating the 'proud, scornful boy' with threats of 'revenge and hate' (l. 164) and insisting not only that Bertram marry Helena but also, quite unreasonably, that he love her too (ll. 182–3). Even allowing for the contemporary custom of arranged marriages and a ward's undoubted duty to obey his king, such a display of angry, personal pressure antagonizes us. As E. K. Chambers put it: 'Even young asses have their rights, and one cannot but feel some sympathy for Bertram.'[12]

The recoil from sexuality beneath Bertram's social outrage issues in his determination not to bed Helena but to escape from marriage and the court to the masculine preserve of war. There is genuine, if slightly comic, adolescent despair in his cry,

> O my Parolles, they have married me!
> I'll to the Tuscan wars and never bed her
> (ll. 268–9)

and he determines to escape 'to those Italian fields / Where noble fellows strike' because 'Wars is no strife / To the dark house and the detested wife' (ll. 286–8). The grounds for this decision are supported (but not, it should be noted, caused) by Parolles, who agrees that

> He wears his honour in a box unseen
> That hugs his kicky-wicky here at home,
> Spending his manly marrow in her arms,
> Which should sustain the bound and high curvet
> Of Mars's fiery steed
> (ll. 275–9)

and sums the situation up epigrammatically, 'A young man married is a man that's marr'd' (l. 294). Interestingly, the same argument is also advanced later by Lavache. At the point when the Countess receives Bertram's letter saying he will never sleep

with Helena, the clown comments (playing like Parolles on 'stand'),

> ...your son will not be kill'd so soon as I thought he would...if he run away, as I hear he does; the danger is in standing to't; that's the loss of men, though it be the getting of children.
> (3.2.36–41)

Again military terms are used about a sexual situation, and it should be noted that the speech inverts Helena's praise of Parolles's cowardice earlier (in metaphors that also mocked his clothing): 'the composition that your valour and fear makes in you is a virtue of a good wing, and I like the wear well' (1.1.199–201). Helena approves of running away from war, Lavache from sexual debility.

In the parting scene (2.5) we feel great sympathy for Helena, whom Bertram harshly calls his 'clog'; but the situation is presented as awkward and embarrassing for both of them, particularly when Helena works up courage to request a kiss and Bertram nervously evades her by insisting that she must immediately 'haste to horse'. Once she is gone, his comment emphasizes what has become the basic opposition for him:

> Go thou toward home, where I will never come
> Whilst I can shake my sword or hear the drum
> (2.5.90–1)

– where, for the first time, military life is associated with the drum which will later become the central symbol for experience of war in the play. Undoubtedly, as Richard Wheeler has recently argued,[13] what we have here is a familiar picture of war embraced as a deflection of sexuality and a release for adolescent aggression, idealized by an 'honour' associated with bravery in the face of death and by the bonding of male companionship; but we oversimplify the situation if we forget the esteem in which such warrior courage was also held by Elizabethans or refuse sympathy to Bertram himself for the painful situation the King has placed him in.

This basic antagonism also emerges in Bertram's

---

[12] See *Discussions of Shakespeare's Problem Plays*, ed. Robert Ornstein (Boston, 1961), p. 40.

[13] Wheeler, p. 37.

next scene, in which a new father-figure, the Duke of Florence, promotes him with unrealistic speed to be 'general of our horse' (a very appropriate position for a character representing Mars). Bertram's response again polarizes love and war, the latter symbolized once more by the drum:

Great Mars, I put myself into thy file;
Make me but like my thoughts and I shall prove
A lover of thy drum, hater of love   (3.3.9–11)

and the Duke, in turn, invests war with sexuality when he bids fortune 'play upon thy prosperous helm / As thy auspicious mistress!' (3.3.7–8). At the same time, Shakespeare stresses that this promotion recognizes genuine achievement on Bertram's part. We hear later that he has 'taken their great'st commander, and...with his own hand he slew the duke's brother' (3.5.5–7); he is called 'gallant'; his service is 'honourable' and 'worthy'; people speak 'nobly' of him; the Duke sends letters to the King setting Bertram 'high in fame' (3.5.3–7, 48, 50; 5.3.31); and, at his return, Lafew is very willing to see the scar on his left cheek as 'a good liv'ry of honour' (4.5.95–6), ignoring Lavache's suggestion of a syphilitic incision (though we must remember also Parolles's boast of 'Captain Spurio's' cicatrice, also on his 'sinister' cheek, at 2.1.43, and Helena's disparagement of all such war scars at 3.2.121–2).

However, this masculine war honour is undermined in several ways: Shakespeare adds a certain ambiguity to the war itself; and nearly all act 4 is concerned with what Bertram calls the interlude of 'the Fool and the Soldier' (4.3.95), the exposure of Parolles's cowardice and treachery, during which the braggart makes some interesting accusations of sexual corruption throughout the army. These in turn reflect on Bertram's efforts to seduce the young Florentine whom Shakespeare has significantly named 'Diana'.

The purpose and grounds of the Italian war are not only vague but more than a little dubious. The King of France, for mysterious 'reasons of...state' (3.1.10), refuses to send official aid to Florence because of a warning from his 'cousin Austria' (1.2.5–9), though the Duke of Florence appears able later to persuade the French volunteers that his cause

is 'holy' (3.1.4). The drum that Parolles equates with war honour is lost because the cavalry (which are under Bertram's command) have mistakenly charged their own soldiers (3.6.46–7). And the conflict ends very vaguely with the Second Lord's announcement 'there is an overture of peace' capped immediately by the First Lord's 'Nay, I assure you, a peace concluded' (4.3.37–8), without further explanation. The war, in fact, is merely a convenience, a backdrop without clear purpose, circumstances, or outcome; so it is hard to take wholly seriously its danger or the honour won in it, especially since it is presented mainly as an outlet for the French courtiers' aggression and yearnings for fame, which are spoken of as a sickness of youth (as the Countess speaks of love). The war, we are told, serves as 'A nursery to our gentry, who are sick / For breathing and exploit' (1.2.16–17); it is 'a physic' for the 'surfeit' of their 'ease' (3.1.18–19). Moreover, as Parolles points out to Bertram, to volunteer is also very fashionable (2.1.49 ff.). Thus, war honour is qualified by the unsure principles behind the conflict, by the wholly self-centred, 'sick' motives of the volunteers, and by a sense of their conforming to fashion in this as in their clothes.[14]

This latter point is forcefully presented in the character of Parolles, Shakespeare's most significant addition to the source, who virtually dominates act 4. The spuriousness of Parolles is dramatized in three main ways. As his name suggests, he is a creature of words, not deeds; then, there is his costume, a confection of gaudy colours, feathers, and especially scarfs (2.3.246, 2.5.43–4, 3.5.85, 4.3.138–9, 312–13), which ensures that his first appearance is comic in itself, a discordant (but lively) blob of colour among the mourning clothes of Roussillon (like an inversion of the Marcade or Hamlet effects), as he elaborately salutes Helena while she anatomizes him aside; and lastly, there is the drum with which Parolles becomes identified and whose military summons is heard frequently throughout act 4, signifying the noisy virility but ultimate emptiness of the whole Italian

---

14 For discussion of ironic aspects in the war, see Alexander Leggatt, 'All's Well That Ends Well: The Testing of Romance', Modern Language Quarterly, 32 (1971), 21–41.

escapade. Appropriately, it is with the oath 'I'll no more drumming. A plague of all drums!' (4.3.288) that Parolles surrenders his pretensions as a soldier.

Helena and Lafew see through Parolles from the start, so Bertram's continued support of him in the face of Lafew's warning (2.5.7–8) indicates a serious immaturity of judgement; and it is mainly to disabuse this complacency that the French lords scheme to expose the braggart (4.3.30–3). It distorts Parolles's role, however, to condemn him too severely in terms of Bertram's evil angel or a vice figure. Though the Countess (3.2.87), Lafew (4.5.1), Mariana (3.5.16) and Diana (3.5.82) all alibi for Bertram by blaming Parolles's influence, in fact Bertram makes his own mistakes; Parolles merely supports them, and acts as a parodic reflection, not a cause, of Bertram's evils. Moreover, Parolles is a very amusing stage-figure: it should be noted that *both* French lords urge the drum trick not only to disabuse Bertram but also 'for the love of laughter' (3.6.32, 39); and the scene of the trick itself is kept from being painful by the fantastic gibberish with which his captors bewilder Parolles, by the impudent extravagance of his own lies, which makes the Second Lord exclaim gleefully 'I begin to love him for this' and 'He hath out-villain'd villainy so far that the rarity redeems him' (4.3.253, 264–5), and by the farcical breaking of stage decorum which has the First Lord's *aside* 'How deep?' apparently answered by Parolles's 'Thirty fadom' (4.1.56–7) and the braggart's wish for 'A drum now of the enemy's –' eliciting a prompt *Alarum within* (4.1.63). At the end, moreover, Parolles reaches a disillusioned level of self-knowledge and acceptance of shame that can throw light on similar elements in the accommodations forced not only on Bertram but also, I would argue, on Helena as well.

The unmasking of Parolles is very carefully placed. It is preceded in act 4, scene 3 by the French lords' criticism of Bertram's callousness to Helena and his attempt to 'pervert' Diana (4.3.13–17). This leads them to a statement of the way that mankind proves a traitor to itself, drowning in its very virtues by swimming against their current, as the Countess warned earlier when she said that misused 'virtues' could be 'traitors too' (1.1.38–40). To the First

Lord's 'Now, God delay our rebellion! As we are ourselves, what things we are!' (whose phrasing will be echoed later in Parolles's 'Simply the thing I am'), the Second Lord replies, in what is perhaps the crucial statement of the play:

Merely our own traitors. And as in the common course of all treasons we still see them reveal themselves till they attain to their abhorr'd ends; so he that in this action contrives against his own nobility, in his proper stream o'erflows himself. (4.3.20–4)

Within this context of reproof, it is carefully emphasized that the tricking of Parolles between 10.00 p.m. and 1.00 a.m. (4.1.24) overlaps with Bertram's deception in the bed-trick between midnight and 1.00 a.m. (4.2.54–8, 4.3.28–9); so the parallels between them are obvious, though Bertram's realization of his disgrace will not occur till the end of the play. Parolles's treachery and increasingly desperate lies prefigure Bertram's ignoble contortions in the final trial scene; and, interestingly for the theme of Mars and Venus, it is sexual corruption that Parolles chiefly criticizes beneath the military show. Bertram, the heroic general of horse, becomes 'a foolish idle boy, but for all that very ruttish' (4.3.207), 'a dangerous and lascivious boy, who is a whale to virginity, and devours up all the fry it finds' (4.3.212–13); and a poem found in the braggart's pocket warns Diana that Bertram is 'a fool…Who pays before, but not when he does owe it' (4.3.221–2). It is not only Bertram who provokes such criticism, however. Captain Dumain too is accused of 'getting the shrieve's fool with child, a dumb innocent that could not say him nay' (4.3.181–3), and of the common soldiers, Parolles claims, 'the muster file, rotten and sound…amounts not to fifteen thousand poll; half of the which dare not shake the snow from off their cassocks lest they shake themselves to pieces' (4.3.162–5). Parolles's extravagances must not be taken at face value, of course, but his comments offer a comic reflection of the way that war can distort and be a distortion of sexual instinct, reminding us that Bertram himself describes his lust for Diana as his 'sick desires' (4.2.35). As the First Lord comments at the beginning of Parolles's exposure (more truly than he realizes), ''A will betray us all unto ourselves' (4.1.92).

The resolution of the drum trick is also important for the light it sheds on the main dénouement. Parolles, who has several times, like a diminished Falstaff, pleaded 'let me live' (4.1.83, 4.3.236, 299), learns to welcome life as a value in itself and to accept his shameful defects for what they are, without more pretension. 'Safest in shame', he decides, 'Simply the thing I am / Shall make me live', since 'There's place and means for every man alive' (4.3.322–8); while his bitter 'Who cannot be crush'd with a plot?' (l. 314) looks forward to Bertram's later collapse in a way that mitigates some of its sharpness. Man is not the ideal, invulnerable creature he pretends to be, and, as the First Lord wonders about Parolles, it is indeed 'possible he should know what he is, and be that he is' (4.1.44–5) – or as Lavache says cynically about cuckoldry, 'If men could be contented to be what they are, there were no fear in marriage' (1.3.48–9). And it is on this level that Parolles is later accommodated by Lafew. Ironically, though earlier he repudiated Lafew's suggestion that Bertram or anyone else could be his 'lord and master' (2.3.186 ff.) – a title Helena was only too eager to bestow (1.3.153) – now he accepts Lafew's patronage with abject gratitude, anticipating in the farcical mode the chagrin with which Bertram will be brought to recognize his shame and the relief with which he too will finally acknowledge Helena as wife.

The shaming of Parolles runs counterpoint, in carefully matched scenes, to Bertram's attempt to seduce Diana and his own deception by the bed-trick. This seduction has both its bad side and its good. The bad is obvious. Bertram is trying to satisfy sexual relations impersonally in terms of war, translating male aggression into promiscuity, in which sex is treated as the taking and possessing of a woman's 'spoil', repudiating responsibility and abandoning the woman as soon as she has surrendered. As the Second Lord puts it, Bertram 'fleshes his will in the spoil of her honour' (4.3.15). The sexual double standard emerges clearly in Parolles's attempt to justify Bertram in the final scene, when he explains that Bertram 'did love her, sir, as a gentleman loves a woman . . . . He lov'd her, sir, and lov'd her not' (5.3.243–5). The emptiness of the seducer's oaths and promises is exposed by Diana, who recognizes them as mere 'words' (4.2.30), which her mother warned her all men swear to get their way (4.2.70–1); and the struggle between Bertram and Diana is consistently described in metaphors of war. Bertram's love gifts are 'engines of lust' (3.5.19), but Diana is 'arm'd for him and keeps her guard / In honestest defence' (3.5.73–4). Though he 'Lays down his wanton siege before her beauty, / Resolv'd to carry her' (3.7.18–19), Diana tells him when he talks of honour,

> your own proper wisdom
> Brings in the champion Honour on my part
> Against your vain assault. (4.2.49–51)

Setting him up for the bed-trick, she talks of the time 'When you have conquer'd my yet maiden bed' (4.2.57); and confronted by Diana at the end, Bertram tries to excuse himself with a last flicker of this misapplied imagery when he says he only 'boarded her i' th' wanton way of youth' (5.3.210). Yet when the issue comes to an open clash between the 'honour' of his ancestral ring, handed down through the males of his family from 'the first father', and the 'honour' of Diana's chastity, he surrenders the emblem of that very nobility he had appealed to as an escape from Helena, in a way that both symbolically, and in terms of plot manipulation, will involve him deeply in the responsibilities of sex that he has been trying to evade.

The attempt on Diana must not be seen as wholly negative, in fact; it has even been called Bertram's 'fortunate fall'.[15] Quite apart from the circumstance that, in the plot, it enables Helena to reclaim him as her husband, psychologically it also marks an effort to assert a sexuality that earlier he ran away from. It is, after all, perverse virility that is misleading him in this situation, a misapplication of the 'virtu' that in war has brought him honour, so that 'in his proper stream he o'erflows himself'. Helena's comments here on his 'important blood' and 'idle

---

[15] See Robert Hapgood, 'The Life of Shame: Parolles and *All's Well*', *Essays in Criticism*, 15 (1965), 269–78. This essay develops the idea of an interconnection between acceptance of life and acceptance of shame.

fire' (3.7.21, 26) are caught up later when the Countess excuses his behaviour as

> Natural rebellion done i' th' blade of youth,
> When oil and fire, too strong for reason's force,
> O'erbears it and burns on   (5.3.6–8)

– catching up the 'oil and fire' imagery of her dead husband, whom the King reported as saying, 'Let me not live . . . After my flame lacks oil . . .' (1.2.58–9). Bertram appeals against 'cold' Diana to his own 'quick fire of youth' (4.2.5) and persists, the Widow says, 'As if his life lay on't' (3.7.43), offering Diana his life as well as his honour (4.2.52); and, importantly, his arguments, though only half sincere, are the same arguments for 'natural' use and procreation that Parolles uses to persuade Helena to part with her virginity in act 1, scene 1, arguments which set her on the path to win 'the bright particular star' she thought too much above her. Mars here is kneeling to Venus–Diana (as in the Renaissance emblems cited by Wind[16]), the irascible is beginning to accommodate itself to the concupiscible.

An important development has occurred, therefore; but its significance will not be grasped till Bertram accepts responsibility for sex and is jolted out of the complacency with which he returns to Roussillon, a confidence nicely caught in Lavache's description of the showy feathers in the hats of the returning volunteers (4.5.100–2 – Bertram, we remember, was identified as 'That with the plume' at 3.5.77–8).

The Countess had earlier sent word to Bertram 'that his sword can never win / The honour that he loses' by leaving his wife (3.2.93–4) and this is repeated at Florence by the Second Lord, on hearing of Helena's supposed death: 'The great dignity that his valour hath here acquir'd for him shall at home be encount'red with a shame as ample' (4.3.65–7). Yet ironically (and this should prevent us assessing the older generation's view too simply), when he first returns, with Helena supposed dead, his elders are quite ready to modify their principles to welcome him. The Countess and Lafew make excuses for his behaviour, laying the blame on Parolles; Lafew even offers his daughter as a second wife; and we hear, for the first time, that this match had been contem-

plated before the marriage to Helena ever cropped up, which Bertram – with wholly new aplomb – cleverly uses both as a sign of his readiness now to submit to the King and as an excuse for his earlier reluctance to accept Helena. He also expresses regret for Helena's death, claiming to have loved her once he lost her; so the King too, admitting Bertram has 'Well excus'd' himself (5.3.55), forgives him – though, significantly, the King now seems to have relapsed into the valetudinarianism from which Helena rescued him.

Remembering the casualness with which Bertram actually received the news of his wife's death (4.3.85) and aware that Helena is *en route* to Roussillon, we anticipate Bertram's deflation. This starts with Lafew's recognition of Helena's ring and the King's suspicions of foul play, is followed by Diana's arrival with Bertram's ancestral ring, and culminates in the appearance of Helena herself, not dead but pregnant with Bertram's child. Bertram's ignoble, Parolles-like failures of nerve under these successive blows turn all his elders against him, but it should not be forgotten that all the apparent disasters are *false*, and that we are perfectly aware of this: irony mitigates censoriousness. The King's suspicion that Bertram must have had Helena murdered, Parolles's blundering attempts to support Bertram that only worsen his case, the growing confusion and exasperation of the King, and Diana's pert, riddling answers, all complicate and lighten the tone,[17] till the delayed but long anticipated entry of Helena herself. Bertram's reply to her comment that as a wife she is only 'The name and not the thing' (5.3.302) – 'Both, both. O, pardon!' – seems as much relief at having escaped from the avalanche of social disapproval that has fallen on him as true love or repentance. He has surely swung from one extreme to the other of Freud's diagnosis of inhibited sexuality:[18] from an attempt to escape into sex with

---

16 See Wind, plate 77.

17 Many of these details are pointed out by Clifford Leech, 'The Theme of Ambition in *All's Well That Ends Well*', *ELH*, 21 (1954), 17–29.

18 'On the Universal Tendency to Debasement in the Sphere of Love', in *Standard Edition of the Complete Psychological Works of Sigmund Freud*, ed. James Strachey, 24 vols. (1953–74), vol. 11 (1957), pp. 179–90.

a woman whom he can consider degraded by it, to the opposite pole of surrender to the 'magical' security of a dominating woman closely associated with his mother. There is no speech of reconciliation, no acceptance of responsibility, merely what Wheeler calls Bertram's 'dismal and conditional final couplet',[19]

> If she, my liege, can make me know this clearly,
> I'll love her dearly, ever, ever dearly
>
> (5.2.309–10)

in which he seems to be trying to reassert some feeble remnants of dignity and choice, only to be put down dourly by Helena's assurance of 'Deadly divorce' if he finds himself unsatisfied. Mars has indeed bowed to Venus, but the balance hardly seems an equal one; and it should surely not be only on Helena's behalf that we feel qualms about this marriage.

III

In fact, if one problem with *All's Well* is that we cannot be reconciled to Bertram, another is that we are tempted to identify with Helena too closely. However, as Bertram has to be educated to sex, Helena too has to cease idealizing her attraction to Bertram, to accept it at its most basic sexual level, and to learn to fight for her love even at some sacrifice of self-respect. And again we must remember Helena's youth: she is presumably younger even than Bertram. In the source, indeed, we are told that Giletta fell in love 'more than was meete for a maiden of her age'.[20]

The persuasiveness of Helena's passion is unquestionable, and it has long been recognized that her experience draws heavily on the emotions explored in Shakespeare's sonnets;[21] but there are qualifications to it even from the start. There is surely an initial shock intended in her denial of sorrow for her father's death (the timing of which Shakespeare changes to emphasize this point), particularly as we see it in the context of the Countess and Lafew's grief and piety:

> I think not on my father,...
> ...What was he like?
> I have forgot him; my imagination
> Carries no favour in't but Bertram's.
>
> (1.1.77–81)

Her feeling is wholly sexual, moreover, and totally visual, concerned with Bertram's 'arched brows, his hawking eye, his curls', with 'every line and trick of his sweet favour' (1.1.92–4), not with any quality of his character; and she herself seems to recognize the superficiality of this by using metaphors of false religion about it: 'But now he's gone, and my idolatrous fancy / Must sanctify his relics' (1.1.95–6). Her recognition of 'ambition' in her love issues in a death-seeking absolutism that is both impractical and servile:[22] 'there is no living, none, / If Bertram be away' (ll. 82–3); the frustration of her love is twice compared to 'plague' (ll. 88, 90); and she concludes with a bizarre image of miscegenation, 'The hind that would be mated by the lion / Must die for love' (ll. 89–90), that reminds one irresistibly of Pyramus' 'Since lion vile hath here deflower'd my dear' (*A Midsummer Night's Dream*, 5.1.284). In fact the emotional extravagances in this first soliloquy are very like those of the earlier, comic Helena in the *Dream*, who, according to Lysander,

> Devoutly dotes, dotes in idolatry
> Upon this spotted and inconstant man.
>
> (1.1.109–10)

The earlier Helena recognized that

> Things base and vile, holding no quantity,
> Love can transpose to form and dignity.
> Love looks not with the eyes, but with the mind;
>
> (1.1.232–4)

she had the same servile persistence as this Helena:

> The more you beat me, I will fawn upon you.
> Use me but as your spaniel, spurn me, strike me,
> Neglect me, lose me; only give me leave,
> Unworthy as I am, to follow you   (2.1.204–7)

---

[19] Wheeler, p. 56.

[20] Quoted in Hunter, p. 145.

[21] This relation is developed at length by Wilson Knight and by Wheeler; see also Roger Warren, 'Why Does It End Well? Helena, Bertram, and the Sonnets', *Shakespeare Survey* 22 (Cambridge, 1969), 79–92.

[22] See Denis de Rougemont, *Passion and Society*, trans. Montgomery Belgion (rev. edn. 1974), for a discussion of the 'liebestod' tradition in Western love literature.

and pushed it to a conclusion in the same sexual–
death imagery:

> I'll follow thee, and make a heaven of hell,
> To die upon the hand I love so well.
>
> (2.1.243–4)

It is in relation to this earlier, comic Helena, as much
as to the sonnets, that we should see Helena's
opening passion; and, indeed, the Countess recognizes that such a state of mind is part of 'nature's
truth' in all young girls: 'Such were our faults...Her
eye is sick on't' (1.3.130–1), where the mature
tolerance but also criticism implied by 'faults' and
'sick' are an important guide to our response.

There is a certain despairing fancifulness about
Helena's first soliloquy, then, but this is radically
changed by the conversation with Parolles about
virginity, in which Helena takes the initiative and
shows an unexpectedly bawdy resilience. She recognizes Parolles as a liar, fool, and coward, but accepts
him for Bertram's sake, and also, very acutely,
recognizes that

> these fixed evils sit so fit in him,
> That they take place when virtue's steely bones
> Looks bleak i' th' cold wind; withal, full oft we see
> Cold wisdom waiting on superfluous folly.
>
> (1.1.100–3)

This is mainly pejorative, of course, but it contains a
recognition of the unloveliness of 'steely' virtue and
'cold' wisdom, and also of something enduring in
Parolles's very 'evils' that prefigures his eventual
survival. It may, perhaps, anticipate a certain element
in her own later compromise with Bertram.

The crux of the virginity discussion is Helena's
question, 'How might one do, sir, to lose it to her
own liking?' (1.1.147), so that, as she puts it less
bluntly to the Countess later, 'Dian' may be 'both
herself and Love'. Parolles's arguments for the
sacrifice of virginity reflect mere libertinism, but
with lines like 'Get thee a good husband, and use
him as he uses thee' (ll. 210–11), he puts the idea of
sexual action into Helena's head. In answer to his
proposition, 'Will you anything with it?', the
phrasing of her 'Not my virginity; yet...' (l. 161)
suggests a determination to use virginity in the

future – 'yet' is an important modifier in this
play – and it is followed by a day-dreaming passage
about the paradoxes of love that Bertram will find
in possessing it[23] which concludes, with obvious
sexual ambiguity,

> 'Tis pity...
> That wishing well had not a body in't
> Which might be felt. (ll. 175–8)

This virginity discussion, which represents
Helena's swing to a more practical frame of mind
with an obliquity typical of her whole characterization, is couched almost entirely in terms of warfare.
Recognizing 'some stain of soldier' in Parolles, she
asks, 'Man is enemy to virginity; how may we
barricado it against him?', and the discussion is
conducted throughout with wording such as 'assails',
'though valiant, in the defence yet is weak',
'warlike resistance', 'setting down', 'undermine',
'blow up', 'blow down', 'military policy', and
'with the breach yourselves made you lose your
city', to conclude with Helena's 'I will stand for't a
little, though therefore I die a virgin', where 'little'
has the same force as the earlier 'yet' (ll. 109–132).
A few lines later, her day-dream of what her
virginity may mean to Bertram includes being his
'captain, and an enemy', 'his sweet disaster', and,
significantly, his 'traitress' (ll. 164–9).

After this military interchange, Helena's second
soliloquy shows a wholly new self-confidence:

> Our remedies oft in ourselves do lie,
> Which we ascribe to heaven; the fated sky
> Gives us free scope; (ll. 212–14)

she now trusts nature 'which mounts my love so
high' to 'join like likes, and kiss like native things';
and picks up the mention of the King's illness earlier
to sketch out a plan of action:

> The king's disease – my project may deceive me,
> But my intents are fix'd, and will not leave me.
>
> (ll. 224–5)

Thus, through Parolles's sexual realism couched in
the imagery of war, Helena has arrived at a plan of

---

[23] The 'There' in 'There shall your master have a thousand
loves' (1.1.162) can be interpreted as either 'at court' or
'in my virginity'.

aggressive action, a 'policy how virgins might blow up men' (ll. 119–20).

Our knowing this creates an ironic undertow in the next Helena scene, where she gradually admits to the Countess her love for Bertram and her plan to cure the King; and the tone of the scene is complicated further because their conversation is preceded by comments from the Countess's clown and steward. Lavache's request to wed Isbel puts Helena's love for Bertram in a decidedly fleshy context. Like Touchstone with Audrey, he says he is driven to marriage 'by the flesh' (1.3.27). Perverting the marriage service, but anticipating the bed-trick, he claims, 'I think I shall never have the blessing of God till I have issue a' my body' (ll. 22–3), then goes on to welcome cuckoldry and to distinguish between marriage and nature's unregulated sexuality:

> Your marriage comes by destiny,
> Your cuckoo sings by kind.   (ll. 60–1)

He also gives as another 'holy' reason, 'that I may repent' the wickedness of merely being a creature of 'flesh and blood', which seems to anticipate, in exaggerated form, the sense of accepted limitations in Helena's marriage at the end.

Lavache also picks up the military vocabulary of the virginity discussion by a song unexpectedly comparing Helena to the Helen of *Troilus and Cressida*, 'King Priam's joy' (as Helena will be the King of France's) who sent Grecians to sack Troy; but perverts the end of the song (according to the Countess) to claim that it is rare to find one good woman in ten (ll. 67–76), concluding with ironic wonder at the fact 'That man should be at woman's command and yet no hurt done' (ll. 89–90; 'hurt' is another key word in the play). This war imagery is then associated with Helena's own state of mind when the steward tells of overhearing her complaint that Diana was '[no] queen of virgins, that would suffer her poor knight surpris'd without rescue in the first assault or ransom afterward' (1.3.110–12).

Though the interview with the Countess is very sympathetic to Helena, there is also a dimension of irony to it because both we and the Countess already know she loves Bertram, and we (though not the

Countess) know also that she has a scheme to win Bertram through curing the King. Her agitated, oblique manoeuvrings thus have a comic, if kindly, tinge to them. Moreover, there is now a reversion to the opening soliloquy's self-abnegation and sexual embrace of death. Of Bertram she exclaims,

> My master, my dear lord he is; and I
> His servant live, and will his vassal die.
>
> (ll. 153–4)

She describes herself as one

> That seeks not to find that her search implies,
> But, riddle-like, lives sweetly where she dies
>
> (ll. 211–12)

and once again the imagery of love's false religion surfaces: 'Thus, Indian-like, / Religious in mine error, I adore...' (ll. 199–200). Such hesitations, and toings and froings, are typical of Helena, as witness her temporary retreats when she is not immediately admitted to see the King, or before she can bring herself to choose a husband, or after Bertram first refuses her. They help to prevent her losing our sympathy as too determined, too 'irascible' a character, a function that obliquity of plotting will be called on to sustain in the second half of the play.

With the Countess's support, Helena turns her negative reflections on religion and death to a positive purpose in venturing to cure the King, in which endeavour she believes she will have heaven's support and for which she is ready to risk her life. It is important to grasp why this is an inadequate enterprise, however, quite apart from Bertram's refusal to be impressed by it. For one thing, she is relying on the father she claimed so undutifully to have forgotten, in other words on an inheritance analogous to Bertram's reliance on social rank yet rebellious relation to *his* father. Then, although there is a very heavy emphasis on the aid of heaven, her comment,

> But most it is presumption in us when
> The help of heaven we count the act of men
>
> (2.1.150–1)

directly contradicts the self-reliance of her second soliloquy:

> Our remedies oft in ourselves do lie,
> Which we ascribe to heaven   (1.1.212–13)

and though the idea of virginity's miraculous healing power is a traditional one, curiously it is less Helena's virginity than her sexual attractiveness that is invoked round the cure. Lafew first describes the 'Doctor She' as

> a medicine
> That's able to breathe life into a stone,
> Quicken a rock, and make you dance canary
> With sprightly fire and motion; whose simple touch
> Is powerful to araise King Pippen, nay,
> To give great Charlemain a pen in's hand
> And write to her a love-line.   (2.1.71–7)

Then, on leaving Helena to cure the King, he provides a second unexpected reminiscence of *Troilus and Cressida* which, at the same time, introduces the seemingly irrelevant term 'traitor' that is so central to the Bertram plot:

> A traitor you do look like, but such traitors
> His majesty seldom fears; I am Cressid's uncle
> That dare leave two together.   (ll. 95–7)

Helena, moreover, not only lays her life as gage for the cure (as in the source), but also, and primarily, stakes her sexual reputation on it, venturing

> A strumpet's boldness, a divulged shame,
> Traduc'd by odious ballads; my maiden's name
> Sear'd otherwise.   (ll. 170–2)

Clearly, for Helena curing the King's fistula presents some sort of sexual risk, though why this should be so is not made clear.[24] After the cure, moreover, Lafew insists on an erotic element in the King's recovery; 'your dolphin is not lustier', he claims, and 'Lustique, as the Dutchman says. I'll like a maid the better whilst I have a tooth in my head. Why, he's able to lead her a coranto' (2.3.26, 41–3). This eroticism then seems to be projected into the King's insistence on Bertram accepting Helena in marriage, even when she demurs (whereas in the source the King makes the match reluctantly), as though Bertram is somehow serving as his guardian's representative or surrogate here and his refusal tarnishes the King's restored virility.[25] Similarly, Lafew also wishes he were young enough to wed Helena (ll. 59–61, 78–9), and would like to 'make

eunuchs' of the 'boys of ice' who seem to be refusing her (ll. 86–8, 93–5). There is thus a strongly sexual aura round the cure, but it is kept mysterious and symbolic.

Having earned her right to choose a husband, Helena hesitates again, then determines to abandon virginity and fly from Dian's altar to 'imperial Love' (ll. 74–6); but when she reaches Bertram her 'irascible' confidence drains away and she reverts catastrophically to the earlier humility:

> I dare not say I take you, but I give
> Me and my service, ever whilst I live,
> Into your guiding power   (ll. 102–4)

and is even willing to back down entirely when Bertram protests (ll. 147–8). It is the King's authority, not Helena's worth or her determination, which forces the marriage through; and afterwards she shows the same masochistic submissiveness to Bertram's refusal to consummate the marriage and his instructions to leave court (2.4.45, 49, 52), agreeing meekly, 'Sir, I can nothing say / But that I am your most obedient servant' (2.5.72–3). She also retains her earlier sense of unworthiness and guilt:

> I am not worthy of the wealth I owe,...
> But, like a timorous thief, most fain would steal
> What law does vouch mine own
>   (2.5.79–82; cf. 75–6)

– an image she will pick up again when she leaves Roussillon after Bertram's letter of rejection in act 3, scene 2: 'poor thief, I'll steal away' (l. 129). Her reaction to that letter is to blame herself for the danger Bertram will run in the war, seeing herself distractedly as his murderer:

> Whoever shoots at him, I set him there;
> Whoever charges on his forward breast,
> I am the caitiff that do hold him to't;
> And though I kill him not, I am the cause
> His death was so effected.   (3.2.112–16)

For all our sympathy with her distress here, we

---

[24] If the fistula were (as often) in the anus, this might be explicable; but it is never said that this is so, and in the source the fistula is in the King's breast (Hunter, p. 146).

[25] Wheeler makes this point very effectively, pp. 76 ff.

know it was not all her fault; Bertram had determined to go to the war before the marriage was proposed. Moreover, her soliloquy is set ironically between scenes showing the high spirits of the volunteers arriving in Florence and Bertram's spectacular promotion to general of the horse. Clearly, Helena's guilty fear of war is no better grounded (at least in this play) than Bertram's fear of sex.

Her defeatism and self-blame are taken further in her letter to the Countess in act 3, scene 4, in which religion is again perverted to serve sexual chagrin. She claims to be going on a pilgrimage as penitence for the 'ambitious love' that has put Bertram's life at risk; she will 'with zealous fervour sanctify' *his* name (3.4.11); and, as usual, she offers to 'embrace' death herself in order to set him free (ll. 16–17). And once again this is ironically juxtaposed to a scene in which we hear of Bertram's further military success from a Florentine girl to whom he is now eager to pay court.

In terms of the concupiscible–irascible balance, therefore, Helena's first attempt to win Bertram has been too half-hearted: too self-doubting, too reliant on the skills and authority of others, too high-minded and self-pitying, and too oblique in its sexuality to succeed. She needs to grapple with her problem in a more aggressively sexual fashion; and this is exactly what she proceeds to do in the controversial bed-trick. However, just as her psychological hesitations softened aggression in the first half, in this part of the play it is diluted by diverting the dramatic focus to Bertram and Parolles and by keeping the exact nature of Helena's intentions at all times vague. The plot, however, reveals a complex and ruthless plan in two movements: the bed-trick and Bertram's public shaming.

Unlike Giletta in the source story, Helena makes no mention in either her soliloquy or the letter to the Countess of any plan to seek Bertram out or fulfil his seemingly impossible marriage conditions, but she does choose as her goal a shrine that will take her through Florence, where the Widow says the pilgrims to Saint Jacques habitually stay (3.5.92–4), and it is left unclear whether this was intentional. It is certainly chance that brings her into the company of Diana, the very girl Bertram is trying to seduce,

but she is remarkably quick to grasp the situation (3.5.69–70) and then to exploit it. As she arranges for the Widow and Diana to aid her first in securing Bertram's family ring, then in the bed-trick, her means of persuasion are no longer the will of heaven and risk of her own life, but gold and the promise of royal favour; and the paradoxes with which she ends act 3, scene 7 reveal her own awareness of ambiguities in a plan that

> Is wicked meaning in a lawful deed,
> And lawful meaning in a lawful act,
> Where both not sin, and yet a sinful fact.
>
> (ll. 45–7)

Helena is mostly kept absent from act 4, which focuses on Bertram and Parolles; but she turns up briefly in act 4, scene 4 with an important and disturbingly realistic reaction to the conventional bed-trick, reminiscent of Sonnet 129 ('The expense of spirit...'):

> O strange men!
> That can such sweet use make of what they hate,
> When saucy trusting of the cozen'd thoughts
> Defiles the pitchy night; so lust doth play
> With what it loathes for that which is away.
>
> (ll. 21–5)

She has prostituted herself to Bertram's desire for a purely physical, impersonal union, and it is not her virginity she is lamenting here but her feelings of damaged self-worth. She no longer idealizes Bertram.

A little mysteriously (and going beyond the source), Helena then persuades the Widow and Diana to accompany her to Marseilles. Ostensibly, this is to get more rewards from the King of France, but she also drops a hint that she has further instructions for Diana and tells them she has spread a rumour of her own death – her romantic death-seeking is certainly being converted to practical uses now. And, echoing the play's title, she argues that means can always be justified by ends. This same argument, again echoing the title, is repeated in the apparently unnecessary scene at Marseilles (5.1), where she finds the King departed for Roussillon; and there she also hands over a letter, already written, to be taken ahead to him, which turns out later to be the letter signed 'Diana Capilet' which claims that Bertram promised Diana marriage. We may conclude, therefore, that a public confrontation of Diana and Bertram before the King was always part of Helena's plan; and all this journeying emphasizes the determination and effort she is putting into it.

She does not appear again till the end of Bertram's public humiliation, but we are aware that it is all stage-managed by her, working through her surrogate, Diana. Not only has she arranged for Diana to produce Bertram's family ring to claim a marriage contract, but there is also the business of the second ring (not in the sources), which Diana promised to put on Bertram's finger during the night (4.2.61–2). We learn now for the first time that this was given to Helena by the King and that she swore to him only to part with it to Bertram in bed. Obviously, Lafew's recognition of it and the King's consequent suspicions are accidental, but by having Diana demand it, it is clear that it was also always part of Helena's plan. Finally, Diana riddlingly announces Helena's pregnancy. We accept this as fulfilling the romance pattern, but it is worth noting that this is the first we have heard of the pregnancy, that it seems an extremely lucky hit (Giletta slept with Beltramo several times and had twin sons before she confronted him), and that there has certainly not been time for the pregnancy to be so advanced that Helena can feel 'her young one kick' (5.3.296).

In other words, though it is kept carefully obscured, oblique, and out of central focus, there are sufficient indications that Helena has a complex and aggressive plan, not only to inveigle Bertram into bed with her (with the double ring trick for validation), but also to challenge and humiliate him before the King. Helena's final comments are also worth more analysis than is usually given them. There is no servility or self-abnegation now, nor, sadly, any idealism. In response to the King's surprise, she says, ''Tis but the shadow of a wife you see; / The name and not the thing' (5.3.301–2), and reacts to Bertram's relieved 'Both, both. O, pardon!' with a reminder of his behaviour during the bed-trick: 'O my good lord, when I was like this maid / I found you wondrous kind' (ll. 303–4).

She follows this with the inquiry, 'Will you be mine now you are doubly won?' (l. 308), by 'name' and 'thing', that is, by ring and pregnancy (and once more confronting the King); and has an equally uncompromising riposte for Bertram's promise to love her if she can prove her story:

> If it appear not plain and prove untrue
> Deadly divorce step between me and you!
>
> (ll. 311–12)

Then she turns away for a greeting to the Countess – 'O my dear mother, do I see you living?' (l. 313) – the affection of which is all the more striking because such feeling is conspicuously lacking in anything she says to Bertram in the scene. To him she has become ironical: at best teasing, at worst distinctly tart.

IV

Plainly, both lovers are now back in the fold of the French court, but the sense of qualified pleasure in their reunion is reflected also in their elders, who, we remember, had been willing to accommodate Bertram earlier when they thought Helena had died because of his desertion. The King is made to seem rather foolish by the convolutions of the plot. We know he is wrong to have Bertram arrested for Helena's murder and that Helena herself will soon appear; so his comment 'I am wrapp'd in dismal thinkings' (l. 128) is apt to get a laugh in performance (and seems phrased with that intention). His growing exasperation with Diana's riddling is also comically pettish ('Take her away. I do not like her now', l. 275) and Diana's replies to him are frankly pert: 'By Jove, if ever I knew man 'twas you' (l. 281; cf. 287). And his final offer to let Diana choose a husband too must surely be meant to seem ironic when we remember what happened to Helena earlier (particularly since Diana swore off marriage at 4.2.74). The wryness of tone here is underlined by Lafew who does *not* weep (as is often claimed) but says 'Mine eyes smell onions, I shall weep anon' (l. 314) and requests a handkerchief from the scarf-bepestered but now filthy and evil-smelling Parolles, only to be exasperated anew at the latter's 'curtsies'. There is also heavy repetition of 'if' and 'seems' at the end. Bertram promises love *if* Helena can prove her story; the King promises Diana a husband *if* she can prove herself a maid; and he concludes the play with the very qualified couplet,

> All *yet seems* well, and *if* it end so meet,
> The bitter past, more welcome is the sweet,

then extends the same note into the epilogue, begging applause with 'All is well ended *if* this suit be won'.

So heavy a repetition must be intentional, and the mixed reaction it requires reflects a generalization made by the First Lord in act 4, in which moral categories are presented in irascible–concupiscible phrasing: 'The web of our life is of a mingled yarn, good and ill together; our virtues would be proud if our faults *whipp'd* them not, and our crimes would despair if they were not *cherish'd* by our virtues' (4.3.68–71). *All's Well* is consummately a play of middle age, written by a poet who belonged to neither of the generations shown in it; it looks back to the golden comedies, and forward to the Romances. Its main effect is one of accommodation and balance, the interweaving of youth and age, vice and virtue, realism and romance; and not the least important part of this 'mingled yarn' is its rueful mixture of war and sex, an accommodation of the irascible and the concupiscible, Mars and Diana–Venus, that remains unsettlingly partial.[26]

---

[26] A version of this paper was delivered at the Shakespeare Association of America meeting at Ashland, Oregon, in April, 1983.

CHANGING PLACES IN 'OTHELLO'

MICHAEL NEILL

But when you come to love, there the soil alters;
Y'are in another Country.
Thomas Middleton, *Women Beware Women*

...in nature things move violently to their place, and
calmly in their place.
Francis Bacon, 'Of Great Place'

Othello is a tragedy of displacement, a drama of
jealousy and resentment which traces the destructive
symbiosis of two men, each of whom is tormented
by a sense of intolerable usurpation. As its very
subtitle ('The *Moor* of *Venice*') suggests, it is concerned with belonging and estrangement, with
occupation and dispossession; and it explores the
psychological connection between the various ideas
of 'place' with which this central pair are obsessed.
Of course there is a sense in which 'place', in its
physical sense, is important in all of Shakespeare's
tragedies – to the point where the character of each
play can seem to be registered in its particular idea
of place. The cold prison of Elsinore with its waiting
graveyard, Macbeth's hell-castle, the imperial panorama of *Antony and Cleopatra* – each substantially
defines the imaginative world of its play. Place may
be employed in a loosely suggestive, symbolic
fashion, as it is in *King Lear*; or it may be realized with
the densely social particularity of *Romeo and Juliet*;
but it is always closely bound up with the metaphoric
structure of the work. *Othello* is no exception: an
essentially domestic tragedy is elevated to heroic
dignity partly by the boldness of its geographic scale.
Like *Antony and Cleopatra* it straddles the Mediterranean; but there the resemblance ends. The action

of the later play is characterized by a continual
advance and retreat, which matches the psychological
vacillation of its protagonist, the flux of his political
fortunes, and the corresponding ebb and flow of the
audience's sympathies. The movement of *Othello*, by
contrast, is as remorselessly one-way as the current
of that Pontic Sea to which the hero compares his
driving passion of revenge. There is, accordingly,
only a single significant change of place – the voyage
from Venice to Cyprus at the end of act 1. This
contrast in part reflects the different power-relation-
ships prevailing in the political worlds of the two
plays: Rome and Egypt are rival constellations,
Cyprus a mere satellite of Venice. Armies and orders
issue from Venice, Cyprus receives them; the
metropolis is a source of power, the colony a passive
object of competing powers. Where in *Antony* the
movement from Egypt to Rome or from Rome to
Egypt always contains the potential for enlargement
of the self – or at least for liberation of those aspects
of the self which one or other of the play's
antithetical worlds suppresses – in *Othello* the translation from Venice to Cyprus leads to self-estrange-
ment and a kind of diminution. It is (as John
Barton's celebrated Stratford-upon-Avon production in 1971 properly emphasized) a movement to a
narrower, more enclosed world, a place of colonial
exile – a movement from city to garrison town. Its
finality is marked by the storm which intervenes
between the first and second acts, dividing the two
worlds of this play as absolutely as the tempest which
concludes the first movement of *The Winter's Tale*;
but here there will be no lucky peripety, no

counter-movement of redemption. The 'foul and violent tempest' which parts the ships of Cassio and the Moor (2.1.34) clearly anticipates the storm of passion which will part their friendship for ever; the voyage itself parts Desdemona and Othello before their marriage can be consummated, and here too the tempest symbolically announces a division which will be resolved only in the perverted consummation of act 5.[1] As so often in Shakespeare, the sea-voyage amounts to a rite of passage: it is as though some fatal boundary had been crossed – from this bourn no traveller returns.

Venice is the city of the play, its metropolitan centre; but the civilization it represents proves, on closer inspection, to be no more ideal than that of its counterpart in *The Merchant of Venice*. Iago's racial slurs and Brabantio's answering outrage make it plain from the beginning that, beneath its ceremonious courtesies, Shakespeare's Venice is a society capable of treating any stranger, any ethnic outsider with the same calculating cruelty it meted out to Shylock. 'There's many a beast then in a populous city, / And many a civil monster', Iago tells Othello in a characteristically veiled sarcasm (4.1.63–4): the remark is doubly Janus-faced, for beyond its glance at the supposed horning of Othello by the urbane monsters Cassio and Desdemona, it means to point at the Venetian Moor himself as a kind of tamed Caliban, a civilized barbarian; while by a further reach of irony Iago identifies himself as the true beast of his populous city, the 'Spartan dog' of Lodovico's final denunciation (5.2.357), a barbarous monster beneath his civil guise of honesty. The fetches of Iago's policy are designed to expose the essential savagery of his 'stranger' general; but what they produce is an Othello remade in Iago's own monstrous image.

Like the Venice of *The Merchant* too, this is a city whose most humane values can seem compromised by its mercantile ethics: its language of love, typically, is tainted by metaphors of trade, purchase, and possession. Here women are to men rather as Cyprus is to Venice and Turkey – objects of competition, possession, and 'occupation': indeed Brabantio's reply to the Duke's sententious consolation on the loss of his daughter – 'The robbed that smiles steals

something from the thief' – makes precisely that equation:

> So let the Turk of Cyprus us beguile,
> We lose it not so long as we can smile.
>
> (1.3.206, 208–9)

It is natural in this world that Iago and Brabantio should concur in seeing Desdemona's abduction as, like Jessica's, the theft of a father's rightful property; it is perhaps more disturbing to notice that even Othello's language, for all its rhetorical magnificence, finally pictures love as a fabulous treasure, an object of erotic commerce:

> The purchase made, the fruits are to ensue:
> The profit's yet to come 'tween me and you.
>
> (2.3.9–10)

However gracefully bantering its expression, the metaphor here is close to that crass possessiveness which lies at the root of all jealousy – as we may quickly feel in the more obviously corrupted language of the temptation scene:

Othello.
> What sense had I of her stolen hours of lust?...
> He that is robbed, not wanting what is stolen,
> Let him not know't, and he's not robbed at all.
>
> (3.3.335, 339–40)

Cruelly enough, the attitude persists even through Othello's finest agonies of remorse, where his imagination seems tormented by the sense of the

---

[1] For a highly persuasive argument that the marriage is never properly consummated, see T. G. A. Nelson and Charles Haines, 'Othello's Unconsummated Marriage', *Essays in Criticism*, 23 (1983), 1–18. To the mass of circumstantial detail on which they rest their case, I would add the suggestive simile with which Iago describes the falling out of Cassio and Montano:

> Friends all but now, even now,
> In quarter and in terms like bride and groom
> Devesting them for bed: and then but now –
> As if some planet had unwitted men –
> Swords out, and tilting one at other's breasts
> In opposition bloody. (2.3.173–8)

All citations from *Othello* are to the edition by Kenneth Muir (Harmondsworth, 1968).

prize he has lost to the virtual exclusion of any sense of the living woman he has destroyed:[2]

> If heaven would make me such another world
> Of one entire and perfect chrysolite,
> I'd not have sold her for it.   (5.2.143–5)

>   one whose hand
> Like the base Indian threw a pearl away
> Richer than all his tribe.   (5.2.342–4)

Even Othello, then, has partly absorbed the values of a Venice which, for all its civilized and heroic airs, is less remote than might appear from Ben Jonson's metropolis of greed, or even Otway's Adriatic Whore, the proverbial capital of European prostitution. Indeed it is precisely upon this sense of the city as a community of 'customers' that Iago, that busy merchant-factor, is able to capitalize in presenting Desdemona to her husband as 'that cunning whore of Venice / That married with Othello' (4.2.88–9):

> I know our country disposition well:
> In Venice they do let God see the pranks
> They dare not show their husbands; their best
>   conscience
> Is not to leave't undone, but keep't unknown.
>   (3.3.199–202)

Yet with all its deficiencies and occasional ugliness, for all the hidden savagery of its 'civil monsters', Venice remains a true *polis*, a civilizing and ordered place where the calm and rational interventions of ducal authority are an effective check against the storms of a Brabantio's wrath or an Iago's envy. No such effective sanctions govern Cyprus: it is another country.

Shakespeare's audience knew Cyprus as the Venetian colony briefly rescued from the Turks by the triumphant Battle of Lepanto in 1571; so that, as Emrys Jones has demonstrated, the action is tied to a fairly precise historical as well as geographical location.[3] It capitalizes, however, on much older associations: Cyprus, the audience might also have remembered, was sacred to foam-born Venus as the place where the goddess renewed her virginity after her adulterous liaison with Mars. This was the island of erotic myth where John Ford would locate his *The Lover's Melancholy* (c.1629); and the Cyprus to

which we are introduced at the beginning of Shakespeare's second act seems at first to be infused with something of that ancient grace. The miraculous tempest which providentially destroys and scatters the Turkish fleet is evoked in Shakespeare's most exuberant and sprightly verse, whose tone contrasts as sharply as possible with the brooding ratiocination of Iago's soliloquy at the end of act 1. Retrospectively we may see the storm as prefiguring the emotional turbulence of the later acts; but in its immediate context it has the effect of a welcome release to the pent-up emotional energies of act 1 – a feeling emphasized by the lively excitement and bustle of Montano and his companions. It is as though the air were suddenly cleared of that murk of slander and intrigue which fouled the atmosphere of Venice; and the marvellous gaiety of the Venetians' arrival helps to confirm the impression that they have indeed been translated to the traditional domain of love. Cassio is at his most spiritedly cavalier, Desdemona full of high, nervous anticipation, and even Iago, playing with disarming insouciance the role of urbane jester in a lady's court, appears for a short time (however misleadingly) liberated from his claustrophobic hutch of resentment; while, as for Othello, he speaks with the relaxed and affectionate confidence of one who has come home:

> How does my old acquaintance of this isle?
> Honey, you shall be well desired in Cyprus:
> I have found great love amongst them.
>   (2.1.197–9)

In fact, of course, as their departure for the citadel quickly reminds us, this is an island prepared not for love but for war; and these voyagers have come to the shut-in society of a garrison town, the sort of place that feeds on rumour and festers with suspicion. Amply fulfilling those sinister confusions of black and white suggested in Iago's teasing riddles at the

---

[2] For further comment on the significance of commercial imagery in the play see Edward A. Snow, 'Sexual Anxiety and the Male Order of Things in *Othello*', *English Literary Renaissance*, 10 (1980), 384–412.

[3] Emrys Jones, '"Othello", "Lepanto" and the Cyprus Wars', *Shakespeare Survey 21* (Cambridge, 1968), 47–52.

harbour (2.1.128–32), this is a world whose whispering can transform the marriage-bed itself to the centre-piece of some luxurious Venetian brothel, and make the 'fair Desdemona' seem indistinguishable from the prostituted Bianca (whose own name, ironically enough, means 'white' or 'fair'). It is a place where no one is truly at home, and where the only native Cypriot we meet is, significantly, the jealous camp-follower, Bianca. 'Jealousy in itself', Northrop Frye remarks, 'tends to create an enclosed prison-world';[4] and this Cyprus is its perfect physical correlative. Far from providing a refuge from urban corruption, it is a colonial outpost of civilization where the worst Venetian values can flourish unchecked by any normative social order. Desdemona above all is a stranger to it; cut off from her family, effectually removed from those 'Of her own clime, complexion and degree', a woman almost alone in a conspicuously masculine realm, she is as isolated and potentially vulnerable as Othello in the subtle world of Venice. To the extent that the Cyprus wars have returned the martial Othello to the military environment he knows best, husband and wife may seem at first to have changed places. But the activity of the civil monster Iago ensures that this impression is short-lived, Desdemona has merely come to share the Moor's continuing isolation; each is a stranger whose only 'place' is in the other's heart. In the first act Othello spoke of his marriage to Desdemona in terms of a willing exchange of freedom:

> But that I love the gentle Desdemona,
> I would not my unhousèd free condition
> Put into circumscription and confine
> For the seas' worth.   (1.2.25–8)

The vicious psychological circumscription of Cyprus will give an ugly new meaning to that careless metaphor, as the action of the play moves from the relative freedom of the city to the cramping confines of a besieged citadel. The siege which seems to be lifted at the opening of act 2 has, in reality, only just begun: Desdemona's virtue is its imagined object, Othello's consciousness its true battleground – for that is the fortified 'place' which Iago will methodically reduce and occupy. Indeed

the whole action of the play might be read in terms of sinister distortions and displacements of the old metaphor of erotic siege.

But 'place' has another, even more potent significance in *Othello* – one which provides the key to Iago's consuming passion of resentment. The importance of Venice as the metropolitan centre of the play world is that it supplies, or offers to supply, each individual with a clearly defined and secure position within an established social order: indeed it is precisely the city's idea of 'place' (a term which includes 'office' and 'rank' as well as 'status') which distinguishes it from the barbarous world beyond, that vaguely imagined wilderness to which Iago consigns his 'stranger' General. The displaced Venetians of the Cypriot garrison are solidly located solely by virtue of the 'place' they bring with them, above all their rank in the state's military hierarchy. In such circumstances 'place' is liable to become an object of unusually ferocious competition; but of course it was already an issue before the departure from Venice. The magnifico, Brabantio, woken by the 'malicious bravery' of Iago and Roderigo, instinctively rebukes them with an appeal to 'My spirit and my place' (1.1.104) – the same lofty 'place' upon whose potency he relies in arraigning Othello before his fellow senators (1.3.53). To be thus confident of one's place is to feel at home in a very important sense: it is to have a particularly firm idea of the rights and dignities attaching to one's function in this society. Neither Iago nor Othello is at home in quite this way: that is the ground of their fatally shared insecurity.

Iago's notion of himself is as a man whose expectations are properly governed not merely by his personal worth, but also by his being native to the place called Venice. This, in his estimate, properly raises him above such outsiders as Othello and Cassio. From Iago's point of view (as to Brabantio's prejudiced eyes) Othello is a man without any true place, 'an extravagant and wheeling stranger / Of here and everywhere' (1.1.137–8), a man whose

---

[4] Northrop Frye, *Fools of Time* (Toronto and London, 1967), p. 102.

undeserved office can be tossed aside with that dismissive mock-honorific, 'his Moorship' (1.1.33). He discovers a special bitterness, therefore, in the fact that it should be this contemptible alien who has conspired to keep him from his own rightful place – and that in favour of yet another stranger, 'One Michael Cassio, a Florentine' (1.1.20). The heavy metrical stress on the first syllable of 'Florentine' exactly catches the force of Iago's scorn, the curl of his lip. In his own estimate he is a man doubly displaced; and this is the theme of his tirades in the opening scene:

> Three great ones of the city,
> In personal suit to make me his Lieutenant,
> Off-capped to him: and by the faith of man,
> I know my price, I am worth no worse a place.
> (1.1.8–11)

Iago's sense of self, as this speech already suggests, is founded upon the treacherous relativities of comparison. For such a man to be bilked of the place which answers to his conviction of his own market price is to be cheated of identity, since the very centre of his being is to be found in that obsessive concern for what is 'wholesome to my place' (1.1.146).

Iago is possessed by comparison: it is hardly too much to say that he has *become* comparison. For him nothing (and no one) has a value in and of itself, but only as a measure or object of comparison – hence his overriding faith in money, that ultimate agent of comparison which offers to place everything within a comprehensive taxonomy of price. Such a construction of the world does, however, invoke its own nemesis, for it commits one to a devouring torment of self-comparison that has, in principle, no end. In act 1 Iago presents himself to Roderigo as a model of rational self-love (1.3.311), one of those who know how to 'Do themselves homage' (1.1.54); he is thus a free man, liberated from those bonds of service, affection and duty which, by putting a man comprehensively in his place, serve as constant provocations of unwelcome comparison, stinging reminders of the price that others put upon one. Yet ironically enough the very speeches in which this claim is most fiercely advanced are full of nagging self-comparison – both with those whose servitude he despises and those whose superior authority he resents:

> We cannot all be masters, nor all masters
> Cannot be truly followed. You shall mark
> Many a duteous and knee-crooking knave
> That, doting on his own obsequious bondage,
> Wears out his time, much like his master's ass,
> For naught but provender, and when he's
>   old – cashiered!
> Whip me such honest knaves. Others there are
> Who, trimmed in forms and visages of duty,
> Keep yet their hearts attending on themselves...
> It is as sure as you are Roderigo,
> Were I the Moor, I would not be Iago:
> In following him, I follow but myself. (1.1.43–59)

Iago dreams of a world without comparison, a bureaucratic Utopia in which place is determined by the 'old gradation, where each second / Stood heir to th'first' (1.1.37–8); yet this ideal of egalitarian succession is contradicted by his wounded sense of superiority to both the braggart Moor, with his 'bombast circumstance / Horribly stuffed with epithets of war', and to the desk-soldier, Cassio, that 'counter-caster' with his 'bookish theoric' (ll. 13–31). The true accountant, endlessly poring over his ledger of 'debitor and creditor', is, needless to say, Iago himself. For Iago is a kind of moral mercantilist: there is only a certain stock of virtue in the world, and by that rule one man's credit must necessarily be another's debit:

> If Cassio do remain
> He hath a daily beauty in his life
> That makes me ugly. (5.1.18–20)

Cassio's charm, Desdemona's goodness, Othello's nobility – none of these can be granted an intrinsic worth or independent significance; each is comprehensible only as an implicit criticism of Iago's life. Intolerable objects of comparison whose very existence challenges his place in the order of things, they must be eliminated.

The villain's preoccupation with displacement is, interestingly enough, one of Shakespeare's principal additions to the story. In Giraldi Cinthio's *Hecatom-*

mithi, Iago's equivalent, the Ensign, is motivated not by thwarted ambition, but by lust; it is not his rival's rank that the Ensign covets, but his favour with Disdemona. It is worth asking why Shakespeare, who seems to have worked with a version of Giraldi beside him and who otherwise seldom departs from his original without good reason, should have chosen to make 'place' the point at issue in this way.[5] Kenneth Muir's explanation (fairly representative of those critics who have troubled to pose the question) is that it is merely a device to complicate the villain's motives. The loss of promotion is one of three stings of envy which have lodged in Iago: it combines with 'pathological jealousy of his wife' and 'a jealous love of Desdemona' to arouse his hatred of the Moor; but in Muir's estimate it is the least important of the three because it 'is not directly mentioned after the start of the play, except once'.[6] I should argue that the sheer dramatic prominence given to the lost lieutenancy by the opening dialogue establishes it as so much an essential *donnée* of the action that it scarcely needs reiteration – particularly since Iago's nagging consciousness of the slight is registered in a self-lacerating punctilio over Cassio's title of rank. He uses the word 'lieutenant' more often than all the other characters of the play together: fifteen of its twenty-five occurrences are from his mouth, where it increasingly sounds like a kind of sarcastic caress. Just as tellingly it is Othello's 'Now art thou my Lieutenant' (3.3.475) – perhaps the weightiest half-line in the tragedy – which announces Iago's moment of supreme triumph. Far from being a mere aggravation of the villain's envious disposition, the question of place lies at the very heart of the play: properly understood it is the only begetter of that 'monstrous birth' which issues from the fertile womb of Iago's resentment.

At the same time as he made the question of promotion the focus of Iago's bitterness, Shakespeare also elected to change his rival's rank. In Giraldi, Cassio's counterpart is called 'the Captain'. The alteration may, at first sight, seem trivial, but its inherent improbability makes it virtually certain that it was done with deliberate purpose: for while captain was a long-established military rank, lieutenant was still something of a novelty; in Shakespeare's own plays where 'captain' is commonplace, 'lieutenant' is relatively rare, occurring only nine times in the rest of the canon. In six of these cases it appears to denote a specific grade of officer, more or less equivalent to the modern rank, in the others it carries its older, more general sense of 'deputy' or 'substitute'; only in *Othello* does it seem to describe a rank immediately below that of general, corresponding to the modern lieutenant-general. Clearly, then, the word had not yet stabilized to its modern meaning and still carried a good deal of its original French sense, 'one holding [another's] place' (*lieu tenant*); and in a play so ferociously preoccupied with place it inevitably develops the force of a peculiarly bitter pun.[7] For Iago in particular it acts as a constant reminder that Cassio is not merely the man appointed to deputize in the general's place, but the one who is standing in his own. While Cassio is in the ascendant, Iago probes the word as one might an aching tooth, goading the pain of his own deprivation; and then, as his rival's star begins to wane, 'lieutenant' becomes a term of contempt, a covert sarcasm anticipating their change of places. Thus the high point of Iago's vindictive pleasure in the drinking scene is reached with Cassio's stumbling recognition that he is behaving in a fashion 'unworthy of his place' (2.3.96), and registered in Iago's softly crowing response, 'It's true, good Lieutenant' (l. 100). His triumph is confirmed by Montano's sober expression of disappointment.

> 'tis great pity that the noble Moor
> Should hazard such a place as his own second
> With one of an ingraft infirmity.   (2.3.133–5)

---

[5] See M. R. Ridley (ed.), *Othello*, the Arden Shakespeare, paperback edn. (1965), Appendix 1, p. 238.

[6] See the introduction to his New Penguin edition, pp. 20, 15.

[7] It is just possible that the pun was emphasized by Shakespeare's preferred pronunciation of the word, since the alternative spelling 'lieftenant', which is thought to represent the usual seventeenth-century pronunciation, occurs only once in the canon (in the Quarto text of *2 Henry IV*, 5.5.95). That Shakespeare was thinking of his titles of rank in this way is given some independent confirmation by the apparent play on Iago's rank (ancient/ensign) at 1.1.157–8: 'I must show out a flag and sign of love, / Which is indeed but sign'.

When Othello enters to check the ensuing brawl, Iago is ready with a rebuke that uses the terms of rank to hint successfully at cashierment while maintaining an air of honest and properly deferential concern: 'Hold, ho, Lieutenant, sir . . . Have you forgot all sense of place and duty' (ll. 160–1). Once the cashierment is achieved Cassio's place must surely follow the old gradation and fall to Iago; and Othello's promise at the end of the temptation scene, 'Now art thou my Lieutenant', sounds almost like a formal commissioning. Iago, characteristically, registers his richly ironic satisfaction at this change of places by continuing to dignify his rival with his lost rank, a joke which develops a special relish in his last veiled jeer at the wounded Cassio (as Q1 prints it): 'O *my lieutenant*, what villains have done this?' (5.1.56).[8] The plot to kill Cassio, after all, has stemmed not (as is commonly assumed) from the desire to get rid of an inconvenient potential witness ('the Moor / May unfold me to him', 5.1.20–1), but from Iago's bitter spite at the discovery that 'there is especial commission come from Venice to depute Cassio in Othello's place' (4.2.219–20). This is lieutenantry with a vengeance! – by a kind of cheating pun it mockingly fulfils the very libel he has put on Cassio, whilst robbing Iago of the coveted place he has just obtained with so much labour. With that final 'my Lieutenant' Iago means to say good night to one who has never done more than hold his own rightful place and is now about to surrender it for ever.

Since Coleridge first accused him of 'motiveless malignity', there has been much debate over the allegedly confused and contradictory nature of Iago's motives. But the problem exists only if one makes the doubtful assumption that, to be psychologically plausible, motivation need be coherent, systematic and rational. What is significant about Iago's various self-explanations is not so much their apparent factual inconsistencies as their deadly consistency of tone and attitude. It hardly matters that the alleged reasons for his behaviour are changeable or even incompatible, since they are, in the last analysis, only stimuli to the expression of that underlying resentment which is the principal defining trait of his personality: they are all, to this degree,

rationalizations for an attitude towards the world whose real origins lie much deeper, within the impregnable fortress of silence into which Iago withdraws at the end of the play. Indeed I take it to be profoundly true of emotions like resentment, envy, and jealousy that they are in some sense *their own motive*. As Emilia puts it, in response to Desdemona's baffled reaching for a 'cause', the jealous

> are not ever jealous for the cause,
> But jealous for they're jealous. It is a monster
> Begot upon itself, born on itself. (3.4.156–8)[9]

Resentment dreams of usurpation as jealousy dreams of cuckoldry, but is itself the cuckoo of displacement: '*it* is the cause' – at once motive, justification and purpose in a system as hermetically closed as the enigmatic syntax of Othello's great soliloquy.

Psychologically speaking, then, there is no conflict between Iago's professional envy and his sexual jealousy: one indeed follows naturally from the other, since both are symptomatic expressions of his core of resentment, the cancer of comparison at the heart of his being. Displacement from one office can seem almost tantamount to replacement in the other; the only doubt concerns the question of who is to be held responsible – the man who has put him

---

[8] In this and all other quotations from the play the italicized emphases are my own.

[9] The idea of jealousy as a kind of 'monstrous birth' seems to have been a potent one for Shakespeare: it lies behind Othello's 'strong conception / That I do groan withal' (5.2.55–6), and is built into the structure of *The Winter's Tale* where a clear parallel is developed between the corrupted 'issue' of Leontes's suspicious mind and the supposedly corrupt 'issue' of Hermione's womb. The self-generating nature of jealousy is noted by Freud in 'Some Neurotic Mechanisms in Jealousy, Paranoia and Homosexuality' (*Works*, vol. 18, p. 223), and is discussed by the American psychologist Leslie H. Farber in 'On Jealousy', *Lying, Despair, Jealousy, Envy, Sex, Suicide, Drugs and the Good Life* (New York, 1976), pp. 188, 193–9; for Farber jealousy is the expression of a personality which has taken refuge from its own felt inadequacy in an excessive dependence on the love and esteem of another – in this sense 'the crucial source of [the jealous person's] pain *is* his corruption' (p. 196); jealousy therefore 'is self-confirming: it breeds itself' (p. 188).

out of his place, or the one who has taken it? To begin with it is Othello who is the single object of a suspicion which seems to grow spontaneously from those fantasies of sexual athleticism which Iago concocts for Brabantio:

> Your heart is burst, you have lost half your soul.
> Even now, now, very now, an old black ram
> Is tupping your white ewe. (1.1.88–90)

The striking thing about this speech is that it presents the abduction of a daughter as though it were an act of adultery – an adultery conceived (like Desdemona's later) in terms of both physical and psychological displacement. The elopement is said to rob Brabantio of half his own soul: it is almost, as the quibble promoted by the relentless hammered stresses on 'your white *ewe*' suggests, as though the rape were on Brabantio's own person. The imaginative intensity of Iago's vision far exceeds what is required by the mere theatre of the occasion: in the 'old black ram', the 'Barbary horse', and the heaving 'beast with two backs', are projected Iago's own loathing and fear of Othello as sexual rival. The imposture works upon Brabantio as effectively as it does only because of the degree of Iago's own emotional engagement with the scene he invents; but equally it is only through the excitement of this invention that he discovers his own sexual insecurity and with it a new torment of comparison to which his soliloquy in scene 3 gives voice:

> I hate the Moor,
> And it is thought abroad that 'twixt my sheets
> He's done *my office*. (1.3.380–2)

The point of promoting Cassio to Othello as a rival for Desdemona is not merely to 'get his place', but to turn the tables on the cuckold-maker by exposing him to the shame of cuckoldry. The wounding comparison to which Iago has been subject by Othello's sexual prowess will be cancelled by subjecting the Moor to a similar denigration. Ironically however the logic of Iago's temperament ensures that his leering recollection of Cassio's 'person...framed to make women false' (ll. 391–2) plants a further seed of resentment and suspicion which matures in the following scene. By now he

has convinced himself that the adultery is a matter of simple fact:

> That Cassio loves her, I do well believe't:
> That she loves him, 'tis apt and of great credit.
> (2.1.277–8)

Resentment typically tends to reduce everything to its own level; and the fantasy is flattering because, by putting Cassio in Othello's place, it puts Othello in Iago's own.[10] Beyond that, it appeals to the perverse eroticism which is a paradoxical constituent of all jealousy;[11] and it is this that produces the parallel fantasy by which Iago in turn takes Cassio's place in Desdemona's bed:

> Now, I do love her too;
> Not out of absolute lust – though peradventure
> I stand accountant for as great a sin –
> But partly led to diet my revenge
> For that I do suspect the lusty Moor
> Hath leaped into my seat, the thought whereof
> Doth, like a poisonous mineral, gnaw my inwards,
> And nothing can, or shall, content my soul
> Till I am evened with him, wife for wife.
> (2.1.282–90)

The shocking way in which the metaphors of eating here ('diet ... gnaw') confuse sexual appetite with the devouring emotions of jealousy and revenge,[12] emphasizes the dangerously volatile interrelation of these apparently opposite drives; but Iago is able to protect himself against the frenzy into which a similar welter of feelings will drive Othello by retreating into the reassuringly objective language of

---

10 For an account of resentment which makes it seem a much more exact description of Iago's ruling passion than the traditional 'envy', see Robert C. Solomon, *The Passions: the Myth and Nature of Human Emotion* (New York, 1976), pp. 350–5.

11 See Freud, pp. 223–4; and Farber, pp. 190–1. The same pornographic excitement can be sensed in the excesses of Othello's imagination – 'I had been happy if the general camp, / Pioners and all, had tasted her sweet body...' (3.3.342–3); and he attempts to give these fantasies a hideous reality in the brothel scene (4.2).

12 Cf. Iago's description of jealousy as 'mock[ing] / The meat it feeds on' (3.3.165–6), where 'meat' includes *both* the psyche on which the monster battens and (at a further remove) the object of sexual appetite itself.

moral accounting ('evened with him, wife for wife'). The calculus, however, leads to its own disturbance, for insofar as Cassio seems a likely usurper of Othello's seat, he may just as well have pilfered Iago's cap of matrimonial office: 'I fear Cassio with my night-cap too' (l. 298). It is a suspicion which, at a casual glance, may seem to disappear as suddenly and arbitrarily as it grips him; but in fact it is another of those extraordinary flashes which fitfully illuminate the dark night of Iago's inner self, making him seem a figure of infinitely greater complexity than the stage devil or vice he is sometimes mistaken for. It is possible to trace his painfully self-wounding fascination with Cassio's sexual potency through the elaborate dream-fantasy of the temptation scene: just as his sexual envy of the Moor was first apparent in the bestial porno-graphy of the 'black ram' speech, so here his jealous hatred of the Lieutenant surfaces through the ambiguous sexual excitements of his concocted night with Cassio:

In sleep I heard him say: 'Sweet Desdemona,
Let us be wary, let us hide our loves';
And then, sir, would he gripe and wring my hand,
Cry 'O sweet creature!' and then kiss me hard,
As if he plucked up kisses by the roots,
That grew upon my lips; then laid his leg
Over my thigh, and sighed and kissed, and then
Cried 'Cursèd fate that gave thee to the Moor!'
(3.3.416–23)

As in the earlier episode with Brabantio, the calumny can lodge its sting so effectually only because of Iago's own intense identification with the sexual humiliation he describes. In this context it is tempting to see his attempt on Cassio's life, his determination to make him 'uncapable of Othello's place' (4.2.228), as constituting in part an act of sexual revenge. The political murder he envisages, as the sardonic pun on 'uncapable' suggests, and as that mysteriously emphasized wound 'in the leg' tends to confirm, is also a physical emasculation, a final and absolute displacement of the hated usurper.[13]

From the very opening of the play, it should be clear, Iago's imagination feeds upon (as it is eaten by) fantasies of displacement – public, domestic, and

sexual: such is the self-devouring nature of that 'green-eyed monster' whose habit he understands so well. But there is another side to his scheming, revealed in the glee with which he contemplates the ingenious symmetries of his vengeful design. In act I, scene 3 the inculpation of Cassio holds out the prospect of a 'double knavery' (l. 338): setting out 'To get [Cassio's] place' (l. 387), he will achieve it by making Cassio appear to have taken Othello's. Cassio's crime against himself will be matched by the Lieutenant's imagined crime against his general – the usurpation of one rightful place being balanced against the usurpation of another; and the effect will be to link Cassio and Desdemona in Othello's mind as seconds who have proved unworthy of their office. The growing conviction that both Othello and Cassio have usurped his own place with Emilia gives a further ironic aptness to the scheme by making Othello his own surrogate as both cuckold-victim and potential revenger. For a time he even dreams of crowning this elaborately witty contri-vance by himself taking the Moor's place with Desdemona; but that is perhaps too commonplace a solution: his last and most perfect usurpation, as we shall see, will be to take Desdemona's place with Othello. Such refinements help one to remember how much Iago owes to the earlier villain-heroes of the Elizabethan stage like Barabas and Richard III. Like them he is a conscious and self-delighting artist in evil (much more than the detached Baconian scientist of Auden's famous essay);[14] and his pleasure in the aesthetic cunning of his creations is matched by a delight in verbal ingenuity, in puns, *double entendre*s and ironic equivoques. Like Richard's tutor-Vice, Iniquity, he has learned to 'moralise two meanings in one word'; and he weaves his net for Cassio, Othello, and Desdemona from the threads of ambiguous hint and ambivalent suggestion. But this verbal duplicity also operates at a deeper and

---

13 A wound in the thigh is, of course, a traditional euphemism for gelding; and the emphasis on the place of the wound seems to gather a special significance from the obscene imagery of Iago's dream-fantasy ('then laid his leg / Over my thigh, and sighed and kissed', 3.3.421–2).
14 W. H. Auden, 'The Joker in the Pack', in *The Dyer's Hand* (1937).

more vicious emotional level. When, for instance, the mechanism of Iago's revenge first begins to move in the drinking scene, his satisfaction at the smoothness of its functioning finds play in a passage of intensely private innuendo. He steers the Lieutenant towards Desdemona in a speech whose apparently innocent language is full of gloating sexual suggestiveness:

Confess yourself freely to her; importune her help to *put you in your place* again. She is so *free*, so *kind*, so *apt*, so blessed a disposition, that she holds it a vice in her goodness not to *do* more than she is requested.

(2.3.309–12)

'Place' here (though Cassio cannot hear it) has begun to carry that obscene sense which Iago will deploy to such deadly effect in the temptation scene:

> Although 'tis fit that Cassio have his place,
> For sure he *fills it up* with great *ability*,
> Yet, if you please to hold him off awhile,
> You shall by that perceive him and his means;
> Note if your lady *strain* his *entertainment*
> With any strong or vehement importunity –
> Much will be seen in that.   (3.3.244–50)[15]

Even the concluding appeal to 'hold her free' (l. 253) seems to involve, beneath its frank concession of Desdemona's probable innocence, a dark suggestion of licentiousness. That these *double entendre*s have found their mark is suggested by Othello's tight-lipped response, 'Fear not my government' (l. 254), tersely asserting his claim not merely to stoical self-control, but to domestic and sexual rule.[16] Othello, as we shall see, has always felt his political 'government' to be in some sense dependent on the private office of his love; now he is being lured into the demented conflation of the two which first appeared in Iago's diseased imagination.

By its wanton insistence on arbitrary associations the pun is a perfect instrument of emotions such as jealousy and resentment which thrive on paranoid connection. It is characteristic of jealousy, with its obsessional reaching after certainties which it at once needs yet cannot bear to face, that it should track the paths of suspicion with the doubtful clews of pun and equivoque; and it is no accident that word-play

should be of special significance both in *Othello* and in Shakespeare's other drama of jealousy, *The Winter's Tale*. In each case the action can be seen to hang upon the fatal doubleness of certain words, the ambiguity of certain signs. There is a kind of awful decorum about this, that jealousy with its compulsive dreams of adulterous substitution should discover a self-lacerating pleasure in what is essentially a form of semantic displacement, in which one meaning surreptitiously, adulterously even, takes the place of another. The pun is a kind of verbal bed-trick – as essential to the process of inner displacement by which an Othello or a Leontes collaborates in his own destruction as to Iago's sleight-of-hand. The very triviality of the device (which Shakespeare seems reflexively to acknowledge in Leontes's murderous teasing of meaning from the innocence of 'play'[17]) corresponds to that ultimate triviality of motive so characteristic of jealousy; it is what carries the drama of jealousy uncomfortably close to the border of black comedy which *The Winter's Tale* often crosses, and helps to make the action of *Othello* the most meanly degrading – in some respects, therefore, the cruellest – of all the tragedies.

It was this aspect of *Othello* which excited Thomas Rymer's notorious indignation. The focus of his scorn was the handkerchief device: the handkerchief provides Othello with the certainty he both craves and fears, it is the pivot of the entire tragic design; and yet, as Rymer saw, there is a kind of desperate frivolity about it.[18] The whole embroidery which Iago weaves about this patch of cloth, culminating in the carefully mounted 'ocular proof' of act 4,

---

[15] For the bawdy meanings of the italicized words in this and the previous quotation, see the relevant entries in Eric Partridge, *Shakespeare's Bawdy* (1969). Nelson and Haines, 'Unconsummated Marriage', 15–16, also notice the importance of bitter sexual punning as a sign of Othello's gathering dementia.

[16] For an equivalent use of 'government', see, for instance, Middleton's *Women Beware Women*, 1.3.45.

[17] *The Winter's Tale*, 1.2.187–90. For a discussion of word-play in *The Winter's Tale* see Molly Mahood's brilliant essay in *Shakespeare's Wordplay* (1957).

[18] See Curt A. Zimansky (ed.), *The Critical Works of Thomas Rymer* (New Haven, 1956), p. 163.

scene 1 and Cassio's contemptuous account of 'Desdemona's' infatuation with him, amounts to nothing more than an elaborate *double entendre*, a piece of perspective juggling, a theatrical *trompe l'oeil*, a kind of enacted pun. What is perhaps less obvious is the way in which the handkerchief develops its grip on Othello's jealous mind through a chain of verbal associations which convert it to a material substitute for the love between himself and Desdemona. The Moor's first encounter with his wife after the temptation scene finds its emotional course through a series of feverish quibbles: 'Give me your hand,' he demands (3.4.36), as if seeking reassurance in the familiar gesture of affection; but hardly is her hand in his than it becomes an object of furious scrutiny, as though the simple flesh itself concealed some treacherous meaning. 'This hand is moist... This argues fruitfulness and liberal heart... This hand of yours requires / A sequester from liberty... 'Tis a good hand, / A frank one . . . A liberal hand! The hearts of old gave hands; / But our new heraldry is hands, not hearts' (3.4.36–47). If the hand will not give up its secret, the words do: 'hand' leads by habitual association to 'heart'; and the condition of the heart in turn is disclosed by those maddening equivoques on 'liberal', 'liberty', and 'frank'; at the same time, by a curious semantic alchemy, hand and heart combine to remind him of that '*hand*kerchief... dyed in mummy . . . Conserved of maidens' *hearts*' (ll. 55–75).[19] Thus the handkerchief becomes for Othello both heart and hand together; it not merely stands for but, imaginatively speaking, *is* all that he has ever given Desdemona, all that she owes to him:

That handkerchief which I so loved and gave thee,
Thou gav'st to Cassio....
By heaven I saw my *handkerchief* in's *hand*!
O perjured woman! Thou dost stone my *heart*,...
I saw the handkerchief.   (5.2.48–66)

Once the poison of suspicion has been planted in Othello, language becomes for him a fabric of mocking duplicities as the world seems a tissue of deceiving appearances; so that by act 4, scene 1, when Iago's medicine has already thoroughly done its work, the most innocent remark can inspire a frenzy of jealous rage: he is like Wycherley's Pinchwife surrounded by that 'power of brave signs' each one of which carries its secret message of cuckoldom. Desdemona's harmless reference to 'the love I bear to Cassio' (l. 231) is heard as an outrageously public declaration of infidelity, provoking his enraged 'Fire and brimstone!'; and her pleasure in Lodovico's ill-timed announcement of the order 'Deputing Cassio in his government' (l. 237) only seems to redouble the public insult. To Othello's ear the order itself sounds as a covert taunt, gratuitous and cruel; and on the sexual *double entendre* lurking in 'government' depends the equally wounding ambivalence of Lodovico's soothing praise of Desdemona as 'an obedient lady' (l. 248), a compliment which Othello instantly converts to the mocking description of a compliant whore:

Sir, she can turn, and turn, and yet go on,
And turn again. And she can weep, sir, weep.
And she's obedient; as you say, obedient,
Very obedient.   (4.1.255–8)

Othello here is close to breakdown; he arrests the collapse briefly by turning away from this seeming travesty of domestic duty to the larger world of political obligation ('I *obey* the mandate', l. 261) only to confront once again the grotesque confusion of the two: language now begins to break upon the rack of equivocation –

Cassio shall have my place. And sir, tonight
I do entreat that we may sup together.
You are welcome, sir, to Cyprus. Goats and
     monkeys!   *Exit.*
                              (4.1.263–5)

Just beneath the surface of this speech there is a thread of frightful association ('Cassio...my place... tonight...sup together...welcome...to Cyprus')

---

[19] For the suggestion that the handkerchief with its strawberry spots constitutes a kind of visual pun on the wedding sheets, see Snow, 'Sexual Anxiety', pp. 390–2, Nelson and Haines, 'Unconsummated Marriage', pp. 8–10, and Lynda E. Boose, 'Othello's Handkerchief: "The Recognizance and Pledge of Love"', *English Literary Renaissance*, 5 (1975), 360–74. In the Nelson and Haines reading the pun becomes especially cruel because Othello's wedding sheets remain unstained with virgin blood until the murder.

which runs like a subterranean fuse towards the explosion of disgust and rage in 'Goats and monkeys'. It is as Iago has warned: Cassio has usurped his function; and by that fact Othello now seems to occupy precisely Iago's position at the beginning of the play, forced to surrender his military rank to one he suspects of having stolen his domestic office. To the baffled Lodovico it is as though the Moor's very self had been displaced: 'Is this the nature / Whom passion could not shake?' (ll. 267–8). He is not altogether mistaken: the deliberately muddy ambiguity of Iago's reaction exposes for the audience his satisfaction at the ironic perfection of Othello's apparent metamorphosis – 'He's that he is... If what he might he is not / I would to heaven he were' (ll. 272–4). The riddling patter takes us back to the beginning of the play and to Iago's 'I am not what I am'; now it is Othello who is not what he might be. As his sudden collapse into Iago's characteristic language of bestiality confirms, they two have changed places.

Othello, it must be said, is peculiarly vulnerable to such displacement. If Iago suffers from the devouring resentment of a man cheated of his place, Othello is threatened from the beginning with the even more radical insecurity of placelessness. He has, it is true, a strongly developed sense of the dignity of his rank: preparing to answer the libels of Brabantio he invokes the pride of his inheritance 'From men of royal siege' (1.2.22);[20] and in requesting 'fit disposition' for Desdemona during his absence at the wars he relies as much upon what is fitting to one of his status ('Due reference of place') as upon the proprieties demanded by 'her breeding' (1.3.234–7). But in Venice Othello's place must always be, to some degree, that of a stranger dependent on the favour of others for 'The trust, the office I do hold of you' (1.3.118); it is given warrant only by appeal to 'My services, which I have done the signory' (1.2.18). This appeal opens Othello's first significant speech in the play, an aria of self-affirmation which is echoed at the end in a splendidly defiant reassertion of the theme: 'I have done the state some service and they know't' (5.2.335). Just as the first act of the tragedy climaxes in Othello's investiture as general

commander against the Turk, so its last concludes with his formal repudiation of that command – a final self-cancelling exhibition of service by a Venetian officer whose very name (with its teasing suggestion of 'Othoman') has an oddly Turkish ring to it:

> And say, besides, that in Aleppo once
> Where a malignant and a turbaned Turk
> Beat a Venetian and traduced the state,
> I took by th'throat the circumcisèd dog
> And smote him thus.   (5.2.348–52)

This strangely triumphant demonstration of the contradictions of his being is the last of the play's enacted puns: it makes of Othello a kind of anamorphic beast with two backs, both Venetian and Turk; it invokes the claims of his military 'place' to declare his ultimate placelessness. What once promised to resolve these contradictions, what seemed to render his place something more than a mere mercenary rank, what properly located him within the order of the *polis* was the love of a Venetian woman – the very thing he has now destroyed. Othello's Venetian self is to a large extent Desdemona's creation; and her love for him seems the more overwhelming because it was awakened by her romantic response to his account of himself as a placeless wanderer:

> Wherein of antres vast and deserts idle,
> Rough quarries, rocks, and hills whose heads touch
>   heaven,
> It was my hint to speak – such was the process:
> And of the Cannibals that each other eat,
> The Anthropophagi, and men whose heads
> Do grow beneath their shoulders....
> She swore, in faith 'twas strange, 'twas passing
>   strange,
> 'Twas pitiful, 'twas wondrous pitiful;...
> She loved me for the dangers I had passed,
> And I loved her, that she did pity them.
>   (1.3.139–67)

It is above all his strangeness and extravagance (the very sources of Iago's resentful scorn) which excite

---

[20] 'Siege' (throne, seat) also carries, as *OED* shows, the standard metaphoric senses of 'class' and 'place of [rule]'.

Desdemona's wonder, pity, and love; and it is precisely this reaction which has awoken Othello to his heroic sense of himself: the wilderness landscapes, the human barbarities he recalls are touched with sublimity because he is seeing them, and by extension himself, through her beglamoured eyes. She is, in this sense, the very foundation of his conscious selfhood, the 'place' or citadel of his vulnerable identity. Not for nothing does Cassio speak of Desdemona as 'our great Captain's Captain' (2.1.74), or Iago sardonically declare that 'Our General's wife is now the General' (2.3.305–6); for it is as though only the self-esteem generated by the love of his 'fair warrior' (2.1.176) can validate the public esteem he is granted, can smother self-doubt of this displaced stranger and enable him to fill his place in the Venetian state with the supreme confidence he at first displays. This is what makes him a man to be reckoned with, one who, outsider though he is, can bear comparison with any man in Venice. But it is this too which opens him so fatally to Iago's attack, for it means that his very being is invested beyond himself, where it can seem peculiarly exposed to the frailty or malice of others.

Othello's passion for Desdemona is, in a radical sense, selfish. This is not to call in question its sincerity or to denigrate its intensity; but it does indicate an essential qualitative difference from Desdemona's love for him. For both of them, marriage is conceived as a form of 'office', involving for Othello a willing 'circumscription' of his 'free condition' (1.2.24–8) and for Desdemona a voluntary submission to her 'duty' (1.3.178–87).[21] But for her this implies a complete abdication of the will, an unqualified surrender of the self to the other of which Othello is incapable ('My heart's subdued / Even to the very quality of my lord', 1.3.247–8) – so much so that on the very point of death Desdemona reasserts herself in an act of quiet self-denial; questioned by Emilia as to who is responsible for her death, she quite simply offers herself in Othello's place: 'Nobody – I myself – farewell' (5.2.125). It is as far from the histrionic display of Othello's self-cancelling end as one could imagine. Yet there is no doubt which of the two has lost himself; for Othello has never been more than what his love and

'occupation' have made him, and from these he has cut himself adrift.

The connection which Othello makes between private and public roles is amply illustrated in his apologia to the Senate:

> If you do find me foul in her report,
> The trust, the office I do hold of you
> Not only take away, but let your sentence
> Even fall upon my life. (1.3.117–20)

The public trust is felt as naturally contingent upon his private faith, his political function upon his domestic office. It is inevitable, then, that any betrayal of his love for Desdemona should strike him as a double displacement, an expulsion from that place where both his public and private identity have been located. This is what is agonizingly glimpsed in the notorious pun which concludes his litany of loss in the temptation scene, 'Othello's occupation's gone' (3.3.354). The 'occupation' at issue at once includes his governorship of Cyprus, his larger military calling, his command over the fortress of Desdemona's affection, and, linked to this last (as John Bayley has rightly insisted), the bawdy meaning of erotic possession.[22] It is unnecessary to argue, as Bayley does, that the sexual *double entendre* is unconscious on Othello's part, since the various senses of the word are linked at a profound psychological level. The word-play marks the point at which, with a shock of terrible insight, Othello recognizes the consequences of that equation of public and private roles upon which he has built his life. He is, from that moment, a man utterly displaced.

Henceforth it is characteristically in terms of a lost or violated place that he imagines Desdemona's betrayal:

> But *there where* I have garnered up my heart,
> *Where* either I must live, or bear no life,
> The fountain from the which my current runs,

---

[21] For a sensitive account of this aspect of the play, see Jane Adamson, *'Othello' as Tragedy: some problems of judgement and feeling* (Cambridge, 1980).

[22] John Bayley, *Shakespeare and Tragedy* (1981), pp. 213–14. The pun emphasizes an underlying symmetry in the power relationships of the play: Desdemona is to Othello and Iago as Cyprus is to the Venetians and the Turks. The analogy is not, I believe, a casual one.

Or else dries up – to be discarded *thence*
Or keep it as a cistern for foul toads
To knot and gender in! Turn thy complexion *there*,
Patience, thou young and rose-lipped cherubin,
Ay, *there* look grim as hell!   (4.2.56–63)

In the condensed language of this speech the obsessively indicated 'there' is both the marriage-bed (that locus of domestic office) and the beloved's breast (that lodging of Petrarchan hearts); but, as the imagery of the speech gathers emotional force, it becomes something else, the equivalent of *Lear's* 'forfended place', the 'dark and vicious place' of begetting – the female well-spring of life itself, obscenely imagined as a reptilian mating pond. The toad-pool grows out of that earlier monstrous image of usurpation,

> I had rather be a toad
> And live upon the vapour of a dungeon
> Than keep a corner in the thing I love
> For others' uses.   (3.3.267–70)

Desdemona is for him not merely the precious 'thing', the stolen treasure of love's corrupted commerce, but herself the lost place of love, a violated paradise, transformed to an imprisoning hell – the very hell which, in the brothel scene, he imagines guarded by that lieutenant of Satan, Emilia:

> You, mistress,
> That have the office opposite to Saint Peter
> And keep the gate of hell!   (4.2.89–91)

This hell-gate, surely, opens on the same torture chamber which the maddened Lear imagines burning between a woman's legs – 'there's hell, there's darkness, / There is the sulphurous pit' (*King Lear*, 4.6.129–30).[23]

The ingenious symmetries of the revenge towards which Iago guides the Moor are precisely designed to answer to the latter's sense of cruel displacement: in the murderous consummation of his passion the place of love itself must become the place of punishment: 'Do it not with poison; strangle her in her bed, even the bed she hath contaminated' (4.1.206–7). For Iago this is perhaps no more than

the counter-casting of resentment: but for Othello the precise ironic 'justice' of the suggestion 'pleases' because it converts the act of murder into a species of abstract ritual: it is not so much the annihilation of a living woman as the ceremonial cleansing of a polluted place ('Thy bed, lust-stained, shall with lust's blood be spotted', 5.1.36) – hence the curiously impersonal grammar of his soliloquy over the sleeping Desdemona, 'this sorrow's heavenly – / It strikes where it doth love' (5.2.21–2). Not 'whom' but 'where'.[24] Desdemona is merely his place – the place which Cassio has taken.

To Othello's ear it is the mocking ambiguity of his orders from Venice ('Cassio shall have my place', 4.1.263) that puts the seal of public knowledge upon the double displacement which occurred when his own Lieutenant ('mine officer!', 4.1.201) usurped him in the office of Desdemona's bed. The audience, however, will recognize that Othello's real displacement is achieved elsewhere, in the great temptation scene; and to their ear it is confirmed in the hideously resonant exchange with which that scene concludes:

> *Othello.*...Now art thou my Lieutenant.
> *Iago.*
>   I am your own for ever.   (3.3.475–6)

Superficially Othello merely offers to confirm Iago in the promotion he has for so long coveted; but Iago's reply, picking up the suggestion of diabolic

---

23 For 'hell' as a cant term for the female pudendum, see Partridge, *Shakespeare's Bawdy* (p. 120), who cites Sonnet 144 ('I guess one angel in another's hell'). For an account of a production which emphasized the sexual significance of the 'place' imagined in these speeches, see Robert Cushman's review of the 1971 Mermaid and Stratford *Othellos* in *Plays and Players*, 19, no. 2 (November 1971), 32–6: Cushman attributed to Bruce Purchase's Moor (at the Mermaid) 'one glory: Othello delivers the speech beginning "Had it pleased heaven to try me with affliction" looking Desdemona straight in the crotch which makes unusual sense of the lines about "The fountain from the which my current runs" and particularly of the instruction "Turn thy complexion there".'

24 The grammatical oddity is the more striking because of its distortion of a familiar text, 'Whom the Lord loveth He chasteneth' (Hebrews 12: 6).

symbiosis in the Moor's earlier 'I am bound to thee for ever' (l. 211), points to his occupation of a very different office – that of second to Othello's jealous passion, the monstrous other-self of Iago's own creation, to which the General has surrendered his self-command. Iago has already hinted at its real nature in the mock reluctance of his engagement to prove Desdemona's treachery ('I do not like the office', l. 407) and the 'service' which he offers to Othello at ll. 460–6 is that of a Mephistophilis whose unholy office is to dispossess his master of his soul, to drive him from the occupation of his own self. If Desdemona is in Othello's mind a usurped place, Othello himself by the end of this scene has become occupied territory. The worst of torments he might otherwise imagine, he will declare to Desdemona, would leave 'in some place of my soul / A drop of patience' (4.2.51–2); but in the dungeon of his self no such place remains – patience has been dispossessed by the spirit of jealousy. Indeed the effect of the temptation is to make real the metaphor of diabolic possession with which Cassio lightheartedly toyed in the drinking scene ('It hath pleased the devil drunkenness to give place to the devil wrath', 2.3.287–8). Iago, evidently, is as much the informing spirit of Othello's revenge as he was that of Cassio's wrath.

The temptation scene, then, is about the sealing of a diabolical bond: it is the psychological equivalent of that episode in Marlowe's tragedy where Faustus signs away his soul to the devil, and Shakespeare constructs it as an elaborate reworking of the old Morality triangle he himself had used in his sonnet of jealous passion (Sonnet 144) with Desdemona as the good angel 'fired out' by the bad angel, Iago. What makes it so painful and shocking to witness is that (as the sonnet parallel suggests) it is also a love scene. Iago's design has grown far beyond the purely mechanical purpose he first announced – to destroy Cassio and punish Othello with the libel of Desdemona's adultery. The full obscenity of his stratagem consists in its methodical attempt to destroy the very bases on which a love such as Desdemona's and Othello's rests. The subject of the scene becomes the expulsion of one kind of love in favour of its corrupted travesty: Iago seeks not only to violate the bond between man and wife, but to put another in its place.

The love espoused by Desdemona and Othello is an affront to Iago's construction of the world. The 'freedom' (generosity, spontaneity, openness) which he discerns in both their characters ('The Moor is of a free and open nature', 1.3.393; 'She's framed as fruitful / As the free elements', 2.3.331–2), and which is most fully expressed in their love for one another, is by its very bounty a rebuke to him, a source of wounding comparison. For Iago freedom consists only in the untrammelled exercise of the independent will, so that the self-abandonment of love can only seem an insupportable tax on the integrity of the self: 'this, that you call love . . . is merely a lust of the blood and a permission of the will. Come, be a man. Drown thyself? Drown cats and blind puppies' (1.3.328–33). Love is simply a blind biological craving which reduces one to the helpless condition of a sightless puppy: that is his contemptuous redaction of the mythology of Blind Cupid. Though 'free' and 'love' are characteristically amongst his favourite words, nothing for Iago is freely given – love least of all, for it can only be understood as a form of humiliating enslavement:

> His soul is so enfettered to her love,
> That she may make, unmake, do what she list,
> Even as her appetite shall play the god
> With his weak function. (2.3.335–8)

If he seeks to make of Desdemona's loving nature the Hephaestus' 'net / That shall enmesh them all' (ll. 351–2), such entanglement is no more than they have already wished on themselves.

One way of reading the temptation scene is as a methodical demonstration of Iago's degraded idea of love: his method is to displace Desdemona as the captain of Othello's will – there can be no slavery more wretched than one subject to so easy and arbitrary a change of masters. At the same time, of course, there are uniquely perverse satisfactions to be tasted in the usurping of Desdemona's place. This is the last and most ingenious refinement of revenge: through it Iago accrues to himself not only the 'price' of which he was bilked by Cassio's promotion, but the supreme price which Othello has put upon the jewel of his love, Desdemona. The temptation is also a wooing, an act of erotic possession, punctuated by protestations of love:

> My lord, you know I love you.
> (3.3.116)

> now I shall have reason
> To show the love and duty that I bear you
> With franker spirit. (ll. 191–3)

> But I am much to blame,
> I humbly do beseech you of your pardon
> For too much loving you. (ll. 209–11)

> I hope you will consider what is spoke
> Comes from my love. (ll. 214–5)

> God bu'y you: take mine office. O wretched fool,
> That lov'st to make thine honesty a vice!...
> I thank you for this profit, and from hence
> I'll love no friend, sith love breeds such offence.
> (ll. 372–7)

> I do not like the office.
> But sith I am entered in this cause so far –
> Pricked to't by foolish honesty and love –
> I will go on. (ll. 407–10)

The attitude struck, with Iago's gift of vicious mimicry, is a surreptitious burlesque of Desdemona's own long-suffering devotion; and by the destructive logic of comparison it is precisely this show of love which most inflames Othello's jealousy – Iago's fidelity rendering doubly intolerable Desdemona's apparent infidelity and Cassio's betrayal of trust. The scene reaches its climax with the Moor's formal repudiation of the bonds of matrimony:

> All my fond love thus do I blow to heaven:
> 'Tis gone.
> Arise, black vengeance, from thy hollow cell!
> Yield up, O love, thy crown and hearted throne
> To tyrannous hate! (3.3.442–6)

The spirit of revenge is here imagined as the usurper of love's royal seat; and the metaphor exactly corresponds to the displacement of the loving Desdemona by the vindictive Iago realized in the stage action which follows. The kneeling exchange of vows is presented as a blasphemous troth-plighting:

> *Othello.* ....Now, by yond marble heaven,
> In the due reverence of a sacred vow
> I here engage my words.
> > *He kneels*
> *Iago.* Do not rise yet.
> > *He kneels*
> Witness you ever-burning lights above,
> You elements, that clip us round about,
> Witness that here Iago doth give up
> The execution of his wit, hands, heart,
> To wronged Othello's service. Let him
> command,
> And to obey shall be in me remorse,
> What bloody business ever.
> > *They rise*
> *Othello.* I greet thy love,
> Not with vain thanks, but with acceptance
> bounteous;...
> ...Now art thou my Lieutenant.
> *Iago.*
> I am your own for ever. (3.3.457–76)

If there is any act of adultery in the play, this surely is it. 'Lieutenant' encompasses not merely Cassio's office, but the role of domestic deputy which patriarchal theory gave to every wife. In Iago's lurid fantasy of sharing Cassio's bed he actually cast himself, in a black-comic version of the bed-trick, as Desdemona's substitute. The intense emotional identification of tempter and tempted reached by that point in the scene ('I am bound to thee for ever', l. 211) ensured that Othello and Iago were virtually interchangeable figures in this fantasy; thus for Othello merely to listen to the speech was to put himself imaginatively in Iago's place and, in effect, to experience Cassio's adultery with Desdemona (as Brabantio was made to experience her seduction by Othello) as a sexual assault upon his own person. The ending of the scene merely confirms in literal terms the psychological lieutenancy appropriated by means of Iago's ugly fiction. Iago has successfully usurped both Cassio's and Desdemona's places, and in that dank corner of the emotional prison which the two men share, Othello and he are bound to one another for ever: they have become in an appalling sense, one flesh – this is hell, nor are they out of it.[25]

---

[25] One might add that this is a consummation which leads to its own obscene kind of pregnancy: the 'monstrous

The Othello of the last two acts is a man without place. The height of his agony of remorse is reached with the recognition of his utter dislocation and estrangement, the understanding that by the act of murder he has encompassed the very displacement he sought to avenge, expulsion from the anchoring haven of Desdemona's love. Before his eyes there burns a vision of future damnation, but what he describes is a state of present torment:

> When we shall meet at compt
> This look of thine will hurl my soul from heaven
> And fiends will snatch at it....
> O cursèd, cursèd slave! Whip me, ye devils,
> From the possession of this heavenly sight!
> Blow me about in winds! Roast me in sulphur!
> Wash me in steep-down gulfs of liquid fire!
>
> (5.2.271–8)

Othello knows his price: here is a final accounting more absolute and unforgiving than anything in Iago's meanly resentful balance-sheet. In the hallucinated landscape of this eternal exile ('steep-down gulfs of liquid fire') is the terrible counterpart of that romantically evoked wilderness ('antres vast and deserts idle, / Rough quarries, rocks, and hills whose heads touch heaven') through which the Moor first won his way to Desdemona's heart. It is as though she had cast him back to that savage and unredeemed world from which he came. Yet there remains a curious ambiguity: like the earlier speech, this one is infused with the full power of Othello's thrilling imagination; and like Faustus's great aria of damnation it rises towards a near rapture of despair – the prospect of punishment seems charged with a kind of ecstasy. What Othello can no longer bear is 'the *possession* of this heavenly sight'; because to possess it is to be possessed *by* it, as one might be by a tormenting spirit. His ill angel has fired the good one out: displaced, dispossessed, his occupation gone, Othello offers himself almost gratefully to a damnation which makes him once again an 'extravagant and wheeling stranger of here and everywhere' – blown in the winds, washed to and fro in seas of fire, adrift, released. By comparison with this vision of magnificent desolation the heroic self-regard of his last speech is likely to appear as emptily rhetorical as Leavis charged: but the comparison is one upon which Shakespeare himself, with all the unflinching clarity of his tragic vision, insists.

---

birth' dreamt up by Iago in act 1, and echoed in Emilia's idea of jealousy as a 'monster / Begot upon itself, born on itself', is finally brought to life in a murder which Othello describes as 'the strong conception / That I do groan withal' (5.2.55–6) – where 'conception' puns on the archaic sense of 'baby' or 'foetus'.

PROSPERO'S LIME TREE AND THE PURSUIT OF 'VANITAS'

ROSEMARY WRIGHT

The lime tree features in one of the odder of *The Tempest*'s anticlimaxes. The plot against Prospero's life appears to be coming to a head, and the enchanter and Ariel confer together for means to overthrow the conspirators. The tone is urgent, the terms martial: one anticipates a mimic war in heaven. Yet the episode dissipates in bathos. Ariel's will-o'-the-wisp chase reduces murderous pursuit to a mere unseemly dance among the gorse bushes. Then Ariel himself is bidden only to deck the lime tree by the cell with trumpery garments: mere 'stale to catch these thieves'. As a decoy the device certainly works, although its success must appear contrived. But it in no way advances the plot; the audience is baulked of the expected dramatic confrontation; and an apparently powerful enchanter is reduced to the role of second-hand clothes merchant. Why?

A first answer seems to lie in the fact that the lime tree is not a piece of plot manipulation but a carefully constructed image. As such, it is possessed of a precise technical function which is thematic rather than narrative. Designed both for immediate theatrical impact and for the later process of contemplation, it first seizes the imagination and then unfolds itself to the audience's understanding. Like others of its kind, it states in compressed (and in this case, somewhat bizarre) form, matters of universal application. Relevant first to its own immediate context, it also acts as a focal point for themes current throughout the play.

A second and more precise answer lies in the image's source – or sources. For there are at least two, and discussion of the possible second source will occupy the bulk of this argument. Both sources also merge happily with the long tradition of theatrical devices: visual constructions, dense with meaning, whose form and content are now equally alien to a modern audience.

To a Jacobean audience, the tree as an emblematic theatrical structure would have been familiar as it can never be to ourselves. Along with its equally emblematic fellows – the cave, the castle, the fountain, the bower – it could figure in banquets or tournaments, pageants or processions, patient of whatever significance its devisers saw fit to entrust to it. More significantly for our purposes, it had figured in the biblical plays of the guilds. Two vital trees – the tree of knowledge and the cross – opened and closed the pattern of man's guilt and redemption as it was played annually in the narrow streets; and pageant Edens, propertied with the emblems of paradise, had processed through the streets within living memory. Their secular equivalents – many of them variants on that other Eden, the 'flourishing commonwealth' – continued to do so.

In a play so concerned with versions of paradise and variants on the fall of man, the lime tree with its meretricious promises and glittering second-hand 'fruit' must have provided a ready reminder of the tree of knowledge. Here, almost certainly, is the first tradition on which the image draws. Strewn with the tempting rubbish of Prospero's cell, it is a miniature of the earlier tree whose appeal was to *curiositas*, power and pride. 'Ye shall be as gods' had been the serpent's promise. Such indeed are the ambitions of those who surround the tree on stage. Stephano has had divinity thrust upon him; Prospero's attempts on the deity are of a rather different order; but both have succumbed to the lure to be as gods. So there is much irony in this emblematic tree. At literal level, it has certainly been set up as a decoy by Prospero; but its wider applications exceed the understanding of its stage-creator. As an image of temptation it can be seen, ironically, to be as relevant to the enchanter as to the man who provides his unkind parody.

The seeds for this relevance are sown in Prospero's first account of his quest for knowledge. The 'liberal arts', whose pursuit he puts before the responsibilities of government, are described by him in near-religious terms. Many scholars take him at his own assessment; and certainly the genuine Renaissance magus laid much emphasis on the fact that his art was powerless without a corresponding integrity of purpose. But nothing that we see or hear of Prospero suggests a genuine unworldliness. Though there is no malice in his endeavours, what he wants is power: not knowledge of God, but God's knowledge. This is the temptation for which he falls; and wrench the account of his activities how he will, his 'secret studies' remain forbidden sorties: raids on a territory not his to command. Like Lucifer before him, like Adam again, he finds himself turned out of his kingdom – as he himself turns out Stephano, and as Stephano threatens to turn out his 'servant monster'. The group around the lime tree is like a complex of distorting mirrors, repeating in parody both themselves and their great originals.

But despite the giant echoes the lime tree releases, what we actually see on stage is no more than a piece of theatrical property: a make-believe tree, hung with tawdry clothes, that recalls its original only by mockery. At this level the lime tree provides a further image – coined by the theatre out of its own acknowledged inadequacies – for both Stephano's relation to Prospero, and Prospero's to the power he attempts to wield. Just as Stephano in his tawdry finery 'acts' a kingship he cannot really aspire to, so Prospero in his role of enchanter masquerades in a power that is not generically his own. Like the actor, he is no more than shadow-king. The magic robe in which he glitters is the empty tinsel imitation of a power not his to command.

These two elements in the first source – temptation, and the mocking imitation – provide the point of intersection with the second. And it is this second source that may provide a clue to the enigmatic appearance of the lime tree, and Prospero's odd undignified descent into the role of second-hand clothes dealer. Once again, the source is an emblem; and once again, it achieves significance beyond its immediate context on stage.

The gaudy clothes that dangle from the branches of the tree seem almost certainly to have derived from the late Gothic device of the pedlar and the apes.[1] In this device, apes descend from the trees to rob a sleeping pedlar of his pack, then hang the resulting booty from the branches. Originally a robust item of folklore, the device became an image for the dangers attendant on both security and *curiositas*; whilst a late Renaissance painting[2] reworks the image to suggest that life itself is no more than the pursuit of folly – a dream in which illusion is mistaken for reality.

So far as I know, no one has pointed to a connection between this device and the lime tree. That there is one must to some extent remain conjectural. However, the numerous points of overlap between the two, at many levels and both visual and thematic, make the possibility a strong one. But the image of the pedlar and the apes is now lost to us. So is the bulk of medieval and Renaissance ape lore from which it derives. A brief résumé of the more fundamental assumptions of the latter is necessary if the implications of the image are to make sense.

Renaissance eyes saw in the ape less an animal than a grotesque parody of the human. The standard reference was to Ennius: '*Simia quam similis turpissima bestia nobis*' – or in Bacon's paraphrase, 'as it addeth deformity to the ape to be so like a man...'. Folklore proffered explanations for this long-observed disquieting similitude. On the one hand, apes had once been human, but for transgression of

---

[1] For details of this device, and the account of ape lore that follows, I am indebted to H. W. Janson's *Apes and Ape Lore in the Middle Ages and the Renaissance*, Studies of the Warburg Institute, vol. 20 (1952).

[2] *The Dream*. See Janson, *Apes and Ape Lore*, pp. 214–16.

18. *The Pedlar Robbed by Apes*. Florentine engraving, c. 1470–90

Behaviour as well as appearance confirmed this conclusion. Chatter parodied human speech. Meddling hands parodied purposeful human putting-together. *Curiositas* (once held to be the original sin) parodied genuine inquiry. Even its skill in imitation was turned against it, since it appeared lacking in any reasoned application. Thus the unfortunate ape, loaded with all the sins of the men it failed to measure up to, became the pattern of impoverished imitation: an automatic reference point for all that was shoddy, gimcrack, would-be, and vain. At the same time its physical characteristics, at once compulsive and obscene, gave it a kind of leering fascination. As with the skull at which he gazed with equally fascinated horror, man looked at the ape and saw himself. The mirror was a buckled and distorted one, but it told the uncomfortable inner truth.

Given this gargoyle likeness at his elbow, medieval man made of the ape a symbol for his own degenerate nature. Apes, bordering the manuals of devotion, offer not only contemporary social comment but a metaphor for the unregenerate in human nature at all times. Clambering in the branches of the tree of knowledge, carved on the Virgin's chair beside the lilies, crouched at the foot of the cross, they provide pungent reminders of that abiding human weakness for which the original sacrifice was made.

Then, fairly late in its development as an emblem, the ape became a synonym for the fool. As such, it entered the much broader tradition of the medieval concern with folly – a wide and shifting complex of ideas, whose last and probably greatest expression is the *Encomium Moriae*. This developing tradition,[3] wide enough to castigate the horrors born of folly on the one hand, and to extol its joyous necessities on the other, comes ultimately to see folly itself as the hallmark of Everyman. It was the one ineradicable component of human nature, weakness rather than sin, without which man would undoubtedly be less harmful, but without which he would also be less endearing, and shorn of most of his greatest

some kind against the gods, or failure to heed some divine injunction, had been reduced to animal condition. Apehood was thus a punishment, and another kind of 'fall'. (This widespread belief in a punitive, rather than a natural, origin for apes may lie behind Caliban's fear that Prospero will punish the conspirators by turning them to barnacles or apes 'with foreheads villainous low'.) On the other hand, apehood was also seen as a kind of animal *superbia*: an ill-conceived attempt to emulate the attributes of man, as man himself with equal folly was prone to ape the knowledge and power of God. Sometimes, for his failure to conform to either human or animal category, the ape was classed as a monster, to be placed outside the natural order altogether. But whether he was seen as fallen human or animal over-reacher, he remained a parody of man.

---

[3] For a comprehensive survey of this tradition, together with its development in England and on the Continent, I am indebted to Barbara Swain's *Fools and Folly during the Middle Ages and the Renaissance* (New York, 1932).

19. *The Pedlar Robbed by Apes*. Engraving by Pieter van der Heyden after Pieter Breughel the Elder, 1562

moments too. The ape, however, is lodged with folly's negatives and linked to the mere fool. Such links, once made, seem inevitable. Both empty fools and those who take delight in them share the ape's poverty of concentration and its delight in trivia. Thus the ape becomes the signature of those who reject the vital for the vain. A further link between ape and fool is achieved through the concept of the *simulacrum*, or empty likeness. Just as the ape is already a gross *simulacrum* of man, possessed of his form but emptied of his reason, so the man who connives at his own loss of reason becomes a *simulacrum* of himself. Emptied by folly of the one ingredient that distinguishes him from the beasts, he is reduced to a grinning parody of himself. Thus, in their common reduction to a form without content, . the ape and the fool are one.

This, very briefly, is the background against which the device of the pedlar and the apes needs to be viewed, together with its later more sophisticated progeny. Janson discusses the device at length.[4] There are a number of variations, the most popular and widespread of which appears to have been an engraving after a design by Pieter Breughel the Elder, published in 1562 – it 'served as the *locus classicus* of our motif from the 1560's until well into the seventeenth century'. The different examples vary slightly, but the basic components of the device remain the same. A pedlar lies asleep on the ground, his pack beside him. Meanwhile apes crowd round from the surrounding trees, busily examining both pedlar and pack. The pack's contents consist of 'exactly the kind of *vanae merces* calculated to give apes pleasure, such as boots, gloves, caps, belts, small

---

[4] Janson, *Apes and Ape Lore*, pp. 216–25.

musical instruments, mirrors, etc.' In some examples, the apes are trying on the clothes and admiring themselves in the mirrors. Other apes meanwhile have returned to the trees with their booty, and garments dangle from the branches beyond the reach of the still sleeping pedlar.

Behind this device lies almost certainly, as Janson points out, the traditional ruse for capturing an ape. This is the first element in the image, and its first and most obvious link with the lime tree. The ruse itself exploited two familiar simian characteristics: love of worthless novelties ('stale to catch these thieves'), and mindless skill in imitation. According to tradition, the man who wishes to catch an ape must first take a pair of boots weighted with lead and put them on in view of his hidden prey. He then takes them off, leaves them on the ground, and goes into hiding. The apes, unable to resist the temptation of novelty, come down from the trees to examine the boots, imitate the hunter by putting them on, and are then prevented by the weight of the lead from running away. They may thus – or so runs the legend – be easily taken. In the device of the pedlar, a 'humorous inversion' of this ruse has taken place, and the apes are 'capturing the objects instead of being captured by them'. However, the point remains of their being attracted in the first place by glittering trifles. Behind the somewhat unpleasant humour of the image there now lurks awareness of both the danger of *curiositas* and a form of temptation that traps by exploiting weakness.

The second element is that of the sleeping pedlar. At first little more than a figure of rather drastic farce, he becomes eventually a figure for the dangers of security. Janson calls him 'a "lazy sleeper", who deserves to lose his merchandise as a punishment for succumbing to the lure of *acedia*'. This somewhat stern conclusion is justified by reference to a later more explicitly didactic title appended to Breughel's original reworking of the image: *L'histoire du songe creux qui perdt son bien en dormant*. The primary meaning of *acedia* is of course inertia or sloth, and the inactivity of the pedlar is certainly in striking contrast to the busy meddling all around him. Moreover, the punning use of the French '*bien*' carries its theological implications more obviously

than the mercantile English 'goods'. At this stage, therefore, the two elements of the image, pedlar and apes, embody the separate dangers of security and *curiositas* respectively, and are engaged in apparently opposite pursuits. With reference to the painting's new title, however, Janson continues: '…the pedlar is not simply asleep; he has become the prototype of the *songe-creux*, i.e., the "idle dreamer" who loses his possessions because he prefers the world of his own fancy to the harsh reality around him.' So, if the tempting and trapping of apes is the immediate visual link with the conspirators, there is now more than a suspicion of link between the sleeping pedlar, obsessed with his dream, and the duke who prized his books above his dukedom.

As the image develops still further, the two apparently separate halves finally merge, to become two variants on a single theme. In the strange reworking of the image called *The Dream*, in which clothed apes cavort around a sleeping youth who is propped against a sphere, the pedlar's *songe creux* has itself become an image for the pursuit of vanity. At first, expectedly, such pursuit implies the activities of the worldling, and the apes of the foreground that are now themselves a part of the *songe creux* embody, according to Janson, vestigial traces of the seven deadly sins. At this level, too, security is the familiar state of mere careless self-indulgence, and responsibility deferred or ignored. But if the sleeper's own pursuit of vanity has now merged with the *curiositas* of the apes (both being attracted to the 'idle'), the apes' innocent un-suspicion of treachery has now merged with the sleeper's security. He is propped against a sphere, symbolic of instability, and reference to the unconscious precariousness of his state is thus made obvious. Temptation to folly, and the unconscious dangers of betrayal thereby, are thus transferred from apes to pedlar. The apes that surround the sleeper now illustrate, rather than contrast with, his own occupations. It is the sleeper who is now betrayed by the pursuit of vanity.

A final development yet remains. Closer inspection of the painting reveals that it is not only the seven deadly sins who dance in ape-guise in the foreground. Behind the sleeper passes a procession of human life from birth to death. It includes the

20. *The Dream*. Flemish (?), early seventeenth century (formerly in the David Richardson Collection,
Cambridge, Mass.)

quest for military glory, as well as the struggle to
reach the head of Fortune's wheel. All the partici-
pants are apes. So, as in the earlier medieval treatises,
all the activities of human life are once more seen as
a species of folly, and folly has once again become
the hallmark of mankind. But just as the earlier lore
concerning apes became absorbed into the medieval
concern with folly, so folly itself is now seen in the
new light of Renaissance scepticism concerning
reason. Reason is no longer an infallible guide, to be
taken almost as folly's opposite. The partial and
subjective images that are all our unreliable senses
can return to us had come to be seen, in respect of
their fallibility, as mere dreams. To trust them was a
brand of folly. To trust the judgements based upon
them was equally foolish. So, with our reason flawed
from birth, not only our picture of the world but
our assessment of our own and others' endeavours
must be suspect. All are thus liable to the charge of

vanity. To the extent that all are illusory, all are
dreams.

In this painting, therefore, there is no distinction
between the contents of the dream and the outside
world. Life itself is seen as a dream. But only we,
the spectators, can see this. Like the audience in the
theatre, or the gods whom Erasmus quotes as
viewing the follies of human life 'from some
promontory', we are privileged with knowledge
beyond that of those we watch. The sleeper himself
is strikingly unaware. So, at this final level, security
itself has been transformed. It has become the
treacherous reliance on human knowledge and
personal judgement, whose inadequacy is not
apparent to those who rely on it.

The Dream does not set up, as *The Tempest* does,
a web of constantly shifting relationships between
illusion and reality; but in its insistence on the
illusory nature of all we normally take for actual and

desirable, it approaches the same haunting and elusive territory *The Tempest* makes peculiarly its own.

To those members of the audience familiar with the emblem, the situation on stage must have been fraught with irony. At a literal level, the conspirators are undoubtedly the apes. The noisy chatter, the failure to hold to a purpose, the squabbling, spoiling and snatching as they rob the tree of its trumpery 'fruit': all these are traditional aspects of the ape. Beyond that, they are fools as well. 'Red-hot with drinking', they are devoid of any reason they might have had. Stephano, the thick-necked swaggering bully, is also the ape as parody imitation: he will displace Prospero and rule in his place. Only Caliban, visually equated as a 'monster' with the ape, displays a reason that his betters fail to maintain. The ironies multiply as, with his *refusal* to fall for temptation, his 'god' threatens to 'turn him out of his kingdom' for the primal sin of disobedience. Caliban will not pursue vanity. Vanity is therefore thrust upon him.

The ironies are greatest for the unconscious Prospero. The two halves of the emblem are displaced on stage, and the pedlar's sleep takes place in flashback in the library at Milan. The ape that robs him is the shadow-duke, the deputy Antonio; whilst Prospero's abdication of responsibility has already rendered him another form of shadow. But what of the dream for which he lost his dukedeom? Is it a *songe creux*? A pursuit of vanity, unperceived?

In some respects, not at all. The power it brings him is real, though it has limits, and these have frequently been remarked. Though forbidden, it is not evil, nor is it ever used for evil purposes. In a play shot through with moments of incomparable loveliness, many such moments owe their being to Prospero's magic. But there is about this magic a constant sense of labour and strain: a power wrested, and not naturally ordained. More significantly, as the many gaps in Prospero's knowledge are made plain, there becomes apparent an aching disparity between his limited human understanding and the fringes of cosmic power he has called to his hand. It was the standard charge against the Renaissance magicians that they sought to enforce an impious, as

well as futile, change in nature. Prospero is no different from the rest. It is beyond him to accept the norm of post-Lapsarian frailty; and in his well-intended insistence on an unnatural perfection, his Utopian plans become Procrustes' bed, stretching and lopping without reference to the natures of those whom he determines to accommodate to a grid of his own design. Ariel must be taxed beyond his natural capacity; Caliban practise a continence not in his nature to understand; whilst Prospero himself, resigning his free authority for a life of ceaseless labour, becomes the ape of knowledge whose efforts turn and mock him. As he remarks bitterly of his brother, and as a higher divinity might ironically note of himself, he has

> new created
> The creatures that were mine, I say, or chang'd 'em,
> Or else new form'd 'em.　　　　(1.2.81–3)

His reward is an apparently tragic waste of 'pains humanely taken', and he blames a 'cankered' nature, not himself.

Folklore deals in its own fashion with this particular instinct to meddle. Those who usurp the divine prerogative of creation and attempt to warp nature from her course turn their victims, or themselves are turned, to apes: ludicrous monsters, who fail every category of creation.[5] Other legends, embodying the same insight, speak of the dual creation: product of the devil who, incapable of creative activity himself yet 'unceasingly ambitious to imitate the Lord', can produce only a distorted echo of the original. Meddler, imitator, fallen himself from his former glory, he is known as the Ape of God – the *Simia Dei*.[6]

Despite the shrill tyrannies and undignified shouting matches that accompany his attempts to change nature, the essential goodness of Prospero is never really in doubt. At the end of the play we witness his resumption of humanity, and the regaining of a

---

[5] See Janson, *Apes and Ape Lore, passim*. The late medieval tale of Christ and the Blacksmith (pp. 97–8) is particularly relevant here. A blacksmith who impiously attempts to emulate a miracle of Christ is punished by the failure of his experiment, the by-product of which is a pair of apes.

[6] Janson, *Apes and Ape Lore*, p. 19.

dignity – even, miraculously, humour – that we feel should always have been his. (The flaws remain, of course: *The Tempest* is not a fairy tale.) But for nine-tenths of the play we see him thrall to the *songe creux*, ludicrous, tyrannical and sad. When, like God, he hounds the conspirators from under the ransacked tree, he is only an unwitting usurper, glittering in a power not his own. The magic robes, so vainly cherished, are no different from Stephano's stolen finery. As Stephano bullies Caliban, and Prospero lets loose his hellhounds on Stephano, the strictures of Isabella apply equally to both:

> But man, proud man,
> Dress'd in a little brief authority,
> Most ignorant of what he's most assur'd,
> His glassy essence, like an angry ape,
> Plays such fantastic tricks before high heaven
> As makes the angels weep.
>
> (*Measure for Measure*, 2.2.117–22)

As an emblem, developed over the years to a high level of sophistication and with many different levels of application, the device of the pedlar and the apes can shed light on many areas in the play. More valuably still, it can alert us to the old and now all but vanished tradition of folly that permeates *The Tempest* at every level.[7] Individual instances of this, many at a high level of erudition, can be quoted in profusion once the tradition is known, and with reference to virtually every member of the cast. But even these, important though they are, are less

important than the cast of mind that they embody: one that would seem to see folly as the final and ineradicable hallmark of mankind, and irony as the inevitable result of its endeavours. Shakespeare's treatment of this theme, sardonic and compassionate both at once, leaves behind even the most sophisticated developments of the pedlar emblem. So it does the other more familiar image, so vital to *The Tempest*, of the *Narrenschiff*, or *Ship of Fools*. Even the *Encomium Moriae*, so close to *The Tempest* in its wit and endlessly shifting ironies, halts behind *The Tempest*'s grasp of the shifting levels of illusion. But out of this long tradition comes Shakespeare's own particular distillation: an awareness of the limitations of human knowledge; of the folly of presuming that we know; of the greater folly of thinking we can leave our folly behind us; and of the strange benefits that folly itself can bring.[8]

---

7 So far as I know, only Jan Kott, in *Shakespeare Our Contemporary* (1964), has noted folly as a major preoccupation of the play. I find his remarks indispensable, both thematically and for their elucidation of the play's mirror structure, although he pays attention only to the darker aspects of folly.

8 Caliban's dream, although much condensed, is an almost verbatim account of the magnificent closing paragraphs of Dame Folly's *Encomium*. Bottom's account of his 'rare vision', with which Caliban's dream is often linked, is even closer. Shakespeare has made his own a Platonism to which Erasmus only refers; but both deal with an 'illusion' that transcends reality, and by which reality can only benefit.

SHAKESPEARIAN CHARACTER STUDY TO 1800

JOHN BLIGH

A recent article entitled 'The Emergence of Character Criticism, 1774–1800' was designed to show that character criticism emerged as a genre in itself in the last quarter of the eighteenth century; during this period 'essays and whole books are devoted to individual characters'.[1] This present essay, viewing a wider temporal spread, will consider character criticism, not as a literary genre, but as one of the principal divisions of dramatic criticism, corresponding to the second of the six parts, elements, or constituents, of drama distinguished by Aristotle. To avoid confusion, I shall talk of 'character study' rather than 'character criticism'. Character study, of course, had emerged long before 1774.

During the period from 1664 to 1800, critics of various nations made valuable contributions to the discussion of Shakespeare's characters; I shall try to do justice to the Scots and Germans as well as to native English writers. The questions which have guided my selection of materials are: What were the aims of the early students of character? What methods did they devise? How far were their discussions dependent upon and oriented to theatrical performance? and, Which philosophers apart from Aristotle influenced their aims and methods?

I

Discussion of Shakespeare's characters no doubt began earlier, but our first record of it is a letter written by Lady Margaret Cavendish in 1664. A friend had passed on to her the opinion of a fatuous critic who had said that Shakespeare's plays 'were made up onely with Clowns, Fools, Watchmen, and the like'. Lady Cavendish indignantly replies that Shakespeare is capable of presenting all sorts of person in every social class right up to Kings and Queens; so clear is his imagination that you would think he must have been a King and Queen to know so well what a King or Queen would feel and say in the circumstances of the story; indeed, the marvel is that he knows better than a King how a King should speak.[2]

The question at issue here is, How does Shakespeare succeed so perfectly in presenting such a complete range and variety of human characters? or, What is it that makes his characters so much superior to those of every other dramatist? – a question which is still being discussed by some of the best critics of the present day.[3] Lady Cavendish's answer, which has been repeated too rarely in later centuries, is that Shakespeare owes his success to his ability to forget himself, project himself into each of his characters, and give them a heightened power of self-expression, which enables them to feel more deeply, to live more intensely, and to communicate more effectively what they are feeling and thinking.

The next attempt to state in general terms what is the distinctive excellence of Shakespeare's characters

---

[1] Brian Vickers, 'The Emergence of Character Criticism, 1774–1800', *Shakespeare Survey 34* (Cambridge, 1981), pp. 11–21.

[2] For the text of Lady Cavendish's letter see Brian Vickers (ed.), *Shakespeare: The Critical Heritage, Volume 1: 1625–1692* (London and Boston, 1974), pp. 42–4.

[3] Kenneth Muir's brilliant essay, 'Shakespeare's Open Secret', in the same number of *Shakespeare Survey*, pp. 1–10, is the latest contribution to this discussion.

is that of Alexander Pope. (There were of course numerous comments on individual characters by writers between Cavendish and Pope, but these do not resolve the general question.) Pope includes in the Preface to his quarto edition of Shakespeare's Works (1725) a short but pregnant passage in praise of the characters.

His *Characters* are so much Nature herself, that 'tis a sort of injury to call them by so distant a name as Copies of her. Those of other Poets have a constant resemblance, which shews that they receiv'd them from one another, and were but multiplyers of the same image: each picture like a mock-rainbow is but the reflexion of a reflexion. But every single character in *Shakespeare* is as much an Individual as those in Life itself; it is as impossible to find any two alike; and such as from their relation or affinity in any respect appear most to be Twins, will upon comparison be found remarkably distinct.[4]

In other words, whereas other dramatists form their characters by copying from one another, Shakespeare does not even copy from nature; he creates new individuals who are as lifelike and distinctive as those in life itself. Pope is of course unable to explain how Shakespeare performs this creative miracle, but his observations lead to a practical suggestion. He proposes a new task for students of the characters: take two who in some respect appear to be 'twins', examine them carefully, and show how different they are. (This may be called the 'comparative method' of character study.) The suggestion was taken up by Thomas Whately, who compared Richard III with Macbeth, and in the early nineteenth century by William Hazlitt both in his theatre reviews and in his more scholarly works.[5] Hazlitt believed that not only readers but actors too, even Edmund Kean, tend to conventionalize Shakespeare's characters by failing to discern how one is distinguished from another.[6]

Dr Johnson's contribution, which is superficially in conflict with Pope's, is the observation that in each of his characters Shakespeare has incorporated some part of his deep and exceptional understanding of human nature, so that every character is a vehicle of moral instruction for those who have ears to hear. In the Dedication which he wrote for a book by his friend Mrs Charlotte Lennox (1753), he makes what he believes to be a new point – and with reason (since he is abandoning the neoclassical demand that each character be true to its specific type).

Among his other excellencies it ought to be remarked, because it has hitherto been unnoticed, that *his heroes are men*, that the love and hatred, the hopes and fears of his chief personages are such as are common to other human beings, and not like those which later times have exhibited, peculiar to phantoms that strut upon the stage.[7]

What this means can best be seen from an illustration. In the opening scene of *King Lear*, Shakespeare presents Lear, not as an heroic king, but as a man – a man growing old and wrathful, from whom we can learn various lessons. At 1.1.166–72, for example, where Lear cries out to Kent,

Hear me, recreant!
On thine allegiance, hear me!
That thou hast sought to make us break our vows,
Which we durst never yet...take thy reward,

Dr Johnson has this fine moralizing comment: 'Lear, who is characterized as hot, heady, and violent, is with very just observation of life, made to entangle himself with vows, upon any provocation to vow revenge, and then to plead the obligation of a vow in defence of implacability.'

---

4 Text from D. Nichol Smith (ed.), *Eighteenth Century Essays on Shakespeare* (2nd edn., Oxford, 1963), pp. 44–5.
5 Thomas Whately, *Remarks on Some of the Characters of Shakespeare*, was first published anonymously in 1785. Whately is mistaken when he says (3rd edn., 1893, p. 25) that the criticism of character 'admits not of such general rules as the conduct of the fable'.
6 Hazlitt felt that Kean did not distinguish Richard and Macbeth as he ought, and that he assimilated Richard III to Iago by making Richard too serious and Iago too merry. See P. P. Howe (ed.), *The Complete Works of William Hazlitt* (1930; repr. New York, 1967), vol. 5, pp. 112 and 206. In *The Examiner* of 12 May 1816, Hazlitt published a letter on 'Shakespeare's Exact Discrimination of Nearly Similar Roles'; it is reprinted in Howe, vol. 20, p. 407.
7 Arthur Sherbo (ed.), *Johnson on Shakespeare* (The Yale Edition of *The Works of Samuel Johnson*, vols. 7–8, New Haven, 1968), p. 49. The next quotation, on *Lear*, 1.1.166–72, is from p. 663.

A further contribution, not entirely new, was made by Lord Kames in his *Elements of Criticism* (1761), where he distinguishes between description and expression of passions.[8] He ranks Shakespeare and Corneille as the two greatest geniuses of the dramatic world and contends that Shakespeare's method of characterization differs from that of all other dramatists, including Corneille. Whereas others describe the passions which they ought to express, Shakespeare's gift, says Kames, is to 'annihilate himself' and find the right sentiment for the expression of each passion by each character. His characters do not talk of themselves as if they were spectators; they give vent to feeling strongly felt. Kames's own examples are too lengthy to be quoted here; a simpler illustration will suffice. When Lear finds Kent in the stocks, a spectator might say, 'This makes Lear furious', and an inferior dramatist might make Lear say, 'This makes me furious!' Shakespeare enters into the mind of his character and makes him express his fury:

> They durst not do't;
> They could not, would not do't. 'Tis worse than
>   murder
> To do upon respect such violent outrage.
>
>   (2.4.21–3)

The principle, though not of universal validity (see, for example, *Julius Caesar*, 2.1.63–9), is on the whole sound and valuable.[9]

Finally, Maurice Morgann, in his *Essay on the Dramatic Character of Sir John Falstaff* (1777), has a long footnote in which he attempts to explain in general terms how Shakespeare's characters differ from those of other dramatists. There are difficulties both in the language and in the structure of this note, but the differences which Morgann discerns appear to be three. First, the characters of other dramatists are conceived as related to one another in 'groups' and are given the qualities which found their relationships, but Shakespeare goes further and makes each a complete person: 'those characters of *Shakespeare* which are seen only in part, are yet capable of being unfolded and understood in the whole; every part being in fact relative, and inferring all the rest.'[10] This may mean that Shakespeare

develops each character fully in his own mind, either before starting or while writing, but does not necessarily reveal every aspect of it fully within the play. If so, it is possible that a discerning critic might be able to infer, from mere hints within the play, qualities of the character which were fully clear and perfectly distinct in Shakespeare's mental picture of him or her. Secondly, Morgann attempts to describe how the characters were formed, or rather how they grew, within the mind of Shakespeare: just as (say) an acorn has within it certain seminal principles which evolve into an ever larger organism by assimilating whatever appropriate elements are available in the particular place where it is planted, with its own soil, containing its own minerals, irrigated by hard or soft water, and enjoying more or less sunlight, so each Shakespearian character grew organically in the mind of its maker from certain innate qualities and capacities by absorbing appropriate elements from the setting in which he placed it. (This argument is a remarkable anticipation of the organicism of Kant and A. W. Schlegel, who may be indebted to Morgann.[11]) Thirdly, developing, perhaps independently, a point already made by Lord Kames, Morgann says that Shakespeare gives life to his characters by entering into them and as it

---

8 Henry Home, Lord Kames, *Elements of Criticism* (London, 1824), pp. 204–8. In a *Tatler* essay (no. 47, 28 July 1709), Steele reports the conversation of a friend who distinguished between description and expression of feelings, but to judge from Steele's illustration he did not fully appreciate the importance of what was said to him.

9 Quotations from Shakespeare are from the Signet editions (general ed. Sylvan Barnet).

10 D. N. Smith (ed.), *Eighteenth Century Essays on Shakespeare*, pp. 230–1. A. C. Bradley once said of Morgann's essay (in *The Scottish Historical Review*, 1, p. 291) that 'there is no better piece of Shakespeare criticism in the world'.

11 According to René Wellek, *A History of Modern Criticism, 1750–1950*, vol. 2 (New Haven, 1955), p. 64, Schlegel had read Morgann's essay in or before 1791; for evidence he refers to A. W. Schlegel, *Sämtliche Werke* (Leipzig, 1846–7), vol. 10, p. 54, which is virtually unobtainable. Morgann's list of examples of organic development (in his long footnote, p. 230) begins, surprisingly, with 'metals'; Schlegel's, a little less surprisingly, with 'the crystallization of salts and minerals'. Are crystals his substitute for Morgann's metals?

were living their lives. He knows them better than they know themselves and makes them act from motives which they themselves fail to understand. Morgann ends with this sentence, which is the conclusion not simply of the paragraph to which it is attached, but of the whole note.

If the characters of *Shakespeare* are thus *whole*, and as it were original, while those of almost all other writers are mere imitation, it may be fit to consider them rather as Historic than Dramatic beings; and, when occasion requires, to account for their conduct from the *whole* of character, from general principles, from latent motives, and from policies not avowed.

If this contention is correct, Shakespeare's characters are so different from those of other dramatists that they can be subjected to types of analysis and psychoanalysis which are inapplicable to the characters ·of other dramatists.

Nearly every one of these contributions needs criticism and qualification for which there is no room here. What has been said should be sufficient to show that character study in the seventeenth and eighteenth centuries was by no means confined to the application of rules inherited from Aristotle and Horace. Critics recognized that Shakespeare's characters differ in some way, easy to recognize but hard to explain, from those of other dramatists.

II

In the period under discussion, the only available system of criticism was the neoclassical. In a very restricted sense, all dramatic criticism was and still remains inevitably neoclassical; we cannot avoid such Aristotelian terms as 'plot' and 'character'. However, the neoclassical critics had particular rules for plot and particular rules for character which caused trouble when applied to Shakespeare's plots and characters: he usually disregards the three unities, and he frequently violates the four rules for character.

The list of four criteria for character, drawn up by Aristotle and Horace, was repeated by Dryden in his excursus on 'The Grounds of Criticism in Tragedy' inserted into his 'Preface to *Troilus and*

Cressida'. He defines character, first, as 'that which distinguishes one man from another', and secondly, as 'a composition of qualities which are not contrary to one another in the same person'. That he is thinking of moral qualities can be seen from his example: 'Falstaff is a liar, a coward, a glutton, and a buffoon, because all these qualities may agree in the same man.' Then he gives the set of four criteria. In a good character the qualities or 'manners' must be: apparent (i.e. distinct or easily recognizable); true to type; true to tradition; and consistent.

First, they must be apparent; that is, in every character of the play, some inclinations of the person must appear; and these are shown in the actions and discourse.

Secondly, the manners must be suitable, or agreeing to the persons; that is, to the age, sex, dignity, and the other general heads of manners: thus, when a poet has given the dignity of a king to one of his persons, in all his actions and speeches, that person must discover majesty, magnanimity, and jealousy of power, because these are suitable to the general manners of a king.

The third property of manners is resemblance; and this is founded upon the particular characters of men, as we have them delivered to us by relation or history; that is, when a poet has the known character of this or that man before him, he is bound to represent him such, at least not contrary to that which fame has reported him to have been...

The last property of manners is that they be constant and equal, that is, maintained the same through the whole design: thus, when Virgil had once given the name of *pious* to Aeneas, he was bound to show him such, in all his words and actions through the whole poem.[12]

The first and second of these criteria are connected with the play as a vehicle of moral instruction. Dryden wants the spectator to be in no doubt as to which persons are good characters and which are bad, which are to be imitated and which are not; and he wants the good characters to be paradigms of the behaviour appropriate to their age, sex, and dignity.

---

[12] Arthur C. Kirsch (ed.), *Literary Criticism of John Dryden* (Lincoln, Nebraska, 1966), p. 134. The analysis of Caliban is on p. 138.

The third and fourth criteria are applicable to the play as a source of pleasure: characters which do not meet these two criteria will offend the spectators' sense of propriety and displease them by frustrating their expectations.

Applying the first two tests, Dryden finds that Shakespeare's characters are better than Fletcher's but inferior to Ben Jonson's. He breaks off with an apology for not applying the fourth criterion (consistency), but it is not clear that he has applied the third either. He does not, for example, discuss whether Shakespeare followed tradition in his portraits of Caesar and of Achilles, or whether he ought to have done so.

In the midst of this discussion, which he himself describes as cursory, Dryden gives the earliest known example of a Shakespearian character sketch, an analysis of Caliban, to illustrate the copiousness of Shakespeare's invention. Here is a part of what he says:

...the poet has most judiciously furnished him with a person, a language, and a character, which will suit him, both by father's and mother's side: he has all the discontents and malice of a witch, and of a devil, besides a convenient proportion of the deadly sins; gluttony, sloth, and lust are manifest; the dejectedness of a slave is likewise given him, and the ignorance of one bred up in a desert island. His person is monstrous, as he is the product of unnatural lust; and his language is as hobgoblin as his person; in all things he is distinguished from other mortals.

In the light of later character studies, the interesting thing about this one is that it is an early example of what may be called 'genetic character study': by pointing to the origins and past history of the person (including his history in the time before the play begins), the critic shows that the seemingly incongruous character is not in fact incredible. Shakespeare has told us enough about Caliban's origins and past history to enable us to understand how the creature we see within the play came to be such as he is. We must use these clues if we want to understand Caliban. A much more extensive example of genetic criticism is given by Morgann in his essay on Falstaff; another is Goethe's attempt to explain Hamlet in *Wilhelm Meister's Apprenticeship*.

Neoclassical criteria were applied systematically by Thomas Rymer in his criticism of *Othello* in *A Short View of Tragedy* (1693). After examining the plot and finding it wanting, he proceeds to the characters or manners. Applying the second and third of the neoclassical criteria, he finds the characters 'unnatural and improper'. They are not true to type: Othello has not the character of a general, Iago has not the character of a soldier, and Desdemona is far too naive for a Venetian lady. Nor is Shakespeare true to tradition: by raising Othello and Desdemona to a social status they did not have in the story by Giraldi Cinthio, he has made their interracial marriage even more improbable. Rymer concludes that such a mass of improbabilities is likely to have a bad moral effect on the audience. He adds: 'Our only hopes, for the good of their Souls, can be, that these people go to the Playhouse, as they do to Church, to sit still, look on one another, make no reflection, nor mind the Play, more than they would a Sermon.'[13]

An excellent answer to Rymer was published by the dramatist and scholar John Hughes in *The Guardian* (no. 37, 23 April 1713). He describes how he took some young ladies to see *Othello*. Setting himself down in the corner of his box, he watched not the actors but the faces of the young ladies. At first, they behaved just like the churchgoers described by Rymer: they found pleasure in looking about them, seeing and being seen. After a while, however, the actors enthralled them, 'and as the distress of the play was heightened, their different attention was collected, and fixed wholly on the stage, till I saw them all, with a secret satisfaction, betrayed into tears'.[14] This already is a refutation of Rymer: put to trial in the theatre, *Othello* stands out all appeals. Hughes goes on to justify the characters of Othello and Desdemona and points out a lesson which the spectators can take home with them: 'the moral of this tragedy is an admirable caution against hasty suspicions, and the giving way to the first transports

---

[13] Curt A. Zimansky (ed.), *Thomas Rymer. The Critical Works* (New Haven, 1956), p. 164.

[14] Quotations from *The Guardian*, *The Tatler*, and *The Spectator* are taken from A. Chalmers, *The British Essayists* (Boston, 1855–7).

of rage and jealousy, which may plunge a man in a few minutes in all the horrors of guilt, distraction and ruin.' Here we have a good example of apologetic character study, a defence of Shakespeare, based on experience of the play in the theatre.

After the Rymer episode, nothing more is heard of Dryden's criteria as a group, though later critics sometimes use one or other of them, usually with a tacit modification. It is to be regretted that no writer of the eighteenth century criticized Dryden's definitions of character or reflected formally on his criteria. His second definition includes Aristotle's *tropoi* or manners, but does not include his *dianoia*, the intellectual qualities; yet these certainly help to distinguish one man from another and therefore fall under his first definition.[15] The study of character became unsystematic and haphazard for want of conceptual tools. In the twentieth century we are still hampered by a clumsy and ambiguous vocabulary.

Some of the eighteenth-century critics use 'character' in a non-Aristotelian sense without adverting to the departure. Steele and Addison, for example, when they discuss what part visual impressions play in the creation of a dramatic character, are talking not about an objective combination of moral attributes in the person on stage but about the impression (another sense of the Greek *charakter*) made on the mind of the spectator – the composite image constructed from all the signals, visual as well as auditory, which the spectator receives from the stage. Steele urges the prospective dramatist not to rely on retinue to make his hero magnificent.

The man is to be expressed by his sentiments and affections, and not by his fortune or equipage. You are also to take care, that at his first entrance he says something which may give us an idea of what we are to expect in a person of his way of thinking. Shakespeare is your pattern. In the tragedy of Caesar he introduces his hero in his nightgown. He had at that time all the power of Rome; deposed consuls, subordinate generals, and captive princes might have preceded him; but his genius was above such mechanic methods of showing greatness.[16]

The principle may be sound (though it needs some qualification), but the illustration is faulty. When Caesar is first introduced, he is surrounded by an entourage of senators and commoners. The words he is given to speak may, when simply read, give the impression that he is a domineering person who must always be issuing small commands, a vain person who loves to be flattered, and a superstitious person worried about his wife's childlessness. In the theatre, these negative impressions may easily be outweighed by the visual impression created by Caesar's splendid entourage, especially if the actor playing Caesar has a dignified bearing. The stage picture should contribute to the 'character' or impression formed in the mind of the spectator. When Voltaire, whose later criticisms of Shakespeare were as intemperate as Rymer's, saw a performance of *Julius Caesar* in London in 1731, his delicate sensitivities were offended by the presence of plebeians and of the bleeding body of Caesar on stage, but he had to admit that the sight of Brutus holding up a bloodstained dagger as he addressed the people, quite ravished him.[17]

The first criterion (character must be 'apparent') was rarely used, no doubt because Shakespeare rarely leaves any doubt as to whether a character is basically good or bad.[18] Francis Gentleman, in his book *The Dramatic Censor; or Critical Companion* (1770), refers to debates about Brutus: Should he be regarded as a bad man, since he murders his best friend for political reasons? Gentleman resolves the

---

[15] See Aristotle, *Poetics*, ch. 6 (1449b36–38).

[16] Steele, *The Tatler*, no. 53 (1709).

[17] Cf. Theodore Besterman, *Voltaire on Shakespeare* (Geneva, 1967), p. 51.

[18] In the twentieth century, we find A. C. Bradley using this criterion. In his *Oxford Lectures on Poetry* (1909), pp. 288–9, he observes that Shakespeare took little interest in the character of Octavius and failed to make it wholly clear. The 'doubtful point' is the state of Octavius' intentions at the time of his sister's marriage to Antony. A. L. French, 'Who deposed Richard the Second?', *Essays in Criticism*, 17 (1967), 411–33, takes Shakespeare to task for his uncertain handling of Bolingbroke: Did he depose Richard II, or did Richard depose himself? Kenneth Muir, in *Shakespeare Survey 34*, p. 1, gives two further examples: 'Leavis's quarrel with Bradley on Othello, and Knights's quarrel with him on Hamlet and Macbeth were largely due to the conviction that these tragic heroes were bad men who had been whitewashed by Bradley.'

dispute in Brutus' favour, but with arguments not drawn from the play.

As the Roman idea of patriotism not only justified, but applauded a man, even in the act of suicide, where the good of his country was essentially concerned, it may easily be admitted an established rule, to sacrifice the dearest friend, nay, the nearest relation, for the same glorious cause; and, in this view, Brutus stands exculpated, for Caesar's usurpation of power, most certainly broke off all social connection between him and every citizen, influenced by principles of liberty.[19]

This is a piece of apologetic criticism of a new sort, deserving a different name. The critic is not defending Shakespeare but justifying or whitewashing Brutus (according to one's point of view). This might be called 'vindicatory criticism'. Morgann's study of Falstaff is of this sort: others (for example Dryden above) have called Falstaff a coward; Morgann tries to vindicate him. In doing so, Morgann uses the word 'apparent' in a new and dangerous sense. Dryden meant 'apparent' as opposed to 'obscure' or 'ambiguous'; Morgann uses it in contrast to 'real': 'perhaps after all the *real* character of *Falstaff* may be different from his *apparent* one' (his italics) – which implies, of course, that Falstaff's real character is not, in Dryden's sense, apparent or easily recognizable.[20] The distinction is dangerous because it opens the door to all kinds of superfluous character criticisms which quietly assume that students left to themselves will misapprehend Shakespeare's characters and therefore need the brokerage of a subtle critic (such as Bradley). The assumption is not flattering either to Shakespeare or to the students.

Dryden's second criterion, trueness to type, was employed by John Dennis, a neoclassical critic and 'corrector' of Shakespeare's plays, almost as clumsily as by Rymer. Shakespeare, he says, has offended against the conveniency of manners: 'Witness *Menenius* in the following Tragedy, whom he has made an errant Buffoon, which is a great Absurdity. For he might as well have imagin'd a grave majestick *Jack-Pudding*, as a Buffoon in a Roman Senator', and so on.[21] These and similar criticisms by Voltaire were brushed aside by Dr Johnson as 'the petty cavils of petty minds'.

Francis Gentleman uses this criterion more intel-ligently in his criticism of *King John*, in the writing of which, he says, 'Shakespeare disclaimed every idea of regularity'. A king should be right royal, but King John is not.

In point of characters King John is a very disagreeable picture of royalty; ambitious and cruel; not void of spirit in the field, yet irresolute and impolitic; from what we can observe, totally unprincipled; strongly tainted with the opposite appellations which often meet, fool and knave; during his life we have nothing to admire, at his fall nothing to pity.

There is no capital character within our knowledge of more inequality; the greater part of what he has to say is a heavy yoke on the shoulders of an actor. His two scenes with Hubert are indeed masterly, and do the author credit; like charity they may serve to cover a multitude of sins; the dying scene is not favourable to action.

Mr. Quin was the first we remember to see figure away in royal John; and, as in most of his tragedy undertakings, he lumbered through the part in a painful manner; growled some passages, bellowed others, and chaunted the rest.[22]

At least this is theatre-oriented criticism: actors are warned to avoid the part if they possibly can. But Gentleman can also be positive and helpful. Another king who earns his strong disapproval is Richard II, but he recognizes this as an excellent acting part and regrets that Garrick never played it. 'This monarch', he says, 'should be represented by an amiable appearance, with a smooth interesting flow of expression.' On the speech, 'What must the king do now?' his comment is: 'Though Richard's behaviour is despicable to the last degree, yet what he has to say is . . . expressed in so masterly a manner, that in public or private it must materially touch sensibility, and we are led to pity where we should contemn' – which anticipates Walter Pater's better-known comment that the meekness of Richard's submission

---

[19] Francis Gentleman, *The Dramatic Censor* (repr. Farnborough, 1969), vol. 2, p. 15.

[20] D. N. Smith (ed.), *Eighteenth Century Essays*, p. 211.

[21] D. N. Smith (ed.), *Eighteenth Century Essays*, p. 24. For Dr Johnson's comment see Sherbo, *Johnson on Shakespeare*, p. 65.

[22] Gentleman, *The Dramatic Censor*, vol. 2, p. 167.

'would have seemed merely abject in a less graceful performer'.[23]

Nicholas Rowe, Shakespeare's first biographer (1709), shows in his comment on *Henry VIII* that for Shakespeare fidelity to history (the third criterion) was not always an overriding consideration in the formation of historical characters. If Shakespeare presents King Henry's good qualities much more clearly than his faults, 'it is not the Artist wanted either Colours or Skill in the Disposition of 'em; but the truth, I believe, might be, that he forbore doing it out of regard to Queen Elizabeth, since it could have been no very great Respect of the Memory of his Mistress, to have expos'd some certain Parts of her Father's Life upon the Stage'.[24] (This principle might easily be generalized: in his delineations of Richard III, of Banquo, of King Philip and Limoges in *King John*, of the Dauphin in *Henry V*, Shakespeare is not an objective historian but a patriot, a poet of the establishment, and a loyal subject of the Tudors and Stuarts.)

Applying this criterion to *Julius Caesar*, John Dennis finds the character faulty and attributes the defect to Shakespeare's inadequate reading: if he had used the Roman sources, Sallust and Cicero, as well as the Greek Plutarch, he would have written a much more moving tragedy. Having failed to present an adequate picture of Caesar's greatness, he failed to mediate to his audiences the emotional impact of the assassination. The death of so great a man ought to move us much more profoundly. These reflections drive Dennis on to speculate about how Shakespeare should have developed the plot in order to realize the full tragic potentialities of the material.[25] Dennis does not consider the possibility that Shakespeare was deliberately revising the portrait of Julius Caesar for some other purpose of his own.

The fourth of the neoclassical criteria is 'consistency', but the word is ambiguous. We need to distinguish between simultaneous inconsistency, the conjunction of incompatible qualities in a person at one and the same time, and successive inconsistency, which occurs when a character established at the beginning fails in later scenes to fulfil the audience's expectations. Dryden includes simultaneous consist-

ency in the very definition of character ('a composition of qualities which are not contrary to one another in the same person'). The fourth criterion of Aristotle, Horace, Bossu, and Dryden is successive consistency. Aristotle's example of a character which does not meet this criterion is the heroine of Euripides' *Iphigenia at Aulis*: 'Iphigenia as a suppliant is quite unlike what she is later.'[26] Dryden's explanation of this criterion, quoted above, is too brief to be clear. His illustration is borrowed from Bossu, whose explanation is much clearer: according to Aristotle, the epic or tragic poet should first describe what sort of person the hero is and then show him making a decision which agrees with his previously established character. Virgil describes Aeneas from the start as *pius*, i.e. faithful, loyal and submissive to the gods. Then he falls in love with Dido and is put to a test: an express order of the gods commands him to Italy. His fidelity to the gods overcomes his strong natural inclination to stay. 'If nothing had foreshewn me the Resolution of Aeneas, nor what side he had taken to, nor the contrary, in this case there would have been no *Manners*.'[27]

When Rymer criticizes Desdemona, he is accusing Shakespeare of successive inconsistency: first introduced before the Venetian senate as a noble Venetian lady, she does not act like one when she arrives on Cyprus. Other critics recognize that Shakespeare shows extraordinary skill in 'developing' his characters through successive scenes. 'Development' is another regrettably ambiguous term. In one sense, it means progressive disclosure of an unchanging character; in the other, it means presentation of a person whose character changes as a result of decisions, actions and sufferings occurring within the time represented.

Rowe gives a good example of Shakespeare's skill

---

[23] Cf. Francis Gentleman's Introduction and notes to *Richard II* in *Bell's Edition of Shakespeare's Plays with Notes Critical and Illustrative by the Authors of the Dramatic Censor*, vol. 7 (1774; repr. 1969), pp. 3, 50 and 55. Walter Pater, *Appreciations with an Essay on Style* (1897), p. 202.

[24] D. N. Smith (ed.), *Eighteenth Century Essays*, p. 17.

[25] D. N. Smith (ed.), *Eighteenth Century Essays*, p. 35.

[26] Aristotle, *Poetics*, ch. 15 (1454a31–33).

[27] René Le Bossu, *Treatise on the Epick Poem* (1695), p. 170.

in the progressive disclosure of character when talking of Cardinal Wolsey.

Certainly nothing was ever more justly written, than the Character of Cardinal *Wolsey*. He has shown him Tyrannical, Cruel, and Insolent in his Prosperity; and yet, by a wonderful Address, he makes his Fall and Ruin the Subject of general Compassion. The whole Man, with his Vices and Virtues, is finely and exactly describ'd in the second Scene of the fourth Act.[28]

Rowe is here opening up what a twentieth-century critic has called the rhetoric of character construction.[29]

The first critic to dwell at length upon Shakespeare's skill in the presentation of changing characters was William Richardson, who deserves a much more prominent place in the history of Shakespearian criticism than he has ever had.[30] His 'philosophical analysis' of Shakespearian characters marks a new departure. It does not pretend to be dramatic criticism or to be theatre-oriented; it is unashamedly philosophical. The writer, Professor of Humanity at Glasgow, approaches the characters as a philosopher interested in ethics and psychology, especially at the point where the two disciplines meet. His first book, entitled *A Philosophical Analysis and Illustration of Some of Shakespeare's Remarkable Characters* (1774), starts from the conviction that the phenomena of mind are no less worthy of philosophical attention than the phenomena of the material world; if the knowledge of human nature has been slow to develop, the reasons are that experiment and observation are difficult when the object of inquiry is as unstable as human passion, and that the mind which is calm enough to analyse the passions cannot simultaneously feel them. Therefore the mental philosopher needs the assistance of a dramatist who excels, not in describing, but in imitating the passions, and such, as Lord Kames pointed out, is Shakespeare. His poetry gives the necessary fixity to the fleeting passions, so that we can analyse them minutely and at leisure.

'In the character of Macbeth', says Richardson, 'we have an instance of a very extraordinary change.'[31] An initially honourable man weakens, dallies with temptation, yields, and becomes through his own evil choices a moral wreck. With the aid of ideas learned from the philosopher David Hume, Richardson is able to explain how the change comes about. This type of character study or analysis is interesting, and more will be said about it below, but it has had a questionable influence on some later critics. The result which Richardson hopes to achieve is not a keener appreciation of the plays but some advancement of the sciences of psychology and ethics. Various later critics, including Bradley, have assumed that by leading their students through lengthy psychological disquisitions (for example, on the causes of Hamlet's delay) they would enhance their 'dramatic appreciation' of the tragedies.[32]

Many of the late eighteenth-century students of character were concerned with simultaneous consistency: Is it credible that a Prince who is noble, sensitive and honourable, should be at the same time cruel to his mother and Ophelia and positively satanic in his hatred not only of Claudius whom he wants to send to hell but also of the pair of vipers whom he sends to execution 'not shriving time allowed'? This is the sort of problem which genetic criticism tries to solve in Shakespeare's favour. The earliest known example is Dryden's explanation of Caliban, quoted above. Another excellent example is Dr Johnson's explanation of Polonius. This starts as a piece of corrective (not apologetic) criticism: Warburton gave an inadequate analysis of Polonius in terms of two specific types which are not obviously compatible (a weak pedant and a minister of state); Dr Johnson characteristically turns from

---

[28] D. N. Smith (ed.), *Eighteenth Century Essays*, p. 17.

[29] Giorgio Melchiori, 'The Rhetoric of Character Construction', *Shakespeare Survey 34*, pp. 61–72.

[30] R. W. Babcock, 'William Richardson's Criticism of Shakespeare', *Journal of English and German Philology*, 28 (1929), 117–36, does not do justice to Richardson, who is also a pioneer in the study of Shakespeare's manipulation of the audience, a subject investigated by E. A. J. Honigmann, *Shakespeare: Seven Tragedies: The Dramatist's Manipulation of Response* (1976).

[31] Quoted from a microfilm of the original edition (kindly supplied by the University of Illinois Library), p. 45.

[32] On the first page of his Introduction to *Shakespearean Tragedy* (1904) Bradley says that his one aim will be 'dramatic appreciation'.

the specific to the generic: Polonius is an old man in whom dotage is encroaching on wisdom. To show how one and the same person can be a giver of sound advice in one scene and a foolish pedant soon after, Dr Johnson reconstructs his past, explaining how he came to be such as he is.

Polonius is a man bred in courts, exercised in business, stored with observation, confident of his knowledge, proud of his eloquence, and declining into dotage... Such a man is positive and confident, because he knows that his mind was once strong, and knows not that it is become weak. Such a man excels in general principles, but fails in their particular application. He is knowing in retrospect, and ignorant in foresight.[33]

Richardson applies the genetic method to Hamlet, placing the blame on Claudius and Gertrude: the scandal of their sin has unbalanced Hamlet's personality.[34] In our century, Freud characteristically removes the blame from the older generation: the trouble arises from Hamlet's own failure to resolve his Oedipal complex. Now that Freud's blame-shifting technique is being discredited, perhaps we shall see a return to the position of Richardson.[35]

As was mentioned above, Morgann applied the genetic method to Falstaff in his essay published in 1777. Since Goethe did not publish *Wilhelm Meister* until 1796, it is possible that he may have learned the genetic method from Morgann, but on the whole it is not likely, since he began work on *Wilhelm Meister* in 1776 and the genetic explanation of Hamlet seems to belong to the original conception of the novel.[36] Goethe's explanation is proposed, not as a piece of apologetic criticism, but as the solution to an actor's problem. The hero Wilhelm joins a group of players, persuades them to mount a production of *Hamlet*, and himself undertakes to play the Prince. As he studies the part, he finds it harder and harder to understand – until at length he discovers a 'new way', which turns out to be just the same as Morgann's way with Falstaff. From hints within the play Wilhelm reconstructs Hamlet's life before the death of his father.[37] Again like Morgann, Goethe writes as advocate of the character he analyses: he places Hamlet in the most favourable light he can, praising his good qualities and excusing his faults.

III

Of the two philosophers who influenced the development of character criticism during the eighteenth century the earlier is David Hume, who proposed in his *Treatise of Human Nature* (1739–40) his theory of the conversion or transformation of the passions. It is simply a generalization reached by induction from countless instances where a person stirred to one passion is seen to be easily moved to another. Psychic energy, once stirred up, can be diverted into a new channel; violent love, for example, can be converted into violent hate, or furious indignation can be transformed into pity. Moreover, when two passions are aroused simultaneously, the weaker tends to be converted into the stronger, to become, as it were, fuel for the stronger; and this happens even if the weaker is painful and the stronger pleasant: if jealousy or impatience is stirred up at the same time as love, the weaker emotion is converted into the stronger, and love is intensified.

When two passions are already produced by their separate causes, and are both present in the mind, they readily mingle and unite...The predominant passion swallows up the inferior, and converts it into itself. The spirits, when once excited, easily receive a change in their direction; and 'tis natural to imagine this change will come from the prevailing affection.[38]

---

33 Arthur Sherbo (ed.), *Johnson on Shakespeare*, p. 974.
34 Richardson, *A Philosophical Analysis*, pp. 135–6.
35 During the few years before he wrote his *Interpretation of Dreams* (1900) Freud wrote letters to his friend Dr Wilhelm Fleiss which show that he was torn between two theories of the origin of neurosis in adults: either it is due to sexual seduction (in a broad sense) by parents, or it is due to an innate Oedipal drive. Freud decided not to believe his patients' stories about the behaviour of their parents. See Marianne Krull, *Freud und Sein Vater* (Munich, 1979).
36 Cf. William Diamond, 'Wilhelm Meister's Interpretation of Hamlet', *Modern Philology*, 23 (1926–27), p. 93. Bradley, *Shakespearean Tragedy*, p. 86, applies the genetic method to Hamlet.
37 The relevant sections of *Wilhelm Meister* can be read in Frank Kermode (ed.), *Four Centuries of Shakespearian Criticism* (New York, 1965), pp. 422–7.
38 David Hume, *A Treatise on Human Nature*, II, 4 (ed. L. A. Selby-Bigge, 1888; repr. Oxford, 1967, p. 420).

In his essay *Of Tragedy* (1757), Hume applies this principle to the working of tragedy, in an effort to explain the paradox that the presentation of painful events can give pleasure.[39] He does not himself apply the principle to Shakespeare's characters – his illustration is from Cicero's Second Verrine Oration – but he could very easily have found examples in Shakespeare. In *King Lear*, for instance, when Cordelia is cruelly rejected by her father, the King of France is moved to pity her and finds to his surprise that this pity has greatly intensified his love for her.

> Gods, gods! 'Tis strange that from their cold'st neglect
> My love should kindle to inflamed respect.
>
> (1.1.256–7)

'Tis not strange at all according to Hume's theory; it is a typical example of the conversion of one passion into fuel for another. Something similar happens in *Romeo and Juliet* (3.5), where Capulet's cruelty to Juliet excites our indignation; after his exit, Juliet stirs our pity, and all the force of our indignation against her father is converted into pity for her.

William Richardson made good use of this theory in his analysis of the change in Macbeth's character. The speeches of the Captain and of Lady Macbeth exhibit him as being at first, says Richardson, brave, loyal to his sovereign, mild, gentle, and ambitious without guilt. 'Soon after we find him false, perfidious, barbarous and vindictive.'[40] Richardson shows how this comes about: at first ambition is in conflict with conscience, and conscience is strong enough to restrain it; but ambition becomes stronger and stronger till it prevails. Success itself strengthens it. The temporary and accidental emotion of joy, occasioned by success against Macdonwald, is converted into and enhances the passion of ambition from which it grew. Then the promotion of Malcolm arouses feelings of impatience in Macbeth, and these too are converted into fuel for ambition. At the time of the soliloquy, 'If it were done', Macbeth is already degenerating: he still sees the malice of the act contemplated, but he is deterred chiefly by dread of punishment and regard for public opinion. After this, the taunts of his wife and her explanation of

how he can escape punishment give to ambition its final victory over conscience. But conscience, though defeated, is not destroyed; once the deed is perpetrated, conscience returns with violence to accuse and condemn. Conscience now begins to assimilate all other emotions and passions; its terrors gradually overwhelm Macbeth.[41]

Secondly, there is Immanuel Kant, who set forth his aesthetic philosophy in his *Critique of Judgment* (1790). This dealt the death-blow to neoclassical criticism of Shakespeare by demonstrating once and for all that in the development of any art genius creates works from which rules can be extracted for the guidance of beginners, but genius will always transcend existing 'mechanical' rules.[42] Kant also pointed the way towards the 'organic' criticism of the Romantics by contending that 'beauty is the form of the purposiveness of an object, so far as this is perceived without any representation of purpose' (i.e., in plain English, we see that each part of a beautiful object or artefact contributes purposefully to the whole, without feeling impelled to ask what is the purpose of the whole).[43] The development of a work of art in the mind of an artist is comparable to the growth of an organism; it is a groping, partly conscious and partly instinctive, towards a final organic unity. The artist's mind, from the start, is

---

39 David Hume, 'Of Tragedy', ed. John W. Lenz, *Of the Standard of Taste and Other Essays* (Indianapolis, 1965), p. 32.

40 Richardson, *A Philosophical Analysis*, p. 45.

41 Richardson's footnotes are few and far between, about half a dozen to a book, but each book has a footnote acknowledging indebtedness to Hume. See *A Philosophical Analysis*, p. 53; *Essays on Shakespeare's Dramatic Characters of Richard III, King Lear, and Timon of Athens* (1874; repr. New York, 1974), p. 8; *Essays on Shakespeare's Dramatic Character of Sir John Falstaff and on His Imitation of Female Characters* (1789; repr. New York, 1973), p. 7. He also has three footnotes acknowledging indebtedness to Lord Kames.

42 Kant was anticipated here by J. G. Herder's section on 'Shakespeare' in his *Von Deutscher Art und Kunst* (*Sämtliche Werke*, vol. 5, 1891; repr. Hildesheim and New York, n.d.), pp. 208–31.

43 Kant, *Critique of Judgment*, ss. 62–3, as translated by F. C. Copleston, *A History of Philosophy*, vol. 6/2 (1962; repr. New York, 1966), p. 152.

groping towards a half-unknown end, just as a plant assimilates matter into its system and works towards an end which it does not know.

The relevance of this theory to Shakespearian criticism was quickly seen by A. W. Schlegel: the critic should look at a play as an organic whole and try to show how each scene and each character fits into the organism, or harmonizes with the overall tone. In an essay, 'Romeo und Julia', published in Schiller's periodical *Die Horen*, 1797, Schlegel, applying the new method, shows among other things that the qualities given to the minor characters are dictated by the total design of the play.[44] Why, for example, is old Capulet made so irascible and cruel? Schlegel's answer is that 'it saves Juliet from any conflict between love and filial affection... After such treatment, she can no longer respect her parents; henceforth, when compelled to dissemble, she does so resolutely and without scruples of conscience.'

It is no less regrettable than amazing that this epoch-making essay, which inaugurated a new era in Shakespearian criticism, should have passed into oblivion. In our century, Harley Granville-Barker tries to explain the violent anger of Capulet by saying that Elizabethan fathers were often like that.[45] And much more recently, T. J. Cribb could write on 'The Unity of *Romeo and Juliet*' without showing any awareness of the existence of Schlegel's treatment of the same subject.[46]

An English translation of Schlegel's essay was published anonymously in the first and only issue of *Ollier's Literary Miscellany*.[47] The anonymous translator, Julius Charles Hare, after paying a generous tribute to the two Schlegel brothers, August Wilhelm and Friedrich, declares that the business of criticism henceforth,

when it is employed upon a single work, will be to effect, what is effected in the present criticism of Romeo and Juliet, – to discover the seminal principle, the detection of which alone can make the whole poem intelligible, and then watchfully to follow the process of the creative power lodged in that principle, as it gradually expands itself, until in the fulness of its blossoming it 'dedicates its beauty to the sun.'

Schlegel's treatment of *Romeo and Juliet* set the pattern for Hermann Ulrici's treatment of six tragedies in *Shakespeare's Dramatic Art* (1839) and for G. G. Gervinus's *Shakespeare Commentaries* (1849–50) – though both these authors prefer to trace 'organic criticism' back to the short passage in Lessing's *Hamburg Dramaturgy*, quoted in the last paragraph of Schlegel's essay, rather than to Schlegel himself.[48] In 1873, F. J. Furnivall, founder of the New Shakspere Society, declared Gervinus's work (translated into English by F. E. Bunnett, 1863) to be 'still the only book known to me that comes near to the true treatment and dignity of its subject, or can be put into the hands of the student who wants to know the mind of Shakespeare'.[49]

To sum up: during the first two centuries, students of Shakespeare, recognizing the superiority of his characters over those of other dramatists, discovered at the same time the inadequacies of the four neoclassical criteria; some of them turned to good use the work of philosophers other than Aristotle; and they pursued a wide variety of purposes: to explain in what ways Shakespeare's characters are superior to those of other dramatists (laudatory criticism); to defend the reputation of

---

[44] Schlegel gives a short summary of this article in his *Lectures on Dramatic Art and Literature* (trans. John Black, 1815; repr. London, 1881), p. 361. The German text is reprinted in Emil Staiger (ed.), *A. W. Schlegel, Kritische Schriften* (Zurich, 1962), pp. 92–113.

[45] Harley Granville-Barker, *Prefaces to Shakespeare*, 2 vols. (Princeton, 1946–7), vol. 2, p. 334.

[46] T. J. Cribb, 'The Unity of *Romeo and Juliet*', *Shakespeare Survey 34*, pp. 93–104.

[47] There is a copy of *Ollier's Literary Miscellany*, No. 1 (1820) in the British Library. It is defective: pp. 37–8 are missing – apparently a printer's error. The quotation is from p. 12.

[48] Cf. G. E. Lessing, *Hamburg Dramaturgy*, No. 15 (ed. V. Lange, New York, 1962, pp. 40–1), on which see J. G. Robertson, *Lessing's Dramatic Theory* (1939; repr. New York, 1965), p. 209, quoting a remarkable criticism of Lessing by a certain W. Wetz.

[49] Furnivall quotes this passage from his Society's Prospectus in the Introduction which he wrote for Bunnett's translation (1863, from the second German edition of 1862), p. xxi.

Shakespeare against charges of unskilful dramatization (apologetic criticism); to defend the reputation of a loved character against adverse moral judgements (vindicatory criticism); to correct the inadequate character sketches of earlier critics (corrective criticism); to help actors to discriminate one role from another (comparative criticism); to help actors to find self-consistency in difficult roles (genetic criticism); to help actors, particularly in minor roles, to see how their parts fit into the unity of the whole (organic criticism); to help theatregoers to derive moral profit from their visits to the theatre (moralizing criticism); to extract laws about the workings of the human mind for the advancement of psychology and ethics (philosophical criticism). One thing no critic was able to do: to pluck out the heart of Shakespeare's mystery and tell future dramatists how to create comparable characters.

HOW GERMAN IS SHAKESPEARE IN GERMANY? RECENT TRENDS IN CRITICISM AND PERFORMANCE IN WEST GERMANY

WERNER HABICHT

When in World War II dramatists of enemy nations were banned from German theatres, an exception was made for Shakespeare. For, as the Nazi Ministry of Propaganda decreed officially, Shakespeare was to be treated as a German author.[1] This, however, was by then the confirmation of a hardly contested fact rather than a vicarious invasion of British territory. Affinities between Shakespeare and German culture had been enthusiastically acknowledged and bardolatrously celebrated throughout the preceding two centuries, ever since eighteenth-century intellectuals had discovered his plays. These had then left their imprint on the work of the major German classics, from Lessing through Goethe to Kleist and Büchner. Shakespeare was considered as the catalyst that brought German literature into its own – a view which in the course of the nineteenth century grew into something of a myth, the fullest presentation of which was to be Friedrich Gundolf's influential book *Shakespeare und der Deutsche Geist* (1911). It is true that throughout the nineteenth and early twentieth centuries there had also been patriotic objections to the mania with which a foreign dramatist was thus extolled at the expense of the national classics and of the respect due to the classical Greek subsoil of German culture. But Shakespeare's potent German defenders, even when sharing the xenophobia of such attacks, retaliated by arguing that it was indeed in Germany that Shakespeare had found his real spiritual home, since in England the Puritans had deprived him of his natural platform. As a consequence Shakespeare was firmly integrated into the concept of national literature and literary national-

ism, which itself was a heritage of German Romanticism. And Shakespeare had also passed into the hands and minds of both Hegelian art-philosophers and positivistic philologists, only a few of whose products have proved as enduring as Alexander Schmidt's *Shakespeare-Lexicon*.

All this was of course helped, and the reception of Shakespeare by the general public was facilitated, by the existence of the excellent metrical translation by Schlegel and Tieck, another product of the Romantic period deriving from a concept of organic poetry; it eventually established itself as the apparently invulnerable standard version, was disseminated in popular editions and used for most stage productions, and yielded the Shakespearian quotations that became common parlance. When in the 1930s a new translator thought it was high time to introduce a radically modernized German Shakespeare and, encouraged by disintegrationist textual theories then current, offered somewhat freely adapted new versions which some theatres performed successfully, his efforts elicited conservative vituperation and led to so heated a public controversy that Goebbels himself put a dictatorial end to it in 1936 by ruling that no other than the old Schlegel–Tieck translation was thenceforth to be admitted on German stages.[2] Shakespeare the German classic was not to be tampered with.

---

[1] Press conferences of 20 September 1939 and 16 July 1940. Cf. Ilse Pietsch, 'Das Theater als politisch-publizistisches Führungsmittel im Dritten Reich' (unpublished dissertation, University of Münster, 1952), p. 228.

[2] Cf. editorial in *Die Literatur*, 38 (1935/36), pp. 452–3.

The story of the German Shakespeare myth from Shakespeare's appraisal as a catalyst of German literary and cultural identity, through his appropriation as a national culture hero, down to the abuses of him for purposes of nationalist propaganda is, one would hope, a thing of the past.[3] But it has left us with a cumbersome heritage, and perhaps also with a warning of what may happen when identity-seeking nations turn to Shakespeare as an idol.

The ghost of that myth still walks occasionally; some ten years ago, for instance, it lurked behind a full-page review article in West Germany's leading weekly paper, a review that tore to shreds a new German 'Shakespeare Handbook' for the very reason that it allegedly failed to exhibit specifically German achievements of Shakespeare scholarship worthy of the glorious nineteenth-century tradition.[4] That the reviewer was no other than the (by then) aged modernist translator of the 1930s whose work had been banned by Goebbels was not entirely coincidental. His victims, however, the authors of the *Shakespeare Handbuch*,[5] were young enough to be relatively unaffected by the nationalist past; they had endeavoured to present a conspectus of the state of international research and critical discussion, within which the German contribution proved indeed less conspicuous than it may have appeared in the isolation of national self-adulation (which, on the other side of the Atlantic, had already caused the irritations of H. H. Furness documented in the early New Variorum volumes). The only Teutonic characteristic one might still diagnose in that *Shakespeare Handbuch* is, apart from the German language, its lengthy thoroughness, which amounts to nearly one thousand pages, though this has not prevented it from being republished in an augmented edition in 1978, nor from being supplemented, in 1982, by yet another handbook, on Teaching Shakespeare, in three volumes, 1150 pages in all.[6]

Obviously there is a demand for the reliable information provided by laborious publications such as these, and also for the output of Shakespeare primers, surveys, casebooks, and the like, some more innovative than others.[7] The fact that Shakespeare continues to be the most frequently played dramatist on the German stage (as he has been for many decades) and that his plays also appear quite frequently on German television may account for a certain amount of public – not merely academic – interest. German publications on Shakespeare also include, as Ruth von Ledebur has pointed out in her study of the first twenty-five years of post-war German Shakespeare reception,[8] a steady stream of more or less popular books, pamphlets, and articles lovingly written and often privately published by lawyers astounded at Shakespeare's familiarity with the courts, by clergymen proving Shakespeare's either Catholic or Protestant convictions, or by journalists guaranteeing ample press coverage to major Shakespeare productions and minor Shakespeare sensations. Some of these are not at all favourably disposed towards what they tend to look down upon as the official Shakespeare industry. But even the organized body of the latter, the Deutsche Shakespeare Gesellschaft (which prides itself on 120 years of continuous history, though in 1963 it was divided for political reasons) is supported by mem-

---

[3] For a more extensive discussion of these developments see Werner Habicht, 'Shakespeare in Nineteenth-Century Germany: The Making of a Myth', in *Nineteenth-Century Germany: A Symposium*, ed. M. Eksteins and H. Hammerschmidt (Tübingen, 1983). A convenient survey of Shakespeare's influence in Germany is available in Horst Oppel, *Englisch-deutsche Literaturbeziehungen* (Berlin, 1971), vol. 1, pp. 98–125. The most recent of many documentations is Hansjürgen Blinn (ed.), *Die Shakespeare-Rezeption: Die Diskussion um Shakespeare in Deutschland*, vol. 1 (Berlin, 1982).

[4] Hans Rothe, 'Rangierbahnhof für Shakespeare', *Die Zeit*, 16 February 1973, p. 22.

[5] Ed. Ina Schabert (Stuttgart, 1972; 2nd edn. 1978).

[6] *Shakespeare: Didaktisches Handbuch*, ed. Rüdiger Ahrens, 3 vols. (München, 1982).

[7] Among the more innovative surveys are Walter Naumann, *Die Dramen Shakespeares* (Darmstadt, 1978); Gerhard Müller-Schwefe, *William Shakespeare: Welt – Werk – Wirkung* (Berlin, 1978); Wolfgang Weiss, *Das Drama der Shakespeare-Zeit* (Stuttgart, 1979); Ulrich Suerbaum, *Shakespeares Dramen* (Düsseldorf and Bern, 1980); Dieter Mehl, *Die Tragödien Shakespeares: Eine Einführung* (Berlin, 1983).

[8] Ruth Frfr. von Ledebur, *Deutsche Shakespeare-Rezeption seit 1945* (Frankfurt, 1974), pp. 208–311.

bers from many walks of life, professors of English being in a distinct – though dominating – minority.

Academic Shakespeare critics, on the other hand, would tend today to consider themselves as humble mediators within the international concert rather than as promoters of national glory. Besides, the German university system (in whatever state of reform it may happen to be) hardly permits the exclusive and lifelong Shakespeare specialist to develop. But the assimilation since 1945 of work on Shakespeare carried out in England and America has not only helped to put typically German preconceptions into their proper perspective, but has also provided cues for further inquiries, which, conditioned by the central European background as they naturally tend to be, have yielded the occasional noteworthy result that might deserve to be re-channelled into even the specialist discussion in English.[9]

In the early post-war years, for instance, the influence of the New Criticism caused a movement away from historicism; and yet those who probed into the subtle textures of the individual literary work of art usually considered the historical dimensions of their findings, too, especially when trained in classical scholarship, so that the professional distinction between the critic and the scholar that used to be emphasized in England was not really applicable. Shakespearian fruits of that movement included studies such as Wolfgang Clemen's interpretative commentary on *Richard III*, E. Th. Sehrt's penetrating analysis of play openings,[10] and numerous books and printed dissertations (not to mention articles) on individual dramatic motifs and devices and their literary background and Shakespearian use, many of them written under the guidance or influence of Clemen,[11] whose *Shakespeare's Dramatic Art* (1972) itself contributed essays on, for instance, the art of preparation, dramatic past-future links, and soliloquies. Among the more recent additions (since about 1970) are book-length studies dealing with the significance of elements of magic,[12] with dramatic verse and dialogue,[13] with various types of dramatic speech,[14] scene,[15] and character,[16] or with the function of costume and stage properties.[17] There have also been new approaches to the study of Shakespearian imagery (the multi-faceted developments of which Clemen has summarized in an introduction to the second edition of his well-known seminal work[18]), among them particularly detailed and intensive explorations of Shakespeare's uses of personification, of his book

9 A checklist of German-language contributions to Shakespeare studies covering the post-war period up to 1967 is available in Hans Walter Gabler's *English Renaissance Studies in German 1945–1967* (Heidelberg, 1971). See also W. Habicht and H. W. Gabler, 'Shakespeare Studies in German: 1959–68', *Shakespeare Survey 23* (Cambridge, 1970), pp. 113–23. The ensuing period is covered by the annual bibliographies of studies published in central Europe (including theatre reviews) in *Shakespeare Jahrbuch* (West), 1971–82, and by the fairly extensive English summaries of German-language monographs and dissertations published annually in *English and American Studies in German* (supplement to *Anglia*), ed. Werner Habicht (Tübingen, 1969, etc.).

10 Wolfgang Clemen, *A Commentary on Shakespeare's Richard III* (1968); E. Th. Sehrt, *Der dramatische Auftakt in der elisabethanischen Tragödie*, 2nd edn. (Göttingen, 1973).

11 See the list of Munich dissertations on Shakespeare directed by W. H. Clemen in the latter's *Commentary*, pp. 240–1.

12 Kurt Tetzeli v. Rosador, *Magie im elisabethanischen Drama* (Braunschweig, 1970).

13 Werner Sedlak, *Blankversveränderungen in Shakespeares späten Tragödien* (Diss. München, 1971); York-Wedigo M. Schwarz, *Das Aneinandervorbeireden in der Dialoggestaltung Shakespearescher Dramen* (Diss. Göttingen, 1978). Several articles on versification are in *Shakespeare Jahrbuch* (West), 1977.

14 Peter Rohrsen, *Die Preisrede auf die Geliebte in Shakespeares Komödien und Romanzen* (Heidelberg, 1977); Wolfgang G. Müller, *Die politische Rede bei Shakespeare* (Tübingen, 1979).

15 For example, Hans Otto Thieme, *Die Zornesszene in Shakespeares Historien* (Diss. Marburg, 1972); Hans W. Thum, 'Staged Scenes' in Shakespeares Dramen (Diss. München, 1973).

16 For example, Thomas Häntsch, *Der Berater des Herrschers im dramatischen Werk Shakespeares* (Diss. Göttingen, 1975); Blanca-Maria Rudhart, *Die Frauen in Shakespeares Königsdramen* (Frankfurt, 1982).

17 Gerhard Neuner, *Die Bedeutung des Kleides in Shakespeares Dramen* (Diss. München, 1968); Evelyn Hentschel, *Die dramatische Funktion der Requisiten bei Shakespeare* (München, 1981).

18 *The Development of Shakespeare's Imagery*, 2nd edn. (1977).

metaphors, and also of the impact of the history of London import trade on the imaginative world of Elizabethan drama.[19] English counterparts of some of these works were usually arrived at independently. Studies of Shakespearian themes and their Renaissance intellectual contexts, which abounded in English until they came under attack from Richard Levin,[20] have also had occasional German equivalents, some focused on single plays, others on specific concepts; these were to some extent affected by the *Geistesgeschichte* tradition.[21] Again, since the mid-sixties a performance-oriented awareness of Shakespeare's stagecraft has arisen in the German-language area as elsewhere; to this Rudolf Stamm and several of his pupils in both Switzerland and West Germany have made a special contribution by attempting a kind of systematic grammar of the theatricality implicit in the texts of Shakespeare and his contemporaries.[22]

When in the 1970s a younger generation of scholarly critics of literature deplored the lack of theoretical foundations of previous practical criticism and turned for orientation to structuralist or semiotic, communicative or rhetorical, hermeneutic or sociological, or, more recently, deconstructionalist models that were in the air, drama was relatively seldom a central concern. But the occasional overall theory of drama did come forward, such as the one based on communicative principles propounded by Manfred Pfister,[23] and new perspectives, or rationalized ways of assessing what used to be intuitively recognized, seemed to offer themselves and have yielded various further studies raising if not clarifying problems of construction and dramaturgy, such as dramatic perspective,[24] role-playing,[25] the dramatist's control of audience sympathies and his devices of audience surprise,[26] action and plot in the light of structuralist, sociological, or rhetorical theories,[27] problems of dramatic time[28] and dramatic genre,[29] or the relation between Shakespeare's

[19] Heinz Zimmermann, *Die Personifikation im Drama Shakespeares* (Heidelberg, 1975); Theo Grüttner, *Buch und Schrift bei Shakespeare* (Diss. Köln, 1970); Hildegard Hammerschmidt, *Die Importgüter der Handelsstadt London als Sprach- und Bildbereich des elisabethanischen Dramas* (Heidelberg, 1979). See also Jürgen Beneke, *Metaphorik*

[20] *New Readings vs. Old Plays* (Chicago, 1979).
[21] See, for instance, the poetological assessment of *A Midsummer Night's Dream* in Rainer Lengeler, *Das Theater der leidenschaftlichen Phantasie* (Neumünster, 1975), or the monograph on *The Winter's Tale* by Friedrich Oberkogler, '*Das Wintermärchen' von William Shakespeare: Eine geisteswissenschaftliche Studie* (Stuttgart, 1976). See also Günter Rohrmoser, *Shakespeares Erfahrungen der Geschichte* (München, 1971) (on Shakespeare's sense of history), and, on specific themes, Hans-Wilhelm Schwarze, *Justice, Law and Revenge: 'The Individual and Natural Order' in Shakespeares Dramen* (Bonn, 1971); Karl Ohm, *Shakespeare und das Gewissen* (Frankfurt, 1975).
[22] Some of Rudolf Stamm's articles on the subject are included in his *The Shaping Powers at Work* (Heidelberg, 1967). See also Jörg Hasler, *Shakespeare's Theatrical Notation: The Comedies* (Bern, 1974); Renate Stamm, *The Mirror Technique in Senecan and Pre-Shakespearean Tragedy* (Bern, 1975); Georg Rudolf, *The Theatrical Notation of Roman and Pre-Shakespearean Comedy* (Bern, 1981); and, from a different point of view, Andreas Höfele, *Die szenische Dramaturgie Shakespeares* (Heidelberg, 1976).
[23] *Das Drama: Theorie und Analyse* (München, 1977). See also Norbert Greiner, Jörg Hasler et al., *Einführung ins Drama*, 2 vols. (München, 1982), which is more eclectic. Both are clearly of Shakespearian interest.
[24] Manfred Pfister, *Studien zum Wandel der Perspektivenstruktur in elisabethanischen und jakobäischen Komödien* (München, 1974).
[25] Dietrich Schwanitz, *Die Wirklichkeit der Inszenierung und die Inszenierung der Wirklichkeit* (Meisenheim, 1977).
[26] Werner Habicht and Ina Schabert (eds.), *Sympathielenkung in den Dramen Shakespeares* (München, 1978); Sybille Jobin, *Shakespeare: Die Dramaturgie der Zuschauerüberraschung in seinen Komödien* (Bonn, 1979).
[27] Dieter Ramm, *Die Phasenstruktur der Shakespeareschen Tragödien* (Frankfurt, 1974); Peter Hasenberg, '*By What You See Them Act': Probleme der Handlung in Shakespeares 'Macbeth', 'Othello' und 'King Lear'* (Amsterdam, 1981). The 1981 volume of *Shakespeare Jahrbuch* (West) is also devoted to problems of plot and action.
[28] Bernard Lenz, '*The Time Has Been': Die Vergangenheitsdimension in Shakespeares Dramen* (Frankfurt, 1974). See also Franz H. Link, *Dramaturgie der Zeit* (Freiburg im Breisgau, 1977).
[29] For example, Volker Schulz, *Studien zum Komischen in Shakespeares Komödien* (Darmstadt, 1971); Astrid Kirchheim, *Tragik und Komik in Shakespeares 'Troilus and Cressida', 'Measure for Measure' und 'All's Well that Ends Well'* (Frankfurt, 1971); Susanne Stamnitz, *Prettie Tales of Wolues and Sheepe: Tragikomik, Pastorale und Satire im Drama der englischen und italienischen Renaissance 1550–1640* (Heidelberg, 1977).

im Drama: Dargestellt an Shakespeares 'Pericles' und 'Cymbeline' (Bonn, 1975), and cf. note 38.

Elizabethan background and present response as in Rolf Breuer's mediation between historicism and Jan Kott.[30] Little in this category of Shakespeare criticism would seem to be specifically German; even the German language is in some cases partially obscured by jargonese accretions. Analyses of Shakespeare's language have perhaps even more naturally been indebted to the general developments in modern linguistics; a number of these originated in the context of Marvin Spevack's work in Münster on the *Complete and Systematic Concordance of the Works of Shakespeare*[31] and on the project of a Shakespeare Dictionary (SHAD).[32]

The most prolific activities, however, would seem to have been propelled by a theoretical interest in the reception of literature, which in Germany has to some extent been indebted to Gadamer's hermeneutic aesthetics and its extensions into literary theory by H. R. Jauss, Wolfgang Iser, and others. Recognition of the indefinitenesses of the transmitted literary text and of the frame of reference by which its reception and concretion is conditioned has encouraged the acknowledgement of how much the impact of Shakespearian drama owes to the context in which it is read and performed. Even if existing theories of literary reception may not be clear-cut enough to be readily applicable, a good deal of practical field-work has been done in the last decade or so. Most of it came in the wake of comparable work in English, but, especially when tilling the Central European ground, was able to add a few pieces of genuinely researched extra information not only on Shakespeare's influence and his affinities with modern drama, but also on the history of Shakespeare adaptations[33] and on the remote and recent stage history of Shakespeare or of specific plays such as *A Midsummer Night's Dream*, *Measure for Measure*, or the Histories.[34] Shakespeare illustrations, too, have been studied as documents of Shakespeare interpretation, on principles outlined by the late Horst Oppel,[35] who also assembled an archive of pictorial material upon which several useful scene-by-scene commentaries on individual plays in the light of pertinent illustrations of various periods are based.[36] Moreover, Shakespeare criticism

30 *Vorgeschichte des Fortschritts: Studien zur Historizität und Aktualität des Dramas der Shakespearezeit* (München, 1979).

31 8 vols. (Hildesheim, 1968–75).

32 See, for example, Dietrich Rolle, *Ingenious Structure: Die dramatische Funktion der Sprache in der Tragödie der Shakespearezeit* (Heidelberg, 1971); Jürgen Schäfer, *Shakespeares Stil: Germanisches und romanisches Vokabular* (Frankfurt, 1973); *Documentation in the OED: Shakespeare and Nashe as Test Cases* (Oxford, 1980); Annegret Staufer, *Fremdsprachen bei Shakespeare* (Frankfurt, 1974); Dieter Stein, *Grammatik und Variation von Flexionsformen in der Sprache des Shakespeare-Corpus* (München, 1974); Gertrud Scholtes, *Umgebungsstrukturen von Verben im Shakespeare-Corpus* (Frankfurt, 1978).

33 Apart from countless studies on numerous German (and Austrian) authors' indebtedness to, and involvement with, Shakespeare see particularly Heinrich Huesmann, *Shakespeare-Inszenierungen unter Goethe in Weimar* (Graz, 1968); Ilse H. Reis, *Gerhart Hauptmanns Hamlet-Interpretationen in der Nachfolge Goethes* (Bonn, 1969); Paul Kussmaul, *Bertolt Brecht und das englische Drama der Renaissance* (Frankfurt, 1974); Martin Brunkhorst, *Shakespeares 'Coriolanus' in deutscher Bearbeitung* (Berlin, 1973); Horst Oppel, *Die Vorgeschichte zu 'King Lear' im Lichte moderner Adaptationen*, Akademie der Wissenschaften und der Literatur, Mainz (Wiesbaden, 1978); Bruno von Lutz, *Dramatische 'Hamlet'-Bearbeitungen des 20. Jahrhunderts in England und den U.S.A.* (Frankfurt, 1980); *Anglo-Amerikanische Shakespeare-Bearbeitungen des 20. Jahrhunderts*, ed. Horst Priessnitz (Darmstadt, 1980). The *Shakespeare Jahrbuch* (West), too, in the 1970s gave considerable space to articles on Shakespeare reception, production, and adaptation past and present; see particularly vols. 1970, 1972, 1974, 1976.

34 See, for example, Jörg Fenkohl, *Dramen Shakespeares auf der Bühne des deutschen Expressionismus* (Diss. Berlin, 1973); Christiane Vielhaber, *Shakespeare auf dem Theater Westdeutschlands 1945–1975* (Diss. Köln, 1977); Hans-Joachim Troeber, *Shakespeares 'Sommernachtstraum' auf der Bühne des 20. Jahrhunderts* (Diss. Trier, 1977); Ulrike Dibbelt, *Vom Mysterium der Gnade zur Korruption durch Macht: Shakespeare 'Mass für Mass' in Westdeutschland* (Bonn, 1980). Horst Zander, *Shakespeare 'bearbeitet'* (Tübingen, 1983) is a particularly informative examination of West German productions of the Histories between 1945 and 1975.

35 *Die Shakespeare-Illustration als Interpretation der Dichtung*, Akademie der Wissenschaften und der Literatur, Mainz (Wiesbaden, 1965).

36 Heidemarie Spangenberg, *Illustrationen zu Shakespeares 'Macbeth'* (Diss. Marburg, 1968); Rolf Pfeiffer, *Bildliche Darstellungen der Elfen in Shakespeares 'Sommernachtstraum'* (Diss. Marburg, 1971); Ingold Dutz, *Shakespeares 'Pericles' und 'Cymbeline' in der Bildkunst* (Diss. Marburg, 1975). Horst Oppel himself has evaluated pictorial

itself has been subjected to stern metacritical treatment, both with relation to some controversial plays[37] and in an attempt to redefine such critical terms as 'baroque' or 'imagery'.[38] The methodology of teaching Shakespeare is about to grow into a discipline of its own anyway and has begun to yield elaborate reflections upon the problems encountered by German Gymnasium teachers in coping in the classroom with the Shakespearian challenge provided by the recently reformed curricula.[39]

A sensitivity for Shakespearian drama as an open form has doubtless resulted from all this, and has in turn inspired confidence into the search for Shakespeare's 'relevance'. This search now takes place both in the study and on the stage and has doubtless contributed to bridging the traditional and institutional gap between the two. A changing attitude towards Shakespeare translation is perhaps the most salient case in point. The very idea that there should be such a thing as a standard translation has become profoundly suspect. The Romantic translation by Schlegel and Tieck already referred to did of course have that status up until the 1960s, despite numerous rival efforts which, ever since the Romantic period itself, had – in vain – sought either to improve on it or to provide alternatives for it. To scholarly critics accustomed to working (and teaching) on the basis of an English text, that standard translation had been relatively uninteresting anyway, while on the other hand popular writers on Shakespeare had simply taken it for granted; and it had also been used unproblematically for most theatre productions. If it is still used in productions today, however, this now tends to be an indication of a conventional performance style. When recently the German Television decided to use the Schlegel–Tieck translation for the dubbing of the televised BBC Shakespeare (with emendations required by lip-synchronization), the choice was made deliberately because the particular stance of that series suggested it.[40] The general attitude has indeed changed; translation has come to be felt as both an obstacle and a fresh opportunity – as an obstacle, because a 'received translation' would seem to obscure the potential of the original text; as an

opportunity, because a flexible approach to the plays via their retranslation can be an efficient way of interpreting them. Hence, new German versions now follow one another more rapidly than ever. Recent translators such as Rudolf Schaller, Erich Fried, Wolfgang Swaczynna, Maik Hamburger, Hermann Motschach, and, particularly, Frank Günther have indeed had their impact via the stage rather than via the book. Nevertheless, Shakespeare translation and its history have also become an object of analysis from various linguistic and literary points of view, as by now an array of learned studies testifies.[41] Another symptom of the present state of affairs is the appearance of multi-volume bilingual editions which present the English text along with annotated literal prose translations meant to facilitate German readers' direct access to Shakespeare's original meanings, and to help them bypass the

---

material in several treatises on *King Lear*, especially in *Die Gerichtsszene in 'King Lear'*, and in '*Those Pelican Daughters*': *Wanderungen und Wandlungen eines Sinnbildes*, both Akademie der Wissenschaften und der Literatur, Mainz (Wiesbaden, 1968 and 1979 respectively).

[37] Peter Bettinger, *Shakespeares 'Othello' im Spiegel der literarischen Kritik* (Frankfurt, 1977); Peter Wenzel, *Die 'Lear'-Kritik im 20.Jahrhundert* (Amsterdam, 1979); Michael Steppat, *The Critical Reception of Shakespeare's 'Antony and Cleopatra' from 1607 to 1905* (Amsterdam, 1980).

[38] Brigitte Barcklow, *Die Begriffe Barock und Manierismus in der heutigen Shakespeare-Forschung* (Diss. Freiburg, 1972); Maria Rauschenberger, *Shakespeares 'Imagery': Versuch einer Definition* (Amsterdam, 1981).

[39] See note 6 above. Recent book-length publications also include Klaus Busacker, *Shakespeares 'Julius Caesar': Vorschläge zur Behandlung des Dramas im Leistungskurs* (Würzburg, 1982); Reiner Küpper, *Shakespeare im Unterricht* (Würzburg, 1982).

[40] Cf. Gert Rabanus, 'Shakespeare in deutscher Fassung', *Shakespeare Jahrbuch* (West), 1982, p. 71.

[41] For instance, H. J. Koyro, *A. W. Schlegel als Shakespeare-Übersetzer* (Diss. Marburg, 1966); Peter Gebhardt, *A. W. Schlegels Shakespeare-Übersetzung* (Göttingen, 1970); Balz Engler, *Rudolf Alexander Schröders Übersetzungen von Shakespeares Dramen* (Bern, 1974); Norbert Hofmann, *Redundanz und Äquivalenz in der literarischen Übersetzung, dargestellt an fünf deutschen Übersetzungen des 'Hamlet'* (Tübingen, 1979). See also *Shakespeare Jahrbuch* (West), 1971, the main theme of which is Shakespeare translation.

standardized elegance and shortcomings of the Schlegel–Tieck version.[42]

All this has also affected Shakespeare performance. Many directors now tend to work out their conceptions on the basis of a new Arden or a New Penguin edition, and then go on either to select a published translation that suits their purposes or to do the translating themselves, sometimes engaging literary consultants. Peter Palitzsch, a pupil of Brecht, for his memorable production of the first tetralogy of Histories (*Die Rosenkriege*) in Stuttgart in 1967 used a German text prepared by his dramaturg, Jörg Wehmeyer, who says that his translation was inspired by the avant-garde stage designs of Wilfried Minks, which had impressively stylized the image of the English court as a slaughterhouse.[43] More recently, Dieter Dorn, in an interview of 1981 on his Munich productions of *A Midsummer Night's Dream* and *Twelfth Night*[44] which emphasized the creation and destruction of illusions, has described his need for a translation which was to offer the actors more resistance than was to be expected from the suave Romantic poetry of Schlegel, and which was also to avoid the latter's elegant rhyming and unintentional humour. The most consistent use of translation as an instrument to formulate directional intention, however, has been made by Peter Zadek, whose daring productions of *The Merchant of Venice, Lear, Hamlet, Othello,* and *The Winter's Tale* electrified – and polarized – German audiences of the seventies. Zadek starts out (as documentations of his theatre work amply testify) with an English prompt-book plus a rough German prose translation prepared by his assistants; this preliminary German text is then intensely tested and shaped in the course of rehearsals.[45]

Translation under these circumstances is part of practical theatre work. It involves a total dissection of the Shakespearian text, the theatrical reassembling of which then draws on materials provided not only by the expected target language, but also (particularly in Zadek's case) by the actors' individual, collective, and ritualistic body language, and by visual associations derived from the circus, the variety show, the iconography of comics, and the real world. The process of translation thus becomes an essential impulse in productions that seek to relate Shakespearian substance to the preconceptions, fantasies, and nightmares of a modern audience. Most significant Shakespearian directors since the late sixties have shared this experience, even though the reassembling of the playtexts deconstructed in a conscious act of translation has of course been achieved in various theatrical idioms. Peter Stein in his grand-scale 1977 Berlin production of *As You Like It*, for instance, found his style by exploring Shakespeare's intellectual background in seminars and preliminary theatrical exercises to which his entire team was subjected in order to enable them to state the present significance of Elizabethan history.[46] Hansgünter Heyme for his 1981 production of *Hamlet* in Cologne had the stage furnished with dozens of video monitors that projected the hero's disintegrated image, while his lines were spoken by the director from the auditorium. The verbal level of the play was – in these and other productions – subordinated to the total performance. In order to emphasize the deformity of Richard III, for example, Wilfried Minks in a Frankfurt production of 1981 had him raise the pitch of his voice to such an extent that the words became grotesquely incomprehensible.

How German is it, then – this transformation of Shakespearian messages received with late twentieth-

---

42 The *English-Deutsche Studienausgabe der Dramen Shakespeares*, general editors W. Habicht, E. Leisi, R. Stamm (Bern and München, 1977, etc.) also provides full annotation and commentary. Five volumes have appeared to date.

43 Cf. J. v. G., 'Shakespeare heute – übersetzt oder bearbeitet?', *Heidelberger Tagblatt*, 3 July 1967, p. 13.

44 Published in *Shakespeare Jahrbuch* (West), 1982; see pp. 32–3.

45 Cf. Volker Canaris, *Peter Zadek: Der Theatermacher und Filmemacher* (München, 1979).

46 For full descriptions of Stein's theatre work and productions see Peter Iden, *Die Schaubühne am Halleschen Ufer 1970–1979* (München, 1979), and, particularly, Michael Patterson, *Peter Stein: Germany's Leading Theatre Director* (Cambridge, 1982).

century antennae in a non-English environment and in a revitalized, performance-oriented theatre? Probably not particularly German at all, since even directorial approaches and acting styles, idioms, and devices are no longer confined within national boundaries. For instance, virtually no German production of *A Midsummer Night's Dream* since Peter Brook's (1970) has refrained from doubling the parts of Hippolyta with Titania and Theseus with Oberon,[47] or from introducing elements of the circus. Giorgio Strehler's Italian precedent of having an actress play the part of the Fool in *King Lear* has been followed in several recent renderings of this tragedy, as, for example, in the one directed by Jürgen Flimm in Cologne in 1982. And there are all those apparently innovative devices, the origins of which may be hard to trace, but which suddenly abound in German performances as well as in English or American ones, such as nineteenth-century costumes for the comedies, the symbolical use of mirror sets, the archetypal use of running, dripping, or splashing water, etc.

Perhaps some of the Shakespearian experimentations in Germany have been slightly more radical than elsewhere, and perhaps this radicalism has after all been encouraged by the distancing effect of the linguistic target medium (though similar experiences are doubtless available to the English-speaking world, too, as the recently published translation of a Shakespeare play into American would seem to suggest).[48] Significantly the German theatre in the last decade has attracted, and proved a fruitful ground for, such powerful Shakespearian fragmentators and reassemblers as Peter Zadek, who had begun his career in England, or Charles Marowitz and the Hungarian-born George Tabori, who came from America. At the Hamburg opera house, another American, John Neumeier, has developed an elemental choreography for Shakespeare ballets to supersede the pantomimic idiom of John Cranko.

It may well be that the theatrical impetus of the late sixties and the seventies has made German performances not only of Shakespeare, but also of other classics, internationally more acceptable, or at least more interesting, than they used to be. It has rendered obsolete if not superseded the traditional styles of acting the classics, particularly tragedies – those declamatory spiritualizations of timeless human dilemmas and philosophical significances, which in Germany had remained relatively unaffected even by the Stanislavsky method, and which still prevailed in the early post-World War II years. And yet there are indications that the free play of fragmentation and association, of deconstruction and reconstruction, propagated by progressive directors (which has also been duly recorded and even emulated by academic critics) will not quite go to post-modern extremes. The early 1980s have so far seen remarkable rediscoveries of the literal level of Shakespeare's plays, and of their actual stories, as points of departure for spectacular explorations of their imaginative worlds, as in two noteworthy *Hamlet*s in Renaissance costume, directed by mellowed avant-gardists. One of these, Rudolf Noelte, treated the tragedy (in Bonn, 1981) as an opulently furnished closet drama. The other, Klaus Michael Grüber, in 1982 presented, on the vast empty stage of Peter Stein's Berlin Schaubühne, an uncut six-hour version, which seemed to include a range of previous reactions to the play, both German and otherwise. This may be indicative of yet another trend that goes to confirm the availability of Shakespearian drama as a productive challenge. No nationalist spirit is needed to deal with a challenge such as this.

---

[47] The fact that this casting device had already been used in a German-language production directed by Leopold Lindtberg at Salzburg in 1966 remained comparatively unnoticed.

[48] It must be admitted, however, that William T. Betken in *The Other Shakespeare: 'The Two Gentlemen of Verona'* (Rhinebeck, NY, 1982) is far from being aware of the range of possibilities inherent in the translation process.

SHAKESPEARE PERFORMANCES IN STRATFORD-UPON-AVON AND LONDON, 1982–3

NICHOLAS SHRIMPTON

It would be hard to imagine a more perfect illustration of our current uncertainty about the interpretation of Shakespeare's comedies than the productions of these plays presented at Stratford in the Royal Shakespeare Company's 1982–3 season. Barry Kyle's interpretation of *The Taming of the Shrew* opened in October 1982. John Caird's *Twelfth Night* and Adrian Noble's *The Comedy of Errors* followed in the April and August of 1983. If you rearrange the first and second of these productions you are left, not merely with a sketch map of contemporary disagreement, but with a sequential history of recent critical thought.

Twelfth Night was a thoughtful, often moving, production which could in principle have been offered in this theatre at any time in the last fifty years. On an exquisite picture stage, actors in Jacobean costume offered a coherently thematic reading of the play. The assumption upon which such performance relies is the widely held belief that Shakespeare's comedies are serious poetic statements designed, in H. B. Charlton's words, 'to elucidate the moral art of securing happiness'.[1] The director's duty is to elicit such meaning from the text and, on this occasion, 'A great while ago the world began' and 'Youth's a stuff will not endure' were taken as the keynotes of a strikingly melancholic interpretation. The set, the music, and the placing of dramatic emphasis stressed the sense of the passing of time, while a noisy Malvolio supplied broad comedy to keep the groundlings happy.

The Taming of the Shrew based itself on the first substantial challenge to this view of Shakespearian comedy. C. L. Barber's article 'The Saturnalian Pattern in Shakespeare's Comedy' originally appeared in *The Sewanee Review* in 1951 but became better known eight years later as the introduction to his book *Shakespeare's Festive Comedy*. Noting the way in which a criticism of the comedies based on 'character and story and moral quality' had often 'fallen back on mere exclamations about poetry and mood', Barber proposed instead an examination of the 'structure' of the plays.[2] What he found was, famously, a 'festive' or 'holiday' pattern in which the process of restraint and release embodied in such social institutions as Candlemas, May Day, Midsummer Eve or Halloween was re-enacted in the design of Shakespeare's plays. I saw Barry Kyle's *The Taming of the Shrew* on the very evening of the winter solstice and was therefore, perhaps, unusually open to its holiday stresses. But no audience can have missed the festive implications which troupes of carol singers, mugs of mulled ale and a brazier of burning coke thrust (literally in the last case) under our noses.

If this 'festive' *Shrew* might loosely be described as a structuralist production, Adrian Noble's *The Comedy of Errors* marked the arrival on the Stratford stage of some post-structuralist assumptions. At first sight the ruthless defamiliarizing of the play – most of the characters in some form of clown costume, the Antipholus brothers established as twins simply by having their faces painted blue, an arbitrary use of a flying platform – seemed Brechtian. But there was

---

[1] H. B. Charlton, *Shakespearian Comedy* (1938), p. 290.

[2] C. L. Barber, *Shakespeare's Festive Comedy* (Princeton, 1959), p. 4.

no social message on offer. Meanings of any kind were steadily resisted and in their place we had what Barthes might call the play of signifiers.

The withdrawal from interpretation which such techniques reflect began, in Shakespeare criticism, with John Holloway's attack on the treatment of plays as 'a fount of…moral informativeness'[3] in 1961. It reached a peak with the appearance of Richard Levin's *New Readings vs. Old Plays* in 1979. And, as Norman Rabkin pointed out in his book *Shakespeare and the Problem of Meaning*, Levin's questioning of 'thematism' in the interpretation of Jacobean drama coincided with a more general intellectual crisis:

The reader-response theories argued in various ways by such critics as Stanley Fish and Norman Holland call into question the power of an imaginative work to elicit a uniform response from its audience; Jacques Derrida and his deconstructive allies see language and art as so intractably self-reflexive as to be incapable of analyzable significance; Harold Bloom argues that all reading is misreading, that one reads well only to find oneself in the mirror.[4]

Such shifts of opinion in literary criticism were bound, sooner or later, to affect that most practical branch of the trade, theatrical direction. The Royal Shakespeare Company's programme for *The Comedy of Errors* was generously equipped with background material on the links between the play and St Paul's epistle to the Ephesians. The production itself had no truck with such traditional interpretative techniques. Whether we wished it or not, Adrian Noble thrust us into a new era in the presentation of Shakespeare's plays.

When a theatre company offers us three productions as diverse as these, in the space of a single year, one might begin to wonder whether the concept of a 'company' still has any meaning. A more appropriate response would be gratitude for the intellectual vitality which enables this theatre to reflect so vividly the contentious state of contemporary thought. Seeking a house style in an age of uncertainty is probably an unconfessed desire for ossification.

Whether the productions were as good as they were interesting is, of course, another matter. Intellectual pioneering is not necessarily a guarantee of a pleasurable evening in the theatre. By the same token, *Twelfth Night* is not to be dismissed simply because it seemed the conservative voice in an innovatory chorus. If we are to have thematism, this is what thematism should be like. Every detail of Robin Don's set and Ilona Sekacz's score, every nuance of the playing contributed to the idea of time the bringer of ruin. On the title-page of the programme we found Sonnet 12 ('nothing 'gainst Time's scythe can make defence'). And on stage, as Feste spoke his strikingly bitter account of time's whirligig bringing in revenges, the thunder spoke too. The cyclorama filled with clouds and we heard the gutters of Illyria awash with rainwater.

The set was part ruined garden, part graveyard. A vast autumnal tree overshadowed (for Orsino's court) a pair of rusting gates and (for Olivia's house) a mortuary chapel. Sarah Berger's black-gowned Olivia was ostentatiously in mourning for her dead brother, while Miles Anderson gave us an appropriately violent, sombre, and austere Orsino. Fabian was an old man, Feste a pensive intellectual.

Malvolio apart, the other clowns were correspondingly subdued. Daniel Massey played a gawky but soft-hearted Aguecheek, afflicted by fits of depression and easily moved to tears. John Thaw, as Toby Belch, was an upper-class thug, hearty rather than jovial, more cruel than comic. The drunk scenes were very drunk indeed and the uproar so uproarious that it could only be curtailed by blasts on Maria's pocket whistle.

As that detail suggests, Gemma Jones's Maria was the most original piece of characterization in the production. She was as tall as her mistress and substantially taller than Viola, so the references to her as a 'wren' and a 'giant' went for nothing. But her lanky elegance gave the clue to her social role. This was a high-spirited, horsey girl from a county background, now living in reduced circumstances as a paid companion. Part games-mistress, part romp,

---

[3] John Holloway, *The Story of the Night* (London and Lincoln, Nebraska, 1961), p. 16.

[4] Norman Rabkin, *Shakespeare and the Problem of Meaning* (Chicago and London, 1981), p. 1.

21. *Twelfth Night*, Royal Shakespeare Theatre, 1983. Zoë Wanamaker as Viola and Miles Anderson as Orsino

her worship for this Flashman of a Sir Toby was pure reversion to type.

Zoë Wanamaker was a touching, husky, gamine of a Viola, capable of shrewd comic touches (a wild shriek of panic on 'She loves me', for example) but very much in tune with the pervasive melancholy of the production. 'I am all the daughters of my father's house' reduced her to tears and prompted a disturbing cuddle from her handsome master. Unfortunately her Olivia was not up to her weight. Rushed and sometimes squeaky, Sarah Berger's lack of subtlety significantly reduced the erotic tension of their interviews.

Malvolio's extravagance of manner had a similar effect on his exchanges with Sir Toby. 'Dost thou think, because thou art virtuous, there shall be no more cakes and ale?' was delivered with great weight and force, but to such a fool of a steward that

the clash between profligacy and puritanism remained elusive. Emrys James's interpretation of Malvolio involved a great deal of comic biz ('If this fall into thy hand, revolve' – spins round on the spot). The audience clearly adored it. But he and Olivia between them gave an oddly coarse-grained effect to what was otherwise a memorably picturesque, sensitive and sad production.

Barry Kyle's festive *The Taming of the Shrew* was, by deliberate intention, coarse-grained throughout. The play-within-a-play status of the action was stressed by inserting the first four Sly scenes from *The Taming of A Shrew* and the 'travelling players' involved were presented as a distinctly scratch company. As a consequence both their costumes and their manners were a job lot. In act 1, scene 1, for example, Lucentio was a late-Victorian schoolboy in blazer and boater, Gremio was one the Three Kings

22. *Twelfth Night*, Royal Shakespeare Theatre, 1983. Daniel Massey as Sir Andrew
Aguecheek, Gemma Jones as Maria, and John Thaw as Sir Toby Belch

of Orient from a nativity play, Kate wore a puce Jacobean gown with a wild blonde wig, and Biondello arrived dressed as (what else?) Grimaldi.

If you could once get over the paradox of an expensively subsidized national company spending a great deal of money in order to look like an incompetent amateur dramatic society, then there was much here to relish. Connoisseurs of vaudeville could certainly not have gone home unhappy. As a scrapbook of music hall technique it contained everything from the low comedy of the 'Walk this way' joke (Baptista's 'But gentle sir, methinks you walk like a stranger' delivered as an outrageously camp Tranio minced about the stage) to the most elaborate slapstick acrobatics. The first encounter between Katherina and Petruchio involved some genuinely dangerous tumbling. Kate responded to his insinuating 'Marry, so I mean, sweet Katherine, in thy bed' by pushing him backwards into a tank of water hidden in the stage. He emerged, dripping

23. *The Taming of the Shrew*, Royal Shakespeare Theatre, 1982. Petruchio (Alun Armstrong) and Katherine (Sinead Cusack), with Baptista (David Waller)

and shivering, and planned his revenge. On 'Kiss me, Kate' she kneed him in the groin. But 'we will be married o'Sunday' so took her breath away that he was able to seize her by the hand and throw her, in her turn, full length into the pool.

Other effects of this unsophisticated kind included staging Gremio's account of his wealth as a scene from *The Generation Game*, with luxury items moving across the back of the stage on a conveyor belt, and allowing the Pedant (a schoolmaster on a mountaineering holiday) to make his first entrance by abseiling down the side of the proscenium arch.

A comic style so whimsically diverse as this might perhaps lead one to think that *The Taming of the Shrew* was as anti-interpretative as *The Comedy of Errors*. In fact it had two clear strands of meaning.

One was the festive stress – the carols and chestnuts and 'improvised' costumes. The other, lurking within the slapstick, was a serious study of the relationship between the shrew and her bridegroom. Sinead Cusack's Katherina was gorgeously unkempt and passionate rather than genuinely curst. But her transition to sweetness was delicately observed, and convincingly attributed to the gradual acquisition of a relish for Petruchio's particular brand of rough practical joke.

Petruchio, as this suggests, was by turns Groucho Marx and a Boy From The Blackstuff. It wasn't only his sense of humour, however, that enabled him to tame his wife. The director obliged Alun Armstrong to take his 'falcon' imagery literally. This was a man who understood the grim techniques of sensory deprivation and he entered to give the speech in which he explains them with a live falcon on his wrist. Stanley Wells recorded the way in which the bird's 'grave beauty awes the house into silence'.[5] But for all its power as a *coup de théâtre*, it was hard not to remember it as one trick among many in a generally tricksy production.

Tricks and jokes were even more prominent in Adrian Noble's *The Comedy of Errors* and here they were the whole point. It's not quite true to say that every character was a clown – Adriana, for no very obvious reason, was a twentieth-century housewife. But she was the exception which proves the rule. On the whole the director who had discreetly imported the spirit of Grock to his production of *King Lear* in the previous season proceeded on the principle of 'Send in more clowns'.

Critics (though not, it must be said, audiences) responded to this decision with irritation. Robert Cushman made the case against the production most eloquently, accusing it of pedantry: 'This, the production seems to be saying, is *clowning*; aren't you impressed?'[6] Certainly, it was not as funny as it might have been had the jokes been less forced. The style was pushed beyond farce to circus and the pace was frantic. Every tumble or pratfall was underlined with a drumroll or a swanee whistle, every serious speech sent up with music from the pit orchestra. Dr Pinch's scene was played as a full-scale cod opera. Though Richard O'Callaghan and Henry Goodman clowned legitimately, and very skilfully, as the two Dromios, they had too much competition to shine out as they should.

The intention, however, was probably less to make us laugh than to shake us out of our habitual expectations of the text. This was not realism – the familiar simulacrum of human behaviour which a willing suspension of disbelief allows us briefly to accept as life itself. Instead it was language at play, insisting on its artificiality and perpetually postponing significance. The actors were mouthpieces rather than characters. The action was a string of gags.

The most vivid illustration of this process was the treatment of the relationship between Antipholus of Syracuse and Luciana. Sometimes stressed as a fragment of romantic comedy in what is otherwise a heartless Roman farce, it was here ruthlessly undercut. Antipholus did his wooing in act 3, scene 2 while hanging upside down by his knees from a second floor window. Luciana responded by performing some acrobatic tricks with a step-ladder. Zoë Wanamaker as Adriana and Joseph O'Conor as Aegeon attempted, doggedly, to establish character and express emotion. A tide of slapstick washed their humane endeavours away. James Fenton, in *The Sunday Times*, wondered what the consequences would be of applying the same technique to *Hamlet*.[7] Unless the fashion for the *nouvelle critique* undergoes a very sudden reversal, it cannot be long before we know.

The other major production of a comedy in the 1982–3 season was *A Midsummer Night's Dream*, directed by Bill Bryden for the National Theatre. Originally conceived for the Cottesloe, it toured in the winter of 1982 to Bath (where it was the first production in the restored Theatre Royal), Cardiff and Glasgow. In April 1983 it transferred to the wide open spaces and proscenium arch of the Lyttleton Theatre, attempting to retain its initial intimacy by seating members of the audience on cushions around the stage. In the course of this complicated process the original Oberon, Paul Scofield, was replaced by Robert Stephens.

I saw it at the Lyttleton and the first thing I must report is that it does not fit into the neat map of changing production styles provided by the Royal Shakespeare Company. This was an eclectic production, full of good ideas and rich performances but without any particular axe to grind. The set was a white box, but a white box picturesquely overgrown with vines and lavishly strewn with rose petals. Spectators in twentieth-century clothes sat round the walls, but the play's costumes were Edwardian (with Edmund Dulac fairies). The cast responded to its on-stage audience, but also provided a good deal of conventional dramatic illusion.

[5] *Times Literary Supplement*, 22 October 1982.
[6] *The Observer*, 14 August 1983.
[7] *The Sunday Times*, 14 August 1983.

24. *The Comedy of Errors*, Royal Shakespeare Theatre, 1983. Luce (Frankie Cosgrave) refuses admission to Dromio of Ephesus (Henry Goodman, left), watched by Dromio of Syracuse (Richard O'Callaghan)

This is not to suggest that it was muddled or incoherent. Rather, it stood back from both interpretation and the ostentatious rejection of interpretation to provide a space in which actors could express themselves. Casting a black Hippolyta (Marsha Hunt), for example, produced some hints of pre-marital resentment – Theseus's 'What cheer, my love?' (1.1.122) was nervously delivered as she stalked prematurely off stage in a state of high dudgeon. But it was not developed into a deliberate portrait of marriage as conquest and enslavement. When the Duke and his new Duchess came on at the beginning of the final act, they waltzed together in elegant harmony.

The two major directorial decisions of the pro-

duction were similar exercises in the unpicking of recent accretions to our expectations of *A Midsummer Night's Dream*. Theseus and Hippolyta were not doubled with Oberon and Titania. As a consequence the interpretation of the woodland scenes as the subconscious experience of the daytime characters was only there if the audience wished to find it. Nearly twenty years of theatrical practice (since Frank Dunlop's production of 1967) was thereby reversed. Equally significant was the playing of the fairies. These have tended to be sinister ever since Robert Helpmann's innovatory Oberon of 1937. Bill Bryden turned them back into the benign creatures which their blessing of the bride bed has always suggested they should be. Gentle, curious and coy, they actually seemed far stranger than the hissing monsters fashionable in the last half-century.

The King and Queen of the Fairies were both magnificent. I saw Robert Stephens's mellow, self-satisfied, *sportif* Oberon, not Paul Scofield's ('grizzled, solicitous, sonorous and quietly self-mocking'[8]). Susan Fleetwood's subtle and tender Titania clearly complemented both of them. These were not ethereal beings but substantial personalities: vital, complex, and vocally superb. As Titania woke from her fascination with Bottom, her horror and her husband's sense of hurt generated a powerful and appropriate impression of adult marital quarrel.

The lovers were Edwardian silly asses, chiefly distinguished by Jennifer Hall's pert but touching Helena. The mechanicals were the production's most significant weakness. You can tell whether or not the 'hard-handed men' are going to be intelligently interpreted the moment they open their mouths. If the director has allowed them all to do different funny voices, then disaster looms. Here Quince was Irish (a pocket George Bernard Shaw), Flute Lancastrian, Starveling Yorkshire and Bottom a Cockney. This insensitivity about their status as a group of local workmen carried over into their comic style.

The play-within-a-play had a live dog (another bad sign), much intrusive music, and laboriously elaborate slapstick. Its one redeeming moment was an attempt to make sense of the textual crux 'Now is the mural down between the two neighbours' (5.1.204). A few moments after Wall, heavily laden with loose bricks, had staggered off, a loud crash came from the wings. An officious Philostrate bustled out to inspect the damage and returned, covered in dust, to point Theseus's line.

On the whole, however, the funniest scene in Shakespeare was spoiled by over-doing and, though a Wilson, Keppel and Betty sand-dance for the Bergomask cheered things up slightly, it could not quite compensate for the lost jokes. The conclusion involved much 'festive' handshaking with the audience, confirming the sense of a lively but wildly diverse dramatic style. The other matter of note was that this production (two and a quarter hours long) was played without an interval. The Royal Shake-

speare Company announced a similar policy for *The Comedy of Errors*, but did not go through with it.

What the Royal Shakespeare Company did go through with was three very different kinds of history play, ranging from the patriotic pageantry of *Henry VIII* to the Roman tragedy of *Antony and Cleopatra*. It is tempting to think that the recent birth of an heir to the throne was what suggested the return of the first of these plays to the repertoire. If so, the director, Howard Davies, had cast himself as the wicked fairy at the christening. Taking as his justification Cranmer's ambiguous prophecy of the political qualities of the infant Elizabeth ('Peace, plenty, love, truth, terror', 5.5.47), he set out to supply a consistently ironic and disillusioned reading of the text.

The style was Brechtian, with music in the manner of Kurt Weill by Ilona Sekacz and pseudo-Victorian cut-out flats by Hayden Griffin. Against this alienating and anachronistic background, actors in sixteenth-century costume set out to demonstrate the brutality of Tudor realpolitik. Richard Griffiths played a burly but youthful Henry, slowly feeling his way towards the exercise of absolute power. John Thaw was a stately and calculating Wolsey.

The early scenes were chaotic. Dispassionate performance of the political speeches tended to make them merely dull, and Tudor dances done to the tango (as Henry meets Anne Bullen at Wolsey's party) did little to relieve the tedium. Director's notes, reproduced in the programme, suggested that we should find hints of Mrs Thatcher ('There is no alternative') in Wolsey's attitude to taxation, and a ground bass of Tawney's *Religion and the Rise of Capitalism* under the entire action. Neither of these ambitions was successfully achieved on stage.

Human drama, rather than political alienation, was what rescued this production from itself, and it first began to be manifested in the courtroom (2.4) as Wolsey clashed with Gemma Jones's eloquent Katherine of Aragon. Clear, passionate, and un-affectedly tragic, Katherine gave a sense of shape to this scrapbook of a play. 'Go thy ways, Kate' (2.4.133) was Henry's first good moment. The

---

[8] Robert Cushman in *The Observer*, 28 November 1982.

25. *Henry VIII*, Royal Shakespeare Theatre, 1983. John Thaw as Cardinal Wolsey

subtlety and precision which had provoked it were shown even in details as fine as the faint hint of a twenty-year-old Spanish accent which lingered in Katherine's voice.

John Thaw sustained this intensity in 'Farewell, a long farewell, to all my greatness', speaking with strength rather than plangency and to very good effect. The spirit of Brecht blew back into the theatre for the coronation procession, which was mounted with tailor's dummies and declaimed stage directions rather than with extras and action. But two remarkable scenes remained to come. One was the dying Katherine's conversation with her gentleman usher Griffith, skilfully played by Clyde Pollitt. The other was an excellent account of the accusation of Cranmer in act 5, scene 3. With Oliver Ford Davies as an outstanding Gardiner – a boney, high-browed, over-bearing fanatic – the mood and manner of a committee were superbly caught. An exercise in sustained playing against the spirit of the text, this

26. *Antony and Cleopatra*, The Other Place, 1982. Michael Gambon as Antony and Helen Mirren as Cleopatra

production will chiefly be remembered as a perverse curiosity. It should also be remembered for some brilliant fragments of closely observed behaviour.

Few such fragments could be claimed to redeem Ron Daniels's production of *Julius Caesar*, which opened at Stratford in March 1983. A noisy piece of braggadocio, it offered spectacular gimmicks as a substitute for clear ideas about the play. Its search for such ideas, however, led it to make an unexpected contribution to a general election campaign. Four MPs and three journalists were invited to pronounce, in the programme, on whether or not the conspirators were right to assassinate Caesar. Michael Foot, then Leader of the Labour Party, said that they were and a month later, with an election imminent, found himself under attack on the features page of

The Times for his irresponsible views on political murder.[9]

The production itself could not make up its mind on the question. Caesar was initially presented as a version of Mussolini, and the vast blocks of fake marble which made up Farrah's set hinted at the fascist architecture of the 1930s. This political pointing might lead one to expect that his opponents would emerge as heroic friends of freedom. In fact their leader Cassius (played with splendid energy and force by Emrys James) was rapidly transformed into a melodramatic villain, stamping his feet and shaking his fist at the audience.

---

[9] Ronald Butt, 'Yon Cassius, Foot's unlikely hero', *The Times*, 14 April 1983.

This apparent contradiction might not have mattered had Brutus, the man caught between them, been presented as a character of sufficient depth and complexity. Unfortunately Peter McEnery spoke badly and behaved weakly. What chiefly lingers in the mind from this production is its use of a closed-circuit television system to project details of the actors' faces on to an enormous screen during the murder and the speeches over Caesar's body. Intended presumably to remind us of contemporary political rhetoric (Mark Antony's oration had a faint air of Richard Nixon's 'Checkers' speech) its chief effect was to distract the audience from both words and action. It was abandoned later in the season.

Adrian Noble's production of *Antony and Cleopatra* at The Other Place used no such extravagant devices. Instead it was distinguished by its extreme simplicity, pouring this imperial gallon of a play into the pint pot of studio performance. A bare stage and platform were the only set, though audiences hungry for spectacle could content themselves with the sight of Helen Mirren's sumptuous and scarcely concealed physique. Thoughtful speaking and acute reaction to the thoughtful speech of others were the proper preoccupations of the actors.

Just occasionally the thinking was odd. Bob Peck's northern lad of an Enobarbus, for example, spoke 'The barge she sat in' in the outraged tones of a plain man who deeply disapproved of luxury. But elsewhere the fresh ideas were profoundly effective. Romans (and in particular Jonathan Hyde's Octavius Caesar) were presented not as chilly technocrats but as emotional *mafiosi*, swarthy, violent, and sudden.

Michael Gambon's shambling bear of an Antony thereby escaped the customary impression of an eccentric funster kicking over the traces. This was an ageing man from a passionate race, still hungry for passion and aware that time was running out. At times his manner was a touch too pedestrian – 'I am dying, Egypt, dying' was spoken as a bald statement of his symptoms. But all the best effects in this production were achieved in a smoulder rather than a blaze, and he was no exception.

The heart of the play, however, was Helen Mirren's marvellous Cleopatra. More tender than imperious, most impressive when she was most intimate, she gave remarkable depth to the final acts. In mourning for Antony she contrived an extraordinary ruin of her beauty – squatting on a grubby blanket, dressed in black with her hair scraped back and ash and dirt on her face. More astonishing even than this, however, was the subsequent transition to her suicide. As Caesar left at 5.2.191, she suddenly passed (on 'He words me, girls') from an extremity of violent grief to a serene perception of her fate. Only inches from her audience, in a crowded studio theatre, she conducted a complex and tumultuous inner life with complete assurance. A recent analysis of box office returns has revealed that the Royal Shakespeare Company makes more money from extravagant shows than it does from simple ones, and of course it must obey this clear commercial logic. The remarkable achievement of this sparse but striking production argues, none the less, that hard living and high thinking must not yet be allowed to perish utterly from the English theatre.

THE YEAR'S CONTRIBUTIONS TO SHAKESPEARIAN STUDY

1. CRITICAL STUDIES
reviewed by BRIAN GIBBONS

The admirable criticism to be found in the Introductions to some recent editions of Shakespeare's works demonstrates the virtues of orthodox scholarly method as a basis for first-rate critical thought; happily, these virtues are also to be found at large in some of this year's other publications. Ian Donaldson's *The Rapes of Lucretia*[1] offers a lucid, direct, and admirably succinct narrative, accessible to the general reader as well as the specialist. That it does so speaks for the skill and judgement of the author, who surveys a wide and difficult field: literature in several languages and from Roman times to the French Revolution, paintings from Botticelli to David, and some complex issues of cultural and intellectual history. Donaldson's concern, as his subtitle declares, is with 'a myth and its transformations', and for him Shakespeare forms only a part – if an important part – of his whole account. For Shakespearians, on the other hand, the whole book may be viewed as leading up to and then receding from *The Rape of Lucrece*, putting Shakespeare's poem in the context of European painting and a certain strand of European literature and cultural history. The book is intended as 'a critical examination of certain decisive stages in the evolution' of the Lucretia story. Some aspects of this story, which Shakespeare does not deal with in the narrative poem, are touched on, with characteristic Shakespearian sensitivity to the deep centres of European myth, in his Roman plays. To quote a few lines of Donaldson serves to suggest the importance this material could have for the young Shakespeare:

It is a story about public and political behaviour, and about private, sexual behaviour, and about the relationship between these two kinds of behaviour. It is a story about the nature of liberty: liberty for the state, and for the individual . . . it is significant that Brutus vows to free Rome while holding the dagger with which Lucrece has killed herself . . . In many versions of the story the political symbolism is plain: Lucretia is not simply Lucretia, but the figure of violated Rome; the rape epitomises the wider tyranny of the Tarquins...Tarquin lays siege to her in much the same manner as he had once infiltrated himself into the confidence of the people of the Gabii.

(pp. 8–9)

This interest in Lucretia as a symbol could diminish her significance in human terms; another element in the symbolic patterning contrasts Lucrece with Brutus, who in the interests of the state condemned his own sons to death for treason and was celebrated after his death as a patriotic hero: 'Brutus, being a man, sacrifices his feelings; Lucretia, being a woman, sacrifices her life.' Ancient society may have seen in Lucretia's suicide a heroic self-abnegation, preventing moral pollution from passing along the family line. In many treatments of the story, however, the suicide is presented as a moral triumph which establishes her superiority to her fate and ravisher. Early Christians found Lucretia's suicide admirable, atoning for shame and sacrificing her life for a high ideal. With Augustine, however, difficulties are raised: if adulterous, why is Lucretia to be praised? If chaste, why put to death? Chastity is essentially a matter of the will not the body. Her suicide becomes for Augustine an act of murder, not

---

[1] Clarendon Press, Oxford, 1982.

heroism. Donaldson quotes the views of John Case in 1596: 'Lucrece's poniard made her neither chaste nor brave', and for Tyndale the pride in which she gloried in her chastity was damnable, and when she lost it she despaired, which was also damnable. Others queried whether her shame arose from having felt furtive enjoyment in the rape (p. 36).

Donaldson's discussion of the treatment of Lucretia in painting is full of interest, and the comment on the illustrated examples (especially those by Lotto, Cranach, and Tiepolo) is imaginative and subtle, leading the discussion directly towards the subtler ambiguities of the myth which are of particular interest to Shakespeare.

Donaldson notes that the problem of the Christian references in the poem cannot be dismissed as one of casual anachronisms, nor are such references systematic; rather Shakespeare gives us 'an alternation between Roman and Christian viewpoints, which generates constant uncertainty as to the way in which the poem is to be read' (pp. 45–6). He continues 'The story is no longer one of moral certainties, though critics often assume it is. Lucrece seems unsure of the moral consequences both of rape and suicide, hesitantly debating her way towards death...the simpler code of honour is complicated by newer, Christian considerations.' Considering lines 1156–76, Donaldson persuasively argues that Lucrece seems to anticipate the way in which her suicide may be regarded from other cultural and religious points of view, glimpsing the Augustinian attitude, then blurring it with vivid but confusing analogies which multiply the points of view from which such a suicide can be considered. Furthermore Shakespeare offers the suggestion that Tarquin wished to rape Lucrece precisely because she is so chaste, so invitingly, arousingly, perfect. Most significantly, Shakespeare explores the idea that Tarquin's rape of Lucretia was finally a reflexive act, more damaging to himself than to his victim; in Shakespeare's words:

A captive victor that hath lost in gain,
Bearing away the wound that nothing healeth,
The scar that will despite of cure remain,
Leaving his spoil perplex'd in greater pain.
She bears the load of lust he left behind,
And he the burden of a guilty mind.   (ll. 730–5)

Donaldson finds that Shakespeare opens up 'a new interior world of shifting doubts, hesitations, anxieties, anticipations, and griefs. No other version of the Lucretia story explores more minutely or with greater psychological insight the mental processes of the two major characters...[Shakespeare] does not take moral repossession of the older story, confidently charging it with new depth and intricacy of significance' (p. 44).

It can be fairly said that The Rapes of Lucretia must be essential reading for all those interested in Shakespeare's narrative poetry, and perhaps for all those, also, concerned with Shakespeare's interest in ancient Rome. In the present context (of critical studies of Shakespeare) this book is important because it shows how much original material remains to be uncovered by the most orthodox scholarly procedures if they are pursued with genuinely sustained vigour and scruple. This book is clearly the product of a single individual's curiosity, and its shape is dictated by the overall arguments whose resolution he pursues. It is not faked, and its questions are not bogus or borrowed. To write upon Donaldson's plan, however, it is at least necessary to read and think. By exploring unusual territory, and a work of Shakespeare's which has a perhaps deceptively youthful style, Donaldson has proved that really original research is still possible; it is not a matter of ditching orthodox techniques but of possessing curiosity and imagination and sensibility.

Arthur Kirsch has written a splendid book in defence of the profundity and seriousness of five plays which have had an uneven press in modern criticism: Othello, Much Ado, Measure for Measure, All's Well, Cymbeline.[2] Kirsch adduces refreshing and powerful material from remarkably familiar places: the Bible, the Prayer Book, Montaigne: and he frequently cites the propositions of Sigmund Freud. He approaches the plays as, in the first place, plays, not peculiar narratives by an Elizabethan patient, and

---

[2] Shakespeare and the Experience of Love (Cambridge University Press, 1981). An article dealing with Cymbeline and discussing Freud's account of dreams along lines similar to Kirsch is D. E. Landry, 'Dreams as History: The Strange Unity of Cymbeline' (Shakespeare Quarterly, 33 (1982), 68–79).

he begins by noticing the importance of the medieval dramatic tradition, in providing a means for the articulation of human experience as psychological as it is moral: medieval theatre audiences were accustomed by dramatic allegorization 'to a way of understanding the primitive components and processes of human behaviour which Freud, in a sense, had to recover through psychoanalytic excavation' (p. 6). Thus in *The Second Shepherds' Play* the conflation of a literal sheep and the Lamb of God in Mak's child can be compared to dream condensation, 'and the whole way in which the plot of Mak and the shepherds not only parallels the Nativity but enacts its meaning is an example of dream displacement. And in the play, as in a dream, both mechanisms provide a means, as well as an expression, of the experience of transformation.' We are also to notice that the conception of time and the immanence of the dream wish in the construction of the whole dream have their connections with the mode of this medieval play. These points are significant to the whole argument of Kirsch's book. He writes

In *Much Ado About Nothing*, for example, as in the medieval mystery drama, the multiple plots have a symbiotic relationship. The spiritual reverberations of the story of Claudio and Hero are displaced onto, as well as realised through, the largely psychological energies of the plot involving Beatrice and Benedick, and both plots draw nourishment from the comedy of Dogberry, whose childlike receptivity to experience suggests the ancestry of the shepherds in *The Second Shepherds' Play*. All three plots represent the play's informing experience, which is the transformation wrought in men and women when they are in love. Similarly, in *Cymbeline* the whole plot involving Cloten is a displacement that both makes possible and expresses the psychic and spiritual process of Posthumus's return to his love for Imogen, and...is dilated into an image of a regenerated human community. (p. 8)

Kirsch begins with *Othello* and there raises the difficult and central issue of representation of tragic conditions as sexual. Freud argues that the dissociation of affection from sensuality, the two currents of erotic feeling, is almost universal in civilized man and is tragic; Freud declares that the fundamental attitude of human beings towards the sexual act is of something degrading. Kirsch relates this to Montaigne's essay 'Upon Some Verses of Virgil' which he argues Shakespeare drew upon in *All's Well*; Montaigne in that essay writes that sexual gratification cannot be harmoniously absorbed into the affection that belongs to marriage, 'this reverent alliance and sacred bond'. Montaigne's attitude to the sexual act is to notice the guilt associated with it and to ask 'Are not we most brutish, to term that worke beastly which begets, and which maketh us?' Cassio, Iago, Emilia, Brabantio, represent a society beset by such guilt and incapable of the ideals commended in the scriptures. Kirsch argues that the imagery associated with Desdemona, the chrysolite (one of the twelve precious stones set in the walls of the heavenly city representing faith, constancy and innocence) and the pearl of great price (Matthew 13: 45–6) powerfully contributes to the sense of primal beauty and power in Othello's reunion with her on Cyprus. Iago represents something in Othello, but it is not something peculiar to him (as critics have urged). It is guilt, a feeling of sexual activity as degrading, a hatred of the body, which Montaigne and Freud concur in finding universal in civilized men. Through Desdemona's final vindication Othello is able to rediscover his own true self. Kirsch despises modern critics who convict Othello of moral or psychic failure and he quotes at length the view of Desdemona expressed by W. H. Auden ('I cannot bring myself to like her . . . ') to expose it mercilessly as cheap and showy twaddle, yet nevertheless comprising the basis of much modern criticism of the play.

The best part of an admirably strong defence of *Much Ado* concerns the demonstration, in written criticism, of something audiences at good performances of the play recognize: Beatrice and Benedick are comically compelling

precisely because they themselves understand, and the play as a whole supports, the significance of what they appear to make light of...the fears and fantasies that inform their jests are in fact acted out in the courtship of Claudio and Hero . . . the inevitability of [their] union expresses the truth that despite real risks and difficulties men and women have no choice but to love one another if they are to remain psychically and spiritually whole. (pp. 42, 57)

The heartlessly chill mirror-glass set, in the most recent Stratford production, only stressed the emptiness which separated its actors from each other; thus it showily followed modern critical assumptions that the play is entertaining but essentially empty. Arthur Kirsch dismisses the school of G. B. Shaw who despise the play and its wit-combats; better than this, he offers persuasive and dense evidence that its concerns with fashion are related to the sermon on apparel in the Homilies and to passages in the scriptures cited in the ceremony of holy matrimony concerning idolatry, spiritual adultery, and the sins of the flesh. The marriage ceremony cites Peter, advising against gorgeous outward apparel, 'with broided hair and trimming about with gold' and commends 'the hid man which is in the heart' (Kirsch, p. 52). Kirsch shows how Borachio's drunken homily on fashion is full of serious sacred allusion (like the Porter in *Macbeth*) concerning baptism, redemption, and idolatry-adultery. As in *All's Well* and *Cymbeline* fashion is deeply connected with slander and men's susceptibility to it; its root (as in *Othello* too) is sexual. Meditation on the double nature of the flesh that clothes the human spirit (flesh 'the fashion of this world', in the phrase of Corinthians 7:31), Kirsch argues,

is the profound biblical note...that Shakespeare strikes in the scene between Borachio and Conrade, holding us still for a few moments, as he often does in his comedies, to contemplate the deep mystery of the libidinal instincts, whose vicissitudes can either unite men in love and community or drive them into the isolation of their separate selves. (p. 53)

In her approach to Shakespeare from the perspective of anthropology, Marjorie Garber has produced a balanced and instructive study of certain rites of passage as they are presented in a large number of Shakespeare's plays.[3] She writes:

rites of passage are individual and non-periodic. The crises which provoke them have to do not with the season, but – in most cases – with some aspect of the family system. Where rites of intensification affect all the members of a group at once, rites of passage affect a single person directly, and others only as a result of their relationship to him...the symbolic pattern of an initiation ritual, like that of an agricultural festival, is

based upon a metaphorical experience of death and rebirth. But the life crisis that provokes that experience occurs not as a result of changes in the external world, but rather as a result of changes in the individual. As he grows to maturity – as he comes of age – the novice is separated from a former identity, and integrated into a new social role. (p. 19)

The non-specialist may be grateful for the brief explanations of modern anthropological concern with thresholds (or 'liminality'!) where the act of crossing from one state to another, becoming a 'marginal person', is both a danger and an opportunity. It is not surprising that Marjorie Garber resorts to the relatively delimited terms and fashioned tools of modern anthropology, sociology, and psychology, given that her true concern is nothing less, actually, than the magic or sacred in Shakespeare. This is approached by considering specific instances collected from all Shakespeare's works under a number of main headings. It is the specific instances which arrest the attention, providing again and again illustration of Shakespeare's creation of deep structures upon which depend individual characters and whole plays.

Certainly what is most interesting in this book is the product of a literary student not an anthropologist; it is the gathering together of Shakespeare's fascinating treatments of the various human repercussions of such events as separation and individuation (twins, brothers and sisters, fathers and daughters), nomination and election (assumption of or loss of a name), mastery of speech, woman's rites, death and dying. It is a strength of the book, as this list of its chief concerns indicates, that it witnesses Shakespeare's habitual rooting of dramatic action in the deepest dynamic experience of the individual and the group. Marjorie Garber can sketch in a pattern deftly; but she does also risk being merely sketchy:

Literal thresholds are occasionally mentioned in Shakespeare's works, and references to them suggest a background in folk custom and superstition. When Richard approaches the gates of York in *3 Henry VI* and finds them barred, he senses a bad omen: 'For

---

[3] *Coming of Age in Shakespeare* (Methuen, London and New York, 1981).

many men that stumble at the threshold / Are well foretold that danger lurks within' (IV vii 11–12). Virgilia, the wife of Coriolanus, refuses to leave the house while her husband is in danger: 'I'll not over the threshold till my lord return from the wars' (*Cor.* I iii 74–5). Here the home becomes a sacred or magical place, assuring protection to its absent master. At the close of *A Midsummer Night's Dream* Puck tells the audience that he is 'sent with broom, before, / To sweep the dust behind the door'...In *The Rape of Lucrece* an anthropomorphised threshold attempts to warn Lucrece of Tarquin's entry. (pp. 8–9)

We learn how the concept of threshold can refer to the foundation of houses to be laid or consecrated, or gates or barriers to be penetrated, as with Romeo and the orchard wall, Coriolanus at Corioli's gates, Duncan at Macbeth's castle. Physical action on stage sometimes embodies the concept literally. In *The Comedy of Errors* the incident of the door separating Antipholus from his rightful house and wife, which produces one comic climax, is repeated when the Priory gate preserves his twin from hue and cry and yields his long-lost mother; as Marjorie Garber's account makes clear, magic, magicians, privileged localities and rites of transition are essential elements in the play. This point is exceptionally important, especially in so early a comic masterpiece; perhaps it deserved more attention. Marjorie Garber seems to prefer exploring later works, where an episode combines detailed depiction of private experience with a socially felt transition. Dealing, later on in the book, with aspects of *Measure for Measure*, Marjorie Garber makes sense of the meaning of shrouds, veils, and masks in the play as part of the symbolic death and rebirth ritual – but her close and specific commentary takes off on a penetrating analysis of the action: Claudio's appearance in the last scene, his face covered, suggests a shroud, prompting an audience to think of the biblical Lazarus restored to life by Christ at the behest of his sisters Mary and Martha. The two symbolic attributes that link Claudio with death, muffling and silence, are part of the condition of religious sisterhood, as the nun tells Isabella early in the play. In the final scene literal and metaphoric unveilings occur several times: even if we do not accept Marjorie Garber's suggestion that

the audience will be aware that in 'initiatory rituals pertaining to puberty and sexual coming of age the novice is often covered with a blanket or rug, and that this act of covering is a symbol of death as the later uncovering signifies rebirth' (p. 222), nevertheless it is clearly right to say that the appearance of the muffled Claudio functions as a visual emblem of the rite of passage he has undergone but also as 'an iconic representation of the transformations undergone by others . . . who speaks (by his very silence) to onstage and offstage audience alike' (p. 224).

Coming of Age in Shakespeare is worthwhile for its emphasis on the incorporation of ritual elements in the story and structure of many plays; it serves to remind the reader that archetypal symbols in drama need not always be static and iconic, but may also be dynamic and represented by process. Often such archetypes are apparent through the subliminal suggestion of stage action, where the book-bound solitary reader will attend only to other kinds of meaning.

Marilyn French, in *Shakespeare's Division of Experience*,[4] shares with Marjorie Garber an interest in anthropology, sociology, and post-Freudian theory in relation to literature. She aims to show the 'gender principles' in Shakespeare, and in the most general terms her subject is obviously important. She separates the gender principles from individual actual men or women, who may manifest qualities associated with either gender principle. In her opening chapters of general propositions the reader may feel at once exhilarated by the spaciousness and disappointed by the frequent, and surely not inevitable, bluntness and oversimplification. There is intelligence and seriousness at the centre of this study, but it feels as if it was written in some haste: the introductory chapters are short, they are followed by very many chapters which take the reader at an unvarying pace through the works in mainly chronological order; nor is the approach freshly thought

---

[4] Jonathan Cape, 1982; quotations cited from the paperback edition of Sphere Books. An approach similar in outline to Marilyn French's, but with its own voice, is Linda Bamber, *Comic Women, Tragic Men: A Study of Gender and Genre in Shakespeare* (Stanford University Press, 1982).

out. A persistent reliance on assertion becomes wearying, and the author's ability to write wittily and vigorously can desert her for considerable stretches; but the book is intermittently punctuated with excellent comment, for example on *All's Well That Ends Well* and *The Comedy of Errors*, which makes one wish it had been revised, much reduced in length, and focused on a selected group of plays or issues. Marilyn French's writing exhibits the strengths and weaknesses of the modern critic with a genuine interest in Shakespeare only to be expressed through the restricted mechanism of the over-determined thesis.

A quite different approach is apparent in Marion Trousdale's account of *Shakespeare and the Rhetoricians*,[5] in which a highly wrought design of argument is devised to serve a sophisticated set of purposes. The book deals with sixteenth-century rhetoric, and gives analysis of the handbooks' contents and theoretical assumptions; for those who do not have (even yet) a conviction that to have read these manuals is necessary for the student of Renaissance literature, Marion Trousdale provides an implicit rebuke; at the same time, her approach to Renaissance rhetoric is not innocent of contemporary literary theory and, in her index, Thomas Dekker is followed by Jacques Derrida (Barthes and Erasmus, Fish and Puttenham have all their part to play in the argument). The book, essentially, attempts to find explanations for the circumstance that Shakespeare's works provoke many different responses and interpretations – indeed are in a sense systems for generating variation as well as being composed according to rhetorical techniques whose aim was to see in a topic as many diversities, from as many different points of view, as possible. Marion Trousdale sets about this task by analysing and quoting from English handbooks, though her star witness is the Erasmus of *De Copia*; she lists the set categories, the 'places', in which things can be defined, as they appear in Wilson (Trousdale, p. 28) and she gives simple examples to explain, early on in her book, why the assumptions of the rhetoricians are important to the critic of the plays. To the Elizabethans, she insists, words are separate from, disjunct from, things. 'If, in the play *Othello*, the Ideal of Othello is as substantial as Othello himself on stage, then he equals the words used to describe him in the play, and there is only one verbal structure, one form, one idea that can truly present what Othello is' (p. 26). Rather than this, we are invited to follow Wilson the rhetorician and use 'places', that is to say categories, to talk about character, our interest in Othello becoming an interest in

those places by means of which his character can be verbally defined. We might, as Wilson suggests, when a man is commended or condemned for an action, consider whether the deed was honest, possible, easy or difficult to do. We might also enquire into his disposition, his studies, his exercises of mind and body. These are not aspects of his character, but intellectual categories by means of which his character can be described. If we use such places, Othello cannot be represented as having one single defining character. He has rather many different defining characteristics or aspects, and as verbal structures these characteristics are discontinuous... they are multiple because they are *forms of discourse*. They are not forms of things.

(p. 10)

This system of places promotes discovery of aspects of a topic, it is more than a mechanical aid to description; it is connected to dialectic in its concern with seeing something in as many ways as possible and from varied points of view. Erasmus taught his students to turn a single thought into many forms, separating the *res* from the verbal forms in which it was decked. This exhibits his attitude to the colours of rhetoric as separable from the kernel thought. His exercises in varying repetitions are related by Marion Trousdale to the semantic repetitions, and indeed to the whole fabric of structural repetition, of a Shakespeare play. Rather than logical sequence the patterning is of repetition and elaboration of a word or idea woven into the fabric of the text. A useful illustration is offered in an analysis of the 'To be or not to be' soliloquy (pp. 58–9). Marion Trousdale suggests that Ascham or Erasmus would have seen Shakespeare as writing plays from a received body of patterns and formulae, finding new ways to vary them endlessly.

To put it like this is to risk making both men

---

[5] University of North Carolina Press, Chapel Hill, and Scolar Press, London, 1982.

appear small-minded pedants and to risk presenting the rhetorical approach as mechanically reductive. Such uncertain moments are not characteristic of this study as a whole, but there is a perceptible difficulty in demonstrating the necessary connection between the frankly routine drill of 'place rhetoric' and the composition of *Richard II*. Arguments about How Elizabethans Would Have Felt need to be modified by the recognition that Shakespeare's plays educate, discover, and can alter a spectator's sensibility and (temporarily) possess and manipulate his beliefs and feelings. Writing on *Love's Labour's Lost* Marion Trousdale asserts that Elizabethans did not censure Berowne for being 'both guilty of courtly artifice and critical of it'. The point is not proven. A strong advocacy of redundant artifice emerges as an important part of this study. Evading such traditional critical concerns as spiritual experience and moral value, Marion Trousdale flourishes instead a commendation of Shakespeare in *Love's Labour's Lost* which was originally applied by Sir Thomas Chaloner to Erasmus's *Praise of Folly*: 'he neuer shewed more arte, nor witte, in any the grauest boke he wrote, then in this his praise of Folie.' Here copious praise seems also excessive.

Shakespeare and the Rhetoricians shows a restrained but real impatience with critics who discuss organic unity, consistency of characterization, and fail to question the nature and strategies of the text from which they would extract monolithically stable character and action. This impatience is quite proper, and it is in accord with the experience of the plays in performance to suggest (with the necessary tentativeness about conscious intent by the artist) that the

kinds of questions Shakespeare might have asked in pursuing such patterns are: not why Richard was deposed, but why he might have been deposed; not how did he feel when it happened, but how might he have felt; not ought he to have been deposed, but what is there in his deposition that would make it possible to present a case on both sides.   (p. 66)

The particular plays chosen to illustrate the dialectical nature of Shakespeare's dramatic designing – *Richard II*, *Love's Labour's Lost*, *Julius Caesar*,

Hamlet – suit the purpose of showing that in Elizabethan drama there is a habit of expounding, and with it 'an essentially prismatic vision', which help to account for 'an almost baffling richness in an often careless, intentionally digressive, and often random dramatic art' where 'all action, all fable if you prefer, was trope – one made metaphors out of it, one drew morals from it . . . it became a point of wit' (pp. 132–3). Of *Hamlet*, thus, it can be urged that 'the play is not representation in any strict sense of the word. Rather, it is a verbal structure in which possible relationships between different pieces of action are suggested by rhetorical elaboration, creating an almost bewildering sense of possible significances within the body of the play.'

Marion Trousdale is not always easy to read, and the concern for exact and scrupulous weaving of a dense argument tends to conceal a central thrust which deserves daylight and champain airing. It is not new, but better than that, it is true to the plays as audiences demonstrably receive them. This central idea is expressed by comparing Shakespeare's art of construction to the Gothic as seen by the art historian Worringer, who saw Gothic structures as articulated in such a way that 'the richness of possible patterns of meaning can never be contained totally by any of the numerous impositions of significant form' (p. 136).

In *Shakespeare and the Rhetoricians* the reader is not surprised to find *Hamlet* described as 'a verbal structure'; in *Shakespeare the Director*[6] emphasis falls on action and gesture, the dramatist's 'second means of communication', and we are directed to consider the complex relationship between verbal and visual in the plays: Ann Pasternak Slater's scheme is to trace Shakespeare's chronological development of technique in devising theatrical effects, focusing on explicit stage directions and on those implicit in the dialogue (for example 'Deere daughter, I confesse that I am old; / Age is unnecessary: on my knees I begge' or 'What man, ne're pull your hat vpon your browes:'). She comments usefully on Shakespeare's devising of

---

[6] By Ann Pasternak Slater (Harvester Press, Brighton, and Barnes and Noble, Totowa, NJ, 1982).

stage business to crystallize the play's themes in visual terms, and plots the alternation between verbal and visual representation of images. Thus she writes

In *Antony and Cleopatra* Philo's description of Antony as 'the Bellowes and the Fan / To coole a Gypsies Lust' is promptly echoed in the authorial stage direction, *Enter Anthony, Cleopatra…with Eunuchs fanning her*. It is a slight instance of the continual traffic between the theatrical and linguistic in Shakespeare's work. But 'in such indexes', as Nestor says,

> (although small pricks
> To their subsequent volumes) there is seene
> The baby figure of the gyant masse…

Behind the rational combination of verbal and visual imagery in a single play there lies a larger sub-conscious cross-flow of metaphor, both visual and linguistic, throughout the canon. The imagery of the stanza from *Lucrece* (lines 1513–19) foreshadows the theatrical paradox of *Othello* in which the 'blackfac'd' naif is ensnared, body and soul, by the 'Saint-like' demi-devil, for no given reason…Edward Armstrong notes that 'My sweete ounce of mans flesh, my in-conie Iew' in *Love's Labour's Lost* is a bizarre premonition of the main action of *The Merchant of Venice*, and Professor Wilson Knight observes that Lear's unusual preference, 'Thou'dst shun a Beare,/ But if thy flight lay toward the roaring Sea,/ Thou'dst meete the Beare i'th' mouth', accurately prefigures two calamities governing the centre of *The Winter's Tale* – both, it might be added, having scant support from Greene's *Pandosto*.

(p. 195)

As this excerpt shows, in *Shakespeare the Director* the organization of detailed illustration from the plays is very efficient, if sometimes pursued to somewhat curious, very academic lengths, and although the card-index basis of the study can be intrusive, the book will prove interesting to those for whom its approach is very familiar (most serious Shakespearians), while for sixth-form and undergraduate readers this book's opening chapters ought to make it impossible, in future readings of the plays, to skip printed stage directions (even in so intense a crisis as that in act 3, scene 1 of *Coriolanus* when the Tribunes orchestrate the crowd's hatred to a peak of pressure, many students[7] will ignore the reaction of Coriolanus because it is a simply phrased stage

direction: Brutus cries 'bear him to the rock', the stage direction is: *Coriolanus draws his sword*).

Ann Pasternak Slater has a worthwhile subject, but she is inclined to make exaggerated claims for her originality, and self-assertiveness mars the tone and damages the quality of the writing. On pages 6–7 there is a particularly distasteful attempt to disparage the contribution to the subject of other scholars and critics: we are told that, for instance, studies of the Elizabethan Stage tend to be concerned only with historical reconstruction, Theatre History with post-Elizabethan staging, the analysis of Shakespeare's stage directions has remained 'almost exclusively bibliographical' while 'the literary critic refers to a few old favourites . . . and is generally uninformed about their textual status'; work on the sources apparently is usually concerned with identifying sources and verbal parallels, that on stage symbolism takes isolated moments and is undermined by an 'ignorance of Shakespeare's standard vocabulary of stage action'. Such charges have little dignity and less accuracy. In any case the view of Shakespeare studies proposed is intolerably intramural; it neglects one major area of Shakespeare criticism, that of reviews of theatre productions.

The kinds of insight into Shakespeare's technique which are the subject of Ann Pasternak Slater's study are the continuous, intense, and expert preoccupation of a large body of Shakespearians; although they may occupy a less institutionalized area of Shakespeare criticism, they compensate by writing with unusual felicity and wit, and draw upon stores of visual memories of staging and acting. Past volumes of *Shakespeare Survey* itself contain admirable examples of this sort of critical analysis (I would pick out the exemplary work of Peter Thomson here); but even *The Times* can print good criticism in this kind: here is Irving Wardle, for instance, describing John Wood as Saturninus in the 1972 production of *Titus Andronicus* at Stratford-upon-Avon:

His performance is spell-binding to watch: endlessly mobile and unpredictable as it drops into the chatty

---

7 This is the experience of GCE A-Level examiners in a recent Shakespeare paper taken by eight thousand candidates in Great Britain.

cadences of modern English or rises into spitty fury: linking blood-drenched inhumanity with domestic realism. Mr Wood arrives for the morning hunt bleary-eyed after his first night with Tamora; and at the news of the Goths' invasion, he raises a finger to his lips warning the messenger not to wake the baby. The performance is a wonderful blend of deadly vigilance, petty rancour, and buffoonery.

This excerpt from Wardle's review of *Titus* is quoted in fact from another book treating of plays in performance, Michael Hattaway's *Elizabethan Popular Theatre*.[8] Whereas in *Shakespeare the Director* the subject is divided into a series of topics – position on the stage, taking by the hand, kneeling, kissing and embracing, weeping, silence and pause, costume, properties, sources, and sub-plots – in *Elizabethan Popular Theatre* successive chapters deal with Playhouses and Stages, Performances, Players and Playing (under these headings come such topics as playhouse economics, acting styles, plays and games, boy players, make-up and costumes, clowns and tragedians, speaking the speech); following these introductory chapters come reconstructions of performances, in their original conditions, of *The Spanish Tragedy*, *Mucedorus*, *Edward II*, *Dr Faustus*, and *Titus Andronicus*. The informing proposition of the book is 'that the value and popularity of this drama owe something to its traffic between the academic and the demotic, the idealised forms of court show and the energies of carnival... between a literary and an oral culture' (p. 1). Hattaway observes that the aristocratic withdrawal from popular culture had not really begun before the turn of the century; he also argues that the ethos of these plays (all of the 1590s) is 'sceptical and anti-authoritarian (although not anti-aristocratic) or, less attractively, chauvinistic and anti-Catholic' (p. 2).

As the list of topics in Hattaway's study makes clear, his approach is practical and provides a scholarly, up-to-date, succinct account of the evidence, tested against modern experience of theatrical production, both professional and experimental. The book was evidently completed before the National Theatre's 1982 revival of *The Spanish Tragedy*, an event which certainly confirms Hattaway's claims that the dramaturgy of this period is

highly sophisticated. It contained modes that ranged 'from the creation of partial illusion by mimicry to the exhibition of performance skills, from representation to presentation, and dramatists delighted in switching from one mode to another'.

Hattaway succeeds in bringing to life – sometimes with pulse-quickening immediacy – the material conditions of performance in a theatre about the time of the first performance of *Titus*:

Actors in modern productions, particularly a long run, come to know their entrances and their exits well, to feel the rhythm of a play. Elizabethan players must have nervously consulted their plots, found themselves suddenly on stage giving a performance based on their individual skills and depending largely on extemporization to establish contact between their own and others' parts...particular players specialized in particular kinds of roles and acting, but having performed the massive task of committing lines quickly to memory, each player must have drawn heavily on his own repertoire of stock gestures or routines.

(p. 54)

Hattaway takes account of the evidence from such familiar sources as the actor's 'part' for the title role of *Orlando Furioso*, the rehearsal scene in *A Midsummer Night's Dream*, the Induction to *Cynthia's Revels*, Henslowe's contract with the actor Robert Dawes, the repertory of fifteen plays for only twenty-five playing days from Henslowe's diary for 1596, and so on, but the use made of this evidence is refreshingly practical, imaginative but not tendentious; we are reminded of the difference, the serious gap, between modern assumptions about the aims of actors or directors and those which prevailed in Shakespeare's own time: 'Audiences tend nowadays for better or worse to expect "interpretations" of plays: the Elizabethan companies did not draw upon a repertory of "classics". At its first performance *Hamlet* was simply enacted and not deliberately interpreted' (p. 53). Hattaway argues that in these plays with their varied modes, their spectacle, song, dance, masque,

---

8 Routledge and Kegan Paul, London, Boston, and Henley, 1982. The subtitle is *Plays in Performance*; it appears in a series, Theatre Production Studies, general editor John Russell Brown.

actors cannot have had time to develop naturalistic character portrayal. The emblematic and the gestural are for Hattaway important elements in composition and in performance; both imply conscious awareness of the distinction between the person represented and the person representing. When giving a commentary on *Titus* as a script for performance, Hattaway shows the play moving 'from set piece, or from one gest or formal dramatic image, to another' (p. 59). He sees Shakespeare in this play trying out the use of the gallery aloft and the pit beneath the stage, but in a Roman play where any Christian connotations of these locations have been banished; also Shakespeare was exploring what happens when the severed hand is repeatedly thrust before the audience 'purely as an object, quite displaced from its usual position in the world and therefore strange and frightening': contrasting with the repetition of words such as 'shadow' and 'face' in *Richard II*, where meanings accrete to generate symbolic significance, 'the hands of Titus and Lavinia remain remorselessly hands. The word designates only its accustomed object and moves towards neither metaphor nor metonym, the thing moves no distance towards emblem. We have therefore an index of the play's peculiar kind of realism' (pp. 188–9). Quotations from reviews of the Brook and Nunn productions by Richard David, Harold Hobson and others vividly emphasize the importance of music, properties, and highly stylized movement to bring out the implications – and the fundamental structure and articulation – of this grand style. By setting *Titus* in the context of the chosen non-Shakespearian plays, and taking into account so many issues with which other students prefer not to get entangled, Michael Hattaway in fact suggests a rich, alternative sense in which Shakespeare the director is to be recognized in his work.

John Russell Brown is also the shaping hand behind another volume, *Focus on Macbeth*,[9] a collection of new essays, by experienced hands, on topics mostly suggested by Brown himself, after his experience as assistant director in a recent production of the play at the National Theatre with Albert Finney and Dorothy Tutin. The volume has an emphasis on performance, with an especially lively example of how a literary approach can make use of non-verbal, visual effects as part of an essentially orthodox critical examination of the play; this essay, by D. J. Palmer, treats the stage directions, explicit and implicit, as carefully and seriously as an earlier tradition treated verbal imagery; in so doing Palmer brings out the rich integrity of the play's design at the same time as he refreshes a reader's memory of how the play works in performance. Other essays are also ready to face the full challenge of this extraordinary work. Thus R. A. Foakes shows how Shakespeare breaks new ground in 'his deeper study of the nature of ambition', and this essay sensitively explores Macbeth's experience of encountering further and ever more terrible images of death, towards which his ambition remorselessly drives him, so that he can escape the prison of his own imagination only 'at the appalling cost of losing his capacity to care' (p. 27). Brian Morris, in the next essay, argues that *Macbeth* as a play concerns guilt without remorse, its hero's 'inability to register the religious dimension of human life narrows and blinkers the scope of the play's vision'; Morris also finds courtesy to be the highest moral value in the play, and its association with extreme violence gives the tragedy 'its unique tone' (pp. 50–2). Other interesting essays include a highly informative account by Peter Stallybrass of '*Macbeth* and Witchcraft' and an interview with Peter Hall on 'Directing *Macbeth*'. This volume should improve the standard of student work on this extremely popular 'set book'; it also contains some excellent original work on the play at the highest levels.

Several interesting essays concern *Othello* this year. Muriel Bradbrook has a new essay in her book *Artist and Society in Shakespeare's England*,[10] in which there is an excellent discussion of the symbolic meanings of the handkerchief, and of depictions of black and beautiful persons in Renaissance art; G. K. Hunter, whose work on the same subject in the past is well known, discusses *Othello* as part of

---

[9] *Focus on Macbeth*, ed. John Russell Brown (Routledge and Kegan Paul, London, Boston, and Henley, 1982).

[10] Harvester Press, Brighton, 1982.

his account of 'Tyrant and Martyr: Religious Heroisms in Elizabethan Tragedy',[11] which has instructive general and particular perceptions; and Barbara Everett[12] explores the Spanish background of the play, beginning from the fact that Iago is a Spanish name, and going on to notice numerous aspects of the play and its hero (with his Shakespearian antecedents) which complicate the presentation of the Moor. Barbara Everett stresses her interest in how the story of the Moor might appear if read within a world 'with a different mental geography' from our own; and 'the heart of the tragedy of the real-life Spanish Moor was the ancient strength of the bonds which linked him to his fellow-Spaniards: bonds which ironically drove him (like Shylock) into a reactively defensive racism and nationalism' (p. 107).

In the same volume is an informative account by Stanley Wells of 'Shakespeare in Hazlitt's Theatre Criticism'. In a long and important article that can be read with profit alongside this, Roy Park deals with 'Lamb, Shakespeare, and the Stage'.[13] He begins by stressing that Lamb, far from disliking theatre, was a constant theatre-goer and that the stage played a more important part in his life than in either Hazlitt's or Coleridge's. Park directs attention to Lamb's criticism of non-dramatic literature, and painting, to illuminate what he sees as Lamb's misunderstood criticism of acting. Lamb attacked the needless or self-inflicted loss of imaginative potential in all these arts; he attacked the 'insipid levelling morality to which the modern stage is tied down', and he felt that acting was intrinsically incapable of rendering the full moral complexity of lived experience embodied in the greatest tragedies. Painting provides an analogy to acting; poetry is superior to both: 'in a reading we are lost in admiration at the respective moral or intellectual attributes of a character...but in a picture Othello is always a Blackamoor; and [Falstaff] only Plump Jack'.

Two other articles deal with our contemporary actors and productions; Stanley Wells surveys 'Television Shakespeare'[14] and shows lively journalistic art; his observations on film technique as applied to the plays are shrewd and his quotations from those involved in television versions of the plays are well worth recording. In much more contentious spirit Alan Sinfield[15] discusses the most recent production of *King Lear* at Stratford-upon-Avon, by Adrian Noble, as symptomatic of the fashion for 'ventriloquising contemporary significance through the plays'. Sinfield thinks dishonest the extensive cutting, manipulating, and breaking-up of dialogue to make contemporary significance (he notes that this is called 'making the scene work' in the trade). Shakespeare did not envisage certain aspects of modern society, and making his texts speak to our condition by major distortions may not be more politically effectual than it is aesthetically honest. Sinfield argues that it cannot be satisfactory for a director to make audiences doubt whether what they are watching is actually Shakespeare or a new work masquerading as the 'basically conservative' original. A director's or actor's preferred dimension of meaning, whether political, social or metaphysical, may be better met by new plays. Sinfield might have noted that Shakespeare himself, in his own time, wrote new plays in reaction to inherited classics of non-dramatic and dramatic literature. Perhaps only such flagrant manipulations of the Shakespeare text as the recent *King Lear* at Stratford call forth such radical demands for playing Shakespeare as remote – as Their Contemporary, not Ours – but Sinfield certainly makes a strong case in defence of Bond's *Lear* and *Bingo*.

An outstanding feature of Adrian Noble's production of *King Lear*, for me, was the detailed accuracy with which the physical characteristics of old age were presented: something about the production's concern with the mood and texture of today's Britain, in which the aged play an increasingly prominent part as their numbers rise, gave a

---

[11] This article is in *Poetic Traditions of the English Renaissance*, ed. Maynard Mack and George de Forest Lord (Yale University Press, New Haven, 1982).

[12] *Shakespeare Survey 35* (Cambridge University Press, 1982), 101–12.

[13] *Shakespeare Quarterly*, 33 (1982), 164–77.

[14] *Ibid.*, pp. 261–77.

[15] '*King Lear* versus *Lear* at Stratford', *Critical Quarterly*, 24 (1982), 5–14.

freshness to the quirks and sudden anxieties, the childish tantrums and the still potent mature passion which shake bodies no longer quite in command of themselves. This aspect of *King Lear* is excellently treated by Susan Snyder in her article '*King Lear* and the Psychology of Dying'[16] which begins by saluting Freud on the theme of the Three Caskets: 'Eternal wisdom in the garb of primitive myth bids the old man renounce love, choose death and make friends with the necessity of dying.' A book by Elisabeth Kübler-Ross, *On Death and Dying* (New York, 1969), is cited for its account of the five stages through which a dying person passes: denial, anger, bargaining, grief, acceptance. The death of Cordelia is an aspect of Lear's own, Susan Snyder argues, but its separateness allows Lear to do the impossible, experience his own death and cry out against its terrible wrongness. No dying person, says Kübler-Ross, ever actually gives up hope, which persists through all the stages of dying. Susan Snyder writes well on the intense physicality of *King Lear*, as the demands of the ailing body thrust aside culture's niceties and abstract concerns. The play represents the human body in anguished movement, tugged, wrenched, beaten, pierced, stung, scourged, dislocated, flayed, gashed, scalded, and finally racked: nor are the smells of mortality excluded. Only through this does a deeper human understanding well up. This serious and perceptive essay quickens our awareness of the play's extraordinary truth of observation.

Three articles contribute interesting information as an integral part of their critical accounts, and are well worth consulting in detail. William Chester Jordan's 'Approaches to the Court Scene in *The Merchant of Venice*' deals with the alternatives of Equity and Mercy or Reason and Nature;[17] Walter Cohen's '*The Merchant of Venice* and the Possibilities of Historical Criticism' explores what is now known about actual conditions in sixteenth-century Venice in relation to Shakespeare's treatment;[18] and Margaret Scott surprises by finding new things to say about '"Our City's Institutions": Some Further Reflections on the Marriage Contracts in *Measure for Measure*'.[19]

To begin with Jordan: he observes that no version of the bond story before Shakespeare involves anyone denying the agreement to render flesh, no question is raised about the validity of the contract. Even in the common law tradition in England from the twelfth century onwards an exception could have been pleaded against Shylock because the Law 'should not suffer vicious contracts in which sin intervenes'; nor would the death or maiming of a debtor have been tolerated merely because of a default on a loan. The play is not concerned with real courts where mutilation would be held unreasonable and against nature; but it obliquely involves these values while dramatizing centrally a confrontation between mercy, the religious equivalent of equity, and justice, the common law.

Walter Cohen sees the crisis in the play arising not from Shylock's insistence on usury but his refusal of it. Antonio the open-handed Christian merchant in conflict with Shylock the tight-fisted Jewish usurer can be seen to represent rising capitalism versus declining feudalism. English history might evoke fears of capitalism, but Italian history allays such fears. In sixteenth-century Venice the government barred Jewish usurers and forced the Jewish community to finance low-interest institutions to serve the poor of the Christian community. The real Jews of Venice contributed to capitalism not as usurers but as merchants. Shakespeare needed to transform materialist problems into idealist ones or project them harmlessly away from his Christian characters. The play is hence anti-Semitic. (I should add that the vocabulary and manner of delivery in this article imply a very much more substantial enterprise than the one actually completed.) Cohen glances towards the problem of *The Merchant of Venice* as a play designed to provoke questions, or, to put it another way, thinks that it escapes standard categories of interpretation by including contradiction. We are reminded that Marxist theory sees in the sense of closure produced by some works of art analogues to 'reactionary corporatist ideologies

[16] *Shakespeare Quarterly*, 33 (1982), 449–60.
[17] Ibid., pp. 49–59.
[18] *ELH*, 49 (1982), 765–89.
[19] Ibid., pp. 790–804.

designed to suppress awareness of class conflict'. Cohen's theoretical preoccupations do not systematically produce his interpretation, however.

The essay by Margaret Scott begins by noting that the Law in *Measure for Measure* is 'story-book law', unlike any actual law. The play is based on Cinthio and Whetstone, not closely attentive to any set of historically verifiable conditions, although beguiling prospects of such exactitude have attracted attention in past scholarship on the play: it has been noticed that Shakespeare's friend William Russell contracted an informal marriage in 1603 and his aunt Agnes Arden was recognized as wife by Thomas Stringer for three months before her church wedding. Margaret Scott notes that in the first place the law in *Measure for Measure* is foreign and it is Catholic; the play emphasizing cloisters, Friars, allegiance to Rome. The Tridentine decree of 1563 wrought major changes in the laws of Catholic marriage, contrasting with the law in Protestant nations. Clandestine marriage was decreed invalid in Catholic countries; but in England marriage of consent continued until Lord Hardwicke's Marriage Act of 1753. Thus in a Catholic city after 1563 neither Claudio and Juliet nor the pre-contracted Angelo and Mariana would have been deemed validly married. An English ecclesiastical court in 1604 would however have accepted Claudio's plea; Scott believes the same view would have been taken of Angelo's case. Shakespeare could have known about the European background in this matter, and have stressed it to reinforce the ambiguity of the central issue in a play concerned with shifts of judgement and changed appearance: Isabella's Church has considered a man a husband on one day then decreed him a fornicator on the next; in the eyes of Catholics of the time Mariana would be a fornicatress in the bed-trick. Why does not Isabella ask Claudio if there was a pre-contract? This article adduces relevant and interesting information to sharpen our awareness of the undertow in this absorbing image of an action done in Vienna.

By contrast two other essays in *ELH* display an over-eager concern to live up to that journal's reputation for theoretical disquisition. Thus Barry Weller[20] begins promisingly with general observa-

tions about 'Identity and Representation in Shakespeare'; he declares that 'Drama is more "realistic" than fiction which pretends to unfold the complexities of human conduct: that is, it reproduces the circumstances under which human beings ordinarily meet and know each other – as appearances not as essences, through intuition and surmise, not through certain and immediate entry into another consciousness.' The actual discussion of particular plays is disappointing and does not develop the interesting points made to begin with. David Marshall's essay 'Exchanging Visions: Reading *A Midsummer Night's Dream*'[21] sees the comedy as a play about the problems of representing and figuring, but drama inevitably involves an element of disfiguring as poetry is 'joined' to the stage; the play also reflects upon the circumstance that spectators must allow themselves to be silenced and impressed by someone else's vision and way of seeing. Marshall talks of Titania being transformed into a blank page to be written and figured upon by someone else's fancy, a figure for the conditions of theatre.

William Rossky somewhat more straightforwardly says that we should see '*The Two Gentlemen of Verona* as Burlesque',[22] as the closest thing in Shakespeare to a Gilbert and Sullivan operetta. Having myself been involved in a production of the play which found the high burlesque mode perfectly sustained in the writing, I would support the quoted opinion of Francis Fergusson on the play: 'it is sensible to give Shakespeare credit for knowing just how silly his gentlemen would appear'. Rossky acknowledges the dangers of anachronistic reading of this play and inspects the story of Titus and Gisippus to find no precedent for the compulsive villainy of Proteus; other Elizabethan stories treat the play's topics in a less absurd manner. These differences indicate Shakespeare to be consciously mocking the conventions of friendship's superiority over love. The essay cannot prove its case, but it is sympathetic.

Finally we may notice two lively and individual

---

20 *Ibid.*, pp. 339–62.
21 *Ibid.*, pp. 543–75.
22 *English Literary Renaissance*, 12 (1982), 210–19.

contributions. A chapter in Herbert Grabes's large and compendious study *The Mutable Glass*[23] deals with Shakespeare's use of mirror imagery and mirror properties in his works. This is a useful survey, worth consulting when working on a particular poem or play in which the topic is prominent; Grabes reaches the conclusion that in the seventy or more 'mirror' passages in Shakespeare (a small number given the volume of his output) his use of current conventions proves to be efficient, but he did not luxuriate in them. Grabes writes well on the broken mirror of Antony (p. 206) and on that of Richard II: 'He sees the mirror as a "flattering glass" and symbol of *vanitas*; Bolingbroke sees it as a sign of immoderate self-projection and vanity. The contemporary reader or spectator, however, for whom the broken mirror was an omen of imminent death, would or could view Richard's action as a sign of self-destruction' (p. 215). This is a very large and expensive book which, nevertheless, all libraries should acquire. And the last article to be noticed is Camille Slights's 'The Principle of Recompense in

Twelfth Night'.[24] She writes well on the dream of inviolable autonomy that absorbs characters in the play: Orsino's vision of self-surfeiting desires, Olivia's isolation, 'watering her chamber round', Toby's unconfined pleasure, Malvolio's behaviour to his own shadow, anticipate Claude Lévi-Strauss, who noted 'mankind has always dreamed of seizing and fixing the fleeting moment when it was permissible to believe that the laws of exchange could be evaded, that one could gain without losing, enjoy without sharing'. Yet in *Twelfth Night* money flows more freely and frequently than in almost any other play. The ending is strikingly crowded with action, and reciprocal love culminates not in a private dream world but in the give and take of legal, financial and spiritual transactions of human society.

---

[23] *The Mutable Glass: Mirror-imagery in titles and texts of the Middle Ages and the English Renaissance* (Cambridge University Press, 1983).
[24] *Modern Language Review*, 77 (1982), 537–46.

2. SHAKESPEARE'S LIFE, TIMES AND STAGE
reviewed by LOIS POTTER

This Stage-Play World, by Julia Briggs (Oxford University Press, 1983), embodies in its title most of the themes which have dominated this year's work. Shakespeare's 'Stage' has swallowed up his 'Life' and 'Times'; writers vie with one another to show that life was (and is) theatrical, that politics and theatre are inseparable, and that the visual side of the theatre – its architecture, its staging, its iconography – was after all as important as the words that were spoken there. I shall consider some of the reasons for this emphasis later, but first I shall look at some general works, starting with the one I just mentioned.

Julia Briggs's excellent book is thematically structured, with examples from literary works illustrating chapters on Renaissance politics, religion, society, and so on. Though the theatre gets a chapter to itself, drama is shown to be interwoven with every aspect of the period: it provides an

analogy for the Platonic view of life as a shadow, as well as for the formal and ceremonial nature of society, and it allows the expression, if not necessarily the resolution, of 'passionately conflicting convictions'. One of Mrs Briggs's most interesting suggestions, in the chapter on theatre, is that the very extent of anti-theatrical prejudice made the dramatists themselves hyper-conscious of both hypocrisy and illusion. Thus, both Shakespeare and Jonson express occasional revulsion at their own profession and also exploit their audience's inability to tell truth from fiction. The book is well written as well as subtly organized. Its very subtlety may be a liability to the reader who is an absolute beginner: at times, reading through what was essentially a series of well-chosen quotations linked by an intelligent commentary, I wondered whether an anthology of primary materials would have been more useful. But the book can certainly be recommended for the second stage of study: that is, for the reader who has some knowledge of a few Renaissance works and feels the need to put them into context.

Not particularly easy reading, but certainly a useful new reference tool, is *Brief Lives: Tudor and Stuart Authors*, which appears as a special number of *Studies in Philology* (vol. 79, 1982). Mark Eccles, who compiled these entries (nearly a hundred) from parish registers, legal documents, etc., presents them in extended note form, with each figure scrupulously given all the different names under which he appears in the records. Since much of the material comes from lawsuits, it is hardly surprising that many of the writers appear in a 'dramatic' light: we learn that Tourneur's pocket was picked in 1613 by one Alice Conway, that two burglars stole Fulke Greville's silver in 1615, and that Marston was robbed on the highway in 1616. A particularly exciting discovery is that Marlowe and a companion were arrested for coining at Flushing in 1592 on the basis of evidence given by their 'chamber-fellow', none other than Richard Baines. It also appears that this Baines is the same one who was hanged at Tyburn in 1594 for felony and murder: surely this means that the value of his evidence about Marlowe's blasphemies must become even more questionable than it already was. Mark Eccles's *Brief Lives* are not so chatty as Aubrey's, but they seem a good deal more reliable, and they point to a number of places where future research may be done.

D. Heyward Brock's *Ben Jonson Companion*[1] is bound to become a standard reference work, but prospective buyers ought to wait for the second edition, which is likely to be a good deal better than the first. The book includes a lot of material which everyone will be glad to have: for instance, lists of Jonson's dedicatees and of those who danced in his masques. But Professor Brock's knowledge of Jonson doesn't extend to Jonson's own knowledge. The entries on Chaos, Gargantua (described only as 'the hero of a folk-tale well known in the sixteenth century'), and Owleglass (not identified with Eulenspiegel) are among those which I found inadequate. Astonishingly, Professor Brock's entries on Catullus and Cervantes suggest that he accepts as Jonson's own the dismissive views of these writers expressed

by such characters as Sir John Daw and Kastril. Much space is taken up with long summaries of plays and masques, but every reader is bound to complain about omissions. My own suggestions for the second edition are Argalus and Palemon (in *Bartholomew Fair*), the Gunpowder Plot, and Thomas Rodgers, who was the victim of a Fairy Queen swindle. The entry on Samuel Sheppard ought to be revised in the light of H. E. Rollins's article on him (*Studies in Philology*, vol. 24, 1927).

This year's source studies can be divided into those which use pictorial evidence and those which don't. The split between verbal and visual interpretation, of course, is hardly a new one. After the dumb show in *Hamlet*, Ophelia's reaction to the entrance of the Prologue is the hopeful question, 'Will he tell us what this show means?' In fact, all he does is beg their 'hearing' of the tragedy which is to follow. I shall look first at the writers who seem to have concentrated chiefly on what the audience *heard*, in, between, or behind the lines of the text.

Classical sources get less attention this year than last, though Ovid figures in a brief note pointing out a parallel between Othello's success in love and that which was attributed to Ulysses, another much-travelled story-teller.[2] Two writers are interested in Shakespeare's assimilation of the *Aeneid*. John W. Velz sees Coriolanus as another Turnus, an anachronistic though heroic figure who stands in the way of Rome's fulfilment of its destiny.[3] Gregory des Jardins traces 'The Hyrcanean beast' of Hamlet's 'passionate speech' to Dido's words to Aeneas: the point is that Virgil's hero rejects the thought of revenge on Helen, and will later reject Dido herself, in order to save what is left of his country; Hamlet, on the other hand, ignoring the lesson implicit in his misquotation, will pursue revenge and passion at the expense of his country's future good.[4]

---

[1] Indiana University Press, Bloomington, and Harvester Press, Brighton, 1983.

[2] C. S. Lim, 'An Ovidian Source for Othello's Success in Love', *Notes and Queries*, NS 30 (1983), 127.

[3] 'Cracking Strong Curbs Asunder: Roman Destiny and the Roman Hero in *Coriolanus*', *English Literary Renaissance*, 13 (1983), 58–69.

[4] *Notes and Queries*, NS 30 (1983), 124–5.

Several other points on sources and analogues, all from *Notes and Queries*, 30 (1983), may be conveniently taken together. G. K. Hunter in fact gets rid of a couple of 'sources', since he convincingly reinstates the view of Marco Mincoff that the chapbook version of *Titus Andronicus* is based on the ballad which in turn is based on the play, not vice versa.[5] L. T. Woodbridge suggests the influence of two Erasmian dialogues, published together in translation in 1568, in *Othello*, *As You Like It*, and, less convincingly to me, *1 Henry IV*.[6] Robert A. H. Smith finds in *Richard II* possible echoes of *Friar Bacon and Friar Bungay*, *Dido*, *Faustus*, and *The Troublesome Reign of King John*;[7] J. J. M. Tobin links *Hamlet* with one of Nashe's most colourful passages from *Christ's Tears over Jerusalem*.[8] François Laroque points out that the German Faustbook provides a story similar to the 'pound-of-flesh' one, also involving a Jew and followed, suggestively, by a description of Shrovetide customs, which might provide an explanation for the masquing in Shakespeare's play: Carnival, as its name implies, is obsessed with flesh.[9] David Hopkins finds influence running the other way in Jonson's poem to Sir Robert Wroth, whose references to entering the breach and boasting about one's military prowess he traces to Henry V's orations to his troops.[10] He also finds a possible indebtedness on Milton's part: Sin, in *Paradise Lost*, might derive from *Richard III* ('the kennel of thy womb' and the 'hellhound').[11]

Some of the various explanatory notes in *Notes and Queries*, 30 are discussed elsewhere (see pp. 218–19). Of those which are not, I might mention Martin R. Orkin's use of the proverb 'Children are deceived with comfits and men with oaths' to suggest that Hotspur's dislike for the oaths sworn by a comfit-maker's wife may reflect his subliminal suspicion of Glendower and his too-relaxed household.[12] R. C. Horne finds an autobiographical interpretation for Sonnet 37: by analogy with the initial father–son image, the poet must be saying that he has been 'made lame' by the death of Hamnet Shakespeare, and hence the poem can be no earlier than August 1596.[13]

The Winter's Tale has always been recognized as a 'seasonal' play. But Margaret Hotine draws extraordinary conclusions from the fact that it was performed at court on 5 November 1611. Noting that spiders were associated with treachery, and that Northampton's speech against the Gunpowder plotters contained images of spiders, drugs, and cups, she suggests that Shakespeare is hinting that James I's fear of the Catholics is as irrational as Leontes's account of the nausea produced by the sight of a spider.[14] François Laroque links the play with both Innocents' Day and Easter Week, suggesting that folk ritual provides a bridge between pagan and Christian interpretations of the play.[15] While the relation between folk plays and professional drama is a potentially fruitful area to explore, it needs to be approached with caution; I recommend Thomas Pettitt's article in *Research Opportunities in Renaissance Drama*, 25 (1982), for a wide-ranging and well-balanced survey of the subject.[16]

Other brief notes include R. E. R. Madelaine's attempt to make something of the 'rotten orange' in *Much Ado*.[17] While I don't think much of the suggestion that Hero's blushes are the source of Claudio's image, there *is* something odd about its use by a character who is earlier described as 'civil as an orange'; the connection between the two is likely to be Beatrice's own gloss on her pun ('something of that jealous complexion'), but it may also be

---

[5] 'The "Sources" of *Titus Andronicus* – Once Again', 114–16.

[6] 'Shakespeare's Use of Two Erasmian Colloquies', 122–3.

[7] 'Three Notes on *Richard II*', 116–17.

[8] 'Hamlet and Salary', 125–6.

[9] 'An Analogue and Possible Secondary Source to the Pound of Flesh Story in *The Merchant of Venice*', 117–18.

[10] 'Ben Jonson and *Henry V*', 148.

[11] 'Milton's Sin and Shakespeare's *Richard III*', *Notes and Queries*, NS 29 (1982), 502–3.

[12] 'A Proverbial Allusion and a Proverbial Association in *1 Henry IV*', 120–1.

[13] 'The Date of Shakespeare's Sonnet 37', 130–1.

[14] 'Treason in *The Winter's Tale*', 127–30.

[15] 'Pagan Ritual, Christian Liturgy, and Folk Customs in *The Winter's Tale*', *Cahiers Élisabéthains*, 22 (1982), 25–33.

[16] 'Early English Traditional Drama: Approaches and Perspectives', 1–30.

[17] 'Oranges and Lemans: *Much Ado About Nothing*, IV, i, 31', *Shakespeare Quarterly*, 33 (1982), 491–2.

interesting to know that oranges were sometimes taken to be the golden apples of Venus.

The behind-the-scenes role of women in Shakespeare's writing is suggested by two scholars. R. F. Fleissner sees *As You Like It* as a possible tribute both to Shakespeare's mother and to the Virgin Mary, as evidenced by the poet's habit of punning on names and the conjunction of the words 'merry' and 'Arden' in the same speech.[18] Rolf Soellner offers an explanation for the emphatic insistence, in the dedication to *The Rape of Lucrece*, that the poet belongs exclusively to Southampton: he is distinguishing himself from the writers of other 'suffering heroine' tragedies which were currently being dedicated to noble ladies.[19] This argument depends on the assumption that Shakespeare had read two of these works (Kyd's translation of Garnier's *Cornélie* and Daniel's *Cleopatra*) in manuscript, and it does not quite explain why he *didn't* dedicate his poem to the Countess of Pembroke since, on this account, she would have been the obvious patron for it. Yet the existence of an alternative possibility for patronage, and the intricacies of the relationships involved, might turn out to illuminate some of the Sonnets as well (I am thinking of those which rather smugly assert the superiority of their male dedicatee to the usual 'painted beauty').

John S. Mebane's 'Structure, Source and Meaning in *A Midsummer Night's Dream*',[20] though it reaffirms the importance of *The Knight's Tale* for Shakespeare, is not really a source study so much as a sensitive account of the play in terms of its thematic and philosophical links with Chaucer. Other studies of influences on early Shakespeare include Joan Rees's note on various fictitious characters who share the free-associating garrulity of Juliet's Nurse (she suggests Miso, in *The Arcadia*, as a possible prototype),[21] and Peter Berek's 'Artifice and Realism in Lyly, Nashe, and *Love's Labor's Lost*', which sees *Gallathea* and *Summer's Last Will and Testament* as successive stages in the process which culminates in Shakespeare's play: the integration of pattern and artifice with a sense of ordinary contemporary life, the felt reality of human emotions, and the presence of death.[22] Helmut Bonheim makes out a good case for paying more attention to

the romance as a source for ideas on the drama (after all, the printed book was available for study in a way that the play was not), but he knows less about early drama than about the novel, and thus often fails to recognize that there is a more obvious source (of the interpolated song, for instance) than the one he gives.[23] Joseph Candido's 'Fashioning *Henry VIII*: What Shakespeare Saw in *When You See Me You Know Me*' shows how, in both plays, the character of the King is created through patterns of speech (frequent, abrupt questions) and of scene: his entrance leaning on the arm of an adviser, his presence, in a state of bemused helplessness, during a confrontation between his queen and a churchman.[24]

The type of source study I have just been describing, which depends less on small verbal parallels than on larger analogies and associations, might perhaps be called *A Study in Creative Adaptation*. This is in fact the subtitle of Leah Scragg's *The Metamorphosis of Gallathea*.[25] Verbal parallels are the least convincing part of this analysis of Lyly's long-lasting influence on Shakespeare; the most convincing are the close and sensitive discussions of patterns of rhetoric and dramaturgy: the parallel roles of Diana's ladies and Navarre's lords, the various types of metamorphosis brought about by the *deus ex machina*, the 'supposes' in Lyly and *As You Like It*, the endings of *Endymion* and *The Winter's Tale*. Mrs Scragg keeps a sense of proportion when she admits that 'it would be perverse to suppose that Shakespeare was more aware of Lyly's work than his own', and she tries to show the ways in which themes drawn from the earlier dramatist are mediated sometimes through other writers (like

---

18 '"Arden and...Merry"/Mary Arden: Calling on Shakespeare's Mother in *As You Like It*', *Marianum*, 44 (1982), 171–7.

19 'Shakespeare's *Lucrece* and the Garnier-Pembroke Connection', *Shakespeare Studies*, 15 (1982), 1–20.

20 *Texas Studies in Literature and Language*, 24 (1982), 255–70.

21 'Juliet's Nurse: Some Branches of a Family Tree', *Review of English Studies*, 34 (1983), 43–7.

22 *Studies in English Literature 1500–1900*, 23 (1983), 207–21.

23 'Shakespeare and the Novel of his Time', *Deutsche Shakespeare-Gesellschaft West: Jahrbuch 1982*, 133–45.

24 *Cahiers Élisabéthains*, 23 (1983), 47–59.

25 University Press of America, Washington, DC, 1982.

the Euphuistic Lodge of *Rosalynde*) and sometimes through Shakespeare's own reworkings of them. My main complaint about Mrs Scragg's book is not about its contents but about a habit which I have also noticed in other writers this year: I mean, complaining that other critics have not, in effect, written her book for her. If I were to say that I was sorry she didn't see the 'virgin sacrifice' theme of *Gallathea* as a possible explanation for that rather odd moment where Orsino seems about to drag Viola off to a similar fate, the reader might well mutter, 'The tears live in an onion that should water this sorrow'. In fact, of course, I'm delighted to have a chance to make this point for myself: a book can be valuable not only for what it says but also for what it suggests.

Gary Taylor also demonstrates a complex case of creative adaptation – in this case, the unlikely combination of *Eastward Ho!* and *The Miseries of Enforced Marriage* in the gestation of *King Lear*.[26] The incidents which *Lear* has in common with *Eastward Ho!* – the storm, the trial scene, the movement of all the characters toward a specific point, the tripping up someone's heels, the bad servingman – can be shown to arise naturally out of the plot of the comedy, whereas they are totally irrelevant to that of the tragedy. The same can be said of the parallels with the Wilkins play, which are more verbal in nature. The very fact that the three works have so little in common is itself the strongest argument for unconscious influence, as opposed to the commonplace-book type of borrowing. Always assuming that no common source turns up, Mr Taylor seems to have succeeded in showing that there is 'borrowing', and that Shakespeare is the borrower; the conclusion is that *Lear* can't have been composed before the second half of 1605.

Studies of political thought in Shakespeare used to restrict themselves to a verbal approach, but this year most of them dwell on the conjunction of politics and pageantry. An exception is Donna B. Hamilton's careful study of 'The State of Law in *Richard II*',[27] which draws on Fortescue, Bracton and Hooker to show that the concept of kingship and law in the play is that of Shakespeare's own time, not a piece of self-conscious medievalism. That is,

a ruler's authority was taken to rest on the law and he became weaker, not stronger, by setting himself above it. Richard's sense that he has gone pale because the blood of twenty thousand men has fled from his face shows his belated recognition that 'a king is, or should be, one with his people'; the analogy between the people and the lifeblood of the body can also be found in Fortescue.

To illustrate the difference between the verbal and the visual approaches, we can turn to Minoru Fujita's *Pageantry and Spectacle in Shakespeare*,[28] which also dwells on the passage about the blood which triumphed in Richard's face. Words like 'triumph', 'royal', 'show', and 'wonder', are, as Professor Fujita points out, part of 'the lexicon of pageantry'; when examined in this context, they sometimes yield interesting results. Richard's triumph is linked to words like 'pomp' and 'pride' and the concept of wearing one's best clothes; Fujita pursues this conjunction through the play, noting that Bolingbroke's entry into London vulgarizes the idea of triumph, as does Hal's reported decision to wear a prostitute's favour at the royal tournament. At the end of *2 Henry IV*, we may be meant to see (as a stage direction in the Quarto suggests) the coronation procession of the new king. The entrance of Falstaff and his cronies in their scruffy clothes would then form a 'shocking contrast' with the 'gorgeous garment, majesty' and Hal's rejection of Falstaff would enact the image of the sun breaking through the clouds. These are some examples of the interesting conjunction of iconography and imagery which this book offers. I should add that it gets better as it goes on; the unevenness of the writing and proof-reading, particularly noticeable in the first chapter, presumably reflects the varying degrees of editorial attention given to the different chapters in the journals where they first appeared. The approach is at least as much critical as scholarly; at times Professor Fujita turns Shakespeare into a fellow-academic, forever 'trying to show' something or

[26] 'A New Source and an Old Date for *King Lear*', *Review of English Studies*, 32 (1982), 396–413.

[27] *Shakespeare Quarterly*, 34 (1983), 5–17.

[28] The Renaissance Institute, Sophia University, Tokyo, 1982.

other. Shakespeare didn't try to show anything, he just showed it.

Another good example of how pageantry and politics can go together is Katherine Eisaman Maus's comparison of *The Tempest* with its Restoration successor.[29] By replacing Prospero's masque of Ceres with a final scene in which he shows the winds and waves completely at his bidding, Dryden and Davenant, she argues, imply that Prospero has no intention of resigning his power. His intransigence towards the other characters is only one aspect of the play's tense background – the Neapolitan court is returning not from an interracial marriage but from war with the Moors – which Professor Maus sees as a counterpart of Restoration political insecurity.

I cannot devote as much space as I would like to Stephen Greenblatt's collection, *The Power of Forms in the English Renaissance* (originally a special number of *Genre*).[30] Though the essays are not confined to drama, and indeed show a welcome range of reference, a number of them are of Shakespearian interest. As the title indicates, the volume is not primarily concerned with generic studies but with an exploration of the ways in which power is used within, or against, or in collusion with, the worlds of art and the court. Not surprisingly, *Measure for Measure*, *Lear*, *Macbeth*, and *The Tempest* come in for a particularly large share of attention, but there are lively studies of *Much Ado* and *The Comedy of Errors* (here, the 'power' in question is primarily that of the playwright). In fact, as Stephen Orgel points out in his contribution, 'Making Greatness Familiar', the players and the ruler were really engaged in the same activity, a fact which made the relationship between them a particularly delicate and dangerous one.

The constantly expanding field of theatrical iconography probably owes something of its popularity to the fact that recent technology has made it easier and cheaper to add visual interest both to articles and to lectures. *Shakespeare and the Arts* is a selection of papers given at the 1981 Ohio Shakespeare Conference.[31] Most of these use visual evidence of some kind, and were presumably given as slide lectures. I am sure that these were highly successful at the conference. In the cold light of print they do not always seem so persuasive. The least

useful are those which borrow a term like 'mannerism' from art history and then apply it to a play. Others point out visual patterns which certainly exist, but leave me in doubt as to whether they could be conveyed in performance. How likely is it that audiences murmured, 'Ah, yes, *Veritas Filia Temporis*' at the end of *The Winter's Tale*?[32] Or that they recognized the striking parallel which Catherine M. Shaw has drawn between the masque in *Romeo and Juliet* and its tragic parody in the tomb scene where Romeo, again a torchbearer, again in the presence of Tybalt, again kisses Juliet?[33] Elizabeth Truax provides a wealth of information about Renaissance paintings of Venus and Adonis and the Lucretia story, and the mannerist tastes of Bess of Hardwick,[34] but doesn't convince me that either of these factors necessarily had anything to do with Shakespeare's poems.

Other papers dealt with music (Patricia K. Meszaros argues that the music of the spheres in *Pericles* is meant to be audible only to the hero: the audience's effort to hear, for which pauses are provided, is part of its struggle for faith),[35] with televised Shakespeare (I shall consider this topic separately later), and with acting theory and practice. I enjoyed Ellen J. O'Brien's account of Ophelia's mad scene in performance.[36] Jane L. Donawerth's 'Shakespeare and Acting Theory in the Renaissance' attempts to trace a movement from the definition of acting as a means of rousing emotion to a concept of 'judicious' acting which serves a moral purpose;[37] at times, this sounds like a restatement of the old Alleyn-versus-Burbage polarization, but when she

---

29 'Arcadia Lost: Politics and Revision in the Restoration *Tempest*', *Renaissance Drama*, 13 (1982), 189–209.

30 Pilgrim Books, Norman, Okla., 1982.

31 Ed. Cecile Williamson Cary and Henry S. Limouze (University Press of America, Washington, DC, 1982).

32 See Clifford Davidson, 'The Iconography of Illusion and Truth in *The Winter's Tale*', 73–91.

33 'The Visual and the Symbolic in Shakespeare's Masques', 21–34.

34 'Venus, Lucrece, and Bess of Hardwick: Portraits to Please', 35–56.

35 '*Pericles*: Shakespeare's Divine Musical Comedy', 3–20.

36 'Ophelia's Mad Scene and the Stage Tradition', 109–25.

37 Pp. 165–98.

notes Prospero's praise of the 'grace' in Ariel's performance as the harpy she seems to point towards something like neoclassical style. Richard C. Snyder writes well on the psychological aspects of role-playing in *Troilus and Cressida*,[38] and J. S. Lowry, in a more sympathetic treatment of the Duke and Isabella than they are usually given, argues that the title of *Measure for Measure* is part of a pattern which implies the possibility of a dramatic cure through 'a homeopathic imitation of the disease'.[39]

There is plenty of art-orientated criticism elsewhere too. An interesting reply to Roland M. Frye's suggestions about the Alleyn portrait of Richard III (about which I expressed some mild reservations last year) is supplied by S. P. Cerusano who has done some work on the actor's accounts. The unfinished look of the portrait, he suggests, is likely to be the result of Alleyn's having bought it on the cheap, as part of a set, and perhaps at a reduced price because of its condition.[40] Frye has, meanwhile, come up with some good examples of how pictorial evidence can help interpretation:[41] the most interesting of these is his evidence that Hamlet's inky cloak may have been a mourning one, which would have covered him from head to foot and thus have made him a conspicuous figure even in a court where many people were wearing black. In another curious piece of pictorial detective work, Karen Newman shows how the various treatments of the play scene in *Hamlet*, both in pictures and stage sets, remain remarkably constant in their iconography; she also suggests that the absence of the figure of the Prince himself in Francis Hayman's painting may be explained by the fact that the scene was meant to be viewed through Hamlet's eyes.[42]

Éliane Cuvelier's essay on '"Perspective" in *The Winter's Tale*' follows Gilman's *Curious Perspective* in mixing literal and figurative uses of the artistic term.[43] She draws learnedly on the Elizabethan psychology of fantasy as a source of strange images, and relates these to the distorted images of anamorphosis; the world, for Leontes, becomes a 'reversible portrait' where everything is the opposite of itself, a view which finds its counterpart in many linguistic uses in this play. John Doebler summarizes most of the evidence, iconographic and literary, which has

been used to account for Shakespeare's unconventional treatment of Venus and Adonis; he offers one new parallel between Titian and the poet – the use they both make of animals for implicit comment on the scene.[44]

A number of studies draw on emblems, usually as part of an analysis of symbolism. Thus, Deborah Baker Wyrick finds that the ass could stand for humility and sacrifice *or* stupidity *or* a sex symbol.[45] Dromio of Syracuse, she thinks, is simply a fool; Dromio of Ephesus is a suffering ass; and Bottom, of course, combines all three roles. Jeff Shulman likewise finds a double view of a symbolic figure – Hercules could represent 'manly courage' or (with Omphale) 'effeminate amorousness', a buffoon or a symbol of moral choice.[46] As applied to *Love's Labour's Lost*, this analysis of the legend helps to show the inseparability of the various qualities which Navarre and his lords attempt to compartmentalize. Joan Hartwig also provides visual evidence, this time in the form of illustrations of a scold's bridle, to show that Petruchio's method of wife-taming is metaphorically the same as the Renaissance method of taming horses.[47] (She also notes that *A Shrew*, unlike *The Shrew*, has relatively little of this sort of imagery.) Kate ends up as a 'wonder', like the Dauphin of France's manageable horse, which is also

[38] 'Discovering a "Dramaturgy of Human Relationships" in Shakespearean Metadrama: *Troilus and Cressida*', 199–216.

[39] 'Imitations and Creation in *Measure for Measure*', 217–29.

[40] 'More on Edward Alleyn's "Shakespearean" Portrait of Richard III', *Shakespeare Quarterly*, 33 (1982), 342–4.

[41] '"Looking Before and After": the Use of Visual Evidence and Symbolism for Interpreting *Hamlet*', *Huntington Library Quarterly*, 45 (1982), 1–19.

[42] 'Hayman's Missing Hamlet', *Shakespeare Quarterly*, 34 (1983), 73–8.

[43] *Cahiers Élisabéthains*, 23 (1983), 35–46.

[44] 'The Reluctant Adonis: Titian and Shakespeare', *Shakespeare Quarterly*, 33 (1982), 480–90.

[45] 'The Ass Motif in *The Comedy of Errors* and *A Midsummer Night's Dream*', ibid., 432–48.

[46] 'At the Crossroads of Myth: the Hermeneutics of Hercules from Ovid to Shakespeare', *ELH*, 50 (1983), 83–105.

[47] 'Horses and Women in *The Taming of the Shrew*', *Huntington Library Quarterly*, 45 (1982), 285–94.

a 'wonder of nature'. Donn Ervin Taylor explores the composite figure of Fortune and Time in *As You Like It*, where wrestling becomes an image for the need to seize the fortunate moment. Rosalind's sense of the passing of time contrasts with Orlando's indifference to it and Jaques's tendency to waste it.[48]

Lawrence Danson's 'Henry V: King, Chorus, and Critics' starts from the premise that this was the first play to be done in the Globe, and thus that the Chorus's disclaimers are really a way of drawing attention to the marvellous new theatre, just as Henry's apparent modesty in his wooing of Katherine is only a more subtle way of selling himself.[49] Another article which combines awareness of performance conditions with visual imagination is Gordon P. Jones's remarkably convincing explanation for the curious moment in *Antony and Cleopatra*, act 1, scene 2, when Enobarbus mistakes the entering Queen for Antony: the hero and heroine had been wearing each other's clothes in the first scene.[50]

The image of Jupiter on an eagle and an emblem describing his statue in Crete provide Peggy Munoz Simonds with an explanation for his presence in *Cymbeline*.[51] The statue was said to have no ears, thus symbolizing the need for a ruler to avoid flattery or slander. But good as well as evil can enter by the ear: music, prophecy, and the emblematic association of the eagle with St John's Gospel, suggest a Word (the Incarnation which will occur in Cymbeline's reign) audible to the audience but not to the characters. Not iconographical, but a useful complement to this essay, is Robert Y. Turner's study of 'Slander in *Cymbeline* and other Jacobean Tragicomedies'.[52] The 'slandered heroine' plot is seen as a reaction against the vogue for satiric drama; Turner also points out that James I's 'Act Against Scandalous Speeches and Lybellis' dates from 1609. Tragicomedy, with its emphasis on faith (whether in the very absurdities of the plot or in the apparently guilty heroine), shows 'the impulse to affirm trust and fidelity against the impulse to debase'.

This has been a particularly good year for stage history. New evidence has come to light about several indoor playhouses, we have probably got as close as we are ever going to get to the building of

the Globe, and a lot of new material on Shakespearian performances has been made available. A good general study of the Elizabethan theatre in practice was badly needed, and now one has appeared: *Shakespeare's Theatre*, by Peter Thomson, an admirable book which I shall be recommending to all my students.[53] His style is lively, he mixes a good deal of scholarship with occasional flights of wild speculation to provoke discussion (my favourite is the suggestion that the Globe possessed a theatre barge, which could have been used to advertise *Antony and Cleopatra*). Above all, he has lots of practical theatre sense, which comes out in such comments as his analysis of the handling of entrances and exits: 'It is precisely because the audience is attending to the action downstage that the upstage entrances have to be prepared for.' He surveys the Globe's repertory, year by year, including new plays and revivals (unlike Danson – above – he thinks that the 'flirtatious' epilogue of *As You Like It* indicates that this play is 'wooing a new audience' and was the first one to be produced at the Globe); he discusses the production of a play scene by scene, with lists of the props required for each. This is just the sort of thing to bring dramatic history alive for the inexperienced theatre-goer. I am less happy with some of what he writes about the plays themselves – the familiar denigration of Orsino and Olivia, the suggestion that *Troilus and Cressida* and *All's Well That Ends Well* were 'notable documents in the submerged Puritan campaign to raise the status of women'. But he certainly knows, as well as anyone, how they were put on.

John Orrell's *The Quest for Shakespeare's Globe* aims at a more specialized audience than Peter

---

48 '"Try in Time in Despite of a Fall": Time and Occasion in *As You Like It*', *Texas Studies in Literature and Language*, 24 (1982), 121–36.

49 *Shakespeare Quarterly*, 34 (1983), 27–47.

50 'The "Strumpet's Fool" in *Antony and Cleopatra*', *ibid.*, 62–8.

51 '"No More...Offend Our Hearing", Aural Imagery in *Cymbeline*', *Texas Studies in Literature and Language*, 24 (1982), 137–54.

52 *English Literary Renaissance*, 13 (1983), 182–202.

53 Theatre Production Studies (Routledge and Kegan Paul, London, Boston, and Henley, 1983).

Thomson, but is equally exciting to read.[54] The book incorporates material already used in *The Third Globe*, which I reviewed last year, and in the article on Christ Church performance which I shall be discussing shortly. But it is more than the sum of its parts; John Orrell is the sort of scholar (like Leslie Hotson and C. Walter Hodges) who wants his readers to share the process of discovery at every stage, even to the point of inviting them to 'take precise bearings' for themselves on a window or a map of London. Plenty of critics have tried to turn themselves into actors or directors in order to understand Shakespeare's theatre, but few have turned themselves into Elizabethan draughtsmen and surveyors in order to understand how that theatre was built. Orrell has reconstructed the process by which Hollar made his famous panoramic view of London, establishing exactly where he was standing and exactly what distortion his system of linear perspective would have caused in the diameter of the Globe. He makes the practical suggestion that all the public theatres, except the square Fortune, were basically the same in their dimensions, and thus that the second Globe was much the same as the first, on whose foundations it was built. Drawing on the evidence of seating capacity at the Christ Church performance he is able to arrive at an estimate of the numbers which the Globe could hold at each level. Aware that his constant use of mathematical calculations may not be as much fun as, say, Frances Yates's 'Theatre of the World' hypothesis, he ends with some speculations of his own: one is that the theatre was orientated due east, like a church, and 'aligned toward the midsummer sunrise'.

Another bonus of his research, though he makes surprisingly little fuss about it, is the claim to identify the exterior of Blackfriars playhouse on the Hollar engraving. It is true that this tells us nothing about the interior, but other evidence that has come to light may eventually help to provide a similar sense of the basic pattern for this type of building. David George's work on 'Jacobean Actors and the Great Hall at Gawthorpe, Lancashire' is a contribution to a relatively unexplored area: the touring companies of the period.[55] Lancashire had a public

playhouse in Preston until 1609; the Great Hall, which he thinks could seat about 100, went out of use in 1619. From the payment given to actors and other entertainers, he deduces that the average size of a touring company was ten actors, and he notes that those known to have visited Gawthorpe, apart from a touring branch of Queen Anne's Men, were northern players, belonging to the Earl of Derby and his relations. Professor George thinks that this hall, which is still standing and very little restored, may have been built specifically as a theatre. I look forward to hearing more about it.

Another, better-known, indoor theatre is the Whitehall Cockpit. John H. Astington has been examining the records of the Office of the Works to establish the nature of the alterations made by Inigo Jones in 1629.[56] He concludes (rather as Orrell does about the second Globe) that it was basically a refinement rather than a complete alteration of the earlier interior, which was already an elaborately carved, gilded, and painted structure. The stage, probably a platform made up of several movable units, would have been a more permanent version of what was used when the Cockpit was converted into a temporary theatre. A German theatre plan, which bears some resemblance to the Jones design for the Cockpit, is described by Graham C. Adams.[57] Built in 1604–6, the Ottoneum in Kassel was used by English actors until 1613, and is still standing, though much altered. Professor Adams finds evidence that the original building was constructed on Vitruvian principles and thinks that it may be evidence for 'an international knowledge of theatre design'.

Ironically, it was the assumption that it depicted a German theatre that caused the design for the Hall at Christ Church, Oxford, to be ignored for so many years. Professor Orrell identified it on the basis of the dimensions given on the plan, and recognized that it

---

54 Cambridge University Press, 1983.
55 *Theatre Notebook*, 37 (1983), 109–21.
56 'The Whitehall Cockpit: The Building and the Theatre', *English Literary Renaissance*, 13 (1982), 301–18.
57 'The Ottoneum: A Neglected Seventeenth-Century Theater', *Shakespeare Studies*, 15 (1982), 243–68.

must have been intended for the visit of James I to Oxford in 1605.[58] The many curious features of this plan, such as the raked auditorium and stage, naturally raise questions about their use in other private theatres. The Vitruvian perspective stage, complete with periaktoi, may well have been suggested to Jones, as Professor Orrell thinks, by the Oxford scholars' plans to include *Ajax Flagellifer* (a play discussed in the commentary to the edition of Vitruvius which Jones is known to have possessed) as part of the royal programme. But the existence of so near-contemporary a theatre as the Ottoneum may indeed be witness to a tradition of classical design. What will catch the eye of most readers is the evidence about the cramped seating conditions (I hope the builders of the Third Globe do not decide to emulate them): the design allows ladies and royal servants a board eight inches wide, while everyone else has to manage with six inches. The drawing also brings into question the common assumption that the Chief Spectator had a perfect viewpoint of the perspective. It is clear that the precise position at which the King was to sit occupied a good deal of the attention of the Chancellor, Vice-Chancellor and the designer, not to mention the workmen who had to cope with a last-minute decision to move the seat further back so that he could be seen by more of the spectators. But it is equally clear that it would have been impossible for James simultaneously to be at the centre of the circular composition, be visible to as much of the audience as possible, and be in the best possible position for viewing the scene.

The theatre in which W. Reavley Gair envisages the Children of Paul's is not at all like any indoor theatre described above, a fact which may cast some doubt on his reconstruction.[59] Professor Gair thinks that the stage at Paul's was set up diagonally across a corner and he provides extensive detail of its other arrangements. He tends to work on the assumption that everything mentioned in a play must have been literally present on the stage. On the strength of one line in *A Trick to Catch the Old One*, he goes so far as to suggest that the theatre eventually acquired an on-stage staircase that was visible to the audience, despite the fact that, as he himself admits, this

staircase would have cut down the acting space, blocked entry from one of the doors, and required extensive structural alterations. Similarly, he assumes that all the pictures discussed in the plays were visible to the audience and painted by a gifted artist who happened to be a member of the company. Professor Gair has collected a lot of evidence about the state of the cathedral at the end of the sixteenth century, the population of the surrounding area, and some interesting bits of social history; the material is interesting, though not always obviously relevant. He is not well informed on the earlier part of the period: his account of early Tudor drama assumes that progress is to be identified with increasing psychological realism, and when he says that Martin Marprelate was identified on the Paul's stage 'by costume or mannerism or both' he gives a totally false impression: Martin's real identity has *never* been known. His conviction that boys didn't wear false beards at Paul's has been effectively countered by R. E. R. Madelaine, who draws evidence from a wide range of plays known to have been performed there.[60] And, while I share his view that the boy actors must have been more than a joke (no one comes to a theatre regularly just to watch plays being made ridiculous by bad acting), and I like his suggestion that the induction to *Antonio and Mellida* was partly designed to introduce a new company to its audience, I find it hard to believe that the actors' apologies are the expression of a real conviction of inadequacy on their or their author's part. The 1983 production of *The Fawn* at the Cottesloe Theatre showed how teasing and elusive Marston's relationship with his audience could be.

A few brief notes on other aspects of the Elizabethan theatre. David McPherson, who has compared attacks on the stage in England and Spain,

[58] 'The Theatre at Christ Church, Oxford, in 1605', *Shakespeare Survey 35* (Cambridge University Press, 1982), 129–40.

[59] *The Children of Paul's: the story of a theatre company, 1553–1608* (Cambridge University Press, 1982).

[60] 'Boys' Beards and Balurdo', *Notes and Queries*, NS 30 (1983), 148–50.

shows that these were remarkably similar, despite the many differences (not least the religious one) between the two countries.[61] David Bergeron's 'Gilbert Dugdale and the Royal Entry of James I (1604)' notes that this author, who was related to Robert Armin, mentions the royal family's patronage of acting companies, a fact which allows slightly greater precision in dating the transfer of Nottingham's and Worcester's men.[62] John H. Astington's study of 'Gallows Scenes on the Elizabethan Stage' suggests, plausibly enough, that the technique involved a basketwork harness and pulley, probably developed for episodes like the hanging of Judas in the mystery cycles.[63] (Professor Astington brightened my reading considerably when he wondered whether Horatio in The Spanish Tragedy actually played his love scene with Belimperia while wearing this basketwork harness under his clothes.)

Information about English actors abroad in Shakespeare's time is still scattered and relatively hard to come by; a book which collected all the available material would be very welcome. Gunnar Sjögren's posthumously published volume of essays, Hamlet the Dane,[64] includes an account of players and instrumentalists at the Danish court in the 1580s: among these were Kempe, Bryan, and Pope, who later became members of Shakespeare's company. A troupe of English actors based in Germany also attended the coronation of Christian IV in 1596. Some of the other essays in this volume are rather lightweight, but there is much valuable material about the Danish aspect of Hamlet, though it must be said that not much of it was missed by Harold Jenkins in his Arden edition (for instance, the number of Danish nobles named Rosenkrantz or Gyldenstiern, and the fact that 'Dansker', strictly speaking, meant a native of Danzig – with all that this may imply for the play's references to Poland and Polonius). Sjögren's chapter on 'The Genesis of Hamlet', which compares the versions in the Danish chronicles with those of Saxo and Belleforest, will have to be taken into account by anyone working on the subject.

According to Sjögren, English actors were such a common sight in Germany that one religious tract found it necessary to point out that not all Englishmen followed this profession. Willem Schrickx provides some new information, including transcripts of hitherto unpublished documents from Frankfurt and Augsburg, which helps to build up a picture of their wanderings.[65] One petition, for instance, 'not only reveals that there was often considerable rivalry among the companies of wandering actors but . . . also shows unmistakably that they also included Aachen, Liège, Antwerp and Brussels in their itinerary.' Some of the material also has implications for the history of boy actors and for the dating of performances in which the strolling actors are known to have taken part before their departure from England.

I now come to post-Elizabethan productions. This means mainly post-1800, in fact, though I can't resist mentioning the lying-in-state, with specially composed music, which was transferred to the end of Hamlet at Goodman's Fields after having previously commemorated the death of the young Duke of Buckingham in 1736/7.[66] Maarten van Dijk contributes two useful articles on John Philip Kemble, one on his vocal technique and one on the critics' attitudes to his work.[67] The latter is a useful warning for all stage historians against relying too much on purely evaluative theatrical criticism. As Russell Jackson rightly notes in his survey of work on the nineteenth-century theatre, the subject has come of age: 'A field in which anecdote dominated

---

[61] 'The Attack on Stage in Shakespeare's Time: An International Affair', Comparative Literature Studies, 20 (1983), 168–82.

[62] Journal of Medieval and Renaissance Studies, 13 (1983), 111–25.

[63] Theatre Notebook, 37 (1983), 3–9.

[64] Publications of the New Society of Letters, Lund, Sweden, 1983.

[65] 'English Actors' Names in German Archives and Elizabethan Theatre History', Shakespeare Jahrbuch 1982, 146–61.

[66] Norman Gillespie, 'Henry Carey's "Missing" Music to Hamlet, 1736', Theatre Notebook, 37 (1983), 124–7.

[67] 'The Kembles and Vocal Technique', Theatre Research International, 8 (1983), 28–42; 'John Philip Kemble and the Critics', Theatre Notebook, 36 (1982), 110–18.

. . . has been transformed into an academic discipline.'[68] Dr Jackson provides an introduction to the 1982 *Shakespeare Survey* which featured a number of essays on Shakespeare in the Nineteenth Century. Not all the contributors are as sympathetic as he to the theatre of that time; Dennis Bartholomeusz, in particular, tends to compare nineteenth-century Australian productions with his own ideas of what the plays 'really' are like.[69] Michael Booth's examination of the effect of the Meininger Company on subsequent practice in the English theatre finds that much of what the German company was doing corresponded to an ideal shared by Charles Kean and Macready.[70] What impressed the critics most, he adds, was the evidence of something which English theatrical traditions did not yet permit: long rehearsal periods and generous subsidies. On the evidence of Simon Williams, Shakespeare production in Vienna was becoming astonishingly 'modern' in the 1890s.[71] The Burgtheater's leading actor of the mid-1890s, Mitterwurzer, 'seemed to begin each act as if he were playing a totally different person, in this way revealing rather than obscuring contradictions in character'; his successor, Kainz, played Richard II as a 'study in megalomania' and Antony as a schemer whose Forum speech had clearly been planned in advance.

Dennis Bartholomeusz has followed his stage history of *Macbeth* with *The Winter's Tale in Performance in England and America, 1611–1976*.[72] It is always useful to have this sort of book – splendidly illustrated, if less splendidly punctuated and proofread – and much of its information is fascinating. I was glad to read Garrick's alterations to the text (not abandoned until 1856, when Time was at last restored to the play), the excellent accounts of Macready and Helen Faucit in the tragic part of the play, and the gags used by various Autolycuses. It is interesting to see that the rocking horse, so memorable a feature of Trevor Nunn's 1969–70 Royal Shakespeare Company production, was also used by Kemble in 1811, and that Phelps, in following Coleridge's concept of the play, was anticipating some present relationships of director and critic. I am less happy about the assumptions underlying some

of Bartholomeusz's statements: he declares that most eighteenth-century Perditas are 'deservedly no longer remembered' (surely a circular argument), and he praises Theophilus Cibber as 'ahead of his time by nearly fifty years' because he was one of the few who objected to Garrick's *Florizel and Perdita*. This is a good example of the need to put a critic into context: Cibber was consistently hostile to Garrick and, on top of that, Garrick's Perdita was Cibber's estranged wife. Generally speaking, the more visually spectacular a production was, the more the audience seems to have liked it, and the more Bartholomeusz objects to it. Spectacle, of course, tends to date, and it is easy to ridicule the 'Pyrrhic dance' which opened the Charles Kean version, or his procession of the chariots of the Moon, Time, and the Sun, or the volcanic eruption which a New York director, mindful of the Sicilian setting, used to symbolize the violence of Leontes's jealousy. Yet these represent a response to the imagery of the play no less valid than that of modern iconographical critics.

This dichotomy between the popular taste for spectacle and the academic's insistence on something as purely verbal as possible has been highlighted by the steady succession of Shakespeare productions in the BBC TV series, now nearing completion. The Shakespeare Gesellschaft West devoted its 1981 conference to the theme of Audio-Visual Shakespeare, and the title of one of its papers, 'Shakespeare heute: zwischen Wort und Bild',[73] indicates its recognition of the problem. Stanley Wells, in his survey of the BBC series, comments that at times he

---

[68] 'Before the Shakespeare Revolution: Developments in the Study of Nineteenth-Century Shakespearian Production', 1–12.

[69] 'Shakespeare on the Melbourne Stage, 1843–61', 31–41.

[70] 'The Meininger Company and English Shakespeare', 13–20.

[71] 'Shakespeare at the Burgtheater: From Heinrich Anschütz to Josef Kainz', 21–9.

[72] Cambridge University Press, 1982.

[73] Gerhard Müller-Schwefe, in *Shakespeare Jahrbuch 1982*, 36–55.

wished the texts had been rewritten.[74] This has in fact been the case in non-English-speaking countries, none of which, to my knowledge, uses a version earlier than that of Schlegel and Tieck; in most cases the translation is twentieth-century, and the need to match actors' lip movements sometimes conflicts with the requirements of strict accuracy. (Several of the contributors to the Shakespeare Gesellschaft conference discussed the business of choosing a translation, displaying in the process a degree of inwardness with the English text which puts most English-language directors to shame: Maximilian Schell describes how he and Gustav Gründgens debated whether to translate the 'conscience' that makes cowards of us all by 'Gewissen' or 'Bewusst-sein';[75] Dieter Dorn, who directed *A Midsummer Night's Dream* in 1978, prepared for the task by collaborating on a new translation.[76]) In an interesting discussion of the problems of dubbing TV Shakespeare, Gert Rabanus explains that he chooses his actors to match, not the voice of the original performer, but his physical appearance in the role.[77] A medium which permits so total a disjunction between the visual and the verbal must necessarily raise questions about the relationship between them.

Most English-speaking critics who discuss the television series concentrate mainly on the setting and its implications; John Wilders, speaking as its literary consultant, rightly identifies this as the main problem which each director has had to resolve.[78] *Shakespeare and the Arts* (see p. 193) also contains two discussions of the BBC series; one, Susan Willis's 'Making *All's Well that Ends Well*', is a good account, not only of the finished production (which we can all see for ourselves on our video-recorders) but also of the thought and experiment which went into it, some of which ended up on the cutting-room floor.[79] To compare her account with what Bernice W. Kliman tells us about Maurice Evans's early TV Shakespeare productions would probably say more about the different economic conditions of British and American television than about Shakespearian production as such.[80] One critic has already used the BBC *Julius Caesar* to support his view that it is possible for Brutus to play both versions of Portia's death without losing audience sympathy.[81] In fact,

his argument is based partly on textual analysis and partly on assumptions about Brutus' motivation; evidence from performance really adds nothing to it.

I have included this digression on TV Shakespeare by way of introduction to the last two books in this year's batch, both of which demonstrate ways in which Shakespeare's visual impact can be divorced from his words. One is about an Irish actress who performed Shakespeare in Paris in English; the other is a study of an English designer–director who produced *Hamlet* in Russian. Peter Raby's *Fair Ophelia: Harriet Smithson Berlioz* studies the influence not only of one culture but of one art form on another.[82] It is well written, makes good use of illustrations, and provides enough context – accounts of the little-known works in which Harriet first appeared, and of the state of the French stage at the time – to fill out her story without overwhelming it. Because much of the Parisian audience had an imperfect knowledge of English, the impact of the English actors must, Mr Raby suggests, have been similar to that of the Berliner Ensemble in London in 1956, working through stage pictures and business rather than words. He takes Harriet seriously as an artist, though nothing quoted here from her correspondence suggests that she was particularly interesting off the stage. Yet Berlioz's passion for her seems to have survived longer than one would have expected if it had been directed simply at a romantic symbol. She was already becoming fat before he married her, perhaps following the accident in

74 'Television Shakespeare', *Shakespeare Quarterly*, 33 (1982), 261–77.
75 'Deutschland ist nicht Hamlet', *Shakespeare Jahrbuch 1982*, 9–26.
76 Christian Jauslin, 'Dieter Dorns Shakespeare-Inszenierungen: Gesprach mit dem Regisseur', *ibid.*, 27–35.
77 'Shakespeare in deutscher Fassung: Zur Synchronisation der Inszenierungen fur das Fernsehen', *ibid.*, 63–78.
78 'Shakespeare on the Small Screen', *ibid.*, 56–62.
79 Pp. 155–63.
80 *Ibid.*, 135–53.
81 Thomas Clayton, '"Should Brutus Never Taste of Portia's Death but Once?": Text and Performance in *Julius Caesar*', *Studies in English Literature*, 23 (1983), 237–55.
82 Cambridge University Press, 1982.

which she broke her leg, and it is hard to see what future she would have had in a country whose language she did not know, or in England, where she had never been much of a success. Mr Raby's study of her influence on the music and painting of the period adds a valuable dimension to his book: if it seems remote from Shakespeare, it is also remote from the 'real' Harriet, whoever she was. Feminist critics ought certainly to read this book, and to ponder the implications of the sentence which Raby quotes from Liszt's letter of condolence to Berlioz: 'she inspired you, you loved and sang of her, her task was done.'

Gordon Craig's Moscow *Hamlet* is legendary to the point of being mythical, and it is good to have Lawrence Senelick's reconstruction of its creation and the final product.[83] It must have been a ghastly experience for all concerned. Rarely can so much of what puts people off the theatre – the pretentiousness, self-dramatization, and vicious emotional exploitation – have been gathered together in one book. The trouble is that there is too much material: everyone seems to have been keeping notebooks and diaries, with the result that all sorts of temporary bitchiness and ephemeral 'bright ideas' have been recorded for posterity. One point on which Stanislavsky and Craig seem to have been united, as Senelick notes, was 'their contempt for language'. At one point, Craig mused, 'I think that as a matter of fact we could act *Hamlet* without the text, but I don't suppose anyone would like it.' As it was, he cut about a third of the lines, and divided what remained into 'important' and 'unimportant'. When, even then, he couldn't make it look like his personal fantasy of it, he wrote, 'I begin to believe it is a bad play.' The very detailed account of the production, however much of a compromise or a travesty it may have been, provides an opportunity to decide whether it was worth all the fuss. And, again, it is clear that Craig's visual effects were the source of much of its power. Senelick says nothing of the translation that was used, and no wonder. The real translation was not from English into Russian but from words into images.

I agree with what Brian Gibbons has already said about the excellent criticism often contained in theatre reviews. But it is also true, as anyone who has done any research into stage history knows, that a great many theatre reviews are absolutely useless from this point of view: many critics look not with the eye but with the mind. Even at their most vivid, they are often liable to the comment which Stanley Wells makes on one of Hazlitt's reviews of Kean: 'It is the kind of criticism that makes one wish one had seen the performance – which is something – but does not reach the excellence of almost making one feel one *has* seen the performance.'[84] Since theatre reviewing is a branch of entertainment rather than scholarship, one can hardly blame reviewers for aiming at entertainment. But I welcome the fact that more and more learned journals are now drawing on academics to provide the kind of review which may be of some help to future stage historians. Along with *Shakespeare Survey*, *Shakespeare Quarterly*, the *Times Literary Supplement*, and (more patchily) *Cahiers Élisabéthains*, I can recommend the *Critical Quarterly*, which this year included R. L. Smallwood's detailed and interesting accounts of the RSC in *All's Well That Ends Well* and the *Henry IV* plays,[85] as well as Richard Proudfoot on the National Theatre's *Spanish Tragedy*.[86] Alan Sinfield's critical scrutiny of the political and artistic contradictions in the RSC's 1981 *King Lear* is mentioned by Brian Gibbons;[87] I find it interesting as an indication of something which I think will become more common: a critical backlash against the idea that performance can offer the ultimate test of views about a play.

It is easy to see why this reaction is setting in. Not only is the theatre, particularly the Royal Shakespeare Theatre, becoming virtually a part of the academic establishment; the academic world itself is

---

[83] *Gordon Craig's Moscow Hamlet, a Reconstruction*, Contributions in Drama and Theatre Studies, 4 (Greenwood Press, Westport, Conn., and London, 1982).

[84] 'Shakespeare in Hazlitt's Theatre Criticism', *Shakespeare Survey* 35 (Cambridge University Press, 1982), 43–55; p. 52.

[85] In *Critical Quarterly*, 24 (1982), 25–31, and 25 (1983), 16–20.

[86] Vol. 25 (1983), 71–6.

[87] Vol. 24 (1982), 5–14. See above, p. 185.

becoming more of a stage. Academics do not simply write papers; they read them at conferences. Or rather, if they are wise, they 'perform' them: one effect of the critical emphasis on deconstruction and reader response has been to legitimize self-present-ation, even self-dramatization. On top of that, as can be seen from the number of studies devoted to power and conflict in the Renaissance, these subjects have become more relevant. The Western world has good reason to be conscious of the connection between political and theatrical manipulation, and to be nervous of those who do either too well.

3. EDITIONS AND TEXTUAL STUDIES
reviewed by MacDONALD P. JACKSON

The application of thought to Shakespearian textual criticism can still yield exciting results, as the new Oxford *Henry V* demonstrates.[1] The coupling in a single volume (1979) of *Modernizing Shakespeare's Spelling*, by Stanley Wells, General Editor of the Oxford Shakespeare, and *Three Studies in the Text of 'Henry V'*, by Gary Taylor, Associate Editor, seemed arbitrary to some reviewers, but the two kinds of inquiry were complementary and they unite in the achievement of Taylor's edition.

Wells had deliberated upon the difficulties faced by editors of modern-spelling texts. Recommending more thoroughgoing modernization than has been customary, he set down helpful guidelines toward rational and consistent practice. Taylor's concern was with the relationship between the Quarto and Folio texts of *Henry V* and the nature of textual authority in the Quarto. Most scholars have agreed that behind the Folio *Henry V* lay Shakespeare's foul papers, and behind the 1600 Quarto a memorial reconstruction or report. Taylor demonstrated the inadequacy of A. S. Cairncross's case for supposing that F's use of foul papers was indirect, by way of marked-up copy of a Quarto reprint. He found only the usual authorial loose ends in F, not evidence of the wholesale revision imagined by Dover Wilson and the new Arden editor J. H. Walter.[2] He went on to argue that Q is based on a manuscript written from memory of the play as performed – probably on a provincial tour – in a version abridged and adapted for a cast of nine adults and two boy actors. The reporters could be identified as the men whose chief roles had been Gower and Exeter. By pains-taking analysis Taylor showed that, although many of Q's differences from F were due to the reporters'

forgetfulness, others, including some major omis-sions and misplacements, had arisen in the course of the theatrical adaptation. He was able to account for apparent fluctuations in Q's reliability and to show that this despised 'bad quarto' has considerable textual authority in some scenes, especially those in which both reporters had participated.

Taking full account of the variations in Q's quality, Taylor draws on it to an unprecedented degree for his edition. Editors have always used Q to correct a handful of F's obvious misreadings, but Taylor postulates some thirty-seven occasions on which Q preserves a true Shakespearian reading corrupted in F through simple compositorial error. A bolder assumption is that in over a dozen places Q transmits a Shakespearian afterthought which had been introduced into the original prompt-book.

Taylor's adoption of these fifty or so Q variants is less rash than it may seem. In fact he is betting with the odds, which, when Q is genuinely superior to F, must normally favour the guess that F's variant is a compositorial error or Q's an authorial improve-ment, rather than the supposition that some agent in the transmission of Q – prompt-book scribe, actor,

---

[1] Publishers of the four editions surveyed here are the Clarendon Press, Oxford, 1982 (Oxford English Texts), and Methuen, London and New York, 1982 (new Arden). My line references are to the edition under review or, in discussion of articles and notes, *The Riverside Shakespeare* (Houghton Mifflin, Boston, 1974), ed. G. Blakemore Evans.

[2] Their views have been reaffirmed by Kristian Smidt in a chapter on 'The Disunity of *King Henry V*' in his *Unconformities in Shakespeare's History Plays* (Humanities Press, Atlantic Highlands, New Jersey, 1982), pp. 121–44.

or compositor – has made a mistake that fortuitously improves the text. Of course assessment of the merits of Q/F variants will inevitably differ. Taylor is generally judicious, and justifies his decisions in his commentary. Nobody could quarrel with his preference for 'unmasked his power unto France' (1.2.147, based on Q) over F's 'went with his forces into France'. But in preferring Q's 'regard' to F's 'great State' at 2.4.32 he is almost certainly accepting an actor's recollection of 1.1.23. Both contexts describe the reformed Henry, so could easily have been confused in a reporter's memory. Not only is the Q 2.4 passage linked to the F 1.1 passage by 'regard', 'grace', and 'well supplied', but it also misappropriates from 1.1 the words 'wilde' and 'preuent' ('wildnesse' and 'preuention' in F 1.1).

Taylor's most significant adherences to Q involve the expansion of an exchange between Pistol and Fluellen at 3.6.60–4, the addition of the phrase 'Coup' la gorge', which Q gives Pistol, to striking theatrical effect, at the end of 4.6, and several reassignments of speeches – most importantly those which replace the Dauphin with the Duke of Bourbon in the scenes at Agincourt. As Taylor argues, the enlargement of Bourbon's part cannot be due to faulty memory or to the adaptation of the play to provincial tastes, but must have been Shakespeare's own resolution of an indecision that may be inferred from F. The change that makes Bourbon, rather than the Dauphin, sonneteer in praise of his horse 'radically reorganizes the energies' of 3.7 and modifies our whole impression of the French (p. 25).

Taylor adopts several traditional emendations, including Theobald's 'babbled of green fields' (ably defended in an appendix), and introduces to the dialogue over two dozen new ones, mostly persuasive, such as the addition of 'perforce' in 2.0.32, 'mountant' for F 'Mountaine' at 2.4.57, 'ill' for F 'all' at 4.1.292, 'high-loving' for F 'by louing' at 5.0.29, and the insertion of 'that' to create 'before that [which] it loves' at 5.2.304. Some retentions of F readings are surprising. At 2.3.44 'Pitch and pay' is surely not 'the world' but 'the word' or motto (as is 'Couple a gorge' at 2.1.68). 'Mixed-full eyes' (4.6.34) seem most improbable. 5.2.50, retaining F's 'withal', is metrically too anomalous: 2.2.174 is not strictly parallel as claimed, partly because of the different position of the caesura and partly because the last syllable of 'withal' in 5.2.50 carries appreciably more stress than 'you' which in 2.2.174 can virtually assimilate the final syllable of 'deliver'.[3]

Taylor is meticulous in following Wells's principles of modernization, being especially careful to distinguish between meaningful and meaningless spelling variants in passages of dialect, and substituting commas and full stops for many of the colons and semicolons bequeathed him by three centuries of editorial punctuation. His most contentious modernization is of 'Ancient Pistol' to 'Ensign Pistol' (2.1.3) on the grounds that 'ancient' is a corruption of 'ensign', the forms converging in such spellings as 'enseyne' and 'ancyen'. Presumably Oxford's Iago will become – God bless the mark! – his Moorship's ensign.

The commentary is full and informative, and alert both to the richness of the language and to what is possible in the theatre, as is the sane and subtle introduction, which moves easily between questions of fact and questions of critical interpretation. Nobody these days believes that *Henry V* is the naive jingoism which the adapters behind Q tried to make of it. Taylor takes full cognizance of those sceptical antimilitarist accounts which disparage Henry and his exploits, and his understanding reaches beyond Norman Rabkin's view that *Henry V* is two incompatible half-plays, a Gestalt hawk which at every second blink turns into a dove. Rather, he sees that Shakespeare does indeed celebrate Henry's greatness, while everywhere acknowledging its cost. Shakespeare is no homilist. The play includes positive and negative within the one complex vision. This edition offers more than any other to the student of *Henry V*.

In layout the Oxford volumes closely resemble the new Arden series, but they use a more economical modern typeface, and each contains an index to the commentary. Taylor's *Henry V* runs to 330 pages, H. J. Oliver's *The Taming of the Shrew* in the

---

[3] The text contains one unlucky misprint, 'So' for 'And' in line 17 of the Prologue.

same series to 248 pages. *The Shrew* is the shorter play and linguistically the simpler. The textual situation is not wholly dissimilar from that for *Henry V*, since the Folio text of *The Taming of the Shrew* was, in Oliver's view, set from foul papers, while there survives in *The Taming of a Shrew* (1594) a 'bad quarto' of Shakespeare's play. *A Shrew* (customarily identified by the indefinite article) is not, however, a report of the same type as Q *Henry V*, but a meagre rewrite, cobbled up from an erratic plot outline of *The Shrew*, half-remembered patches of Shakespeare's dialogue, plagiarized lines from Marlowe, and the issue of a theatre hack's own dull mother-wit. The Quarto is thus no help in establishing the wording of Shakespeare's play, but may reveal something about its intended structure, at least at one stage of its existence, since *A Shrew* continues and completes the story of Christopher Sly, who is ignored in F after the end of 1.1.

A Shrew is a derivative quarto, not a source for *The Shrew* – this now orthodox belief Oliver shares with Brian Morris, whose new Arden edition was noticed last year. They agree also that it is the Shakespearian play from which *A Shrew* derives, there being no need to postulate a non-Shakespearian *Ur-Shrew* with a different sub-plot, containing two sisters to Katherine. (The compiler of *A Shrew* relied on invention and a head full of Marlovian bombast when memory failed.) However, Oliver, unlike Morris, thinks that the Shakespearian play did undergo some modification, and that the Quarto is based on an early form of it, in which Hortensio was not disguised as the music-teacher Litio. This he infers both from what Q contains and from clues in F that Hortensio's role has been reshaped. Because he has argued for F's dependence on foul papers, he has to suppose that Shakespeare retained these and used them for a revision a few years after the play had originally been written and produced (p. 34). Morris had considered nothing about Hortensio's role in F anomalous enough to warrant such a first-sketch theory. On the other hand, drawing on Karl P. Wentersdorf's evidence, Morris judged that Shakespeare had indeed written for Christopher Sly four or five interludes and an epilogue, as well as the induction, that *A Shrew* preserves them in garbled

form, but that much of the Sly material was cut from the manuscript behind F as too demanding in personnel. F he took to have been set from a transcript, probably not authorial, from foul papers that had been annotated by the book-keeper. Oliver is sceptical of Wentersdorf's case, and concludes that Shakespeare either never wrote a full Sly framework or, having written one, eventually preferred to discard it, as much on aesthetic as on practical grounds. No one would want to be dogmatic in the face of disagreement between two such experienced editors, but Morris strikes me as marginally more persuasive on all three disputed points.

In editing the text Oliver is conservative in his allegiance to F, refusing to emend in some dozen places where Morris followed other editors in doing so. In most of these instances Morris's decision seems to me clearly correct. At 3.2.16, for example, Oliver, accepting F, has Katherine say that Petruchio will 'Make friends, invite, and proclaim the banns', a line which, as Morris justly asserted, 'defies both sense and metre'. Oliver's one new emendation to the dialogue (if we except '*Bene*', instead of the usual '*Ben*' for F's '*Been*' at 1.2.279) is to the last line of 4.5, where Hortensio proposes to apply Petruchio's training methods to his own widow: 'if she [be] froward, / Then hast thou taught *Hortensio* to be vntoward'. Oliver omits 'to be' and so transforms 'untoward' into an adverb meaning 'unluckily' – unluckily for a froward widow. The alteration does not improve the couplet, and the gloss is strained.

Oliver's commentary is serviceable, and his critical introduction sane in abandoning thematic approaches in order to discuss matters of dramatic function, tone, structure, and style. His account is a shrewd elaboration of the familiar perception that the play, while fundamentally a farce, in which a plot that generates funny situations is paramount, contains at least the germ of something emotionally and psychologically more complex in the relationship between Katherine and Petruchio. Shakespeare cannot help trying to understand Katherine, creating a context for her shrewishness, making her human, arousing the audience's sympathy. He 'was already too good a dramatist for the material he was dramatizing: characterization and farce are, finally, incompatible' (p. 52). Oliver has no use for the notion that Petruchio also outgrows his crude role of animal tamer to become amateur psychologist eliciting the loving woman from behind the shrewish mask. For Oliver, Katherine's final speech is just 'the only fitting climax *to the farce*'. Questions of its credibility in human terms are irrelevant. The play 'has modulated back from something like realistic social comedy to the other, "broader", kind of entertainment that was foretold by the Induction' (p. 57). This is a far cry from Morris's view (Arden edition, p. 149) that Petruchio is 'perilously close to tears, tears of pride, and gratitude, and love' as he responds to the 'unsolicited act of love and generosity' with which Katherine ends her speech! Oliver devotes eleven pages to an entertaining stage history.

Troilus and Cressida is one of the first three Oxford editions and the last play in the new Arden series. The editors are Kenneth Muir (Oxford) and Kenneth Palmer (Arden). Comparison must also take account of Gary Taylor's important reinvestigation of the textual situation for this play.[4] According to current orthodoxy, the 1609 Quarto of *Troilus and Cressida* was set from a transcript of foul papers, and the manuscript behind the Folio was the foul papers themselves, but these had been used to mark up an exemplar of Q which served as printer's copy. Taylor concedes F's dependence upon an exemplar of Q but rejects the other tenets. Q and F differ in some five hundred readings. Neither text is consistently and manifestly superior. As Taylor asserts, the urgent questions are whether any of the variants are due to revision by Shakespeare, and, if so, which is the revised text. His carefully argued conclusion is that Q is based on Shakespeare's foul papers, and that the manuscript authority for F's new readings was the official prompt-book; this prompt-book was a scribal transcript of Shakespeare's fair copy, incorporating his revisions.[5]

Taylor presents his case with vigour and flair. He advances one seemingly irresistible argument against the view that F depends on foul papers. He lists twenty-eight variants in which Q is clearly right and F wrong and similarity of graphic outline points to misreading in F. If the annotator of Q copy for F was transferring readings from foul papers, then on twenty-eight occasions he misread Shakespeare's handwriting with such reckless confidence that he deliberately altered an unambiguously printed Q word corresponding to what was actually written in the manuscript. Such behaviour is incredible. The misreadings must have been in the manuscript itself, which therefore cannot have been foul papers. This disproof of one orthodox tenet could be countered only by disproof of another – that F was set directly from a marked-up exemplar of Q. Yet the influence of Q on F seems certain, and the exertion of this influence through the intermediary of a transcript most improbable.

Taylor's overall hypothesis 'provides editors, for the first time, with a rational basis for the selection of readings'. Since F was largely printed from Q, Q must serve as copy-text for the accidentals of an old-spelling edition. 'But in respect to substantive variants F is the more authoritative text, containing ...the author's own verbal revisions.' An editor may justifiably prefer a Q variant 'if F's reading seems reasonably explicable as a scribal or compositorial error', of which there are doubtless many in F, given the length of its stemma of transmission. 'But where both variants seem authorial . . . an editor should prefer F' (p. 127).

In Muir's judgement Taylor's 'main thesis is convincing' (p. 3). He claims to have 'acted upon it in preparing [his] text', but in fact ignores its implications. At 1.3.91, for instance, he has the sun correcting 'the influence of evil planets' as in Q. F refers to 'the ill Aspects of Planets euill'. As Muir says in his commentary, 'Both Q and F readings were doubtless authorial.' This being so, Taylor's theory obliges him to adopt F's variant, unless he means to challenge the principle that the author's

4 '*Troilus and Cressida*: Bibliography, Performance, and Interpretation', *Shakespeare Studies*, 16 (1983), 99–136.
5 Taylor envisages Shakespeare's sporadic introduction of new readings in the course of preparing a fair copy, plus his participation in a few structural adaptations made in transferring the play from the Inns of Court to the Globe. He believes that for the Globe production Shakespeare deleted Pandarus' epilogue, and that he finally intended the three lines common to 5.3 and 5.10 to stand in the earlier position.

final intentions should prevail.[6] Again, at 2.2.57 he accepts Q's 'attributive' while noting that 'The F reading, *inclineable* = prejudiced, is equally Shakespearian.' Muir's handling of more complex variation is open to the same objections. At 1.3.353–8 Q has Ulysses say:

Giue pardon to my speech? therefore tis meete
Achilles meete not *Hector*, let vs like Marchants
First shew foule wares, and thinke perchance theile
    sell;
If not; the luster of the better shall exceed,
By shewing the worse first: do not consent,
That euer *Hector* and *Achilles* meet.

F reads:

   Giue pardon to my speech:
   Therefore 'tis meet, *Achilles* meet not *Hector*:
   Let vs (like Merchants) shew our fowlest Wares,
   And thinke perchance they'l sell: If not,
   The luster of the better yet to shew,
   Shall shew the better. Do not consent
   That euer *Hector* and *Achilles* meete.

Neither text is limited to regular pentameters.[7] F's wordplay in 'the better yet to shew, / Shall shew the better', similar in vein to the punning on 'meet', may be an attempt to inject some rhetorical life into an unsatisfactory passage. Q's 'the luster . . . worse first' is lame in itself, and its pointless repetition of the earlier 'first' makes it even more so. F's version of the whole passage seems to me a slight improvement on Q's (though in comparison with Achilles, Ajax is one of the Greeks' 'foule' rather than 'fowlest Wares'). Palmer finds Q preferable, as presumably Muir does, since he follows it in defiance of his textual theory. For whatever we think of F's merits, we must surely recognize 'better... better' as authorial. Judging from his note, Muir himself is sceptical of Alice Walker's attempt to blame Jaggard's Compositor B for F's version.[8] If both versions are essentially Shakespeare's, Muir's professed acceptance of Taylor's theory commits him to F.

Muir ventures two new emendations. At 2.2.119 he rightly alters QF 'euent' to the more Shakespearian and idiomatic 'th'event', and he postulates another shared QF error at 3.3.34, where Agamemnon instructs Diomedes to supervise in Troy the

exchange of Antenor and Cressida, and adds (in Q): 'Withall bring word If *Hector* will to morrow / Bee answered in his challenge. *Aiax* is ready.' Muir replaces 'bring word If' with 'bear word that', objecting that 'Diomedes cannot discover in Troy if Hector will be answered in his challenge', and suggesting that an abbreviation for 'that' was misread 'yf' and 'bring' was copied inadvertently from line 31. However, the emendation introduces a third 'bear' within the space of eight lines, and Q and F make good sense if, as Palmer explains, Agamemnon's emphasis falls on 'tomorrow' and 'will' means 'desires to'; arrangements for the combat have been made, and it remains for Hector to agree to the day.

An admirable feature of Muir's edition is the provision of photographic quotations from Q and F for an appendix of textual notes. This appendix might profitably have been much longer.

Whereas Muir pays lip-service to a theory that he neither justifies nor applies, Palmer, after a full and sensitive discussion of the textual evidence, opts to do without one altogether, finding the indications too contradictory: 'Where we cannot identify the nature of copy with certainty, then the nature of the copy can have no effect on an editor's method, except in so far as agnosticism gives him more freedom of choice' (p. 16). A frank admission of defeat is better than allegiance to a theory that ignores uncongenial facts. But the possibility of revision by Shakespeare (one that Palmer concedes) embarrasses a simple eclecticism. An editor needs to distinguish between variants produced by corruption and variants produced by authorial revision. Corruption will have affected both texts, but on any

---

[6] F's chiasmus remedies Q's obtrusive placement of the word 'planets' at the end of two out of three consecutive lines.
[7] The immediately preceding speech ends in F with two full lines and a six-syllable line that are not present in Q; F's opening to Ulysses' speech can thus be seen either as a new start metrically or as completing an alexandrine.
[8] Palmer tentatively writes of 'first and second shots' here, but cannot say which is which (p. 8). In F he sees 'a groping for formulae which proved inadequate' (p. 10), and hints that Shakespeare rejected them for Q's simpler, though still imperfect, formulation.

reasonable hypothesis Shakespeare's second thoughts are likely to be confined to one or the other. Palmer treats all variants alike. Nevertheless, his liberation from theory is far from complete: he thinks that F was 'close to foul papers' and that Q's manuscript copy had been 'edited in some way' (p. 8), and in practice he usually acts as if the 'edited' Q contained the Shakespearian second thoughts. Yet the courage even of his lack of convictions deserts him when he confronts the major variations between Q and F. At the end of act 4, scene 4, for example, F prints five lines not in Q. Palmer pronounces F's lines 'Certainly authorial...but perhaps equally certain to be a first shot, wisely omitted by the time Q (or its copy) was prepared, and injudiciously recovered by F'. And, on Palmer's terms, injudiciously retained in his own text, whether his aim is to realize Shakespeare's final intentions (Palmer seems to imply that the dramatist endorsed the omission) or to choose between Q and F 'on their merits'. Actually, the lines are likely enough to be a late Shakespearian addition. A slightly precious over-elaboration of the dialogue – such as, in his note on the passage, Palmer goes on to deprecate – is an occasional characteristic of Shakespeare's revisions in F *Othello* and *King Lear*.

Besides being the first editor to adopt certain eighteenth-century conjectures and to supply some desirable stage directions, Palmer prints convincing new emendations at 1.3.220, 4.1.67, and 5.5.21.

Readers who dislike editions in which the saucy bark of Shakespeare's text floats on a soundless deep of commentary will approve Muir's economical glossing of unfamiliar words and phrases. Palmer's notes are, however, more instructive; he takes pains to establish the superiority of his chosen variants and he enlivens our awareness of the dialogue's subtleties.

Although *Troilus and Cressida* is longer and more complex than either *The Shrew* or *Henry V*, Muir's edition has only 205 pages. Palmer's has 337. In his clear and commonsensical interpretative account of the play, Muir is anxious to correct partial responses. He quotes Keats's dictum that a dramatic poet has to 'make his mind a thoroughfare for all thoughts', and observes that in the first five scenes we share successively the vantage points of Troilus, Cressida, Ulysses, Thersites, and Hector. He notes that 'one

theme of the play is the attack on idealization. Shakespeare is doing what Ibsen was to do in such plays as *A Doll's House* and *Ghosts*' (p. 31). Yet he recognizes that neither Troilus nor Cressida is a mere object of scorn. 'It is not a cynical play, but a sombre examination of a fallen world, which any contemporary preacher would have applauded' (p. 40).

Palmer's sense of this most dialectical of Shakespeare's plays is not unlike Muir's, but his analysis is close and strenuous, concentrating on ideas and savouring intellectual nuances that even an Inns of Court audience might have missed. After some broad observations about the play's shape and peculiar dramatic idiom, Palmer examines six crucial scenes, treats themes and preoccupations under the headings 'time and time's subjects', 'time, treason and prophecy', 'identity and attributes', and 'pride and envy', and ends with an illuminating section on styles and methods. As Palmer says, it is not surprising that in our sceptical and irreverent age *Troilus and Cressida* has grown in popularity. But his conclusion is worth repeating: 'Many suppose that its assertions are wholly destructive: the Emperor never had any clothes. But it may be, in effect, a little more like Strauss's *Ariadne*: a work which asserts its staginess with bravado: which emphasizes that assertion by confining its first Act to the green room and its quarrels: which puts together two plots at the *fiat* of M. Jourdain, who wishes them to be played *gleichzeitig*: which sets the abandoned Ariadne and her retinue upstage, and leaves the forestage to the parodic mockers from the *commedia dell' arte* (and especially to Zerbinetta, for whom each new lover comes "like a god"); and which finds in the end that the *deus ex machina* was a god indeed' (p. 93).

Muir and Palmer are both informative about the play's sources. Palmer reprints some relevant material from Chaucer, Caxton, Lydgate, and Golding's Ovid, and in another appendix makes out a good case for the influence on Shakespeare of Aristotle's *Ethics*.[9]

---

[9] Palmer also suggests (pp. 304–6) that a disturbance during the setting of Q's sheet F was caused by the acquisition of fresh copy. As presented, the case is not persuasive, but Q might repay further bibliographical analysis. A defect in Palmer's edition is that many line references in Section 1

One question recurs in connection with all three plays edited this year: was the Folio text set from autograph? In each case the chosen answer is a keystone in the construction of a textual theory. Taylor's contention that F *Henry V* is based on the original foul papers, never tampered with, is essential to his argument that Q reports some of Shakespeare's final decisions, including the decision to withdraw the Dauphin from the field at Agincourt. Any hypothesis about the manuscript of F *The Shrew* affects speculation on revision in F and discrepancies between *The Shrew* and *A Shrew*. And Taylor's attack on current opinion about the relationship between Q and F *Troilus and Cressida* springs from the denial that F was set from foul papers. The traditional clues from stage directions, speech pre-fixes, and tangles and duplications in the dialogue often turn out to be ambiguous. Might computer-aided analysis of spellings and misreadings in quartos agreed to be based on Shakespeare's foul papers yield information capable of settling such issues? The question of whether a text was printed from auto-graph arises again with *King Lear*.

Etymologically a *hybrid* is the offspring of a tame sow and a wild boar. Editors of *King Lear* have mated tame sow F and wild boar Q to breed a new animal which they take to be Shakespeare's own legitimate brain-child. Contributors to *The Division of the Kingdoms* think it is no such thing.[10] And they question Q's alleged wildness.

The First Quarto (1608) of *King Lear* has been held to bear signs of memorial corruption, while behind the Folio text lies an official prompt-book. Q not only differs from F in a thousand readings, but contains passages totalling close on three hundred lines that are absent from F, which, in turn, contains more than one hundred lines absent from Q. Since virtually all matter peculiar to either text seems Shakespearian, editors have conflated Q and F to produce a version of the play longer than any printed in the seventeenth century. *The Division of the Kingdoms* substantiates an opinion that has been gaining ground in recent years – that although both versions, Q and F, are Shakespearian, a combined version is not. Q, it is argued, rests on foul papers, while Shakespeare himself was responsible for the

cuts, compensatory additions, reallocations of speeches, and alterations to the dialogue in the prompt-book behind F. Q and F may legitimately be used to correct each other's errors, but full conflation distorts Shakespeare's intentions at either stage of the play's evolution.

The book is a collaboration by eleven scholars. Stanley Wells's introduction is an elegant exposition of just what is at stake. Steven Urkowitz chronicles the history of editorial treatment of *Lear*, noting that it was Pope who in the early eighteenth century began the tradition of conflating Q and F, a tradition to which the Victorian editor Charles Knight de-ferred, despite his conviction that F had benefited from Shakespeare's own reshapings. Roger Warren speculates on possible artistic motives for F's excision from 3.6 of the mock trial in which Poor Tom, the Fool, and the disguised Kent sit in imaginary judgement on Lear's daughters. Designed as a bizarre projection of Lear's knowledge of injustice, this ensemble of madness is in performance all too apt to degenerate into random gags. Shakespeare, he suggests, decided to postpone this vision of 'the great image of Authority' to 4.6, where it is conveyed with more coherent impact as the direct vocal expression of the mad mind of Lear himself; and in 4.6 F amplifies by five lines Lear's main tirade on this theme. Michael Warren's subject is the diminution of Kent's role in F, especially within act 4. He shows that 'The more concentrated dramaturgy of the Folio...has no room for Kent's choric utterances or for the maintenance of serious interest in his function-less disguises' (p. 63). F's cutting brings the part into sharper focus. In a wide-ranging essay, lavishly illustrated by 'photoquotations', Randall McLeod detects 'thematic consistency' in the Q/F variation associated with Goneril.

John Kerrigan's survey of rewritten plays reveals that seventeenth-century adapters of other men's scripts replaced blocks of text without tinkering

---

of his introduction are not keyed to his text; also, a comma in line 1.3.94 makes nonsense of his note, and there is a gap in the collation at 3.3.158.

[10] *The Division of the Kingdoms: Shakespeare's Two Versions of 'King Lear'* (Clarendon Press, Oxford, 1983), ed. Gary Taylor and Michael Warren.

with the dialogue as did revising authors. The pattern of variation between Q and F *Lear* is of the authorial kind. Another section of Kerrigan's essay focuses on the Fool. Interpretations of the Fool have shuttled between 'the extremes represented by Empson's blathering natural and Orwell's canny rationalist'; broadly speaking, the Empsonian view derives from elements already in Q, the Orwellian from ingredients peculiar to F (p. 218). Kerrigan's fine critique vindicates F: its Fool is 'dramatically superior' to Q's (p. 230).

Thomas Clayton's account of revision in the role of the King concentrates on the very different effects of the Q and F versions of the play's opening and close. He compares Lear's dying words in F to Cleopatra's, as ambivalently bespeaking delusion or transcendent vision. In Q, 'O,o,o,o', a conventional notation for Lear's death throes, 'expresses an ineluctable nullity' (p. 133). Yet even Q's assignment to Lear of the words that F gives Kent, 'Breake hart, I prethe breake', may be defended on analogy with Donne's thought in 'A Valediction: Forbidding Mourning' about men who 'whisper to their soules to goe, / Whilst some of their sad friends doe say, / The breath goes now, and some say, no'. Beth Goldring's argument is that in F's added line at 1.1.162, where Lear is about to accost Kent, 'Alb. Cor. Deare Sir forbeare', and in its changed prefix, 'Cor.' for 'Glost.' at 1.1.188, which announces the arrival of France and Burgundy, 'Cor.' is not Cornwall but Cordelia. Understood in this way, the F addition at 1.1.162 creates 'a moment emblematic of the whole first scene' (p. 150).

Two essays are more technical. Paul Werstine undertakes a full-scale investigation into the kinds of error and sophistication perpetrated elsewhere in the Folio by the two compositors, B and E, who set F *Lear*. His results show that little of the variation between Q and F *Lear* can be blamed on corruption of the text in Jaggard's printing house in 1623. In particular, Compositor B's inaccuracy and highhandedness have been exaggerated; though he was prone to 'memorial' substitution, the frequent omissions and interpolations that Alice Walker discovered in B's stints of F *1 Henry IV*, a reprint of Q5, are uncharacteristic of his work; the discrepancy may be the result of editorial interference with B's copy of Q5 *1 Henry IV* and of difficulties inherent in the setting of its cast-off prose. Werstine's meticulous qualitative study of the workmanship of Compositors B and E will be invaluable to editors. My own contribution to the volume looks at the distribution of variants, arguing that the pattern cannot be explained by theories that posit fluctuating degrees of corruption in Q (Walker) or in F (Walton), but is best considered the result of revision. I go on to discuss a series of related variants in 1.1, where F changes nudge the play further away, in word and deed, from its *Leir* source material and emphasize the political implications of Lear's initial acts, thereby foreshadowing F's structural alterations in act 4.

Gary Taylor contributes two essays. In one he inspects all divergences between Q and F that *might* have been caused by the censor, concluding that only F's omission of 1.4.140–55 was made under his influence, and that Shakespeare probably acquiesced. Taylor's long and heavily documented final essay draws together and supplements the various arguments. He believes that Shakespeare wrote *Lear* in 1605–6 and revised it in 1610, beginning his revision on an exemplar of Q. He advances a neat bibliographical argument based on F's combination of readings that are press-variant in Q; furnishes evidence that Q is closer than F to Shakespeare's sources of 1605–6, but that F's additions bear ostensible traces of his later reading; and shows that vocabulary links between Q, F, and other canonical plays indicate Shakespeare's rehandling of *Lear* four or five years after original composition. He applies authorship tests to F's variations from Q: these suggest Shakespeare's responsibility and rule out other available candidates. And he surveys all important literary and dramatic differences between Q and F, so as 'to provide a comprehensive working model of the strategy of the Folio redaction' (p. 354).

In an addendum Taylor proposes four new emendations, all plausible. Most interesting is that to Q1's 'wanst thou eyes, at tral madam' at 3.6.23–4. Q2 turned 'tral' into 'triall', and editors usually read 'Want'st thou eyes at trial, madam?' Taylor would retain Q1's comma after 'eyes' and infer an easy o/a confusion, interpreting the last three words as a reference to troll-madam, a game like bagatelle, mentioned in *The Winter's Tale*, 4.3.87.[11]

Cumulatively the case for revision in *King Lear* is overwhelming. But scholars persuaded by it must beware of imagining purposeful change in F where corruption in Q is more probable. McLeod, for instance, follows Urkowitz in taking issue with Duthie over Q's version of 2.4.182–98, where Goneril's entry interrupts Lear's denunciation of her to Regan. At 2.4.188 F has Lear repeat, in slightly different form, a question that he has just asked and will shortly ask again, 'Who stockt my Seruant? *Regan*, I haue good hope / Thou did'st not know on't.' Then he notices Goneril's arrival ('Who comes here?'), exclaims to the heavens, and remonstrates with Regan for taking her sister's hand. The episode makes perfect dramatic sense. Q gives 2.4.188 to Goneril, immediately after 'Enter Gon.', and has her ask 'Who struck my seruant[?]' McLeod claims that in Q Goneril 'strides in on the offensive ... harping on the same theme as in the third scene, the affront to her retinue' (p. 181). But Goneril's aggression in Q is pointlessly directed at Regan, who has obviously not connived at Lear's striking of Goneril's 'gentleman', and with whom Goneril immediately aligns herself.[12] Moreover, Lear's 'Who comes here?' is theatrically meaningless if Goneril has already delivered a belligerent speech. Duthie seems to me right in thinking Q corrupt here, an easy misreading ('struck' for 'stockt') leading to misattribution of Lear's lines. Even Wells makes one infelicitous choice of variants to illustrate the principle that Q and F may differ yet be equally acceptable. At 5.3.81 F has Regan say 'Let the Drum strike, and [do thou, Edmund] proue my title thine.' Q assigns the speech to Edmund himself, who says 'Let the drum strike, and [let it] proue my title good.' Greg considered Q's line an absurd perversion of Shakespeare's intentions as realized in F. Wells agrees with Urkowitz that the readings are 'merely different' (p. 5). But, as Greg objected, a drum can prove nothing but its capacity for noise. I think that in this particular instance Q really does enshrine somebody's misapprehension of Shakespeare's meaning. Yet it is not necessary to suppose with Greg that Q's 'good' is part of the corruption, adapting the

line to the wrong speaker. Restored to Regan, Q's line, addressed to Edmund, makes the same sense as F's. So 'thine' may be Shakespeare's change to avoid ambiguity.

There is doubtless room for disagreement over the above two variants. But Q was, after all, erratically printed from baffling copy, and inevitably many Q corruptions will make a certain amount of sense; not all Q's 'false readings' will be 'impossible readings', to use Housman's terms. Disinterested attention to literary and dramatic niceties will be required if we are to discriminate between situations in which Q and F are both Shakespearian and situations in which Q has corrupted the one-and-only Shakespearian reading preserved in F.

Peter W. M. Blayney is known to believe that Shakespeare revised *King Lear*, but his study of the *Lear* textual problem has long been 'in preparation'. Publication of the first volume of *The Texts of 'King Lear' and their Origins* (Cambridge University Press, 1982) lets us see why. It is a prodigious accomplishment, complementing Charlton Hinman's great work on the First Folio. Blayney reports the results both of an exhaustive bibliographical investigation of Nicholas Okes's 1608 Quarto and of the most thorough inquiry yet made into the workings of a Jacobean printing-house. His chief aim has been to furnish a background to textual study of Q and its relation with F, but bibliographers with no special interest in *Lear* will find Blayney's volume an invaluable source of information and reflection about quarto printing and about techniques of analysis. He has not only scrutinized Okes's books as physical objects, but has also undertaken historical research, winnowing available records. The book is well illustrated with reproductions of printed texts,

---

[11] In *The Winter's Tale*, 4.3 is Autolycus' scene, and his songs and the context of roguery make for several verbal links with *Lear* 3.6, including the collocation 'wakes [and] fairs'; Shakespeare uses 'wake' = feast on only one other occasion.

[12] Even if Goneril's 'Who struck my seruant' in Q is directed at Lear and 'Regan I haue good hope / Thou didst not know ant' is an implicit rebuke to Lear rather than a challenge to Regan, Goneril's aggression leads nowhere; her next speech is a defence of her own behaviour.

manuscripts, ornaments, and woodcuts, and the second half is given over to appendixes packed with documentation.

In his opening chapters, Blayney provides a brief history of the printing house that Okes purchased from the Snowdons in 1607 and biographies of its owners, and considers early seventeenth-century norms of operation and output, relating his findings to those of D. F. McKenzie about the Cambridge University Press close on a hundred years later. He distinguishes between 'concurrent' and 'interrupted' printing, and stresses the prevalence of the sharing of printing jobs between two or more houses: 'Shared printing, it would seem, was the London solution to the problem of flexibility' (p. 57). Okes's evidently began as 'a one-press printing house of moderate efficiency' (p. 43), turning out an average of 200 edition-sheets per year. Chapter 3 concentrates on 'Okes at work, 1607–8', pinpointing *Lear*'s place in the pattern of production. Chapters 4 and 5 offer a minutely detailed reconstruction of the composition, distribution, and presswork of the *Lear* Quarto. Blayney has employed, with due awareness of their limitations, all the techniques of modern analytic bibliography. Use of a Povey lamp to determine the order in which the formes of each sheet were printed undermines the conjectures of Greg and Bowers. But the most significant data come from the identification of recurrent types. Blayney explains why it is 'essential for a quarto type-recurrence study to be based on *considerably* more evidence per forme than will suffice for a folio' (p. 91). He himself sifted 6,000 potential clues so as to create 'a list of over 2,000 appearances made by 571 types' (p. 94); the list is given in full in an appendix. He shows that most of the Quarto was set by one compositor working from a single case, but that a second case and compositor were employed for some pages and portions of pages from the middle of H4^v onwards. The second compositor set about half of sheet I, two pages of sheet K, and most of sheet L. Spelling, capitalization, punctuation, and 'psycho-mechanical' evidence reinforce the implications of the typographical investigation. Outer formes were printed first, except in the case of sheets C and I. 'The pattern of headline recurrence is apparently unconnected with the use of skeleton formes' (pp. 149–50), and is paralleled by only one other Okes quarto of 1607–8. Blayney connects the abnormality with the fact that, contrary to Okes's normal practice, Q *Lear* was set seriatim. Blayney has not tried to trace the work of the *Lear* compositors through other books printed by Okes; this is a reasoned abstention (pp. 182–5). He insists on the atypical nature of the *Lear* Quarto – 'not only as a quarto, a play-quarto, and a Shakespeare quarto, but as an *Okes* quarto' (p. 185).

Among the exceptional features of *Lear* are the quality and quantity of the press variants in five of its formes. Hinman's study encouraged the view that in London printing shops during the late sixteenth and early seventeenth centuries proof was not read against copy before presswork began, but that only stop-press correction was attempted. In Chapters 6 and 7 Blayney establishes that in Okes's day, no less than in Moxon's, earlier stages of correction were carried out, however perfunctorily. His examination of surviving proof-sheets reveals miscorrection, simple or compound, to be a fertile source of error. Emenders of Shakespearian texts must not be hypnotized by the *ductus litterarum*. Chapter 8 compares the licensed manuscript (preserved in the Bodleian) of Sir Antony Sherley's *Relation of his Travels into Persia* with the 1613 Quarto, of which the first twelve sheets were printed by Okes. The comparison is bedevilled by uncertainty whether printer's copy was the extant manuscript or, as appears more likely, a transcript prepared for the press. Blayney ends with an epilogue recounting Okes's later career.

Lear was the first play quarto printed by Okes, and it is already clear that some of its aberrations result from his inexperience. But for the application of Blayney's bibliographical findings to the *Lear* textual enigma we must await his second volume.

This year has seen the fruition of another major publishing venture. Michael J. B. Allen and Kenneth Muir have collected into one magnificent book photographic reproductions of all twenty-two substantive quartos of Shakespeare's plays, including *The Two Noble Kinsmen* and the acknowledged bad quartos, but not *The Taming of a Shrew*, or *The*

Troublesome Reign of King John.[13] *Titus Andronicus* is reproduced from the unique Folger copy, and *The Contention* and *The True Tragedy* (bad quartos of *2* and *3 Henry VI*) from Bodleian copies, the latter unique. For all other plays Huntington copies have been used[14] – unwisely in the case of *1 Henry IV*, where severe cropping has eliminated most headlines and sometimes even reduced the top line of text. A few other plays are marred by cropped headlines, bottom lines, or initial letters, by excessive show-through, by tears and blotches, or by annotations that obtrude or obscure. Resort to alternative originals of, for example, *Othello, Hamlet* Q1 and Q2, *Richard II, Richard III,* and *Romeo and Juliet* Q1 would have improved readability and completeness, repaying the extra editorial trouble. However, Allen and Muir do list obscured readings, and for most plays the reproductions are beautifully clear. In craftsmanship and design the volume is a notable achievement. Strongly stitched and bound, and complete with slipcase, it is oblong, each page showing one opening. Quarto pages, variable in size in the originals, have been given an appearance of uniformity by being overprinted with a faint tint block.

The editors present *Troilus and Cressida* in its second state, which includes the Epistle. They have supplied the deposition scene first printed in Q4 of *Richard II,* but not, unfortunately, the surviving sheet C from Q0, the lost first edition of *1 Henry IV.* A first issue of *2 Henry IV* omitted 3.1; the incorporation of this scene into the second issue entailed the resetting of some 165 adjacent lines. Allen and Muir print the cancellans, but not the cancellandum, primary authority for this portion of the play. Their introduction is an elementary guide to the nature of the quartos and their place in Shakespearian textual studies. Known substantive, but not accidental, press variants are listed in an appendix. There has been no attempt at a census of extant copies of the quartos, or at a charting of their diverse mixes of corrected and uncorrected formes. Nor is information provided about compositor studies of the quartos reproduced. Page 77 is incorrectly headed with the title 'RICHARD II'.

Inevitably such a weighty volume is cumbersome to handle and easily damaged, and the absence of marginal act, scene, and line numbering (for which an appended guide to conventional divisions is a poor substitute) hampers location of particular words and passages, so many scholars will continue to use the individual Shakespeare Association/ Clarendon Press facsimiles, where these are available. But there are few books on which Shakespearians could better spend their money than this University of California Press publication.

Foremost among willing buyers should be Randall McLeod, whose concern in 'UN *Editing* Shakespeare' is with those 'iconographic' features of the Shakespeare quarto and Folio texts which are obliterated by modern editorial regularization.[15] Discovering an intimate relation between the seventeenth-century printed medium and its message, he argues that we 'must reconceive the status of text in the era of photographic reproduction' (p. 36). McLeod favours greater use of photofacsimiles and begins with an ingenious analysis of some of Keats's annotations on his own facsimile of the Shakespeare First Folio and of the sonnet that Keats penned in the space between the end of *Hamlet* and the beginning of *King Lear.* McLeod demonstrates the benefits of reading Keats's sonnet in its original physical form and context, and argues that Keats's own response to Shakespeare was similarly enriched by his encounter with 'the Folio icon'.

In 'The Marriage of Good and Bad Quartos' McLeod, under the pseudonym Random Cloud, puns his way through a lively airing of the same prejudices.[16] His article combines guerrilla raids upon an orthodox editorial position with shrewd observations on the quarto texts of *Romeo and Juliet.* Some of the particular points are valid – and no editor of *Romeo and Juliet* can afford to ignore them – but

---

[13] *Shakespeare's Plays in Quarto: A Facsimile Edition of Copies Primarily from the Henry E. Huntington Library* (University of California Press, Berkeley, Los Angeles, and London, 1981).

[14] Except that the British Library has supplied its unique last page of Hamlet Q1 and one leaf of *Pericles* that is defective in the Huntington copy.

[15] *Sub-Stance,* 33/34 (1982), 25–55.

[16] *Shakespeare Quarterly,* 33 (1982), 421–31.

they do not necessarily support the general argument, in so far as one is advanced. McLeod would really like to abolish editing altogether. Editors regard the early prints as witnesses, who vary in their reliability, and from whose conflicting, confirmatory, or collusive testimony the truth – a text answering to Shakespeare's 'intentions' – may more or less successfully be reconstructed.[17] Some witnesses earn higher esteem than others: quartos are pronounced good or bad. McLeod objects to the 'prejudicial connotations' of these 'moral categories', and laments that 'our tradition is unwilling to allow multiple textual authorities to rest as a simultaneous set of existential entities to be encountered absurdly by the reader' (pp. 421–2). He finds in the decisions and statements of the new Arden editor of Romeo and Juliet contradictions that 'stem from setting an editorial standard (projected as a hypothetical fair copy) above the actual literary objects, Q1 and Q2 – and of [sic] setting art above its material manifestation' (p. 425). But if we take this line far enough, the concept of 'Q1' itself becomes a pointless abstraction, reducible to individual copies with their peculiar wormholes and flyspots. For me an ideal copy of Q1 is a less adequate material manifestation of 'Shakespeare's Romeo and Juliet' (the quotation marks are a concession to McLeod) than is an ideal copy of Q2; as a literary object Q1 contains less that is Shakespeare's than does Q2. Heminges and Condell, who reviled 'copies maimed and deformed by the frauds and stealths of injurious impostors', had no compunctions about passing moral judgements on contemporary printed texts. In 'UN Editing Shak-speare' McLeod asks, 'But where can be begin?' Is this material manifestation of McLeod's thought sacrosanct, or may the reader venture the editorial guess that he intended 'we', not 'be'? Despite McLeod's extravagancies, his witty provocations are salutary in stressing the instability of dramatic texts, in urging an open-minded attitude to quartos supposed to be bad, and in hinting at what may be gained from familiarity with the early editions as entities.

The late Alice Walker's articles on textual problems in Measure for Measure and All's Well That Ends Well are characteristically trenchant.[18] Endorsing the view that Folio Measure for Measure was set from a Ralph Crane transcript of Shakespeare's foul papers, she examines passages corrupted by serious omissions and confusions, and evaluates or proposes explanations and emendations of cruxes. All editors of the play will want to read these notes. She suspects that two related six-line lacunae in the foul papers – due to damage to head or foot of a leaf – led to the inept transfer from 3.2 to 4.1.59–64 of the Duke's lines on 'place and greatness', and to the garbling of Abhorson's false syllogism at 4.2.43–7. And she believes that the song and opening dialogue of 4.1, which introduce Mariana, were a non-Shakespearian interpolation. The song, 'an artistic blunder' in an otherwise 'ironic and unsentimental comedy', is followed by an artless string of tags.[19] Other difficulties in the text 'seem to be due to the usual errors in transmission' (p. 9), which she estimates at well over a hundred. She supports Rowe's 'brakes of vice' (F 'Ice') at 2.1.39, explaining that since 'brakes' are 'curbs', 'brakes of vice' are the laws; accepts Hanmer's 'injurious law' (F 'loue') at 2.3.40, because 'injurious' shows that the law (and an oxymoron) was intended; would read 'an idle plume / Which the air beats in vain' (F 'for vaine') at 2.4.11–12, rejecting weathercocks as irrelevant and supposing F's 'for' to have been caught from the previous line; and at 4.1.75 favours 'Our corn's to reap 'fore yet our tilth's to sow' (F 'for ... Tithes') – taking 'tilth' from Warburton via Theobald, and

---

[17] In Lear, if the authors of The Division of the Kingdoms are right, Q and F witness to separate truths, for they (imperfectly) represent Shakespeare's fully realized intentions at different periods. So McLeod's upholding of multiple textual authority has some appropriateness to that particular play.

[18] 'The Text of Measure for Measure', Review of English Studies, 34 (1983), 1–20; 'Six Notes on All's Well That Ends Well', Shakespeare Quarterly, 33 (1982), 339–42.

[19] Her suspicions of 4.1 were anticipated by Frank O'Connor, who in Shakespeare's Progress (Collier Books, New York, 1961) classed the scene among those mangled by some hack who had 'not the remotest idea of how to get people on and off the stage' (p. 155). Walker's surmise about a lacuna at 4.1.60 ignores Kenneth Muir's plausible suggestion, in Notes and Queries, NS 13 (1966), 135–6, that what belongs here is the Duke's gnomic soliloquy (which Walker examines) printed in F at the end of act 3.

insisting on "fore' herself. She argues that F's 'prenzie' at 3.1.93 and 3.1.96 must imply 'outward-sainted', but recognizes that her ruminations about 'puree' (an obsolete term for white miniver) leave the crux unsolved. Her two proposals for regularizing metre at 2.4.118 and 2.4.21 are highly attractive. She finds *Measure for Measure* 'remarkable for ... unity of design and sustained attention to details' (p. 19). In an appendix on the date of composition she argues for 1603.

Walker's notes on *All's Well* include a defence of the Folio stage direction, '*Enter a gentle Astringer*' at 5.1.6, and support of the replacement of F 'ne' at 2.1.173 by 'nay', which suits the incremental design of *auxesis* structuring Helena's rhetoric. Walker is least convincing on 4.2.38–9, where F reads: 'I see that men make rope's in such a scarre, / That wee'l forsake our selues.' Misquoting F as reading 'ropes', she alters to 'make rope in such a score', and links the expression 'make rope' to two Latin proverbs. No theatre-goer could have understood the lines as she interprets them, and no editor need look beyond Sisson's solution to this crux. F's 'rope's' = 'rope us' is confirmed by 'wee' and 'our selues', and the simple emendations needed are 'may' for 'make' (a compositorial slip under the influence of 'forsake') and 'snare' for 'scarre' (an easy minim confusion).

At last compositor studies are yielding worthwhile returns. Now that the identification of Folio Compositor E's stints seems firm, his treatment of known printed copy can be compared with the treatment that must be assumed if he set his stints of *Hamlet*, *King Lear*, and *Othello* from corrected quartos. Gary Taylor shows that E habitually retained at least 75 per cent of the punctuation of his copy.[20] His behaviour in F *Lear* is perfectly consistent with his normal practices – if he was setting from Q2; it is less so if he was setting from Q1. Pages attributed to him in F *Hamlet* and *Othello* are thoroughly anomalous if he was setting from corrected quartos: fewer than 40 per cent of the *Hamlet* Q2/F punctuation marks in E's stints match, and for *Othello* Q1/F the figures cluster around 43 per cent. Taylor considers, and deems improbable, alternatives to the obvious conclusion that Compositor E did not set *Hamlet* or *Othello* from quartos. And if the inexperi-

enced E was not given printed copy for these plays, it is unlikely that the other F compositors were given it either. Taylor's evaluation of indifferent variants in which F *Lear* agrees with Q2 against Q1 confirms that Compositor E set from a corrected exemplar of Q2. P. W. K. Stone made the same deduction from evidence that only partly overlaps with Taylor's. Stone's further claim that Compositor B in his portion of F *Lear* worked directly from a manuscript is bolstered by Taylor's analysis of the indifferent variants and of a sample of F spellings that violate B's preferences without being traceable to either Q1 or Q2 copy.

F. D. Hoeniger's new Arden edition of *Pericles* (1963) consolidated the orthodox position that while acts 3 to 5 are of Shakespeare's composition, acts 1 and 2 are remnants of a play not of his authorship but rehandled by him. Twenty years later, Hoeniger lends his considerable authority to another theory.[21] In impressive detail he elaborates the idea that Shakespeare wrote the whole of *Pericles* as an experiment, the arthritic style of the first two acts being deliberate, adjusted to the apt archaism of the Gower choruses, which constitute Shakespeare's solution to the structural problem posed by the chronological and geographical spread of his romance material, and at the same time come close to the heart of the play's concerns. The presence of the resurrected medieval poet, introducing and commenting on a re-enactment of an ancient tale that he had recounted in his own *Confessio Amantis*, is itself testimony to the immortality of art. Shakespeare begins by subduing his style to that of his presenter, but by the third act he feels able to speak in his own voice. Over the last decade several critics have entertained some such notion as Hoeniger's, but his experience as an editor who fully appreciates the stylistic oddness of *Pericles*, acts 1 and 2, gives his revised opinion a special interest.

The scholar who wants to use internal evidence to attribute to Shakespeare some anonymous or

---

[20] 'The Folio Copy for *Hamlet*, *King Lear*, and *Othello*', *Shakespeare Quarterly*, 34 (1983), 44–61.

[21] 'Gower and Shakespeare in *Pericles*', *Shakespeare Quarterly*, 33 (1982), 461–79.

disputed play faces an onerous but straightforward task. He or she must discover a set of variables that differentiate each of Shakespeare's undoubted plays (or at least those of a given period or genre) from a wide range of plays by other dramatists of the time, and show that the doubtful play exhibits the *peculiarly* Shakespearian features. Attribution studies which, like those of Thomas Merriam and Eric Sams, fail to satisfy this common-sense requirement may arouse interest but cannot command assent. Thomas Merriam believes that *Sir Thomas More* is wholly, or almost wholly, Shakespeare's.[22] Merriam's tests on computer counts of selected word-pairs and collocations compare a large Shakespearian aggregate with *Sir Thomas More*, Munday's *John a Kent*, the anonymous *Edward III*, *Pericles*, and a hypothetical Henslowe collaboration created by statistical calculations based on small samples from Dekker, Munday, Chettle, Webster, and Heywood. On these tests *More* and *Pericles* are compatible with the Shakespearian aggregate, but the other three plays are not. These findings prove next to nothing, but the techniques used are not without promise. Eric Sams wants to annex *Edmund Ironside* to the Shakespeare canon. His case rests mainly on the presence in the anonymous manuscript play of concatenations of words and images that recur in Shakespeare plays, mainly early ones.[23]

J. J. M. Tobin has for some years been pointing to just such linkages between works by Nashe and Shakespeare without inviting us to amalgamate the two oeuvres under a single name. His more modest contention is that Shakespeare sometimes drew on his memories of Nashe's writings. His latest researches reveal echoes in *Hamlet* of Nashe's *Christ's Tears over Jerusalem* and *Lenten Stuff*.[24] The first parallel confirms F *Hamlet*'s 'hire and salary' (3.3.79), which could scarcely be doubted at any rate (Q2 has the obvious misreading 'base and silly' and Q1 the vapid 'a benefit'); and the second, more helpfully, lends welcome support to F's 'scullion' against Q2's 'stallyon' (2.2.587). In each case the Shakespeare and Nashe contexts are linked by a complex of associated words and ideas. Tobin notes similar connections between *Macbeth* and *Christ's Tears* (which influenced *1 Henry IV* as well).[25] One set of collocations in

Nashe's pamphlet anticipates the key words in Macbeth's speech referring to 'this bank and shoal of time' (1.7.6), and so suggests that Theobald was right to emend (or interpret) F's 'Schoole' as 'shoal', though the line doubtless carries subsidiary puns.

In last year's *Shakespeare Survey* George Walton Williams assessed John Kerrigan's bold approach to the notorious Rosaline–Katherine puzzle in *Love's Labour's Lost*, 2.1, and concluded that 'the text does not provide enough material for a solution' (p. 187). Manfred Draudt's submission is that there is no puzzle to solve.[26] After a lengthy analysis he concludes that 'Compared with the traditionally emended version of this scene, which has created

---

22 'The Authorship of *Sir Thomas More*', *ALLC Bulletin*, 10 (1982), 1–7. In 'The Master of the Revels and *The Booke of Sir Thomas Moore*', *Shakespeare Quarterly*, 33 (1982), 493–5, G. Harold Metz suggests that the censor's perusal of the play took place *while* it was being revised; his reconstruction of the manuscript's history implies an improbably early date for the additions. T. H. Howard-Hill chaired a seminar on *Sir Thomas More* at a meeting of the Shakespeare Association of America in Ashland, Oregon, April 1983. Papers by Gary Taylor, Charles Forker, and Giles Dawson tended to strengthen the case for Shakespeare's, and against Webster's, authorship of Hand D; and if the three pages are Shakespeare's, they belong to the seventeenth century, as Taylor showed. Conflicting ideas were canvassed about the script's evolution.

23 '*Edmund Ironside*: a reappraisal', *Times Literary Supplement*, 13 August 1982, p. 879. The article provoked correspondence for some months. The play's date of composition is unknown; Sams argues for the 1580s. Sams has also, in 'Shakespeare's text and common sense', *Times Literary Supplement*, 2 September 1983, pp. 933–4, attacked the theory that *The True Tragedy* Q 1595, *The Contention* Q 1594, *A Shrew* Q 1594, and *Hamlet* Q1 1603 are corrupt versions of the Shakespearian plays preserved in F and in *Hamlet* Q2 1604. He regards them as Shakespearian apprentice work. Shakespeare's second attempt at a shrew play, F *The Shrew* (thought by most scholars to have been composed *c.*1590) has been misdated 'by fifteen years or more'!

24 '*Hamlet* and Nashe's *Lenten Stuffe*', *Archiv für das Studium der neueren Sprachen und Literaturen*, 219:134 (1982), 388–95.

25 '*Macbeth* and *Christs Teares over Jerusalem*', *Aligarh Journal of English Studies*, 7 (1982), 72–8.

26 'The "Rosaline–Katherine Tangle" of *Love's Labour's Lost*', *The Library*, 4 (1982), 381–96.

more problems and inconsistencies than it could explain, the original Quarto text is, all in all, superior.'[27] He maintains that Q's 1.2 is 'an actable scene that makes perfectly good sense within the context of the play as a whole'. He is indulgent towards Berowne's flirtatious exchanges with two ladies, and unperturbed by the fact that in Q 'two of the lords do not, from the start, show signs of falling in love with those ladies who favour them: Berowne at first flirting with Katherine, and Dumain inquiring after Rosaline' (pp. 394–5). In Draudt's opinion, compensation for the lack of a neat and immediate pairing of the couples is afforded by an increase in 'comic potentialities'. Could a producer successfully adopt this attitude, or would adherence to Q clutter the exposition and perplex the audience?

Draudt elsewhere discusses the close of *Love's Labour's Lost*, where the song about Winter and Spring is followed in Q by the enigmatic and unattributed statement 'The wordes of Mercurie, are harsh after the songes of Apollo', set in larger type.[28] F assigns the speech to '*Brag.*' and adds *You that way: we this way. / Exeunt omnes.*' Draudt inclines to the view that the Folio addition is authentic and 'directs the Princess and her ladies through the one stage-door to begin their journey back to France, and ushers the remaining characters through the other' (p. 167). Q's line is more mysterious. Commentators have been alert to resonances that it catches from the play as a whole, but slow to discover for it a straightforward denotation in its immediate context. Draudt believes that the reference is to the song that we have just heard and to a lost intervening speech – either a witticism on the performance or an ironic reminder that the ladies are about to depart – by the mercurial Moth. This is possible, but are not 'the words of Mercury' most naturally interpreted as the tidings of a messenger? And can it be coincidental that the play affords a messenger who brings harsh tidings? The Quarto of *Love's Labour's Lost* perpetuates many of the hesitations and reworkings of the foul papers. To me it seems likely that at an early stage of composition Shakespeare intended to let the song end the Pageant of the Worthies, which, in Q as it stands, is interrupted by a quarrel among the performers and by Mercade's bad news; that Q's cryptic line announced Mercade's entry or commented on his message; and that it was accidentally moved with the song when Shakespeare reshuffled and worked over his foul papers in order to end the play with the strains of cuckoo and owl. If Shakespeare not only wrote Q's line but intentionally put it in its present position, then Kerrigan's note in his New Penguin edition (1982) might serve as a last word on the subject.

Kerrigan does agree with Draudt that F's added exeunt line is authentic. In a note that supplements, and sometimes duplicates, his Penguin account of the text, Kerrigan distinguishes between three kinds of authorial revision that have been suspected in *Love's Labour's Lost*.[29] The first is revision within the course of composition, leading to the duplications and loose ends typical of quartos based on foul papers. The second is revision carried out after the foul papers had been completed, but possibly before the play was performed: evidence for this stage is supplied by the Folio alterations to Q, if any of these have authority. Kerrigan thinks that Stanley Wells is right to demand respect for them, but that the person who annotated the exemplar of Q from which F was printed worked not from a manuscript haphazardly consulted but from his memory of the play in performance, his recall being accurate enough for him to introduce into F some Shakespearian contributions to the prompt-book. A third stage of revision is posited by editors convinced that

---

[27] He incorporates into his argument the burden of his note, 'Katherine's "Mask" and "Cap" in *Love's Labour's Lost*, Act II, Scene 1, Lines 124 and 209', *Weiner Beiträge zur Englischen Philologie: A Yearbook of Studies in English Language and Literature*, 78 (1981), 1–6. There he submits that Katherine wears both a travelling mask and a cap as protection against the sun, not primarily as disguise. For his present purposes Draudt minimizes the authority of F's divergences from Q, since he must repudiate F's changes to speech prefixes in 2.1. Compare the next item.

[28] 'Shakespeare's Unpretentious Ending to *Love's Labour's Lost*', *Deutsche Shakespeare-Gesellschaft West: Jahrbuch 1982*, pp. 162–8.

[29] '*Love's Labor's Lost* and Shakespearean Revision', *Shakespeare Quarterly*, 33 (1982), 337–9.

the closing song in *Love's Labour's Lost* is indebted to Gerard's *Herbal* published in 1597, and must therefore be a late insertion in a play written some years earlier. Kerrigan is justly sceptical about the supposed debt, and so about the late insertion.

Dewey Ganzel's fascinating biography of John Payne Collier challenges the accepted view that Collier augmented by forgery his discoveries of manuscript material relating to Shakespeare and his contemporaries.[30] Ganzel makes shrewd use of the techniques of the cross-examining defence lawyer, impugning the motives of Collier's nineteenth-century accusers, and he offers new evidence in support of the authenticity of at least some annotations to the Perkins Folio, arguing that Collier's only fault was to exaggerate their age. He points out that the annotator has introduced readings peculiar to the First Quarto of *Titus Andronicus* (1594), which was unknown in Collier's lifetime, the sole surviving copy having been discovered in Sweden in 1904. However, one crucial instance of alleged agreement between the *Titus Andronicus* Quarto and the Perkins Folio turns out to be illusory, and without this instance the case for the annotator's having cursorily collated Q is weak.[31] Moreover, Ganzel fails to answer the prosecution's other charges against Collier, who can certainly be convicted of at least one act of serious falsification. The Joan Alleyn letter among the Henslowe papers at Dulwich College can be studied in photographic facsimile in S. Schoenbaum's *William Shakespeare: Records and Images* (Scolar Press, London; Oxford University Press, New York, 1981), and though the manuscript is slightly defective it is clear that the portion of Collier's published transcription which includes a reference to 'Mr Shakespeare of the globe' is incompatible with the original, and that the misrepresentation must have been deliberate. Ganzel does not profess palaeographical expertise. Nor does he cite the disinterested twentieth-century judgement of such authorities as Greg and Chambers. Greg had no doubt that several items in Henslowe's Diary were 'modern fabrications'. Collier need not have been the culprit, of course. The time may be ripe for a new analysis of all the suspect documents. If, as still seems probable, the pseudo-secretary hand

identifiable in the Perkins Folio, the ballads of the Hall commonplace book, and the Daborne warrant in the Bridgewater collection is Collier's, he would have to have acquired much greater calligraphic skills in order to perpetrate all the forgeries of which he is currently accused. Ganzel's book serves as a reminder that a handful of the Perkins Folio's conjectures are rather good: in his new Arden edition of *The Shrew* Brian Morris was tempted by 'Aristotle's *Ethics*' ('ethicks') for F's 'Aristotles checks' at 1.1.32, and ought perhaps to have yielded.

A few notes treat technical matters or the choice of variants. In *King Lear*, 4.2.28, Goneril tells Edmund 'My foote vsurps my body' in Q in its uncorrected state, 'A foole vsurps my bed' in Q in its corrected state, and 'My Foole vsurps my body' in F. Editors have debated the claims of the second and third of these readings. Thomas Clayton contends that the first is Shakespeare's and means 'My so-called husband – my sometime "head", now my "foot" – usurps my body'.[32] If he is right, Goneril's speech would have mystified at least two potential patrons of the Globe, the Q press-corrector and the agent in the transmission of F who independently changed 'foote' to 'Foole'. Moreover, if the Q(c) correction is a sophistication, other Q(c) readings hereabouts become suspect and F agreement with Q(u) ceases to imply F's dependence on Q. Nevertheless, Clayton does show that the Q(u) line makes sense.

In a closely reasoned piece on 'Gadshill's Question in *1 Henry IV*', Bob Antoni and George Walton Williams plead for retention of Q's prefix at 2.4.173.[33] In Q (1598) Gadshill asks about the robbery; most editors follow F in reassigning the speech to Prince Hal. Fidelity to Q turns out significantly to increase the parallelism between the play's comic and historical scenes.

---

[30] *Fortune and Men's Eyes: The Career of John Payne Collier* (Oxford University Press, 1982).

[31] See the review by Arthur Freeman, *Times Literary Supplement*, 22 April 1983, pp. 391–3, and subsequent correspondence.

[32] 'Old Light on the Text of *King Lear*', *Modern Philology*, 78 (1981), 347–67.

[33] *Cahiers Élisabéthains*, 23 (1983), 99–103.

In his new Arden edition of *Romeo and Juliet* Brian Gibbons asserted that the Folio text of the play 'is based on Q3 with the exception of a number of passages which follow Q4' (p. 2). Presumably he inferred F dependence on Q4 from a score of Q4/F verbal agreements against Q3. S. W. Reid scrutinizes these readings, and finds no logical reason to believe that Q4 was used in the printing of F.[34] Reid clarifies principles for establishing the descent of printed texts.

Answering his own challenge, issued in the previous year, Richard Levin points out that the word 'Iudeian' occurs in the anonymous *The Tragedy of Claudius Tiberius Nero* (1607), and George Walton Williams adds another instance, spelt 'Iudean', in Elizabeth Cary's *Mariam* (1613).[35] In discussion of Othello's Indian/Iudean (5.2.347) nobody has mentioned that the anonymous *Guy, Earl of Warwick* (1661) has 'Indea' (B1ᵛ) where the context proves that 'Iudea' is intended ('Judea' appears on C1ᵛ and thereafter). This is virtually the same error (of misreading, presumably, since *Guy* observes the modern I/J distinction) that advocates of F's 'Iudean' in *Othello* assume in Q.

Paul Werstine announces that examination of the Bodmer copy of the 1600 First Quarto of *Much Ado About Nothing* – the only copy not collated by Hinman for his Shakespeare Quarto Facsimile – reveals no unrecorded press variants but clarifies two doubtful punctuation marks.[36] And G. V. Monitto finds in three French–English reference works of 1580, 1593, and 1611 evidence that around the time when *Hamlet* was written 'sallied' included senses now contained in 'sullied'.[37]

J. W. Binns's interest is in editorial handling of the one hundred and twenty scraps of Latin in Shakespeare's plays. He suspects that Shakespeare's own Latin was never wrong without just cause, and makes valuable suggestions towards a more systematic and professional treatment of these words, phrases, and quotations.[38]

Though not directly concerned with Shakespeare's text, G. Thomas Tanselle's 'Classical, Biblical, and Medieval Textual Criticism and Modern Editing' is a sustained and powerful piece of cogita-

tion, from which any editor may profit.[39] Tanselle concludes: 'Editing ancient texts and editing modern ones are not simply related fields: they are essentially the same field. The differences between them are in details; the similarities are in fundamentals' (p. 68).

Katherine Duncan-Jones asks 'Was the 1609 *Shake-speares Sonnets* really Unauthorized?'[40] She looks to the text of the sonnets, the career of their publisher Thomas Thorpe, and the structure of the sequence as it appears in Q for an answer, which is that Shakespeare probably consented to publication and may even have sought it. Her article is a model of informed good sense on a topic that rarely attracts it.

Finally may be mentioned some items of exegesis where the text is not in doubt. Michael Warren argues that Albany's 'Fall and cease' at 5.3.265 of *King Lear* 'is not a peculiarly phrased invocation to the heavens but a simple command to kneel in silence'.[41] Derick R. G. Marsh gives pregnant meaning to Hamlet's passing remark to Rosencrantz and Guildenstern that he is 'most dreadfully attended' (2.2.269) by taking it as a covert allusion to the Ghost.[42] Michael Cameron Andrews explains that Hamlet confronts his mother in a private

---

[34] 'McKerrow, Greg, and Quarto Copy for Folio *Romeo and Juliet*', *The Library*, 5 (1983), 118–25.

[35] 'The Indian/Iudean Crux in *Othello*: An Addendum', *Shakespeare Quarterly*, 34 (1983), 72; 'Yet Another Early Use of *Iudean*', ibid.

[36] 'The Bodmer Copy of Shakespeare's *Much Ado About Nothing* Q1', *Notes and Queries*, NS 30 (1983), 123–4.

[37] '"Sallied Flesh" (Q1, Q2): *Hamlet* I.ii.129', *Studies in Bibliography*, 36 (1983), 177–8.

[38] 'Shakespeare's Latin Citations: The Editorial Problem', *Shakespeare Survey 35* (Cambridge University Press, 1982), 119–28.

[39] *Studies in Bibliography*, 36 (1983), 21–68. Also worth recording is Peter L. Shillingsburg, 'Key Issues in Editorial Theory', *Analytical and Enumerative Bibliography*, 6 (1982), 3–16.

[40] *Review of English Studies*, 34 (1983), 51–71.

[41] '*King Lear*, V.iii.265: Albany's "Fall and Cease"', *Shakespeare Quarterly*, 33 (1982), 178–9.

[42] 'A Note on Hamlet's "I Am Most Dreadfully Attended" (II.ii.266)', *Shakespeare Quarterly*, 33 (1982), 181.

apartment much less intimate than a modern bedroom.[43] Frank Fabry glosses some punning between Peter and a musician in *Romeo and Juliet*,[44] and A. Jonathan Bate defends the traditional understanding that in *Romeo and Juliet*, 4.4.5–6, Capulet addresses a woman called Angelica, presumably the Nurse, and is not ordering the herb of that name.[45] In a note on Claudio's vilification of Hero as a 'rotten orange' R. E. R. Madelaine finds that 'the association between oranges and love or lust appears to have had some emblematic currency in the Elizabethan period'.[46]

Touchstone says that failure to understand his verse 'strikes a man more dead than a great reckoning in a little room' (*As You Like It*, 3.3.14–15). R. V. Holdsworth cites two passages by Thomas Middleton which support a suggestion by H. J. Oliver, editor of the New Penguin *As You Like It*, that a 'little room' is a private one in an inn, a secluded table adding to the 'reckoning' or bill for the meal.[47] G. J. Roberts notes allusions in Shakespeare's plays to the belief that to draw blood from a witch's face nullified her spell.[48] Seeking to identify the plant 'Dian's bud' in *A Midsummer Night's Dream*, Marion Cohen picks two candidates, euphrasia or eye-bright and, more enthusiastically, spurge or virgin's nipple.[49] Is preferential voting permitted, or has she spoilt her ballot paper?

---

[43] 'His Mother's Closet: A Note on *Hamlet*', *Modern Philology*, 80 (1982), 164–6.

[44] 'Shakespeare's Witty Musician: *Romeo and Juliet*, IV.v.114–7', *Shakespeare Quarterly*, 33 (1982), 182–3.

[45] 'An Herb by Any Other Name: Romeo and Juliet, IV.iv.5–6', *Shakespeare Quarterly*, 33 (1982), 336.

[46] 'Oranges and Lemans: *Much Ado About Nothing*, IV.i.31', *Shakespeare Quarterly*, 33 (1982), 491–2.

[47] 'Touchstone's Little Room', *Shakespeare Quarterly*, 33 (1982), 492–3.

[48] 'Shakespeare and "Scratching"', *Notes and Queries*, NS 30 (1983), 111–14.

[49] '"Dian's Bud" in *A Midsummer Night's Dream*, IV.i.72', *Notes and Queries*, NS 30 (1983), 118–20.

THE MALONE SOCIETY

The Malone Society was formed in 1906 to make accessible material for the study of pre-Restoration English drama. For thirty-three years its Honorary General Editor was Sir Walter Greg, and the posts of officers and members of the Society's Council have continued to be held by well-known scholars.

So far, the Society has published over 140 volumes. Most of these are facsimile reprints or diplomatic editions of sixteenth- and seventeenth-century plays, from printed and manuscript originals. The introductions are brief and factual, and are largely devoted to clarifying the nature of the texts reproduced. Annotation is confined to such matters as press variants, manuscript alterations and the listing of irregular and doubtful readings. Occasional volumes of 'Collections' – twelve so far – reproduce shorter plays or contemporary documents relating to the drama.

Malone Society publications provide a range of essential texts and source materials, most of which are not otherwise available without consulting original documents. They are noted for their high standards of scholarship and good quality of production.

Annual subscriptions finance new publications on a non-profit making basis. At present, one volume is produced each year and issued to members without further charge. Members may also purchase past volumes (as available) through AMS Press Inc., at a substantial 40 per cent discount on the list prices.

The annual subscription of £10.00 is a modest price for volumes as significant in their content and as scrupulously produced as Malone Society publications. Each subscription helps the Society to give a fuller and more economic service. We therefore hope that you will apply for membership, sending one year's subscription fee to the Honorary Membership Secretary or, if you live in the USA, Canada, Australia, New Zealand or Japan, to the officer for that area.

Honorary Membership Secretary:
Dr John Jowett
The Oxford Shakespeare
40 Walton Crescent
Oxford OX1 2JQ

Honorary Treasurer for Canada:
Professor Anne B. Lancashire
University College
University of Toronto
Toronto M5S 1A1

Honorary Treasurer for Australia and New Zealand:
Mr F. H. Mares
Department of English Language and Literature
University of Adelaide
Box 498D
GPO Adelaide
South Australia 5001

Honorary Treasurer for the USA:
Professor Thomas L. Berger
St Lawrence University
Canton
New York

The Japanese Officer of the Malone Society:
Professor Jiro Ozu
201 Toyotama Mansion
1–8 Toyotama Kita
Nerima-ku
Tokyo

INDEX

Abbey, Edwin Austin, 51, 52
Adams, Graham C., 196
Adamson, Jane, 127n
Addison, Joseph, 146
Ahrens, Rüdiger, 156n
Albert, Prince, 47
Allen, Michael J. B., 211, 212
Alleyn, Edward, 193, 194
Alleyn, Joan, 217
Anderson, Miles, 164, 165
Anschütz, Heinrich, 199n
Antoni, Bob, 217
Archer, William, 14, 21
Arden, Agnes, 187
Aristotle, 13, 14, 141, 144, 146, 148, 152, 207, 217
Armin, Robert, 198
Armstrong, Alun, 39n, 167
Armstrong, Edward, 182
Ascham, Roger, 180
Astington, John H., 196, 198
Aubrey, John, 189
Auden, W. H., 123n, 177
Auerbach, Erich, 72n

Babcock, R. W., 149n
Bacon, Francis, 115, 134
Baines, Richard, 189
Bamber, Linda, 179n
Barber, C. L., 2, 3, 5, 7, 9, 66n, 163
Barcklow, Brigitte, 160n
Barsanti, Jane, 44, 45
Barthes, Roland, 164, 180
Bartholomaeus Anglicus, 86
Bartholomeusz, Dennis, 199
Barton, Anne, 17n: see also Anne Righter and Bobbyann Roesen
Barton, John, 115
Bate, A. Jonathan, 219
Battenhouse, Roy, 88n

Bayley, John, 127
Bean, John C., 6, 33n, 34–6, 39
Beardsley, Aubrey, 53
Beaumont, Francis, 42
Beckerman, Bernard, 38, 40
Belgion, Montgomery, 107n
Beneke, Jürgen, 158n
Bennett, Josephine Waters, 99n
Benston, Alice N., 59n
Bentley, Eric, 35
Berek, Peter, 191
Berger, Sarah, 164, 165
Bergeron, David, 198
Bergson, Henri, 36
Berlioz, Harriet Smithson, 200, 201
Berlioz, Hector, 200, 201
Berry, Ralph, 6, 7, 13n, 39n
Besterman, Theodore, 146n
Betken, William T., 162n
Bettinger, Peter, 160n
Binns, J. W., 218
Black, John, 152n
Blayney, Peter W. M., 210, 211
Blinn, Hansjürgen, 156n
Bloom, Harold, 164
Boas, F., 69n
Boase, T. S. R., 41, 42n
Boccaccio, Giovanni, 99
Boettinger, C. A., 46
Boitard, François, 42
Bonheim, Helmut, 191
Boose, Lynda E., 125n
Booth, Michael, 199
Borgia, Cesare, 96
Bosch, Hieronymus, 50
Botticelli, Sandro, 175
Boucher, François, 43
Bowers, Fredson, 211
Boydell, John, 45–8
Bracton, Henry de, 192

Bradbrook, M. C., 8, 30, 184
Bradbury, Malcolm, 6, 20n, 59n
Bradley, A. C., 143n, 146n, 147, 149, 150n
Brecht, Bertolt, 161, 170, 171
Breuer, Rolf, 159
Breughel the Elder, Pieter, 136, 137
Briggs, Julia, 188
Briggs, K. M., 9
Brissenden, Alan, 9
Brock, D. Heyward, 189
Brook, Peter, 5, 9, 162, 184
Brooks, Harold F., 2, 6, 9
Brown, John Russell, 1, 2, 5, 10, 11, 21, 29n, 56n, 59n, 183n, 184
Brunkhorst, Martin, 159n
Bryan, George, 198
Bryden, Bill, 168, 169
Büchner, Georg, 155
Buckingham, Duke of, 198
Bull, George, 96n
Bullough, Geoffrey, 2, 57n
Bunnett, F. E., 152
Burbage, Richard, 193
Burckhardt, Sigurd, 11
Busacker, Klaus, 160n
Butt, Ronald, 172n

Caird, John, 163
Cairncross, A. S., 202
Calderwood, J. L., 3, 7, 9
Calvert, Louis, 85
Canaris, Volker, 161n
Candido, Joseph, 191
Carroll, W. C., 7, 17n, 18n
Cary, Cecile Williamson, 193n
Cary, Elizabeth, 218
Case, John, 176
Catullus, 189
Cavendish, Lady Margaret, 141, 142

221

Caxton, William, 207
Cerusano, S. P., 194
Cervantes, Miguel de, 189
Chalmers, A., 145n
Chaloner, Sir Thomas, 181
Chambers, Sir Edmund, 2, 7, 102, 217
Charlton, H. B., 66n, 163
Chaucer, Geoffrey, 191, 207
Chettle, Henry, 215
Christian IV, King of Denmark, 198
Cibber, Theophilus, 199
Cicero, 148, 151
Cinthio, Giraldi, 119, 145
Clayton, Thomas, 200n, 209, 217
Clemen, Wolfgang, 14, 157
Coghill, Nevill, 5, 33n
Cohen, Marion, 219
Cohen, Walter, 186, 187
Coleridge, Samuel Taylor, 185, 199
Colie, Rosalie, 4, 72n
Collier, John Payne, 217
Condell, Henry, 75, 213
Conway, Alice, 189
Copleston, F. C., 151n
Corneille, Pierre, 143
Cosgrave, Frankie, 169
Cowper, F. Cadogan, 51
Craig, Edward Gordon, 201
Cranach, Lucas, 176
Crane, Ralph, 213
Cranko, John, 162
Cribb, T. J., 152
Cusack, Sinead, 167
Cushman, Robert, 128n, 168, 170n
Cuvelier, Éliane, 194

Daborne, Robert, 217
Dadd, Richard, 48, 50
Daniel, Samuel, 191
Daniels, Ron, 172
Danson, Lawrence, 58n, 195
Dash, Irene, 33n, 34
Davenant, Sir William, 193
David, Richard, 184
Davidson, Clifford, 193n
Davies, Howard, 170
Davies, Oliver Ford, 171
Davies, Thomas, 85n
Dawes, Robert, 183
Dawson, Anthony B., 66n
Dawson, Giles, 215n
De Loutherbourg, Philip James, 45–7
De Mille, Cecil B., 52

De Rougemont, Denis, 107n
Dean, T. A., 52
Dekker, Thomas, 180, 215
Dennis, John, 147, 148
Dent, R. W., 9
Derrida, Jacques, 164, 180
Derby's Men, Earl of, 196
Des Jardins, Gregory, 189
Diamond, Arlyn, 34n
Diamond, William, 150n
Dibbelt, Ulrike, 159n
Doebler, John, 66, 194
Don, Robin, 164
Donaldson, Ian, 175, 176
Donatus, 13, 15
Donawerth, Jane L., 193
Donne, John, 209
Doran, Madeleine, 13n, 14
Dorn, Dieter, 161, 200
Dowden, Edward, 11
Draudt, Manfred, 215
Dryden, John, 35, 144–9, 193
Du Guernier, Louis, 42
Dugdale, Gilbert, 198
Dulac, Edmund, 168
Duncan-Jones, Katherine, 218
Dunlop, Frank, 169
Dusinberre, Juliet, 4, 55
Duthie, G. I., 30n, 210
Dutz, Ingold, 159n

Eccles, Mark, 189
Eksteins, M., 156n
Edwards, E., 43, 44
Edwards, Lee R., 34n
Elizabeth I, Queen, 148
Else, Gerald F., 14n
Empson, Sir William, 209
Engler, Balz, 160n
Ennius, 134
Erasmus, 138, 140n, 180, 181
Erikson, Erik, 99
Evans, Bertrand, 3, 8, 17n, 95
Evans, Dame Edith, 39
Evans, G. Blakemore, 15n, 70n, 85n
Evans, Maurice, 200
Everett, Barbara, 185
Ewbank, Inga-Stina, 6, 19

Fabry, Frank, 219
Farber, Leslie H., 121n, 122n
Farrah, 172
Farren, Elizabeth, 45
Faucit, Helen, 199

Fenkohl, Jörg, 159n
Fenton, James, 168
Fergusson, Francis, 187
Finney, Albert, 184
Fish, Stanley, 164, 180
Flahiff, F. T., 72n
Flaxman, John, 47
Fleetwood, Susan, 170
Fleiss, Wilhelm, 150n
Fleissner, R. F., 191
Fletcher, John, 42, 145
Flimm, Jürgen, 162
Foakes, R. A., 5, 184
Foot, Michael, 172
Ford, John, 117
Forker, Charles, 215n
Fortescue, Sir John, 192
Fortescue-Brickdale, Eleanor, 51
Freedman, Barbara, 35
Freeman, Arthur, 217n
French, A. L., 146n
French, Marilyn, 179, 180
Freud, Sigmund, 106, 121n, 122n, 150, 176, 177
Fried, Erich, 160
Frost, Robert, 69
Frye, Northrop, 2, 3, 5, 9, 10, 36n, 73, 118
Frye, Roland M., 194
Fujita, Minoru, 192
Furness, H. H., 156
Furnivall, F. J., 152
Fuseli, Henry, 45, 47, 48

Gabler, Hans Walter, 157n
Gadamer, Hans-Georg, 159
Gainsborough, Thomas, 43
Gair, W. Reavley, 197
Gambon, Michael, 172, 173
Ganzel, Dewey, 217
Garber, Marjorie, 178, 179
Garnier, Robert, 191
Garrick, David, 34, 45, 147, 199
Gebhardt, Peter, 160n
Gentleman, Francis, 85n, 146, 147, 148n
George, David, 196
Gerard, John, 217
Gervinus, G. G., 152
Gibbons, Brian, 201, 218
Gillespie, Norman, 198n
Giovanni (Fiorentino), Ser, 56
Girard, René, 70
Giucci, Caetano, 50, 51
Goddard, Harold, 33n

Godshalk, W. L., 20n
Goebbels, Joseph Paul, 155, 156
Goethe, Johann Wolfgang von, 145, 150, 155
Golding, Arthur, 207
Goldring, Beth, 209
Goodman, Henry, 168, 169
Gower, John, 214
Grabes, Herbert, 188
Granville-Barker, Harley, 152
Gravelot, François, 43, 44
Green, William, 1n
Greenblatt, Stephen, 193
Greene, Gayle, 3n
Greene, Robert, 20
Greg, Sir Walter, 2, 210, 211, 217, 218n
Greiner, Norbert, 158n
Greville, Fulke, 189
Griffin, Hayden, 170
Griffiths, Richard, 170
Grimaldi, Joseph, 166
Grimm, Jakob and Wilhelm, 53
Grock, 168
Grüber, Klaus Michael, 162
Gründgens, Gustaf, 200
Grüttner, Theo, 158n
Gucht, Michael van der, 42
Gundolf, Friedrich, 155
Günther, Frank, 160
Gwyn, Nell, 58

Habicht, Werner, 156n, 157n, 158n, 161n
Haines, Charles, 116n, 124n, 125n
Hall, Edward, 27n, 75
Hall, Jennifer, 170
Hall, Sir Peter, 184
Hamburger, Maik, 160
Hamilton, Donna B., 192
Hamlyn, Robin, 45n
Hammelmann, Hanns, 42
Hammerschmidt, H., 156n, 158n
Häntsch, Thomas, 157n
Hapgood, Robert, 105n
Harari, Josué V., 70n
Hare, Julius Charles, 152
Harper, John, 85
Harris, Bernard, 5, 56n
Hart, H. C., 92n
Hartwig, Joan, 194
Hasenberg, Peter, 158n
Hasler, Jörg, 158n
Hattaway, Michael, 183, 184
Hawkins, Sherman, 36n

Hayman, Francis, 194
Hazlitt, William, 142, 185, 201
Hazlitt, W. Carew, 67n
Heilman, Robert, 6, 33, 35
Helpmann, Robert, 169
Heminges, John, 75, 213
Henslowe, Philip, 183, 215, 217
Hentschel, Evelyn, 157n
Herder, J. G., 151n
Herrick, M. T., 14n
Heyden, Pieter van der, 136
Heyme, Hansgünter, 161
Heywood, Thomas, 215
Hibbard, G. R., 23, 25, 36, 38n
Hinman, Charlton, 210, 211, 218
Hobson, Harold, 184
Hodges, C. Walter, 196
Hoeniger, F. D., 214
Höfele, Andreas, 158n
Hofmann, Norbert, 160n
Holdsworth, R. V., 219
Holinshed, Raphael, 75n, 76
Holland, Norman, 164
Hollar, Wenceslaus, 196
Holloway, John, 164
Honigmann, E. A. J., 1, 149n
Hooker, Richard, 192
Hopkins, David, 190
Horace, 144, 148
Horne, R. C., 190
Hotine, Margaret, 190
Hotson, Leslie, 196
Howard-Hill, T. H., 215n
Howe, P. P., 142n
Huesmann, Heinrich, 159n
Hughes, John, 145
Hughes, Leo, 35
Hume, David, 149–51
Hunt, Marsha, 169
Hunter, G. K., 4, 5, 100n, 107n, 110n, 184, 190
Huston, J. Dennis, 15n, 37n
Hutt, William, 85
Hyde, Jonathan, 173
Hyland, Peter, 55, 58n

Ibsen, Henrik, 207
Iden, Peter, 161n
Iser, Wolfgang, 159

Jackson, Russell, 198, 199
Jaggard, William, 206, 209
James I, King (James VI), 197
James, Emrys, 165, 172
Janson, H. W., 134n, 136, 137, 139n

Jauslin, Christian, 200n
Jauss, H. R., 159
Jenkins, Harold, 198
Jobin, Sybille, 158n
John de Trevisa, 86
Johnson, Samuel, 45, 100, 142, 147, 149, 150
Jones, Emrys, 117
Jones, Gemma, 164, 166, 170
Jones, Gordon P., 195
Jones, Inigo, 196, 197
Jonson, Ben, 58, 87n, 117, 145, 188, 189
Jordan, William Chester, 186
Juliá, Raúl, 39n

Kahn, Coppélia, 33n, 34–6, 39n, 40n
Kainz, Joseph, 199
Kames, Henry Home, Lord, 143, 149, 151n
Kant, Immanuel, 143, 151
Kean, Charles, 199
Kean, Edmund, 142, 201
Keats, John, 207, 212
Kemble, Charles, 48, 85
Kemble, John Philip, 198, 199
Kempe, William, 198
Kermode, Frank, 5, 11, 69n, 150n
Kernan, Alvin B., 87n
Kerrigan, John, 18n, 208, 215–17
Kirchheim, Astrid, 158n
Kirsch, Arthur, 101n, 144n, 176–8
Kleist, Heinrich von, 155
Kliman, Bernice W., 200
Knight, Charles, 208
Knight, G. Wilson, 99, 100, 107n, 182
Knights, L. C., 10
Knowles, Richard, 71n
Kott, Jan, 140n, 159
Koyro, H. J., 160n
Krieger, Elliot, 4, 10
Krull, Marianne, 150n
Kübler-Ross, Elisabeth, 186
Küpper, Reiner, 160n
Kussmaul, Paul, 159n
Kyd, Thomas, 191
Kyle, Barry, 163, 165

Lamb, Charles, 10, 185
Landry, D. E., 176n
Landt, D. B., 87n
Lange, V., 152n
Laroque, François, 190

Lascelles, Mary, 90
Le Bossu, René, 148
Leavis, F. R., 6, 131
Ledebur, Ruth von, 156
Leech, Clifford, 5, 20n, 55n, 106n
Leggatt, Alexander, 4, 7, 11, 67, 103n
Leisi, E., 161n
Lengeler, Rainer, 158n
Lennox, Charlotte, 142
Lenz, Bernard, 158n
Lenz, Carolyn, 3n, 33n
Lenz, John W., 151n
Lessing, Gotthold Ephraim, 152, 155
Lever, J. W., 90, 92, 93n
Lévi-Strauss, Claude, 188
Levin, Richard, 158, 164, 218
Lewis, C. S., 14n
Lim, C. S., 189n
Limouze, Henry S., 193n
Lindheim, Nancy R., 72n
Lindtberg, Leopold, 162n
Link, Franz H., 158n
Liszt, Franz, 201
Lord, George de Forest, 185n
Lotto, Lorenzo, 176
Lovejoy, A. O., 69n
Lowry, J. S., 194
Lucas, E. V., 52n
Lupton, Thomas, 92n
Lutz, Bruno von, 159n
Lydgate, John, 207
Lyly, John, 19, 20, 191

McAfee, Helen, 58n
McEnery, Peter, 173
Machiavelli, Niccolò, 96
Mack, Maynard, 72n, 185n
McKenzie, D. F., 211
McKerrow, R. B., 2, 218n
McLeod, Randall, 208, 210, 212, 213
Maclise, Daniel, 48
McLuhan, Marshall, 9
McPherson, David, 197
Macready, William Charles, 199
Madelaine, R. E. R., 190, 197, 219
Mahood, M. M., 1, 124n
Marcuse, Herbert, 9
Margeson, J. M. R., 55n
Marlowe, Christopher, 60, 129, 189, 204
Marowitz, Charles, 162
Marprelate, Martin, 197
Marsh, Derick R. G., 218
Marshall, David, 187

Marston, John, 189, 197
Marx, Groucho, 167
Massey, Daniel, 164, 166
Masuccio, Tommaso, 61
Mathews, Charles, the Elder, 85
Maus, Katherine Eisaman, 193
Mebane, John S., 191
Mehl, Dieter, 156n
Melchiori, Giorgio, 149n
Mendelssohn, Felix, 50
Merchant, W. Moelwyn, 10, 41, 45n
Meres, Francis, 26
Merriam, Thomas, 215
Meszaros, Patricia K., 193
Metz, G. Harold, 215n
Meyer, Russell J., 67n
Middleton, Thomas, 115, 124n, 219
Miles, Rosalind, 90
Miller, Jonathan, 59
Miltitz, Carl Borromaeus von, 46
Mincoff, Marco, 190
Minks, Wilfried, 161
Mirren, Helen, 172, 173
Mitterwurzer, Anton Friedrich, 199
Monitto, G. V., 218
Montaigne, Michel de, 176, 177
Montrose, L. A., 19n
Moody, A. D., 10
Morgann, Maurice, 143–5, 147, 150
Morris, Brian, 2, 23, 25, 29, 33n, 37n, 38n, 39n, 40n, 184, 204
Motschach, Hermann, 160
Moulton, R. G., 13, 20
Moxon, Joseph, 211
Muir, Kenneth, 2, 4, 116n, 120, 141n, 146n, 205–7, 211–13
Müller, Wolfgang G., 157n
Müller-Schwefe, Gerhard, 156n, 199n
Munday, Anthony, 215
Mussolini, Benito, 172

Nashe, Thomas, 190, 191, 215
Naumann, Walter, 156n
Neely, Carol, 3n
Nelson, T. G. A., 116n, 124n, 125n
Neumeier, John, 162
Neuner, Gerhard, 157n
Nevo, Ruth, 3, 13n
Newman, Karen, 194
Nixon, Richard, 173
Noble, Adrian, 163, 164, 168, 173, 185
Noelte, Rudolf, 162

Novy, Marianne L., 33n, 37n
Nunn, Trevor, 184, 199

Oberkogler, Friedrich, 158n
O'Brien, Ellen J., 193
O'Callaghan, Richard, 168, 169
O'Connor, F., 213n
O'Conor, Joseph, 168
Ohm, Karl, 158n
Okes, Nicholas, 210, 211
Oliver, H. J., 2, 23, 28, 29n, 34, 39, 203–5, 219
Olivier, Laurence (Lord Olivier), 59
Oppel, Horst, 156n, 159
Orgel, Stephen, 193
Orkin, Martin R., 190
Ornstein, Robert, 102n
Orrell, John, 195–7
Orwell, George, 209
Otway, Thomas, 117

Painter, William, 99n
Palitzsch, Peter, 161
Palmer, David, 6, 20n, 59, 66n, 184
Palmer, Kenneth, 205–7
Park, Roy, 185
Parker, J., 47
Parker, M. D. H., 92
Parrott, Thomas Marc, 11
Partridge, Eric, 124n, 128n
Pater, Walter, 147, 148n
Paton, Sir Joseph Noel, 48–51
Patterson, Michael, 161n
Peck, Bob, 173
Pembroke, Mary Herbert, Countess of, 191
Pepys, Samuel, 58
Petrarch, Francesco, 70
Pettitt, Thomas, 190
Pfeiffer, Rolf, 159n
Pfister, Manfred, 17n, 158
Phelps, Samuel, 199
Phialas, P. G., 13
Pietsch, Ilse, 155
Plutarch, 148
Poggioli, Renato, 69
Pollitt, Clyde, 171
Pope, Thomas, 198
Preminger, Alex, 35n
Priessnitz, Horst, 159n
Priest, Josias, 41
Proudfoot, Richard, 201
Purcell, Henry, 41, 45
Purchase, Bruce, 128n
Puttenham, George, 180

Quiller-Couch, A., 90n
Quin, James, 85, 147

Rabanus, Gert, 160n, 200
Rabkin, Norman, 8, 55, 56, 164, 203
Raby, Peter, 200, 201
Rackham, Arthur, 52, 53
Ramberg, J. H., 44, 45
Ramm, Dieter, 158n
Rauschenberger, Maria, 160n
Rees, Joan, 13n, 191
Reid, S. W., 218
Reis, Ilse H., 159n
Retzch, Moritz, 46, 47, 50, 53
Reynolds, Sir Joshua, 45, 46
Richardson, David, 138
Richardson, William, 149–51
Ridley, M. R., 120n
Righter, Anne, 3, 24n; see also Anne Barton and Bobbyann Roesen
Roberts, Alexander, 17n
Roberts, G. J., 219
Robertson, J. G., 152n
Robinson, W. Heath, 51–3
Roesen, Bobbyann, 7, 17n: see also Anne Righter and Anne Barton
Rohrmoser, Günter, 158n
Rohrsen, Peter, 157n
Rolle, Dietrich, 159n
Rollins, H. E., 189
Rossiter, A. P., 8
Rossky, William, 187
Rothe, Hans, 156n
Rudhart, Blanca-Maria, 157n
Rudolf, Georg, 158n
Ruhl, Ludwig Sigismund, 46–8, 50, 53
Russell, William, 187
Rymer, Thomas, 124, 145–8

Salgãdo, Gãmini, 14, 17n
Salingar, L. G., 2, 14
Sallust, 148
Sams, Eric, 215
Sanders, Norman, 36n, 75n
Scaliger, 13, 15
Schabert, Ina, 156n, 158n
Schäfer, Jürgen, 159n
Schaller, Rudolf, 160
Schell, Maximilian, 200
Schiavonetti, L., 46
Schiff, Gert, 45n

Schiller, Friedrich, 69, 71, 152
Schlegel, A. W., 143, 152, 155, 160, 161, 200
Schlegel, Friedrich, 152
Schmidt, Alexander, 85, 155
Schoenbaum, S., 2, 217
Scholtes, Gertrud, 159n
Schrickx, Willem, 198
Schulz, Volker, 158n
Schwanitz, Dietrich, 158n
Schwarz, York-Wedigo M., 157n
Schwarze, Hans-Wilhelm, 158n
Scofield, Paul, 168, 170
Scott, David, 47–9, 52
Scott, Margaret, 186, 187
Scragg, Leah, 191, 192
Sedlak, Werner, 157n
Sehrt, E. Th., 157
Sekacz, Ilona, 164, 170
Selby-Bigge, L. A., 150n
Senelick, Lawrence, 201
Shakespeare, Hamnet, 190
Shakespeare, William
    editions
        Arden, 2, 5, 10, 20n, 23, 25, 33n, 59n, 90n, 92n, 100n, 161, 198; textual criticism of, 202–19 passim
        Bell, 43–5, 47, 148n
        Folio, 24, 34, 75, 82; textual criticism of, 202–19 passim
        Hanmer, Sir Thomas, 43, 44, 213
        Johnson, Samuel, 100, 147, 149, 150
        Johnson–Steevens, 45
        New (Cambridge), 85, 90
        New Penguin, 2, 6, 23, 38n, 75n, 120n, 161, 219
        New Variorum, 2, 156
        Oxford, 2, 23, 34n, 202–5
        Pope, Alexander, 71, 142
        Quarto, 83, 120n, 142, 192; textual criticism of, 202–19 passim
        Riverside, 15n, 70n, 85n
        Rowe, Nicholas, 41, 42, 52, 71, 148, 149, 213
        Signet, 143n
        Theobald, Lewis, 43, 44, 203, 213
        Warburton, William, 149, 213
    plays
        All's Well that Ends Well,

99–113 passim, 158n, 176–8, 180, 195, 200, 201, 213, 214
Antony and Cleopatra, 115, 160n, 172, 173, 182, 195
As You Like It, 1, 5, 34, 55, 57, 71, 86, 87, 161, 190, 191, 195, 219
Comedy of Errors, The, 1, 2, 5, 6, 13–17, 19, 21, 163, 164, 167–70, 179, 180, 193, 194n
Coriolanus, 36, 39, 159n, 182, 189n
Cymbeline, 6, 158n, 159n, 176–8, 195
Hamlet, 159n, 161, 162, 168, 181, 183, 189, 190, 194, 198, 200, 201, 212, 214, 215, 218, 219
Henry IV, 87, 88, 201
1 Henry IV, 85, 87, 88, 190, 201, 209, 212, 215, 217
2 Henry IV, 86–8, 120n, 192, 201
Henry V, 148, 190n, 202–4, 207, 208
Henry VI, 26, 30n, 75–83
1 Henry VI, 26, 27
2 Henry VI, 26, 212
3 Henry VI, 26, 212
Henry VIII, 148, 149, 170, 171, 191
Julius Caesar, 143, 146, 160n, 172, 181, 200
King John, 48, 147, 148
King Lear, 36, 40, 69, 72, 87, 115, 128, 142, 151, 158n, 160n, 161, 162, 168, 185, 186, 192, 193, 201, 207–12, 213n, 214, 217, 218
Love's Labour's Lost, 1, 5, 7, 13, 17–19, 21, 181, 182, 191, 194, 215–17
Macbeth, 36, 73n, 115, 158n, 178, 184, 193, 199, 215
Measure for Measure, 38, 89–97 passim, 140, 158n, 159, 176, 179, 186, 187, 193, 194, 213, 214
Merchant of Venice, The, 1, 2, 4, 10, 11, 55–68 passim, 116, 161, 182, 186, 190n
Merry Wives of Windsor, The, 1, 7, 8, 11, 88

Midsummer Night's Dream, A,
1, 5, 8, 9, 11, 41–53 passim,
69, 70, 71, 87, 107, 158n,
159, 161, 162, 168–170,
179, 183, 187, 191, 194n,
200, 219
Much Ado About Nothing, 1,
28, 85, 86, 176, 177, 190,
193, 218
Othello, 9, 36, 115–31 passim,
145, 158n, 160n, 161, 176–8,
180, 182, 184, 190, 207, 212,
214, 218
Pericles, 158n, 159n, 193,
212n, 214
Richard II, 39, 181, 184, 188,
190, 192, 212
Richard III, 157, 190, 194, 212
Romeo and Juliet, 115, 193, 212,
213, 218, 219
Sir Thomas More, 215
Taming of the Shrew, The, 1, 2,
4, 6, 9, 11, 23–40 passim,
163, 165–8, 194, 203, 204,
207, 208, 211, 217
Tempest, The, 22, 73, 74,
133–40 passim, 193
Titus Andronicus, 182–4, 190,
212, 217
Troilus and Cressida, 99, 144,
158n, 194, 195, 205, 207,
208
Twelfth Night, 1, 5, 30n, 39,
55, 71, 161, 163–6, 188
Two Gentlemen of Verona, The,
1, 5, 6, 13, 19–22, 55, 57,
59, 64, 70, 74, 187
Two Noble Kinsmen, The, 211
Winter's Tale, The, 73, 86, 115,
121n, 124, 158n, 182, 190,
191, 193, 194, 199, 210
poems
Rape of Lucrece, The, 175, 176,
179, 182, 191
Sonnets, 107, 108, 190, 191
Shaw, Catherine M., 193
Shaw, George Bernard, 33, 34,
85, 170, 178
Shaw, J. Byam, 51
Sherbo, Arthur, 100n, 142n, 147n,
150n
Sherley, Sir Anthony, 211
Shillingsburg, Peter L., 218n
Shulman, Jeff, 194
Simmonds, Peggy Munoz, 195

Sinfield, Alan, 185, 201
Sjögren, Gunnar, 198
Slater, Ann Pasternak, 181, 182
Slights, Camille, 188
Smallwood, R. L., 201
Smidt, Kristian, 202n
Smith, D. Nicol, 142n, 143n, 147n,
148n, 149n
Smith, Hallett, 73n
Smith, James, 3, 11
Smith, Robert A. H., 190
Snow, Edward A., 117n, 125n
Snowdon, George and Lionel, 211
Snyder, Richard C., 194
Snyder, Susan, 72n, 186
Soellner, Rolf, 191
Solomon, Robert C., 122n
Spangenberg, Heidemarie, 159n
Spenser, Edmund, 10
Spevack, Marvin, 159
Staiger, Emil, 152n
Stallybrass, Peter, 184
Stamm, Renate, 158n
Stamm, Rudolf, 158, 161n
Stamnitz, Susanne, 158n
Stanislavsky, Constantin, 162, 201
Staufer, Annegret, 159n
Steele, Sir Richard, 143n, 146
Stein, Dieter, 159n
Stein, Peter, 161, 162
Stephens, Roberts, 168, 170
Steppat, Michael, 160n
Stoll, E. E., 11, 55
Stone, P. W. K., 214
Story, Alfred T., 48n
Strachey, James, 106n
Strauss, Richard, 207
Strehler, Giorgio, 162
Stringer, Thomas, 187
Suerbaum, Ulrich, 156n
Swaczynna, Wolfgang, 160
Swain, Barbara, 135n
Swedenberg, H. T., Jr, 35n

Tabori, George, 162
Tanselle, G. Thomas, 218
Tawney, R. H., 170
Taylor, Donn Ervin, 195
Taylor, Gary, 192, 202, 203, 205,
208, 209, 214, 215n
Taylor, Michael, 9
Tetzeli von Rosador, Kurt, 157n
Thaler, Alwin, 36n
Thatcher, Margaret, 170
Thaw, John, 164, 166, 170, 171

Theocritus, 69
Thieme, Hans Otto, 157n
Thomas Aquinas, St, 100
Thomson, Peter, 182, 195, 196
Thorndike, A. H., 11
Thorpe, Thomas, 218
Thum, Hans W., 157n
Tieck, Ludwig, 155, 160, 161, 200
Tiepolo, Giovanni Battista, 176
Tillyard, E. M. W., 5
Tobin, J. J. M., 190, 215
Tonson, Jacob, 41, 42
Tourneur, Cyril, 189
Traversi, D. A., 5, 30n
Tree, Sir Herbert Beerbohm, 85
Troeber, Hans-Joachim, 159n
Trousdale, Marion, 180, 181
Turner, Robert Y., 195
Tutin, Dorothy, 184
Tyndale, William, 176

Ulrici, D. Hermann, 46
Urkowitz, Steven, 208, 210

Van Dijk, Maarten, 198
Van Laan, Thomas, 3
Velz, John W., 189
Veronese, Paolo, 99
Vickers, Brian, 8, 30, 31n, 141n
Victoria, Queen, 47
Vielhaber, Christiane, 159n
Virgil, 144
Voltaire (François-Marie Arouet),
146, 147

Walker, Alice, 206, 209, 213, 214
Waller, David, 167
Walpole, Horace, 45
Walter, J. H., 202
Wanamaker, Zoë, 165, 168
Wardle, Irving, 182, 183
Warren, Michael, 208, 218
Warren, Roger, 107n, 208
Webster, John, 215
Webster, Margaret, 33n
Wehmeyer, Jörg, 161
Weill, Kurt, 170
Weiss, Wolfgang, 156n
Weller, Barry, 187
Wells, Stanley, 5, 19n, 168, 185,
199, 201–3, 208, 210, 216
Welsford, Enid, 9
Wendel, Karl-Heinz, 19n
Wentersdorf, Karl P., 204
Wenzel, Peter, 160n

INDEX

Werstine, Paul, 209, 218
Wetz, W., 152n
Whately, Thomas, 142
Wheeler, Richard, 101n, 102, 107n, 110n
Wilders, John, 200
Wilkins, George, 192
Williams, George Walton, 217, 218
Williams, Gwyn, 16n
Williams, Simon, 199
Willis, Susan, 200

Wilson, Thomas, 180
Wilson, Edwin, 34n
Wilson, F. P., 5, 7
Wilson, J. Dover, 5, 9, 85, 90, 202
Wind, Edgar, 99, 100n, 106
Winter, William, 85n, 87n
Wood, John, 52, 53
Woodbridge, L. T., 190
Woodmason, James, 45
Woolf, Virginia, 13
Wroth, Sir Robert, 190

Wycherley, William, 125
Wyrick, Deborah Baker, 194

Yates, Frances, 196
Young, D. P., 4, 9, 72n

Zadek, Peter, 162
Zander, Horst, 159n
Zeffirelli, Franco, 88
Zimansky, Curt A., 124n, 145n
Zimmermann, Heinz, 158n